The American Nonvoter

The American Nonvoter

LYN RAGSDALE

AND

JERROLD G. RUSK

OXFORD
UNIVERSITY PRESS

OXFORD
UNIVERSITY PRESS

Oxford University Press is a department of the University of Oxford. It furthers the University's objective of excellence in research, scholarship, and education by publishing worldwide. Oxford is a registered trade mark of Oxford University Press in the UK and certain other countries.

Published in the United States of America by Oxford University Press
198 Madison Avenue, New York, NY 10016, United States of America.

Library of Congress Cataloging-in-Publication Data
Names: Ragsdale, Lyn, 1954– author. | Jerrold G. Rusk, 1941– author.
Title: The American nonvoter / Lyn Ragsdale and Jerrold G. Rusk.
Description: New York, NY : Oxford University Press, [2017] |
Includes bibliographical references and index.
Identifiers: LCCN 2016048188| ISBN 9780190670702 (hbk : acid-free paper) |
ISBN 9780190670719 (pbk : acid-free paper) | ISBN 9780190670733 (Epub) |
ISBN 9780190670726 (Updf)
Subjects: LCSH: Voting—United States—Abstention. |
United States—Politics and government—1945–1989.
Classification: LCC JK1987 .R34 2017 | DDC 324.973/092—dc23
LC record available at https://lccn.loc.gov/2016048188

1 3 5 7 9 8 6 4 2

Paperback printed by WebCom, Inc., Canada
Hardback printed by Bridgeport National Bindery, Inc., United States of America

To Matthew

CONTENTS

PREFACE

This book grew out of four factors. First, both of us have been keenly interested in people who do not vote. Although nonvoters are often portrayed as the opposite of voters or are not portrayed at all in studies of electoral participation, we wondered about the many facets of their decisions not to vote, who is more likely not to vote, and how nonvoters differ among themselves. We were also drawn to the question of nonvoting historically. How have nonvoting rates shifted over decades of American political history and what has prompted these shifts? Second, we have become fascinated by the importance of uncertainty in decision making. When we mentioned the word "uncertainty" to some people, they often threw up their hands and said, "Well isn't that just life?" But we were intrigued by what we see as a key difference between how people behave under conditions of uncertainty in the economy and in politics. When presented with economic uncertainty, people and companies hold back and remain on the sidelines—they do not make major purchases or investments. When presented with less economic uncertainty, people and firms spend freely. By contrast, we recognize that when presented with political uncertainty, people rush to act. They protest, join groups, donate to causes, and, we hypothesize, vote. When presented with less uncertainty, they are inclined to pay less attention, be less active, and stay home on Election Day. Attempting to understand how political uncertainty unfolds and how it affects electoral participation is the central thread running through the book.

Third, over the course of a number of years, Jerry has devised a large data set on electoral participation, voting, and demographics beginning with the first federal election in 1788. It had everything we needed to pursue this question of nonvoting historically. The book begins in 1920 with women entering the electorate and concludes with the 2012 elections. Fourth, during the past 10 years, Lyn was dean of the Social Sciences in need of an academic project that would offer an intellectual counterbalance to the administrative challenges of a deanship. Working on this book was always the perfect antidote to one too many meetings or memos. So, this combination of empirical question, theoretical interest, data, and deanship became *The American Nonvoter.* We view this as a study of how uncertainty in the national campaign context affects levels of nonvoting and individuals who do not vote. It is both an empirical analysis but also a political history that informs and is informed by the empirical results.

We would like to thank the many fine people at Oxford University Press for their hard work and support in the publication of this book. Angela Chnapko has been an encouraging, thorough, and helpful editor improving the book at every stage. Alexcee Bechthold and Alphonsa James have been indispensable during the editing and production processes, keeping their eyes on many details that went into the final version. Carol Neimann has enhanced the text with her acumen as copy editor. We also greatly appreciate the comments of the reviewers—Erik Engstrom, Helmut Norpoth, and an anonymous reviewer. Their perceptive readings of the book challenged us to think about key issues in a more thorough and thoughtful way and made the book much stronger.

Lyn Ragsdale and Jerrold G. Rusk
Rice University
Houston, Texas

The American Nonvoter

Introduction

In San Antonio, Texas, on a last-minute campaign swing during the midterm elections of 1966, President Lyndon Johnson urged citizens to go to the polls. Waving his cream-colored Stetson up and down, as if to make his point clearer, Johnson extolled the crowd, "Generations ago, Americans were willing to sacrifice their lives and fortunes to secure the vote. In our own time men have marched and prayed and sung to win it and exercise it—often at great risk to themselves. It is precious—and powerful. It is our protection against tyranny and bad government. It is the instrument of peaceful change. It is the way we express our views on the most important questions we face as a people."

As Johnson hastened to point out, the vote "is not self-exercising. The right to vote is only an abstraction if it is not used. The man and woman who stay at home tomorrow will have the right to vote—but they will not have a part in choosing who shall lead them in the next few years. The wisest man who does not vote has less control over his destiny than the one whom, though he may lack understanding, does go to the polls."[1]

Who votes and who stays home on Election Day have a good deal to say about what happens in American democracy. The outcomes of elections hinge on who votes and in what numbers, who does not vote in what states, and how the electorate expands and contracts from one election to the next. The 2000 presidential race in Florida immediately comes to mind as proof that failing to vote matters. The final Florida results tallied 537 more votes for Texas Governor George W. Bush than Vice President Al Gore out of nearly 6 million votes cast. Yet 5 million of the 11 million Floridians who were eligible to vote chose not to. Had a small number of these people gone to the polls and voted for Al Gore, he would have been elected president.

The result, as anomalous as it was historic, is not the only instance in which nonvoting was pivotal. In the 1876 election, if 462 more people in Florida had

[1] "Statement by the President Calling Upon Citizens to Vote in the Forthcoming Elections," *Public Papers of the Presidents*, November 7, 1966, found at www.presidency.ucsb.edu.

gone to the polls and voted for Democrat Samuel Tilden, he would have won the White House rather than Republican Rutherford B. Hayes. If, in 1884, 525 more people had voted in New York for James Blaine, the Republican would have claimed national victory over Democrat Grover Cleveland. In 1916, if 1,983 additional supporters of Republican Charles Evans Hughes had gone to the polls in California, he would have won the presidency from Woodrow Wilson.[2] Such vivid examples of how nonvoting has mattered are, of course, just that—examples of the much broader importance of nonvoting, which has included historic struggles over expanding as well as restricting the vote and high-stakes major party efforts at winning the turnout game. This book is about "the man and woman who stay at home"—the American nonvoter. Its central premise is that uncertainty in the national campaign context affects how many people do not vote and who does not vote.

Uncertainty arises when decision makers are unable to accurately predict future conditions, possible options, or final outcomes based on what they know about present or past circumstances. Decision makers are unsure or doubtful about what will happen next and recognize that many occurrences with significant political repercussions are often beyond their control. The national campaign context is the array of events, economic conditions, technological advances in communication, and changes in legal requirements that exist in the months preceding the election. The campaign context is not the campaign itself—the hoopla, the whistle stops, the money spent, or the latest polls. Rather, it is the "national scene"—the prevailing aspects of the American public sphere in the months preceding the election—in effect, the raw material for the campaign. The national campaign context involves "the workings of quintessentially short term factor[s] that change [their] values at every election."[3]

The very nature of uncertainty in the national campaign context varies from one election to the next. High unemployment, a stalemated war, civil unrest, a personal scandal—important, if not paramount, at the time of one election—may disappear from political salience by the next election. Communication devices introduced in one election create uncertainty and excitement about what the novel messaging means, but may become commonplace in future elections. Some elections take place immediately after a major crisis; other elections take place at a time when little is happening. In political terms, there is a long time between elections. High levels of uncertainty make it difficult for people

[2] For more information on close presidential races in which turnout could have decided the winner, see Jerrold Rusk, *A Statistical History of the American Electorate* (Washington, D.C.: CQ Press, 2001), 143.

[3] Mark Franklin, *Voter Turnout and the Dynamics of Electoral Competition in Established Democracies since 1945* (Cambridge: Cambridge University Press, 2004), 111.

to avoid politics, even if they are not especially interested in it. Low levels of uncertainty make it easier for people to avoid politics, even when they are very interested in it.

We posit that the higher degree of uncertainty in the national scene, the more likely eligible voters will go to the polls. The uncertainty increases the political stakes between the parties, making it more likely that their campaigns will generate greater interest among a broad segment of the eligible electorate who often pay little attention to politics. The cost of staying home effectively increases as uncertainty grows. People do not wish to risk having a party or candidate they dislike win, for fear that campaign promises will become government policy.

Consider the 1960 presidential election when the country was at a crossroads socially, economically, and internationally. A good part of the campaign focused on Democratic candidate John Kennedy's Catholicism and whether a Catholic should be president. Many of the accusations of "taking orders from the Pope," which had saddled Al Smith in 1928, the last time a Catholic ran for president, were leveled again at Kennedy. Conflict over race relations and civil rights also emerged during the campaign when in October 1960 Martin Luther King, Jr. was arrested and jailed during a peaceful sit-in in an Atlanta department store. Kennedy interceded to gain his release while his Republican opponent Richard Nixon remained on the sidelines. The economy was slow to come out of the recession of 1958, and unemployment remained high in 1960 at nearly 6 percent, in sharp contrast to the 4 percent that had existed in the mid-1950s. Cold War apprehensions continued as the candidates debated the role of the United States in response to tensions with the Soviet Union and the People's Republic of China. Nixon insisted that Kennedy was afraid to use nuclear weapons to protect two small islands off the coast of Taiwan from the Communist Chinese. Quemoy and Matsu, names which everyone knew during the election, were little heard thereafter. The high level of uncertainty associated with these various elements of the campaign context created considerable interest in the election and a drop in the number of nonvoters. It is not surprising that nonvoting reached a historic low in 1960—the lowest level of nonvoting between 1900 and 2012.

Conversely, as the degree of uncertainty drops, eligible voters become less likely to participate. The national scene is seen as fairly stable, and specific elements within it are not subject to large swings as the election nears. The political stakes are smaller, and the parties may invest less in their campaigns. So predictions about two key outcomes of the race—who will win and how many people will vote—are not only clearer but also less crucial to eligible voters. With low uncertainty, eligible voters—even some who typically pay attention to politics—find it less compelling to participate.

In contrast to 1960, contemplate the 1996 election between President Bill Clinton, seeking his second term, and challenger Bob Dole, Senator from Kansas.

Dole, 73 years old, looked tired and worn through much of the campaign. This was in decided contrast to Ronald Reagan, who was only a few years younger when he first sought the White House. With the economy strong, the federal deficit down, and trouble spots in the world relatively quiet, Dole unsuccessfully touted his promise to cut income taxes, which Clinton attacked as "blowing a hole in the deficit." Texas billionaire H. Ross Perot, who had captured media attention and public support in 1992, faded in 1996. Not surprisingly, 24 percent of those registered to vote in October 1996 said that they had less interest in the race than they might otherwise have had because Clinton appeared to be well on his way to victory.[4] Indeed, Clinton won by nearly 10 percentage points. This low level of uncertainty produced a lack of interest among those eligible to vote and a high level of nonvoting. Forty-six percent of the eligible electorate did not vote in the 1996 election, close to a historic high. While researchers have linked the 1960 and 1996 elections to show a linear increase in nonvoting in the post–World War II era, we make clear later in the book that the two elections reflect different levels of uncertainty, not an inexorable increase in nonvoting.

This focus on the uncertainty of the national campaign context challenges the prevailing analyses of American electoral participation, which concentrate heavily on individuals and campaigners. Commentators offer four primary explanations for why people fail to vote:

- Nonvoters lack psychological involvement in politics, which blocks their route to the polls.
- Nonvoters lack the personal resources to go to the polls.
- Nonvoters lack the social connectedness that creates a desire for political involvement and participation.
- Campaigners fail to sufficiently mobilize people in the eligible electorate.

Those taking a psychological approach suggest that nonvoters are bedeviled by "declining psychological involvement in politics and declining belief in government responsiveness"; "a lack of motivation to vote, particularly stemming from party decline"; and lack "a capacity to devote some attention to events outside one's immediate life yet which are significant for the broader community."[5]

[4] http://brain.gallup.com, Question qn53a, Tracking Poll 1996 Week 8, 10/21/1996-10/27/1996.

[5] Ruy Teixeira, *The Disappearing American Voter* (Washington, D.C.: Brookings Institution, 1992), 49; Martin Wattenberg, *Where Have all the Voters Gone?* (Cambridge: Harvard University Press, 2002), 67; Philip Converse and Richard Niemi, "Non-voting Among Young Adults in the United States," in William Crotty, ed. *Political Parties and Political Behavior*, 2nd ed. (Boston: Allyn and Bacon, 1971), 461.

Analysts who focus on personal resources indicate that there are certain key characteristics that people have which make them less likely to vote—limited education, low income, and high mobility being among the most crucial. Researchers who explore social connections stress that individuals cannot be viewed as lone political actors but must instead be seen amidst their social connections, group associations, and interpersonal networks. Nonvoters have more limited social networks than do voters. Lastly, experts who examine campaign mobilization maintain that it is not simply individual citizens who are important in the nonvoting calculus but that campaigners also set the stage for voting and not voting. From this perspective, people do not vote unless they are mobilized by parties, candidates, and other political activists. In the study of electoral participation, these four explanations have uncovered rich information on the roles of citizens and campaigners. Yet, none have considered the national campaign context and the uncertainty within it, which both citizens and campaigners face in the months leading up to an election. The balance of this chapter examines in greater detail the four existing explanations of nonvoting and then considers the importance of uncertainty in the national campaign context for citizens and campaigners alike.

Psychological Engagement

The psychological engagement explanation presents the American nonvoter as a person with little, if any, interest in politics and limited concern about the election outcome. Analysts Charles Merriam and Harold Gosnell first charted this direction in 1924 when they uncovered that general indifference to politics or ignorance about elections were primary reasons for people not voting in Chicago mayoral elections.[6] Paul Lazarsfeld, Bernard Berelson, and Helen Gaudet continued this line of reasoning, concluding that "three quarters of the non-voters stayed away from the polls deliberately because they were unconcerned."[7] The authors of *The American Voter* maintained that "the decision to vote, no less than the decision to vote for a given party, rests immediately on psychological forces . . ."[8] These forces of psychological involvement include strength of party identification, interest in politics, caring about political outcomes, and views of one's

[6] Charles Merriam and Harold Gosnell, *Non-voting: Causes and Methods of Control* (Chicago: University of Chicago Press, 1924).

[7] Paul Lazarsfeld, Bernard Berelson, and Helen Gaudet, *The People's Choice* (New York: Columbia University Press, 1948), 47.

[8] Angus Campbell, Philip Converse, Warren Miller, and Donald Stokes, *The American Voter* (New York: John Wiley, 1960), 90.

own impact on politics, namely, political efficacy. Thus, those people who have strong party ties, show interest in politics, care about what happens politically, and have high political efficacy are more likely to vote; those with weak or absent party ties, apathy toward politics, and low political efficacy are more likely not to vote.

In research which follows *The American Voter* approach, these psychological factors are viewed as sources of motivation. "The psychological approach," wrote Martin Wattenberg, "has further identified the problem to be primarily a lack of motivation to vote, particularly stemming from party decline."[9] In short, nonvoters are not sufficiently motivated to participate. According to Wattenberg, this is especially true among peripheral members of the electorate, who often have limited interest in politics but who are at times mobilized by candidates and parties. Specifically examining the impact of lower political efficacy on participation, Wattenberg concluded that "the failure to mobilize peripheral voters appears to be more a problem of motivation than of resources."[10] In other words, these citizens are unconvinced about their own impact on politics and therefore lack the motivation to vote.

Michael Lewis-Beck et al. viewed psychological involvement as critical to determining who will vote, arguing that "each individual develops a characteristic pattern of involvement in politics."[11] This pattern of involvement encompasses interest and concern about the campaign, a duty to vote, and political efficacy. The authors concluded that "Turnout behavior is guided by the following rule: the stronger a person's psychological involvement in politics, the higher the propensity to participate."[12] Andre Blais also maintained that this psychological involvement extends to people's moral beliefs that they have a duty to vote.[13] Thus, the psychological approach views voting and nonvoting as the result of highly personal investments in politics that transcend any given election and to some extent exist independently of the content of any electoral contest. Researchers Warren Miller and J. Merrill Shanks summarized the psychological engagement viewpoint, stating that "it is not hard to understand why most nonvoters don't vote: they are uninterested, uninformed, and uninvolved."[14]

[9] Wattenberg, 2002, 64.

[10] Ibid., 67.

[11] Michael Lewis-Beck, William Jacoby, Helmut Norpoth, and Herbert Weisberg, *The American Voter Revisited* (Ann Arbor, MI: University of Michigan Press, 2008), 92.

[12] Ibid.

[13] Andre Blais, *To Vote or Not to Vote* (Pittsburgh: University of Pittsburgh Press, 2000), Chapter 5.

[14] Warren Miller and J. Merrill Shanks, *The New American Voter* (Cambridge: Harvard University Press, 1996), 39.

Personal Resources

Political scientists Sidney Verba and Norman Nie advanced the personal resources approach by examining the effects of socio-economic status—income, education, and occupation—on various forms of participation.[15] Their argument is straightforward: those with higher socio-economic status participate more; those with lower socio-economic status participate less. The resource model, resting on classical rational choice theory, posits the costs and benefits of voting. The more resources individuals have—whether social, economic, or political—the lower the costs of voting and the greater the benefits to voting. In later work, Sidney Verba, Kay Schlozman, and Henry Brady modified the argument somewhat by examining money, time, and civic skills as central resources but continued to assert that groups with different levels of education, income, and occupational prestige enjoy distinct levels of these resources that separate voters from nonvoters.[16]

Following Verba and Nie, Ray Wolfinger and Steven Rosenstone expanded the sweep of personal characteristics that are viewed as resources: "a variety of personal characteristics have been suggested as resources, including money, time, social status, experience, information, social contacts, and jobs [which] we infer from the individual's demographic characteristics."[17] Later Steven Rosenstone and John Hansen examined income, education, unemployment, age, and political efficacy as resources, along with other demographic variables including race, sex, and region of the country that are also related to these resources.[18] Jan Leighley and Jonathan Nagler, updating the original Wolfinger and Rosenstone work, found that from 1972 through 2008, people with higher incomes, better educations, and who are older consistently vote more than others.[19]

Social Connections

Researcher Ruy Teixeira offered a third account of American nonvoters concentrating on social structure. He observed the cross-cutting impact of social

[15] Sidney Verba and Norman Nie, *Participation in America* (New York: Harper and Row, 1972).

[16] Sidney Verba, Kay Schlozman, and Henry Brady, *Voice and Equality* (Cambridge: Harvard University Press, 1995).

[17] Ray Wolfinger and Steven Rosenstone, *Who Votes?* (New Haven: Yale University Press, 1980), 9.

[18] Steven Rosenstone and John Mark Hansen, *Mobilization, Participation, and Democracy in America* (New York: Longman, 2003).

[19] Jan Leighley and Jonathan Nagler, *Who Votes Now?* (Princeton: Princeton University Press, 2014).

characteristics beginning in the 1960s. Although education and income increased, thereby making more Americans a part of the middle class, the public also became less rooted in various social structures: the population was younger, more mobile, and less likely to be married than during the 1950s. He concluded that "a substantial decline of the 'rootedness' of individuals within the social structure appears to have been a factor within this period."[20] So while increased education and income should have promoted higher turnout, the decline in social connections contradicted this. Nonvoting resulted from people's limited integration and involvement in the community—a lack of "social connectedness."

Others considering the social realm have focused specifically on young people as nonvoters. Political scientist Mark Franklin conducted a cohort analysis of the impact of youth on turnout. He asserted that when 18-year-olds were given the right to vote, this set in motion a cascading effect of lower turnout since 18-year-olds were less "ready" to vote than 21-year-olds, and successive groups of 18-year-olds entering the electorate had the effect of structurally dampening turnout.[21] Eric Plutzer addressed the process by which people develop the habit to vote. He observed that young people typically start as habitual nonvoters, but a variety of factors including marriage, mobility, church attendance, and parental involvement in politics push them toward becoming habitual voters over time.[22]

Another group of scholars considered the importance of social pressure and people's social networks in their decisions to vote. Experimental research showed that when registered voters receive mailings encouraging them to vote by indicating whether they and their neighbors had voted in the past, the social pressure implicit in the mailings increases voting participation not only in the immediate election but in later elections.[23] Meredith Rolfe broadened the analysis to consider the role of social networks in people's decisions to vote.

[20] Ruy Teixeira, *Why Americans Don't Vote* (Westport, CT: Greenwood Press, 1987), 24. See also Ruy Teixeira, *The Disappearing American Voter* (Washington, D.C.: Brookings Institution, 1992).

[21] Franklin, 2004, 64. See also Michael Hout and David Knoke, "Change in Voting Turnout, 1952–1971," *Public Opinion Quarterly* 39 (Spring, 1975): 52–68.

[22] Eric Plutzer, "Becoming a Habitual Voter: Inertia, Resources, and Growth in Young Adulthood," *American Political Science Review* 96 (March 2002): 41–56. See also Donald Green and Ron Shachar, "Habit Formation and Political Behaviour: Evidence of Consuetude in Voter Turnout," *British Journal of Political Science* 30 (October 2000): 561–573.

[23] Alan Gerber, Donald Green, and Christopher Larimer, "Social Pressure and Voter Turnout: Evidence from a Large-Scale Field Experiment," *American Political Science Review* 102 (February 2008): 33–48. Other field experiment studies include Donald Green and Alan Gerber, *Get Out the Vote: How to Increase Voter Turnout*, 3rd ed. (Washington, D.C.: Brookings Institution Press, 2015); Tiffany Davenport, Alan Gerber, Donald Green, Christopher Larimer, Christopher Mann, and Costas Panagopoulos, "The Enduring Effects of Social Pressure: Tracking Campaign Experiments Over a Series of Elections," *Political Behavior* 32 (September 2010): 423–430.

Rather than a single intervention of social pressure, social networks are more encompassing and capture the many interactions people have in their daily lives. Thus, the act of voting or nonvoting is a conditional decision—conditioned on the size and variation within a person's social network. She suggests that socio-economic characteristics provide people with these distinct networks of other similarly situated people. Within a given social network, people are likely to participate at similar levels.[24] The larger and more varied the network, the more likely people discuss politics and vote.

Thus, there are three individual-based approaches to explaining why people do not vote—psychological engagement, personal resources, and social connections. In some research, the first and third approaches are melded into the second, as psychological and social factors become part of an ever-expandable list of personal resources. Efficacy, for example, is no longer a psychological feeling about one's impact on politics but is rather another resource that permits more political participation.[25] Age is viewed as a personal resource—a measure of personal experience—rather than as a degree of social connectedness. This has made the resource model a convenient umbrella under which numerous demographic and psychological characteristics are crowded. Any factor such as age, sex, race, employment, income, education, mobility, marital status, political interest, efficacy, and duty can be readily treated as a resource or liability that may influence the cost or benefit of voting or nonvoting.[26] This has had the unfortunate effect of blurring the theoretical approaches and leaving researchers with little more than a single, omnibus categorization scheme.

Yet, whether researchers acknowledge the separateness of the theoretical approaches or merge them together, the characterization of American nonvoters offered in the three approaches ultimately rests on a single theoretical premise: there is something inherently lacking in nonvoters' political attentiveness that jams their connections to politics and participation. With the right resources, psychological outlook, or social connections, this jam goes away. Even Rolfe's work on social networks ultimately rests on how individuals behave based on the sizes and shapes of those networks.

Campaign Mobilization

Rosenstone and Hansen provided a fourth approach to American nonvoting that involves politicians' mobilization of the electorate. They indicated that "People

[24] D. Meredith Rolfe, *Voter Turnout* (New York: Cambridge University Press, 2013).

[25] Rosenstone and Hansen, 2003, 132.

[26] See also Wattenberg, 2002, 59–64; Wolfinger and Rosenstone, 1980.

participate in politics not so much because of who they are but because of the political choices and incentives they are offered."[27] Thus, "the strategic choices of politicians, political parties, interest groups, and activists" affect people's decisions on participation.[28] Political leaders may well adjust their campaign techniques if they feel they are not mobilizing sufficient numbers to the polls, not sending the right message, or not using the available media to their advantage.

Francis Piven and Richard Cloward began the study of mobilization by examining the extent to which certain groups of eligible voters—specifically, the poor, the working class, and minority groups—were excluded from voting not just by formal restrictions on the franchise, but also by mobilization efforts that in some cases ignored these eligible voters and in other cases expressly appealed to voters with higher incomes and socio-economic status.[29] Michael Avey rejected the personal resources model in favor of the mobilization model, arguing "Individual socioeconomic characteristics are not the building blocks of a model of the causes and consequences of participation . . . The upper-class bias in turnout is the consequence of appeals of parties and candidates over time, not the result of the incompetence in low-status individuals."[30]

Rosenstone and Hansen broaden the discussion beyond the mobilization of the poor, working class, and minority groups to consider on a general level how party contact or involvement in a social movement increases people's likelihood to vote. They found that mobilization efforts do increase participation, but who is mobilized depends heavily on the personal resources eligible voters have, particularly age and education. Thus, they combine the mobilization and personal resources models. According to Rosenstone and Hansen, mobilization offers eligible voters additional benefits for voting and lowers their costs because they do not need to use as many of their own personal resources to vote. They summarized three primary benefits of mobilization for eligible voters. First, as politicians give people a reason to vote, the costs of voting decrease and the benefits increase. This is an expressive benefit—being on the winning side. Second, politicians also provide tangible benefits which "subsidize the cost of electoral participation" through registration campaigns, campaign literature, transportation to the polls, and absentee ballots.[31] Third, mobilization creates social contacts and networks that would not otherwise exist and thereby helps produce

[27] Rosenstone and Hansen, 2003, 5.

[28] Ibid.

[29] Frances Fox Piven and Richard Cloward, *Why Americans Don't Vote* (New York: Pantheon Books, 1988); Frances Fox Piven and Richard Cloward, *Why Americans Still Don't Vote* (Boston: Beacon Press, 2002).

[30] Michael Avey, *The Demobilization of American Voters* (New York: Greenwood Press, 1989).

[31] Rosenstone and Hansen, 2003, 210.

the social connectedness that worried Teixeira. A large body of field-experiment research shows that grassroots mobilization efforts in the form of get-out-the-vote drives, especially door-to-door canvassing and phone calls, by partisan and nonpartisan groups, increase turnout. Other experimental work points to how the framing of messages about the importance of voting mobilizes individuals to vote.[32]

Others have explored various aspects of mobilization. Thomas Patterson maintained that the mobilization of voters is both candidate- and journalist-centered rather than party-oriented. Candidates say what they feel they can get away with to get people to the polls; journalists work to uncover the "story behind the story."[33] The result is increasing pessimism among the eligible electorate on the state of campaigns and elections. According to Patterson, nonvoters have every reason to stay home. Also, Leighley and Nagler examined how the policy differences between candidates serve as key mobilizing factors—the larger the differences, the more likely people will vote.

The National Campaign Context

While the mobilization model is a helpful addition to works that focus on individuals' psychological involvement, personal resources, and social connections, its spotlight nonetheless remains on individual voters and nonvoters. Campaigns attempt to attract individuals; individuals respond to those campaigns based on their psychological outlooks, personal characteristics, and social networks. In addition, the mobilization model does not investigate the causes and antecedents of the mobilization but instead treats mobilization as predetermined. We turn the tables on this individual perspective and focus instead on the election rather than the individual. In particular, we concentrate on the context of the campaign as Election Day approaches. The national campaign context confronts both campaigners and the eligible electorate.

Campaigners must adjust and respond to these matters, over which they often have little control. Campaigners can only mobilize the electorate by being mindful of this context—its problems, ambiguities, and opportunities. And

[32] E.g., Alan Gerber and Donald Green, "The Effect of a Nonpartisan Get-Out-the-Vote Drive: An Experimental Study of Leafletting," *Journal of Politics* 62 (August 2000): 846–857; Richard Matland and Gregg Murray, "An Experimental Test of Mobilization Effects in a Latino Community," *Political Research Quarterly* 65 (March 2012): 192–205; Donald Green and Alan Gerber, "Introduction to Social Pressure and Voting: New Experimental Evidence," *Political Behavior* 32 (September 2010): 331–336; Gerber, Green, and Larimer, 2008; Green and Gerber, 2015.

[33] Thomas Patterson, *The Vanishing Voter* (New York: Vintage Books, 2002), 69.

their mobilization strategies will be more or less successful depending on how effectively they address the national scene. This national context may disrupt candidates' mobilization strategies, often planned well before the central features of the campaign context become clear. Candidates have proceeded into elections basing their mobilization efforts on images and issues from that past that typically play well among their base supporters. Yet, if the campaign context veers in unexpected directions and uncertainty mounts, the campaigners' lack of nimbleness in the face of these challenges may make their mobilization efforts difficult.

Furthermore, if the context encompasses national "bad times"—economic problems, international crises, or an unpopular president—for which the party in power is typically blamed—then the party out of power is much more likely to be successful raising money, sending out its message, and getting voters to the polls. That is, the party out of power does a better job of mobilization, not because it is necessarily better at mobilization strategies or techniques but instead because the campaign context creates an advantage for these efforts. If the context encompasses national "good times"—a prosperous economy, little friction in the world, and a popular incumbent president—for which the party in power is typically given considerable credit—then the party in power is likely to be more successful in its mobilization efforts in fundraising, campaigning, and getting out the vote, again regardless of how truly effective their methods are. In short, the mobilization efforts that the candidates and parties can undertake are directly tied to the nature of the campaign context.

The campaign context also affects the eligible electorate. Although individuals choose whether or not to vote, they do so in a collective environment that is larger than even their largest social network. An uncertain set of national circumstances draws people to the polls, as they are concerned about the broader context. By contrast, a stable set of national circumstances may keep some people at home because the context is insufficiently grave or uncertain to bother to vote. This is not simply campaigners' efforts to get the right people to the polls, but it is people's own exposure to the campaign context.

Thus, the uncertainty of the national campaign context shapes and reshapes the electorate, helping to define those who vote and those who do not. Under one set of national circumstances, the future is unclear and much is at stake. At other times the national situation is less unsettled, and stability rather than uncertainty prevails. Thus, we expect nonvoting to move up and down across elections as the degree of uncertainty changes from one election to the next. Uncertainty is never absolute or absent but moves along a relative continuum from high to low. In turn, nonvoting moves down and up as levels of uncertainty from the campaign context swell and diminish. When uncertainty is high, more people will vote; when uncertainty is low, fewer people will go to the polls. From the perspective of personal characteristics or social connections, it is less easy to see how nonvoting would shift from one election to the next. Neither people's personal characteristics nor their social networks shift dramatically from one election year to the next. Certainly campaign mobilization can vary from one election to the next, but, as we argue, these differences may reflect changes in the campaign context as campaigns do a better or worse job in keeping ahead of the changing national scene.

Overview

In the following nine chapters, this book offers the first opportunity to investigate the impact of uncertainty in the national campaign context on how many people do not vote in America and who does not vote. We assess the effect of this uncertainty relative to indicators employed in the psychological, personal resource, social, and mobilization explanations of electoral participation. Our approach offers an in-depth longitudinal analysis that combines political history with aggregate and individual empirical analyses. The aggregate analysis begins in 1920 (when women gained the right to vote), and the individual analysis begins in 1968 (when key variables in the American National Election studies become available). As such, this places our work squarely in the literature that examines historical trends in electoral participation.[34] Other equally valuable approaches such as field experiments,[35] formal models,[36] and cross-sectional analyses based on a single election[37] are relevant to the current study but outside its scope. Chapter 1 examines in detail a campaign context theory of nonvoting and more fully considers how elections take place in a specific national campaign context that has greater or lesser degrees of political uncertainty. The higher degree of uncertainty in the campaign context, the lower nonvoting rates will be.

Chapter 2 explores the history of aggregate nonvoting in American presidential and midterm House elections from 1920 through 2012. Often, commentators bemoan a decline in participation in American elections over time. This chapter debunks this observation using an exhaustive dataset about the demography, economics, technology, legal requirements, and election results of the American states.

[34] E.g., Wattenberg, 2002; Leighley and Nagler, 2014.

[35] E.g., Gerber, Green, and Larimer, 2008.

[36] E.g., William Riker and Peter Ordoshook, "A Theory of the Calculus of Voting," *American Political Science Review* 62 (March, 1968): 25–42.

[37] E.g., Wolfinger and Rosenstone, 1980; Rolfe, 2012.

Chapter 3 studies the impact of the national campaign context on nonvoting across the entire time period in presidential and midterm elections and compares states in the South with those outside the South. The chapter also explores prior models of participation that involve demographics, social involvement, and mobilization. The analyses presented suggest that the national campaign context has a greater effect on nonvoting than do some of the demographic, social, and mobilization factors.

Chapter 4 examines the impact of the national campaign context on individual nonvoting from 1968 through 2012. The national campaign context has a strong influence on what citizens perceive about the candidates, and these perceptions, in turn, help explain why certain people do not vote. In addition, the chapter uncovers that there are several different types of nonvoters who vary in the degree of information they have about the national campaign context and the opinions they form about the candidates.

Chapter 5 begins an in-depth analysis of the national campaign context in individual elections. We first estimate the overall effect of the national campaign context on nonvoting in individual elections from 1920 through 2012. From this discussion, four distinct political periods emerge: a period of government expansion from 1920 through 1944, the postwar period from 1946 through 1972, a government reassessment period from 1974 through 1990, and the Internet technology years from 1992 through 2012. During the remainder of the chapter, we estimate the effect of factors within the campaign context—including economic conditions, technological advances, wars, and legal requirements, relative to education and party competition—on presidential and midterm House nonvoting during the first period. Chapters 6, 7, and 8 consider the national campaign context model in the other three time periods. In each of these chapters, the impact of the campaign context on individual nonvoting is also considered within a specific time period. Chapter 9 concludes by summarizing the key findings of the earlier chapters and their importance for American politics.

This book reveals that the national campaign context has a very powerful effect on the American nonvoter. The stability or instability of the economy, technological advances, looming national crises or calm, and shifts in federal legal requirements directly influence nonvoting levels. We find that economic uncertainty decreases the number of people who do not vote in the American states. But, when the economy is stable or stagnant, more people stay home. In addition, people's perceptions of economic conditions influence their individual participation decisions. When people perceive economic stability rather than change, they are much more likely to stay home. Technological shocks with the introduction of radio, television, and the Internet also decrease aggregate nonvoting. Yet, when everyone has access to these devices, their differential effects on participation end. Individuals' use of media directly affects whether they will vote or not. The fewer forms of media they pay attention to, the more likely they will not vote. The uncertainty of war tends to diminish nonvoting at the aggregate and individual levels. The more the war rages—and implicitly the outcome becomes less certain—the more people go to the polls. Finally, we find that national suffrage laws designed to expand the electorate to women, African Americans, and the young do not always meet their objectives. While the Voting Rights Act of 1965 eliminating intimidation against African-American voter registration profoundly increased participation among African Americans, the 19th Amendment granting women the right to vote and the 24th Amendment granting 18-year-olds the franchise did not decrease nonvoting levels.

1

A Theory of Uncertainty in Nonvoting

In this chapter, we present a theory of uncertainty in nonvoting that rests on five premises:

- The key element of the national campaign context is uncertainty that prohibits candidates and the eligible electorate from accurately predicting the future.
- This uncertainty arises from political novelty or surprise—how drastically elements of the national scene change in the months leading up to the election.
- This uncertainty produces risk—the likelihood of making a decision that leads to a negative result—the election of the candidate least likely to reduce uncertainty.
- People choose to vote to reduce uncertainty and risk in response to the novelty of political occurrences.
- The higher (lower) the level of uncertainty, the more (less) likely eligible voters will go to the polls.

Uncertainty

Uncertainty is a ubiquitous phenomenon in society and individuals' daily lives. As defined in the Introduction, uncertainty involves the inability of decision makers to accurately predict future conditions, options, or outcomes based on what they know about the present or the past. Weeks after the stock market crash in 1929, the *Magazine of Wall Street* proclaimed "Uncertainty is worse than knowing the truth, no matter how bad."[1] As Claudio Cioffi-Revilla (1998)

[1] Quoted in Christina Romer, "The Great Crash and the Onset of the Great Depression," *The Quarterly Journal of Economics* 3 (August 1990): 597.

wrote, "Uncertainty means that in politics outcomes are neither predetermined (with probability 1) nor impossible (with probability 0), but lie somewhere in between . . . No area of politics is immune from chance."[2]

There are three key dimensions to uncertainty in the national campaign context. First, uncertainty rests on a continuum from high to low. Barry Burden (2003) observed that uncertainty is a matter of "degree rather than a quality that is present or absent."[3] The degree of uncertainty arises from existing circumstances in the campaign context that change slowly or quickly, dramatically or slightly. In this vein, uncertainty changes over time. It is, thus, a dynamic, time-dependent phenomenon. In a broad-ranging literature, economists view high levels of uncertainty as volatility or a set of shocks that disrupt the current state of affairs.[4] "The rate of information arrival" typically lags behind the volatility, making it difficult, if not impossible, to predict what will happen next.[5] Thus, with high uncertainty there is a greater dispersion of possible outcomes and an increase in forecast errors.[6] Forecasters become uncertain about their own forecasts. While under conditions of low uncertainty, there is one clear path; under conditions of high uncertainty, there are many possible next steps, directions, and blind alleys.

Second, uncertainty in the campaign context can be reduced, but it cannot be eliminated. In some situations, uncertainty is easily removed by acquiring information that clarifies next steps. For example, if a person awaits job offers from two companies and the deciding factor is salary, the job-seeker merely needs to hear the salaries being offered by the prospective employers to remove the uncertainty and take one of the jobs. But the national campaign context is unique in that uncertainty is ever present about two pivotal outcomes upon which the entire election rests: how many people will go to the polls and who will win the race. No matter how much information campaigners and voters acquire, some uncertainty about these two results persists until the votes are counted. And this is in

[2] Claudio Cioffi-Revilla, *Politics and Uncertainty* (Cambridge: Cambridge University Press, 1998), 5–6.

[3] Barry Burden, "Everything But Death and Taxes," in B. Burden, ed. *Uncertainty in American Politics* (Cambridge: Cambridge University Press, 2003), 6.

[4] Ben Bernanke, "Irreversibility, Uncertainty, and Cyclical Investment," *The Quarterly Journal of Economics* 98 (February 1983): 85–106; Romer, 1990; Nick Bloom, Stephen Bond, and John Van Reene, "Uncertainty and Investment Dynamics," *Review of Economic Studies* 74 (2007): 391–415; Michelle Alexopoulos and Jon Cohen, "Uncertain Times, Uncertain Measures," Working Paper 352, University of Toronto, February 11, 2009, 1–56; Nicholas Bloom, "The Impact of Uncertainty Shocks," *Econometrica* 77 (May 2009): 623–685; Nicholas Bloom, "Fluctuations in Uncertainty," *Journal of Economic Perspectives* 28 (Spring 2014): 153–176.

[5] Ben Bernanke, 1983, 86.

[6] Bernanke, 1983, 93; Bloom, 2012, 156.

part because the two outcomes are highly interrelated. A candidate may know that she is well ahead in the polls and be fairly certain about the outcome of the campaign, but she does not know precisely who will vote. If a large number of her supporters fail to go to the polls, she may lose. Generally, candidates and parties lack certainty about how many people will vote, no matter how aggressively they attempt to mobilize them.

In addition, when unforeseen events define the national campaign context or circumstances change quickly, information gathering may actually increase uncertainty. New information may directly contradict older information, intensifying the difficulty for decision makers (whether campaigners or citizens) to predict what will happen next. Moreover, not all politicians find it in their interest to reduce uncertainty. In some situations, some politicians may believe that fanning fear and ambiguity about the future may permit them to gain the upper hand.

Third, there are two types of uncertainty—external and internal. Some analysts consider only internal uncertainty because they argue that uncertainty exclusively involves individuals' perceptions of unfolding situations. This is consistent with Anthony Downs (1957) who wrote "uncertainty is any lack of sure knowledge about the course of past, present, future, or hypothetical events."[7] But we assert that politics is inherently indeterminate, and there is what Cioffi-Revilla calls "natural uncertainty." Thus, uncertainty is both categorical and perceptual—external and internal.

External uncertainty involves the degree to which the national scene changes in unpredictable and unmeasurable ways, beyond the control of government leaders, groups, and individual citizens. At one end of the uncertainty continuum, a high level of external uncertainty arises when startling events occur that people assumed were impossible. These shocks in the national campaign context may involve both downside uncertainty and upside uncertainty. Downside uncertainty encapsulates crises that jar the ordinary course of events. These crises may occur across any number of dimensions—the economy, world affairs, and domestic politics. A financial collapse like the stock market crash of 1929 was viewed as inconceivable until the global crash in 2008. It was widely assumed that foreign terrorism could not unfold on American soil until the events of September 11, 2001. In contrast, upside uncertainty involves pleasant surprises or positive innovations. One of the most dramatic international relations events of the latter half of the twentieth century was also one of the least anticipated—the break-up of the Soviet Union in December 1999. An average annual increase of 7 percent in housing prices

[7] Anthony Downs, *An Economic Theory of Democracy* (New York: Harper and Row, 1957), 77.

from 2001 through 2006 was at once unheard of and then widely assumed to continue indefinitely. Upside uncertainty involves questions about finality. At what point will the good times end? Bubbles are seldom observed until they burst.

At the other end of the uncertainty continuum, as noted in the Introduction, a low level of uncertainty exists in elections in which a popular incumbent is running against a weak opponent. But there are also low levels of uncertainty when the economy is stable or the world relatively peaceful. At points in between along the continuum, differences in economic change, mass communication innovations, disruptive world events, and new suffrage laws make the national campaign context more or less surprising. Thus, external uncertainty is the degree of unpredictability in the national situation.

Internal uncertainty involves individuals' lack of clarity about how they should respond to these changes in the national scene. Individuals must not only assess the national campaign context but also how well the candidates in the race will address the external uncertainty in that context. Are the candidates equally competent (incompetent) in handling the situation? Is one better than the others? With high external uncertainty comes high internal uncertainty. And to alleviate high internal uncertainty, individuals collect information and form opinions about the candidates, determining who is best to alleviate the external uncertainty. With low external uncertainty comes low internal uncertainty. With a stable campaign context, citizens have less to worry about and likely gather less information and form fewer opinions about the candidates. In this case, citizens may know little about the candidates and, with low internal uncertainty, see little reason to vote.

Yet, external uncertainty does not have a one-to-one connection with internal uncertainty, nor do high levels of internal uncertainty automatically prompt an individual to vote. Individuals differ in the level of internal uncertainty they have and how they handle it, even if they were to perceive the external uncertainty in exactly the same way. If, in collecting information and forming opinions about the candidates, an individual is unhappy with one or both politicians—seeing little difference between them or being dissatisfied with one or both, there is no particular incentive to vote. Thus, the connection between the national campaign context and the individual breaks down.

Novelty

The external uncertainty of the campaign context arises from novelty—the degree to which elements of the political environment categorically break with the past. This novelty throws campaigners and the eligible electorate off guard and generates political tension and excitement. It limits the ability to look back to past experience for guideposts on future success or failure. Novelty is a relative phenomenon based on what has happened in the past and rests on the magnitude of change that is created in the political environment—how much the unexpected happens.

At its most obvious, novelty involves the first time that something happens or a one-of-a-kind event that occurs within the campaign context—the first time the country faces a particular threat, the introduction of a new form of technology or legal requirement, or the occurrence of a catastrophic natural disaster. At a more subtle level, novelty also includes a condition quickly worsening, a dramatic event occurring near Election Day, or the government's commitment of a larger amount of resources to address a problem than has been done previously. The novelty of the campaign context is conceptualized as broad-based: it may result from a single event, but it may also involve significant shifts in long-term conditions in the economy or noticeable changes in foreign policy success that take place over the months leading up to and during the campaign period. The novelty may include good or bad news—a war victory or defeat, an economic upswing or downturn, major accomplishments or scandals. The key is a significant change in the context from some time in the past which produces high levels of external uncertainty. What will happen next is unclear.

Campaigners must adjust to and respond to this novelty, often upending their campaign game plans. As much as John McCain, the Republican contender in 2008, wanted to make the campaign about Barack Obama's qualifications to be president, economic turmoil and the uncertainty encircling it overran this strategy and, indeed, brought into question McCain's own skills at coming to grips with the severity of America's economic problems.

In the absence of novelty, politics is routine, incremental, and predictable. The campaign context has continuity from the past; there is little change over time; and little that is going on as Election Day approaches differs from what has happened in the past. Predictability means that conditions remain roughly the same or are improving incrementally, no dramatic events arise, or the government's commitment of resources continues as before. The key is that little unforeseen occurs in the campaign context from the immediate past. Thus, with lower uncertainty, politics generates limited public interest and nonvoting is likely to increase.

In 1972, with Republican Richard Nixon seeking his second term against Democratic Senator George McGovern of South Dakota, per capita personal income remained relatively strong and steady. Unemployment, while up from 1968, was still low at 5.6 percent. Casualties in the Vietnam War were at all-time lows. And there were no dramatic events that took place. Even though operatives from the president's reelection committee had broken into the

Democratic National Committee headquarters at the Watergate office complex in Washington, D.C., few people associated the incident with Nixon himself. Meanwhile McGovern fumbled on revelations that his first vice presidential nominee, Senator Thomas Eagleton of Missouri, had undergone shock treatment for depression and unceremoniously replaced him on the ticket with R. Sargent Shriver of Maryland. Little uncertainty existed in the campaign context and, perhaps, even less existed about the outcome of the race. Nonvoting increased in 1972 to 43 percent from 37 percent in 1968.

The level of novelty dictates not only the level of external uncertainty but also the internal uncertainty people feel about the national campaign context. The greater the degree of novelty, the more (internally) uncertain people are about their perception of events and candidates. Without familiar cues and guideposts, people may perceive the nature of the situation as more (or less) dramatic than it really is. And candidates may attempt to capitalize on this internal uncertainty. As an example, when three individuals in the United States were infected with the Ebola virus in October 2014, many people perceived that a national epidemic would ensue. Several House and Senate candidates used this possibility and the fear associated with the disease in their campaigns during the midterm elections of 2014 to get people to the polls. Thom Tillis, successful Republican Senate candidate who ousted incumbent Senator Kay Hagan (D-NC), told a debate audience: "We've got an Ebola outbreak, we have bad actors that can come across the border. We need to seal the border and secure it."[8] In fact, no national epidemic occurred, nor did any cases come into the United States from Mexico.

Risk

Novelty produces uncertainty, but, in turn, uncertainty creates risk—making a choice among a range of options which "contains a threat of a very poor outcome."[9] The clearest risk is for eligible voters to see their least-preferred candidate win the race. However, the difficulty is that decision makers do not know whether they correctly perceive the costs and benefits of one candidate winning over the other, as the Ebola scare example makes clear. This is the core of internal uncertainty. The costs may be much higher or lower than anticipated. It is also

[8] Igor Bobic, "Scott Brown wants to secure the border from Ebola," *Huffington Post*, October 9, 2014, found at http://www.huffingtonpost.com/2014/10/09/scott-brown-ebola_n_5959200.html.

[9] James March and Zur Shapira, "Managerial Perspectives on Risk and Risk-Taking," in J. March, ed. *Decisions and Organizations* (Oxford: Basil Blackwell, 1988), 81.

easy to overestimate the benefits of one candidate's victory. During many campaigns, a particular candidate may generate incredible excitement and make numerous promises, which lead to disappointment once the candidate is in office. In general, because of internal uncertainty, people do not really know how good their least preferred candidate will be in office, nor can they readily assess how bad their most preferred candidate will be if elected. According to researcher Jack Gray, the most dangerous type of risk "is unchallenged or insufficiently challenged views, the risk that we deny or heavily discount evidence and arguments that challenge our views and selectively accept or place a premium on evidence and arguments that confirm them."[10] This aspect of our theory aligns with the "minimax regret" model of participation developed by John Ferejohn and Morris Fiorina, in which they assert that people vote in order to minimize their maximum regret (of their least preferred candidate winning).[11] However, in two ways our approach moves beyond Ferejohn and Fiorina. First, their model rests solely on individuals' assessments of the candidates and not the broader campaign context within which the candidates campaign. Second, their model does not consider how external uncertainty in the campaign context and internal uncertainty of individuals combine to produce participation decisions.

The risk of the "wrong" candidate winning is heightened in political campaigns because there are typically multiple perspectives on how to deal with the external uncertainty.[12] Partisan and ideological perspectives may differ radically on what to do. For eligible voters who often pay most attention to politics only at election time, these potentially contradictory perspectives increase the risk of not voting. In other races when the candidates agree on the major issues or people perceive little difference between candidates, then uncertainty lessens, because even the least preferred candidate may not be all that bad. People are less likely to see the stakes in the race as pivotal, so there is less risk regardless of who wins, and nonvoting increases.

Party Competition and Uncertainty

Party competition is integrally linked to external uncertainty in the campaign context. To be sure, party competition is not a one-election phenomenon. Over many years and multiple elections, parties compete for a variety of offices. Much of what they can accomplish in a given election depends on how well they have

[10] Jack Gray, "Meta-Risk," *Journal of Portfolio Management* 26 (Spring 2000): 20.

[11] John Ferejohn and Morris Fiorina, "The Paradox of Not Voting: A Decision Theoretic Analysis," *American Political Science Review* 68 (June 1974): 525–536.

[12] Roy Boyne, *Risk* (Buckingham, UK: Open University Press, 2003).

fared before. But, just as the uncertainty of the campaign context defines the mobilization efforts of the parties it also helps set how close a race will be. As the campaign unfolds, party insiders and the general public do not know whether party fortunes will shift and whether circumstances will derail an otherwise well-run campaign. No one is ever quite sure how much effort the parties will undertake, how well they will do, or what mistakes they will make.

The long time frame for most American campaigns also contributes to this facet of external uncertainty. Unlike the short campaign periods in most countries, US election campaigns go on for months and, most recently, presidential campaigns go on for years. This means that there is likely to be volatility in the campaign context as changes occur from one month to the next, all of which can have repercussions for party competition.

Thus, the interconnections among novelty, external uncertainty, and risk are the backdrop for party competition in any election. The degree of uncertainty shapes the competitive environment for the parties, and inter-party conflict responds accordingly. With greater uncertainty comes higher stakes; the parties have greater incentives to take risks and commit resources to win, because a race is too pivotal to lose. If dramatic events jar the political scene, with considerable media attention nationwide, this creates particular consequences for the party in power. The uncertainty is likely to disproportionately affect the incumbent party as it becomes associated with the unfolding novelty. The incumbent party will be blamed if the uncertainty yields failure and heralded if the uncertainty yields success. Often this provides the party out of power a built-in campaign strategy—attacking the party in power for not handling the uncertainty appropriately and creating mobilization strategies accordingly.[13] There are also other factors that contribute to party competition—the demographics of certain states, the personalities and experience of party politicians, the issues they use to connect with voters over the long term. But, uncertainty becomes a key focus of the campaign—something candidates and parties cannot ignore.

Lesser uncertainty means that there are more limited incentives for the parties to target the race as a must-win. With greater predictability in the campaign context, it is unlikely that the party out of power will expend resources at the same level as it would under conditions of uncertainty. Parties can run their campaigns on the issues that appeal to their base supporters. With lower uncertainty in the campaign context, parties and candidates are more likely to stick to familiar issues and familiar formulas for victory that have worked for them in the

[13] David Mayhew, *Partisan Balance: Why American Parties Don't Kill the U.S. Constitutional System* (Princeton: Princeton University Press, 2013); Thomas Mann and Norman Ornstein, *It's Even Worse than It Looks* (New York: Basic Books, 2013); John Aldrich, *Why Parties?* (Chicago: University of Chicago Press, 2011).

past, often based on imagery, values, and mood. For example, the Republican Party's focus on social issues since the 1980s—abortion, gay marriage, gun control—played well when the campaign context offered few surprises.[14]

Nonvoting

The level of external uncertainty of the campaign context creates conditions for voting and nonvoting. As noted above, one of the central points of external uncertainty in any election is "who will win?" Thus, it makes sense that turnout rises in elections when the outcome hangs in the balance and falls when the outcome is suspected months in advance. The external uncertainty and rising party competition generate interest among people who may otherwise pay little attention to politics. It prompts people to enter the polls who typically do not vote, who only vote sporadically, or who decide whether to vote for the first time. Likewise, with heightened party competition produced by external uncertainty, eligible voters are more inclined to vote when the parties offer distinct approaches to alleviating this uncertainty. The net result is that nonvoting is likely to decline in situations of high external uncertainty and concomitantly high party competition.

Conversely, under conditions of low external uncertainty, party competition is likely to be lessened, and this lowers incentives for people to vote. In conditions of low uncertainty, the election, in effect, fails to provide people with a clear choice between alternative views on central policy directions for the country or a state. The direct benefit that the election should provide people—determining an outcome that is favorable to their way of thinking or preventing an outcome that is harmful to their viewpoint—is clouded by limited party competition. In that sense, they perceive benefits to not voting.

Thus, we offer the central hypothesis of the book: the higher the level of uncertainty in the national campaign context, the lower the level of nonvoting. In order to firmly anchor this hypothesis, explore a comparison between economic and political behavior under uncertainty. Under conditions of high uncertainty, economists observe a "wait and see" approach among businesses and consumers. "There is an option value associated with avoiding irreversible actions."[15] Businesses exercise an option to wait, postponing investments and

[14] Earl Black and Merle Black, *Divided America: The Ferocious Power Struggle in American Politics* (New York: Simon and Schuster, 2007).

[15] Bernanke, 1983, 88. See also Rudiger Bachmann and Christain Bayer, "Wait and See Business Cycles," *Journal of Monetary Economics* 60 (September 2013): 704–719; Bloom, Bond, and Van Reene, 2007.

hiring because these actions, once taken, are expensive to reverse. Instead, they retain the option of choosing among alternatives in the future. Similarly, consumers also wait amidst high levels of uncertainty because they do not wish to spend income, also an irreversible act. "When consumers are making decisions on buying durables like houses, cars, and furniture, they can usually delay purchases relatively easily."[16]

In contrast, in the political case there is no value to waiting amidst high uncertainty. Election Day passes, and nonvoters cannot change their minds and decide they should have gone to the polls after all. In this sense, the political decision is irreversible and fixed in time. Even in the current era of early voting, people have little leeway regarding when they vote. While being on the sidelines is an appropriate place to be to wait out economic uncertainty, in the political case there is a moment at which individuals can do something to address the uncertainty, which ends when the polls close. So unlike the "wait and see" response in the economic case, there is a "go and act" response in the political case. Eligible voters must act on Election Day or forgo the ability to respond to the uncertainty by directing who wins and who loses. Unless individuals believe they are not competent to judge the uncertainty and leave that assessment to others, nonvoting is not an apt response to high levels of uncertainty.

Continuing the comparison, economists observe that under conditions of low uncertainty, firms and consumers are much more likely to make irreversible investments. The value of staying on the sidelines drops. A shock does not disrupt the flow of information. According to economist Ben Bernanke, "As knowledge accumulates and priors concentrate, the propensity to invest increases."[17] But in the political case, staying on the sidelines in the midst of low uncertainty makes more sense. Eligible voters find less to worry about and do not feel that the election outcome dramatically alters the future.

While our focus is on nonvoting in national elections, the theory of uncertainty is quite general and can be applied to local and state elections and also elections in other countries. As long as accurate data on nonvoting and key shocks to the economic, technological, legal, and international arenas can be identified, the theory can be tested in a variety of electoral settings. As one example, the 2016 British referendum election on whether to remain in the European Union encapsulated high levels of political and economic uncertainty about what would happen if Britain did in fact leave the European Union. Nonvoting dropped 6 percentage points from that observed in the 2015 parliamentary elections.

[16] Bloom, 2014, 164. See also Romer, 1990. This research documents that as businesses and consumers wait, the economy inevitably slows down.

[17] Bernanke, 1983, 95.

Conclusion

The hallmark of the campaign context is the degree of uncertainty that unfolds in the months before the election. The antecedent of this external uncertainty is novelty; its consequence is risk. This suggests that the emphasis in previous research on the resources, motivations, and social networks of voters and nonvoters must be placed in the broader national campaign context. Even people with substantial personal resources—education, income, interest in politics, and social networks—are less likely to vote if external uncertainty and party competition are low. Understanding the influence of external uncertainty helps better explain how nonvoting levels rise and fall from one election to the next. It is difficult to suggest that people's personal resources radically swing between elections. People with high education in one election year cannot suddenly lose their education in the next. Yet implicitly this is what would need to happen in the individual resource models of the existing literature. This is why researchers often observe that as education levels in the United States have gone up, nonvoting has not necessarily gone down. Considering the campaign context, when there are conditions of high external uncertainty, people of all education levels are more likely to be drawn to elections. When conditions of low external uncertainty prevail, people across all education levels are less likely to be interested in politics. Even people with high education may find it less important to vote when predictability reigns.

Neither party mobilization efforts nor party competition exist in a vacuum. They derive squarely from the novelty and uncertainty of the campaign context. What parties and candidates are able to accomplish during the campaign period is tied to the circumstances that present themselves in the campaign context.

Thus, the campaign context theory increases understanding of both aggregate nonvoting levels and how individuals within the eligible electorate decide whether or not to vote. People choose the candidate they feel will best alleviate significant uncertainty in the political environment. This provides the central incentive to vote. Conversely, if uncertainty is low or no candidate is addressing the uncertainty in a manner consistent with what an individual wants, then this provides a central disincentive to vote.

2

Measuring Nonvoting

At 4 o'clock in the morning of November 9, 1960, no one knew who would succeed Dwight Eisenhower as President of the United States. People who had stayed up all night to watch the results saw the networks sign off at 2 AM without a clear victor. John Kennedy remained with family members and advisors at his house overlooking Nantucket Sound at Hyannisport, Massachusetts, where the group had gathered some nine hours before. Richard Nixon and his team alternated drinking coffee and scotch hour by hour as they milled around a penthouse suite at the Ambassador Hotel in downtown Los Angeles. There were signs on both sides: Mayor Richard J. Daley of Chicago had called Kennedy to say that there was nothing to worry about: Chicago, and thereby Illinois, was in the Kennedy column. Still that did not assure victory. Nixon received encouraging reports from precincts in the suburbs of Los Angeles, not yet known as the conservative political entity "Orange County," which was then the fastest growing county in America. This meant that Nixon would take his home state. Not until some seven hours later were the results known. Kennedy had won, but there was no clear victor. Kennedy prevailed by .17 percent, with 49.72 percent of the national vote; Nixon lost with 49.55 percent. In 14 states, the race was roughly 50–50. Had a mere 12,000 votes shifted in five states—Hawaii, Illinois, Missouri, Nevada, and New Mexico— Richard Nixon would have been president in 1960, not 1968.

Theodore White described the tension within the country: "Four states held center stage: Michigan, Minnesota, Illinois, California—three in the Midwest, one in the Far West. And in each, the same pattern of voting rose from the same style of life and the same prejudices—city against countryside, old stock against new. Los Angeles and San Francisco had voted Republican in 1956; now they were giving Kennedy a lead. But in the Central Valley, where Stevenson had led Eisenhower in 1956, Kennedy was barely abreast—the Central Valley is inhabited by Oklahomans and transplants from the southern Bible Belt. In Los Angeles' suburbs, Kennedy was being overwhelmed. In the three Midwestern states, the big cities had all given him the expected plurality; but in the farms and in the suburbs and the small towns it was going abruptly against him."[1] Although commentators like White knew that the 1960 election was an intensely competitive one, they would not have known that it would stand as the closest race of the entire twentieth century. Even the disputed election of 2000 was not as close. Indeed, the 1960 contest stands as the single closest presidential election since 1880 when James Garfield won the office by 1,898 votes. It also marks the election with the lowest nonvoting of any election since 1900.

Trends in Nonvoting?

This chapter considers the nature of aggregate nonvoting from 1920 through 2012, defined as *the percentage of a state's eligible adult citizens who do not vote in presidential and House midterm elections.* The measure is based on citizen population rather than voting-age population, because only US citizens—those born in the country or naturalized—are permitted to vote.[2] Figures 2.1 and 2.2 chart nonvoting in presidential and House midterm elections for the nation as a whole, southern states in the old Confederacy and the Border South, and states outside the South.[3] Tables 2.1 and 2.2 present the corresponding tabular data and include changes in nonvoting rates between adjacent elections. The figures display how nonvoting moves up and down across elections but within a defined range. During the 24 presidential elections from 1920 to 2012, mean national nonvoting for the entire period is 42 percent, with between one-third and one-half of the eligible electorate not voting. During the 23 midterm House elections from 1922 to 2010, mean national nonvoting is 58 percent. Midterm nonvoting moves in a band from one-half to two-thirds of the eligible electorate. The defined range within which nonvoting moves is consistent with uncertainty in the national campaign context, which is neither absolute nor absent but moves along a continuum from high to low.

The measure of nonvoting allows us to confront commentary over the past several decades which suggests that there is an increasing trend in nonvoting. In a wide array of work, researchers have suggested that voters are vanishing, disappearing, and exiting the body politic. Analysts have maintained that

[1] Theodore H. White, *The Making of the President 1960* (New York: Atheneum Publishers, 1961), 23–24.

[2] The full discussion of our measure of nonvoting begins with the section "How to Measure Nonvoting."

[3] The southern states include Alabama, Arkansas, Florida, Georgia, Kentucky, Louisiana, Mississippi, Missouri, North Carolina, Oklahoma, South Carolina, Tennessee, Texas, Virginia, and West Virginia.

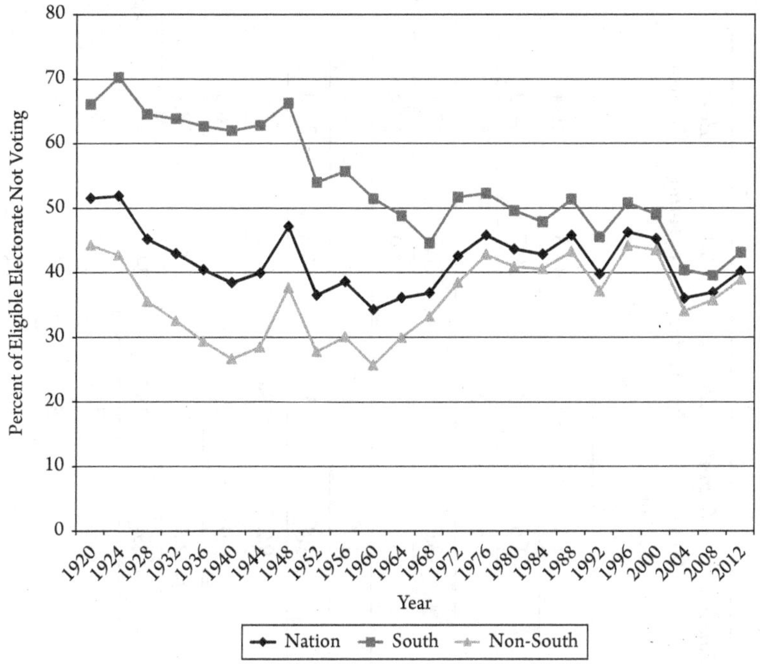

Figure 2.1 Nonvoting in Presidential Elections, 1920–2012

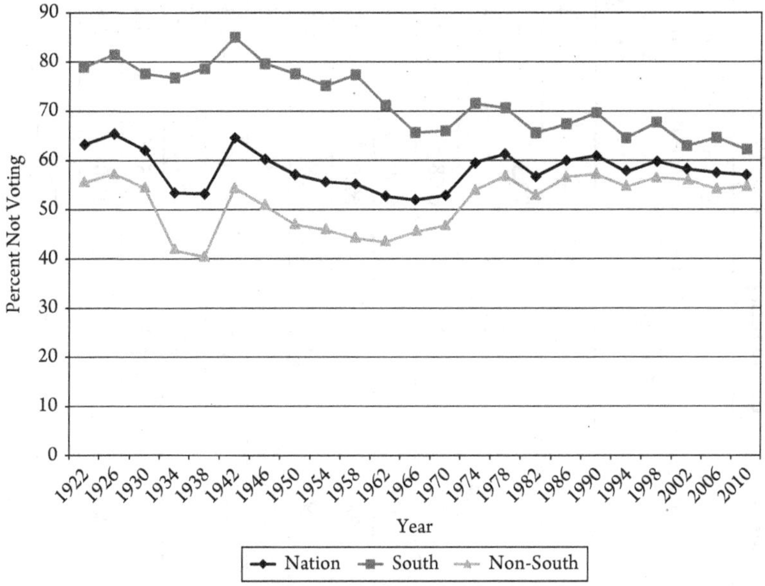

Figure 2.2 Nonvoting in Midterm House Elections, 1922–2010

Table 2.1 **Nonvoting in Presidential Elections, 1920–2012**

Year	*Nation Nonvoting*	*Nation Inter-Election Change*	*South Nonvoting*	*South Inter-Election Change*	*Non-South Nonvoting*	*Non-South Inter-Election Change*	*West Nonvoting*	*Midwest Nonvoting*	*East Nonvoting*
1920	51.5	11.9	66.1	–2.4	44.3	11.3	45.1	41.5	46.4
1924	51.9	0.4	70.3	4.2	42.7	–1.6	43.7	39.7	44.9
1928	45.2	–6.7	64.6	–5.7	35.5	–7.2	40.8	33.1	32.4
1932	43.0	–2.3	63.8	–0.8	32.5	–3.0	33.6	30.9	33.1
1936	40.4	–2.5	62.6	–1.2	29.3	–3.2	33.1	27.0	27.9
1940	38.4	–2.0	62.0	–0.7	26.7	–2.7	28.2	24.7	27.2
1944	39.9	1.5	62.8	0.8	28.5	1.8	31.6	26.8	27.0
1948	47.2	7.3	66.3	3.5	37.6	9.2	38.0	37.3	37.6
1952	36.5	–10.7	54.0	–12.3	27.8	–9.9	29.7	27.0	26.5
1956	38.6	2.1	55.7	1.7	30.0	2.3	32.2	29.0	28.7
1960	34.3	–4.3	51.5	–4.2	25.7	–4.4	28.7	24.1	24.1
1964	36.1	1.8	48.8	–2.6	29.9	4.2	31.3	29.0	29.3
1968	36.9	0.8	44.6	–4.2	33.2	3.3	35.7	31.5	31.9
1972	42.6	5.7	51.7	7.1	38.4	5.2	40.1	35.9	39.0

1976	45.8	3.2	52.3	0.6	42.8	4.4	46.6	38.2	43.0
1980	43.7	−2.2	49.6	−2.7	40.9	−1.9	42.5	37.2	42.8
1984	42.9	−0.8	47.9	−1.7	40.6	−0.3	41.8	37.9	41.8
1988	45.8	2.9	51.4	3.5	43.3	2.7	44.8	40.5	44.3
1992	39.8	−6.1	45.6	−5.8	37.1	−6.2	38.7	34.8	37.6
1996	46.3	6.5	50.8	5.3	44.2	7.1	45.0	42.2	45.2
2000	45.2	−1.0	49.0	−1.8	43.5	−0.7	44.2	45.1	41.1
2004	36.0	−9.2	40.4	−8.6	34.0	−9.5	36.3	31.6	33.7
2008	36.9	0.9	39.6	−0.9	35.7	1.7	38.2	33.9	34.7
2012	40.2	3.3	43.2	3.6	38.9	3.2	41.7	36.5	38.0
1920–2012									
Mean	41.9		53.9		36.0		38.0	34.0	35.7
Standard Deviation	4.8		8.8		6.1		5.8	5.9	7.0
Slope	−0.1		−0.3		0.1		0.1	0.1	0.1
Inter-Election Change	−0.5		−1.0		−0.2		−0.1	−0.2	−0.4

Note: Due to rounding, entries in the Inter-Election Change column may not always exactly equal the subtraction of nonvoting values between adjacent elections.

Table 2.2 **Nonvoting in Midterm House Elections, 1922–2010**

Year	*Nation Nonvoting*	*Nation Inter-Election Change*	*South Nonvoting*	*South Inter-Election Change*	*Non-South Nonvoting*	*Non-South Inter-Election Change*	*West Nonvoting*	*Midwest Nonvoting*	*East Nonvoting*
1922	63.2	3.7	78.9	4.2	55.4	3.5	54.2	55.4	56.8
1926	65.3	2.1	81.4	2.5	57.3	1.9	53.9	59.3	58.7
1930	62.1	–3.3	77.6	–3.8	54.3	–3.0	53.9	54.8	54.1
1934	53.4	–8.7	76.7	–0.9	41.7	–12.6	43.3	39.6	42.3
1938	53.1	–0.3	78.6	1.9	40.4	–1.4	41.7	40.8	38.4
1942	64.6	11.4	84.9	6.3	54.4	14.0	55.8	53.3	54.0
1946	60.3	–4.3	79.6	–5.3	50.6	–3.8	51.3	51.1	49.4
1950	57.1	–3.2	77.5	–2.0	46.9	–3.7	46.9	46.8	46.8
1954	55.6	–1.5	75.2	–2.4	45.8	–1.1	45.2	47.4	44.8
1958	55.2	–0.4	77.3	2.2	44.1	–1.7	44.6	44.5	43.0
1962	52.6	–2.5	71.2	–6.2	43.4	–0.7	43.4	43.8	42.9
1966	51.9	–0.8	65.7	–5.5	45.4	2.0	44.9	46.7	44.7
1970	52.8	1.0	66.0	0.3	46.7	1.2	47.0	46.2	46.8
1974	59.6	6.7	71.5	5.5	53.9	7.3	53.7	53.1	55.2
1978	61.3	1.7	70.6	–0.9	56.9	2.9	57.3	55.4	57.9

1982	56.7	–4.6	65.6	–5.0	52.8	–4.1	52.0	51.3	55.4
1986	59.9	3.2	67.3	1.7	56.7	3.9	54.3	54.9	61.8
1990	61.0	1.0	69.7	2.4	57.2	0.5	56.6	56.1	59.0
1994	57.6	–3.3	64.5	–5.1	54.6	–2.6	53.2	53.8	57.4
1998	59.8	2.1	67.6	3.1	56.5	1.9	54.7	55.1	60.4
2002	58.3	–1.5	62.9	–4.7	56.1	–0.5	56.2	55.0	57.1
2006	57.5	–0.8	64.6	1.7	54.2	–1.9	56.7	52.9	52.3
2010	57.1	–0.4	62.2	–2.4	54.6	0.5	54.1	54.2	55.1
1922–2010									
Mean	58.1		72.1		51.3		51.1	50.9	51.9
Standard Deviation	3.7		6.4		5.3		5.7	5.1	6.5
Slope	0.0		–0.2		0.1		0.0	0.1	0.1
Inter-Election Change	–0.1		–0.5		0.1		–0.5	0.3	0.1

Note: Due to rounding, entries in the Inter-Election Change column may not always exactly equal the subtraction of nonvoting values between adjacent elections.

nonvoting has risen since 1960—touted as the watershed year for high voter turnout. Researcher Thomas Patterson commented that "the period from 1960 to 2000 marks the longest ebb in turnout in the nation's history."[4] He attributed this to increasingly candidate-centered rather than party-centered politics. Scholars Steven Rosenstone and John Mark Hansen observed that "participation in American national elections has declined steadily since the 1960s."[5] They suggested that this has resulted from a combination of lessened political interest among citizens and less effective mobilization efforts of politicians. Mark Franklin found nonvoting increased among successively younger cohorts.[6] Other researchers looked to demographic changes to explain changes in nonvoting. Peter Nardulli, Jon Dalager, and Donald Greco commented that large metropolitan areas were responsible for the post-1960 increase in nonvoting.[7] Analyst Ruy Teixeira wrote that "Not only are American turnout levels low, but they have been going down steadily for the last three decades [since 1960]." He maintained that fewer social ties connecting people, especially the young, to family and place precipitated the nonvoting problem. Teixeira summarized much of the literature by writing "contemporary United States is a very low turnout society." [8]

Researchers further viewed this upswing in US nonvoting as part of a more general increase in nonvoting among established democracies from the 1960s to 2000. Political scientist Martin Wattenberg suggested that all nations experienced a rise in nonvoting, but the US rate started higher and increased more sharply. He described a monotonic decrease in nonvoting up to the 1960 election and a monotonic increase thereafter. Wattenberg maintained that the "relatively high turnout of 1960 represented not an anomaly, but rather the continuation of a well-established forty year trend. In the decades since 1960, the trend has been in the opposite direction."[9] While placing the United States in the context of other nations is important, such an analysis must contend with numerous variations across countries, some of which have compulsory voting, automatic

[4] Thomas Patterson, *The Vanishing Voter* (New York: Vintage Books, 2002), 4.

[5] Steven Rosenstone and John Mark Hansen, *Mobilization, Participation, and Democracy in America* (New York: Longman, 2003), 1.

[6] Mark Franklin, *Voter Turnout and the Dynamics of Electoral Competition in Established Democracies since 1945* (Cambridge: Cambridge University Press, 2004).

[7] Peter Nardulli, Jon Dalager, and Donald Greco, "Voter Turnout in U.S. Presidential Elections: A Historical View and Some Speculation," *PS: Political Science and Politics* 29 (September 1996): 480–490.

[8] Ruy Teixeira, *The Disappearing American Voter* (Washington, D.C.: Brookings Institution, 1992), 9; 24.

[9] Martin Wattenberg, *Where Have All the Voters Gone?* (Cambridge: Harvard University Press, 2002), 28.

registration, and door-to-door registration. Also, gathering data over time across countries is complicated and often inconsistent.[10]

But trends are tricky. Defining a trend is intuitively straightforward: "a line of general direction or movement or a prevailing tendency or inclination." [11] Identifying a trend is more difficult. Basic statistics measure a trend as a general movement in a variable over time, controlling for other factors. Past values of a variable predict the underlying direction and the rate of change in future values of the variable. Thus, the identification of a trend depends heavily on the selection of a starting point. The choice of one starting point may lead to a set of conclusions that are far different from, even the opposite of, conclusions based on another starting point.

In this regard, while many analysts begin studies of turnout with the 1960 election—the lowest level of nonvoting since 1900—it is a false starting point, which makes nonvoting in all elections that follow look worse by comparison. Indeed, there are significant reasons why 1960 would *not* be the place to start a discussion of American nonvoting. There are accurate data for elections well before 1960. The 1960 election carries with it no historical marker: it is not 1920, the first election after World War I when women entered the electorate; it is not 1946, the first post-World War II election; it is not 1966, the first election after the passage of the Voting Rights Act of 1965; it is not 1972, the first election when 18-year-olds entered the electorate. The 1960 campaign is significant in the introduction of the televised debate, but television itself was already a feature of presidential elections earlier, as Eisenhower's hiring of an acting coach in 1952 and Nixon's own "Checker's Speech" to a nationwide audience in the same year attested. The debate itself set no precedent, not repeated again until Ford and Carter in 1976. Similarly, if we were to begin an analysis of nonvoting with the 1996 election—with one of the highest levels of nonvoting in the twentieth century—we would surely observe a trend toward declining nonvoting. Yet, both of these starting points are at best arbitrary and have no particular conceptual or empirical rationale for being employed.

Before 1960 there was actually no "well-established forty year trend" of diminishing nonvoting. As seen in Table 2.1, from 1920, the year in which women entered the electorate, through 1948, nonvoting went below 40 percent only once—in 1940 when the nonvoting rate was 38 percent. American nonvoting did reach its lowest levels in the 1950s and 1960s, when it fell below 40 percent of eligible Americans in each of the five presidential elections from 1952 through 1968. But, as Tables 2.1 and 2.2 clarify, after the 1960s, nonvoting

[10] Because our primary interest is a historical accounting of nonvoting in the United States, this comparative analysis, while worthwhile, is outside the scope of our research.

[11] http://www.m-w.com/dictionary.htm, Merriam-Webster Online Dictionary.

looked remarkably similar to that observed prior to the 1950s. Nonvoting during the 1970s, 1980s, and 1990s, like that before 1950, never went below the 40 percent mark.

As Figure 2.1 and Table 2.1 show, in the seven elections from 2000 to 2012, political leaders and policy analysts have had less to be concerned about than in the elections that preceded them as nonvoting has gone down. Nonvoting in the 2000 presidential election was 45 percent, a small 1 percentage point decline from 1996. Then, in the 2004 presidential election, nonvoting dropped steeply by over 9 percentage points to 36 percent, and it remained roughly the same in 2008 at 37 percent, numbers commonplace during the Kennedy and Johnson years. In 2012, nonvoting ticked up slightly to 40 percent, but this was lower than nonvoting had been during any of the presidential years of the 1970s and 1980s. While nonvoting is notoriously high in American midterm House elections, as Table 2.2 reveals, it nevertheless nudged downward in 2002 by 2 percentage points from 1998, down again by a percentage point in 2006, and remained stable in 2010 when 57 percent of the electorate did not vote in House elections, on par with midterms of the 1950s, when nonvoting was low, although not quite as low as the 1960s.

To amplify this, consider several facts about American nonvoting:

- Nonvoting in the 1960 election was 34 percent.
- Mean nonvoting for the 11 presidential elections from 1920, with the advent of women's suffrage, through 1960 was 43 percent.
- Mean nonvoting for the 13 presidential elections from 1964 through 2012 was 41 percent.[12]
- Mean nonvoting for presidential elections across the entire period from 1920 through 2012 was 42 percent.[13]

These statements simultaneously highlight how unique the 1960 election was and how stable American nonvoting has been. No election since 1960 has had a lower nonvoting rate, but this does not prove that nonvoting has fatally increased. No election before 1960 had lower nonvoting either since women gained the right to vote. Indeed, this is true since 1900 when nonvoting was roughly the same as that in 1960. The stability of American nonvoting is evident in that there

[12] Others have also observed the consistency of voter turnout. See Jan Leighley and Jonathan Nagler, *Who Votes Now* (Princeton: Princeton University Press, 2014) in examining presidential elections from 1972 through 2008.

[13] The standard deviations for these means are also small, providing further evidence of the stability. For the entire period 1920–2012, the standard deviation is 4.8. For the period from 1920–1960, the standard deviation is 5.6. For the period 1964–2012, the standard deviation is 3.8. See Table 2.1.

is virtually no difference in the nonvoting levels between the pre-1960 and post-1960 time period. This is not to suggest that commentators should abandon their concerns about nonvoting, but rather that the worries should be put in the proper historical perspective. Starting an analysis with 1960 heightens the problem artificially, making it more dramatic than it actually has been.

Moreover, the national campaign context suggests that long-term trends toward increasing nonvoting are unlikely. As noted in Chapter 1, the uncertainty of the campaign context shapes and reshapes the electorate, defining those who vote and those who do not. Under certain national circumstances the future is unclear, and much is at stake. At other times the national situation is less unsettled, and stability rather than uncertainty prevails. Thus, as the degree of uncertainty changes from one election to the next, we expect nonvoting to move up and down across elections. When uncertainty is high, more people will vote; when uncertainty is low, fewer people will go to the polls. This counters the presumption that there is, or can be, a long-term trend of increasing nonvoting. Such trends would require that the degree of uncertainty in the campaign context goes down consistently over time and, as a result, more people feel more comfortable leaving Election Day decisions to others. This is not to suggest that it is impossible for nonvoting to move in a single direction across a sequence of elections. Particularly when legal requirements are relaxed, we would expect declines in nonvoting among certain groups within the eligible electorate. Conversely, when legal requirements are made more stringent, we would expect nonvoting to increase. But even with these structural declines, variations in nonvoting across the electorate will remain as uncertainty remains.

How to Measure Nonvoting

To measure nonvoting, we devise a state-level data set on turnout and nonvoting beginning with the 1920 election, the year in which women entered the electorate. Constitutionally, all age-eligible adults were in the electorate. Thus, the voting-eligible population and the voting-age population converged for the first time.[14] To be sure, significant numbers of African Americans were still excluded from voting by state literacy tests, poll taxes, and other impediments that were not eliminated until the Voting Rights Act of 1965. Yet, the 1920 election marks the beginning of modern elections with significant numbers of immigrants in the country, the urbanization of major industrial cities, the United States as an established world power, both politically and economically, and the earliest

[14] Jerrold Rusk, *A Statistical History of the American Electorate* (Washington, D.C.: CQ Press, 2001), 50.

beginnings of radio as the first form of mass media. The state elections data set assembles measures across the 1920–2012 time period of votes cast, voting-eligible population, turnout and nonvoting levels, party competition, suffrage laws, and other statewide indicators on age, race, sex, education, religion, marriage, income, unemployment, and technology in households.

We do not examine elections prior to 1920 because during this pre-modern era there was considerable corruption through unofficial party ballots, bribery, and intimidation which artificially inflated participation numbers to record highs. It was not until the secret ballot and personal registration were introduced sporadically by the states beginning in the 1890s that the corruption abated.[15] Thus, prior to 1920, it is impossible to obtain accurate data on nonvoting because of rampant repeat voting and voting from the graveyard. While the theory of uncertainty in the national campaign context has relevance to any election in any era, it can be empirically tested only when accurate nonvoting data exist.

State-level data enhances scholarship which has focused primarily on national turnout rates. The most appropriate measurement of nonvoting occurs at the state rather than the national level since registration and voting take place in states. Considerable research has underscored the importance of the state as a key unit of analysis. Early researchers considered state differences across ballot types, poll tax and literacy tests, and registration laws.[16] More recently, analysts Erik Engstrom and Samuel Kernell have examined state-level turnout and voting decisions in ascertaining the impact of ballot reforms on participation and party victories during the nineteenth century. Others have considered the impact on electoral participation of state laws such as "motor voter" programs, early voting, and Election Day registration.[17] While motor voter laws have only

[15] See Jerrold Rusk, "The Effect of the Australian Ballot on Split-Ticket Voting," *American Political Science Review* 64 (December, 1970): 1220–1238; Jerrold Rusk, "Comment: The American Electoral Universe: Speculation and Evidence," *American Political Science Review* 68 (September 1974): 1028–1049. An excellent analysis of nineteenth-century voting institutions and reforms is found in Erik Engstrom and Samuel Kernell, *Party Ballots, Reform, and the Transformation of America's Electoral System* (New York: Cambridge University Press, 2014).

[16] See Rusk, 1970; Jerrold Rusk and John Stucker, "The Effect of the Southern System of Election Laws on Voting Participation," in Joel Silbey, Allan Bogue, and William Flanigan, eds., *The History of American Voting Behavior* (Princeton: Princeton University Press, 1978), 198–250; Walter Dean Burnham, "The Changing Shape of the American Political Universe," *American Political Science Review* 59 (March, 1965): 7–28.

[17] Engstrom and Kernell, 2014; Robert Brown and Justin Wedeking, "People Who Have Their Tickets But Do Not Use Them: 'Motor Voter' Registration, Turnout Revisited," *American Politics Research* 34 (July, 2006): 479–504; Michael Hanmer, *Discount Voting: Voter Registration Reforms and Their Effects* (New York: Cambridge University Press, 2012); Ray Wolfinger and Steven Rosenstone, *Who Votes?* (New Haven: Yale University Press, 1980); Benjamin Highton, "Easy Registration and Voter Turnout," *Journal of Politics* 59 (June 1997): 565–575; Paul Gronke, Eva Galanes-Rosenbaum,

modest impact on increasing voter registration, early voting has a stronger effect on increasing voter turnout in some states. In a comprehensive analysis of state influences, political scientist Melanie Springer found "an asymmetry in the effects of institutional change," with restrictive electoral institutions, especially in the South, contributing to low voter turnout, but expansive reforms in other states having modest and varied effects on increasing participation.[18]

The state vantage point not only underscores the importance of the variations among electoral institutions across the American states, but it also affords insights into regional variations that are distinct from and underlie the national summation. Earl Black and Merle Black pointed to region as one of the most defining elements in national elections.[19] They demonstrated the significance and stability of regions as political units beginning in the 1950s and continuing through the early 2000s. Not only is there value in charting the systemic differences between the South and the non-South, but there is equally important information to be gleaned from considering regions within the North. We analyze three regions—the East, the Midwest, and the West—within the North, along with ongoing breakdowns between the South and the rest of the country.

On its face, district-level data would seem to be a more appropriate unit of analysis for House midterm nonvoting, but this is not necessarily the case. Parties typically mount statewide get-out-the-vote drives in both midterm and presidential years. Although some highly competitive districts may be targeted, most congressional districts are not. Too, there are likely to be statewide races going on at the midterm for Senate or governor, which may influence turnout in House races. Thus, the state level incorporates district effects both analytically and empirically. Although there is some loss of information by not calculating

and Peter Miller, "Early Voting and Voter Turnout," in Bruce Cain, Todd Donovan, and Caroline Tolbert, eds., *Democracy in the States: Experiments in Election Reform* (Washington, D.C.: Brookings Institution Press, 2008); Leighley and Nagler, 2014.

[18] Melanie Springer, *How the States Shaped the Nation: American Electoral Institutions and Voter Turnout, 1920–2000* (Chicago: University of Chicago Press, 2014), 163. This result occurs across an array of state voter laws during the period from 1920 through 2000 including voting qualification laws (such as property and residency requirements, poll taxes, and literacy tests), voter registration laws (encompassing frequency of periodic registration, nonvoting purge, mail-in registration, motor voter registration, Election Day registration), voting procedures (poll opening hours), and laws setting the electoral calendar.

[19] Earl Black and Merle Black, *Divided America: The Ferocious Power Struggle in American Politics* (New York: Simon and Schuster, 2007). See also James Gimpel and Jason Schuknecht, *Patchwork Nation: Sectionalism and Political Change in American Politics* (Ann Arbor, MI: University of Michigan Press, 2003); Ruy Teixeira, ed., *America's New Swing Region: Changing Politics and Demographics in the Mountain West* (Washington, D.C.: Brookings Institution Press, 2012); Sean Cunningham, *American Politics in the Postwar Sunbelt: Conservative Growth in a Battleground Region* (Cambridge: Cambridge University Press, 2014).

nonvoting at the district level, it is outweighed by the advantages offered by the state data.

Computing Eligible Population

The measurement of nonvoting as eligible citizens who did not go to the polls involves two sets of decisions: one defines eligibility, and the other accounts for the number of votes cast. Eligibility encompasses four factors:

1. People must be adults in order to vote.
2. People must be citizens in order to vote.
3. People in mental institutions and felons in prisons are not permitted to vote.
4. Americans who reside outside the United States, but who retain their American citizenship, are eligible to vote.

In the state elections data set, the voting-eligible population (the denominator) is calculated by first determining a state's adult population (21 years of age and older prior to 1972 and 18 years of age and older since 1972) and then subtracting from that aliens (those who are not US citizens) and prisoners incarcerated in state and federal correctional facilities within a state who are barred from voting.[20]

This measure is similar, but not identical, to that adopted by political scientists Michael McDonald and Samuel Popkin, whose work underscored how misleading research using voting-age population rather than voting-eligible population was in showing low voter turnout rates in the United States. Instead, McDonald and Popkin constructed the eligible pool by subtracting aliens, prisoners, and parolees, and then adding Americans overseas to the national voting-age population.[21] By measuring turnout with voting-eligible population rather than voting-age population, they observed that turnout was

[20] State citizen data are taken from successive years of the U.S. Census for all years except 1960 when the Census did not inquire about citizenship. The 1960 data are obtained from the Immigration and Naturalization Service Alien Address Program. The number of prisoners incarcerated in state and federal correctional facilities within a state is then subtracted from the number of adult citizens. Prisoners are reported in successive volumes of the *Statistical Abstract of the United States* and taken from Department of Justice prison statistics. Some states also do not restore voting rights to ex-felons once their incarceration and parole are completed, but those data are not available. Reliable state-level data of people in mental institutions across the time period is not available.

[21] A comparison of the McDonald state data set with the current data set for eligibles in presidential election years from 1980—2012 (the years McDonald has state data) reveals that the McDonald data estimates on average 25,489 more eligibles per state per year than the current data set (a small .135 percent difference). The difference likely lies in the counting of Americans living abroad.

much higher than previously depicted. When moving to a state-level analysis, we modify McDonald and Popkin in two ways. First, counts of people on parole and probation, prohibited from voting in some states, are not always available and so are not included in our analysis. Second, Americans living abroad—"ex-patriots," active-duty military personnel, and civilian US government employees stationed outside the United States—are required by law to retain a state residence. So, adding them to the voting-eligible population, as McDonald and Popkin do, actually inflates the eligible population by double counting these people.[22]

Determining Votes Cast and Nonvoting

To ascertain the number of votes cast and the number of nonvoters, we employ the states' final certified results reported to the Clerk of the House of Representatives. The Clerk certifies statewide tallies for all presidential candidates in presidential election years and the statewide House vote in midterm years, which includes votes for all minor candidates and scattered write-in returns.[23] The total number of people who fail to vote (the numerator) is calculated as the difference between the eligible citizen electorate and the total votes cast for each election for a given race in each state based on the Clerk of the House data. Nonvoting rates are, then:

(Total eligible population – Total votes cast) / Total eligible population

These data are distinct from those found in a variety of other sources featured in Table 2.3. As seen in the table, there is considerable disagreement among the

[22] The Federal Voting Assistance Program notes that Americans living abroad—whether military personnel or civilians—must claim a "legal state of residence," which is the state in which they resided before moving out of the country. This is the state in which they register to vote (http://www.fvap.gov/reference/laws/vote-reg-guide/index.html). There are also data availability problems during some of the years of the study in which a count of Americans living abroad is not consistently available at the state level.

[23] http://clerk.house.gov/members/electionInfo/elections.html. A small portion of votes cast are not counted in these final certified tallies. These include improper write-in or mail-in ballots or damaged ballots, which are, by law, excluded from the final count in some states There is, however, no way to determine how many spoiled ballots were discarded for the elections during this time period. But, as an example, spoiled ballots amounted to 2% of the total votes cast in the contested 2000 Florida presidential vote. See Lance De Haven-Smith, *The Battle for Florida* (Gainesville: University Press of Florida, 2005). While this means that the final tallies represent an undercount of the true number of people who went to the polls, they in effect offer a conservative measure of the votes cast.

Table 2.3 **Variations in Turnout by Source, 1960–2012 (Voters as a Percent of Voting-Age Population)**

Year	*CPR—Standard*[a]	*CPR—Revised*[b]	*CRS*[c]	*EAC*[d]	*IDEA*[e]
1960	62.8	NA	62.8	63.1	63.1
1964	61.9	69.3	61.9	61.9	61.9
1968	60.9	67.8	60.9	60.8	60.8
1972	55.2	63.0	55.2	55.2	55.2
1976	53.5	59.2	53.5	53.6	53.5
1980	52.0	59.2	52.8	52.6	52.6
1984	53.3	59.9	53.3	53.1	53.1
1988	50.3	57.4	50.3	50.1	50.1
1992	55.1	61.3	55.0	55.1	55.2
1996	48.9	54.2	48.9	49.1	47.2
2000	54.7	54.7	51.2	51.3	49.3
2004	NA	58.3	55.3	58.2	56.9
2008	NA	58.2	56.8	57.5	58.3
2012	NA	56.5	53.6	54.2	54.6

Note: NA=not available.

[a]CPR—Standard=U.S. Census, Current Population Report (drawn from original reports).

[b]CPR—Revised=Current Population Reports, "Voting and Registration in the Election of November 2000" P20-542, issued February 2002, found at http://www.census.gov/population/www/socdemo/voting.html.

[c]CRS=Congressional Research Service as reported at http://elections.gmu.edu/voter_turnout.htm.

[d]EAC=Election Assistance Commission (created by the Help America Vote Act of 2002 as an independent agency), found at http://www.eac.gov/program-areas/research-resources-and-reports/additional-elections-research.

[e]IDEA=International Institute for Democracy and Electoral Assistance (a multi-nation organization that monitors elections), found at http://www.idea.int/vt/country_view.cfm?CountryCode=US.

sources on exactly how to measure voting and nonvoting. As a striking example, turnout figures for the 1996 election range from 47 percent, as reported by the International Institute for Democracy and Electoral Assistance, to 54 percent, as recorded by *Current Population Reports. Current Population Reports,* the source most frequently used by researchers, is problematic because the data are taken from a nationally representative sample survey conducted two weeks after a given election in which people are asked if they were registered and whether they voted.[24] The *Current Population Reports* notes "significant discrepancies occur each election between the Current Population Survey estimates and the official numbers," ranging from less than 1 percent in 2000 to 5 percent in 1992.[25] Specifically, *Current Population Reports* indicates that the difference between their estimates and official counts may result from a combination of under-reporting in the official counts, as some ballots are invalidated or do not include a vote for a specific office, and over-reporting by *Current Population Reports* respondents who say they voted when in fact they did not.

In addition, *Current Population Reports* routinely and without comment updates its numbers, based on adjustments to the age-eligible population. A major update was reported in 2002 for the period from 1964–2000 which shows considerably higher turnout than had previously been reported. In the update, the *Current Population Reports* re-estimated upward the number of votes cast and re-estimated downward the voting age population.[26] With the *Reports* revision, presidential turnout has never fallen below 50 percent since 1960. Yet researchers often have not employed this update, continuing to use the older *Current Population Reports* data and offering the original lower figures instead.

The Congressional Research Service presents data collected through an outside vendor, Election Data Services, which contacts state officials to obtain election tallies.[27] The Election Assistance Commission, an independent agency established by the Help America Vote Act of 2002, also uses Election Data Services in its surveys of registration and voting. The Commission indicates that its counts may be lower than other sources because "not all local jurisdictions provided data." In addition, both the Congressional Research Service and the Election Assistance Commission examine turnout for the highest office on the ballot. While this poses no problems during presidential election years, there is a loss of comparability in the data during midterm elections, when the highest office varies. The visibility of a gubernatorial race in one midterm may

[24] The *Current Population Reports* is a subset of a much larger data set called the *Current Population Survey* which examines American households on a monthly basis to ascertain a variety of characteristics of Americans including employment, age, education, marital status, and locale. The data were used in Wolfinger and Rosenstone, 1980 and Leighley and Nagler, 2014.

[25] U.S. Census Bureau, *Current Population Reports,* "Voting and Registration in the Election of November 2000," February, 2002, p. 11.

[26] This was first reported in U.S. Census, *Current Population Reports,* P20–542, "Voting and Registration in the Election of November 2000," Table C, issued February 2002 for the period 1964–2000. It appears in updated form for 1964–2004 at http://www.census.gov/population/www/socdemo/voting.html, Voting and Registration, Historical Time Series Tables, Table A-1; A-9.

[27] These data are used by McDonald and Popkin, 2001. See also Michael McDonald, "The Turnout Rate Among Eligible Voters in the States, 1980–2000," *State Politics and Policy Quarterly* 2 (Summer 2002): 199–212.

be quite different than the visibility of a US Senate race in another. Finally, the International Institute for Democracy and Election Assistance uses a mix of data sources. But the Institute does not make clear what sources are used in a given election.

All of these measures also have a built-in problem because they are based on the voting-age population rather than the voting-eligible population. Consequently, the percentages posted in Table 2.3 do not reflect those people who are actually eligible to vote, only those who are old enough to vote.

Thus, building the data set with the Clerk of the House reports has the advantage of employing consistently available data on comparable races across a span of over 90 years. Also, use of the Clerk's data affords a more conservative measure of turnout than the *Current Population Reports* data. The *Current Population Reports* has an over-reporting problem, as people say they voted when in fact they did not. The Clerk's data essentially has an under-reporting problem, in which states often make questionable decisions about which ballots they reject as invalid.[28]

The Focus on Nonvoting

In one sense, nonvoting is simply equal to 100 percent minus the percent voting, but we suggest that our attention on nonvoting provides three new insights not afforded by the typical concentration on turnout. First, on a theoretical level, uncertainty becomes a key mobilizing force that brings nonvoters off the sidelines. While uncertainty also affects voters, many voters participate habitually, regardless of the circumstances in the national campaign context.[29] As discussed in Chapter 1, under conditions of high uncertainty, a "wait and see" approach, appropriate in an economic setting, is not appropriate in a political setting because Election Day is an irreversible, fixed moment at which people must weigh in or lose the opportunity to do so. Thus, the focus on nonvoters permits a better way of ascertaining the effects of uncertainty on electoral participation.

Second, on an empirical level, as we discuss in depth in Chapter 4, specific profiles that distinguish among nonvoters indicate that nonvoters are not simply the opposite of voters. For instance, as seen in Chapter 4, it is not the case that

[28] The Clerk's data are very similar to the data adopted by the Congressional Research Service. The two data sets differ by just 310 votes per state per year with the CRS data counting more votes cast than the Clerk data.

[29] Franklin, 2004; Donald Green and Ron Shachar, "Habit Formation and Political Behaviour: Evidence of Consuetude in Voter Turnout," *British Journal of Political Science* 30 (October 2000): 561–573; Eric Plutzer, "Becoming a Habitual Voter: Inertia, Resources, and Growth in Young Adulthood," *American Political Science Review* 96 (March 2002): 41–56.

voters are well informed and nonvoters are not. Instead, some nonvoters are as knowledgeable as voters. Many nonvoters remain at home because they do not believe that any of the candidates adequately address the uncertainty in the national campaign context.

Third, in comparing our model to the other models in the literature, the focus on nonvoters allows us a better way to assess the demographic characteristics including age, education, and residential mobility that are at the core of the personal resources approach reviewed in the Introduction. As we examine in Chapters 5 through 8, while it is true that nonvoters are younger, less educated, and more mobile than voters, this does not actually tell us much about the reasons they stay home.[30]

Presidential Nonvoting

The national campaign context of elections suggests three generalizations about aggregate nonvoting. First, nonvoting varies by election year. The degree of uncertainty in the campaign context varies from one election to the next, prompting shifts in nonvoting. Second, nonvoting varies by election type. The degree of uncertainty present during presidential elections is likely to be far greater than that found in House elections, especially at the midterm. As observed in the Introduction, House members want to make their races as small and local as possible to avoid confronting uncertainty from the national campaign context and any questions that may arise from it. Finally, nonvoting varies by region and state. The national campaign context plays out differently across the country. A sharp drop in oil prices, while good for most of the country, is not necessarily good for oil producing states. In addition, state and regional politics may have independent effects on nonvoting.

We consider the results for the nation as a whole in greater detail in Figure 2.3 and turn to the regional results later in the chapter. The national graph underscores the overall stability of presidential nonvoting over time. As initially discussed in the Introduction, mean national nonvoting for the entire period from

[30] Unfortunately, the existing aggregate data do not permit us to delve into the differences between registered nonvoters and unregistered nonvoters. Data from the U.S. Census *Voting and Registration* are available to distinguish between the two types of nonvoters from 1978 through 2012. However, while the Census asks people who are registered why they did not vote, it does not ask people who are not registered why they did not vote. Not being registered is a necessary condition for not voting, but it may not be a sufficient condition for not voting. See Barry Burden and Jacob Neiheisel, "Election Administration and the Pure Effect of Voter Registration on Turnout," *Political Research Quarterly* 66 (March 2013): 77–90.

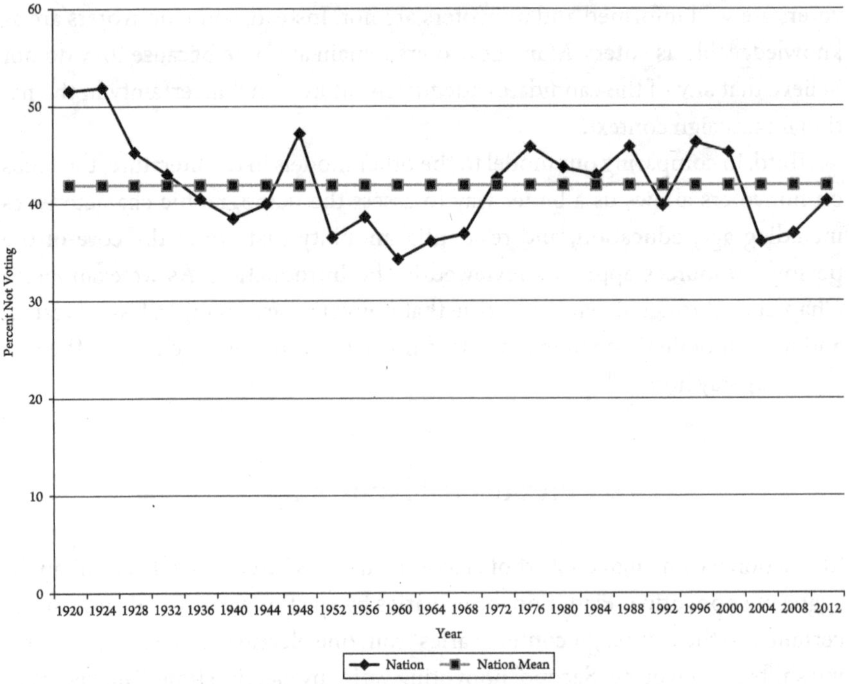

Figure 2.3 National Nonvoting in Presidential Elections, 1920–2012

1920 through 2012 is 42 percent, with a relatively low standard deviation of 5 percentage points. Nonvoting has moved up as well as down, as levels of uncertainty from the campaign context shift, but within a well-defined range. As seen in Table 2.1, national nonvoting was at its highest in 1920 and 1924 (52 percent) and at its lowest in 1960 (34 percent), 1964, and 2004 (36 percent).

Inter-Election Change

In four ways, we consider the question of whether there has been a trend in nonvoting at the national level. First, in Figure 2.3, the slope of the line over the time period equals –.082. It is roughly flat, suggesting no clear direction since 1920.[31]

[31] Between 1960 and 1996, the slope of presidential turnout is –.268. This indeed suggests turnout decline. But considering the slope from 1920 to 1996, the slope is .044. Examining just the post–World War II period from 1948 to 1996, the slope is –.123. Of course, writers analyzing turnout in the late 1990s and early 2000s cannot be held accountable for what happened after the 1996 election. Still, these comparisons illustrate the importance of the proper starting point in an electoral time series. Starting in 1960, a sharp turnout decline appears. Starting in 1920 or 1948, more appropriate years for a variety of reasons, no such decline is apparent.

There is perhaps no more important indicator of this than nonvoting in 2004 and 2008, which reached lows last seen in 1960, 1964, and 1968.[32] Second, we estimate a simple time series model and find no autocorrelation of the residuals; the pattern is stationary and random, with a very low stationary $R^{2=}.006$. This indicates, then, the absence of any trend. In addition, the time series model reveals that the best forecast for future nonvoting based on current nonvoting patterns is the mean for nonvoting of 42 percent, suggestive of stable long-term levels of nonvoting.

Our final approach to considering electoral trends is to examine inter-election change in nonvoting between two adjacent elections as shown in Table 2.1. If these inter-election shifts are in one direction in successive years, then a trend might be in evidence. Yet, the importance of the campaign context suggests that uncertainty changes from one election to the next. Thus, we would expect inter-election nonvoting change to be haphazard and erratic, yielding no trend.

Two points are evident from the national results. First, there is no consistent direction to nonvoting change for the nation as a whole over the time period. There have been 11 negative shifts during the time period and 13 positive shifts. Second, the magnitude of the change from one election to the next varies widely. Nonvoting change is greater than 5 percentage points for eight elections—1920, 1928, 1948, 1952, 1972, 1992, 1996, and 2004. Yet the 1924, 1968, 1984, 2000, and 2008 elections have nonvoting change of 1 percentage point or less. Overall, the results of these inter-election analyses indicate that since 1920 there has been no national trend in nonvoting in presidential elections.

At the Midterm

How does nonvoting differ between presidential and midterm election years? Too often presidential elections are discussed with no mention of midterm contests. When midterm years are analyzed, they are typically discussed with few references to the presidential elections that come before and after. To be sure, presidential and midterm elections have different campaign contexts. A central part of the midterm campaign context are local concerns that generate limited media attention and are likely to create minimal uncertainty. Highly successful incumbent members of the House work to ensure this, as they present campaigns featuring their successes in bringing projects and pork back home rather than lamenting the problems left unresolved on Capitol Hill.[33] They thus protect

[32] Nonvoting in 1904 and 1908 was just slightly above that for 1960 (see Rusk, 2001).

[33] David Mayhew, *Congress: The Electoral Connection* (New Haven: Yale University Press, 1974).

themselves from national swings in party fortunes. So, structurally, many House midterm races involving venerable incumbents are calibrated to have lower degrees of uncertainty and, consequently, higher nonvoting rates.

However, midterm campaign contexts are not all about local politics, and at times uncertainty dominates the campaign context. Congressional incumbents of the president's party find themselves unable to avoid troubles that the president has created. During the period from 1922 through 2010, the president's party lost House seats at the midterm in all years except 1934, 1998, and 2002. And many of these losses were arresting:

- 1922 77 seats
- 1930 52 seats
- 1938 72 seats
- 1942 45 seats
- 1946 54 seats
- 1958 48 seats
- 1966 47 seats
- 1974 48 seats
- 1982 26 seats
- 1994 54 seats
- 2006 30 seats
- 2010 63 seats

So, the predicaments presidents often find themselves in two years into their terms may get people to the polls and compromise the insularity of House incumbents.

Table 2.2 reveals that mean midterm nonvoting for the nation as a whole is 58 percent, fully 16 percentage points higher than presidential nonvoting. But nationally, midterm nonvoting is somewhat more stable than presidential nonvoting, with a small standard deviation of 4 percentage points.[34] The high point for midterm nonvoting occurred in 1926, when 65 percent of the eligible electorate did not vote. This is consistent with the high presidential nonvoting rates in 1920 and 1924 and, as we explore thoroughly in Chapter 5, is the result of eligible women not voting. The low points for midterm nonvoting occurred in the 1962, 1966, and 1970 elections, making these elections the midterm counterparts to the 1960, 1964, and 1968 elections. During the 88 years from 1922 to

[34] The autocorrelation function shows no trend in the data. The Box-Ljung Q statistic is not statistically significant at the .05 level at lags 4 through 7. In a simple model, the stationary R-squared is .045. Considering the period from 1962 to 1998—the years most comparable to the 1960–1996 presidential election period—the slope is –.215. However, the slope from 1922 to 1998 is .030.

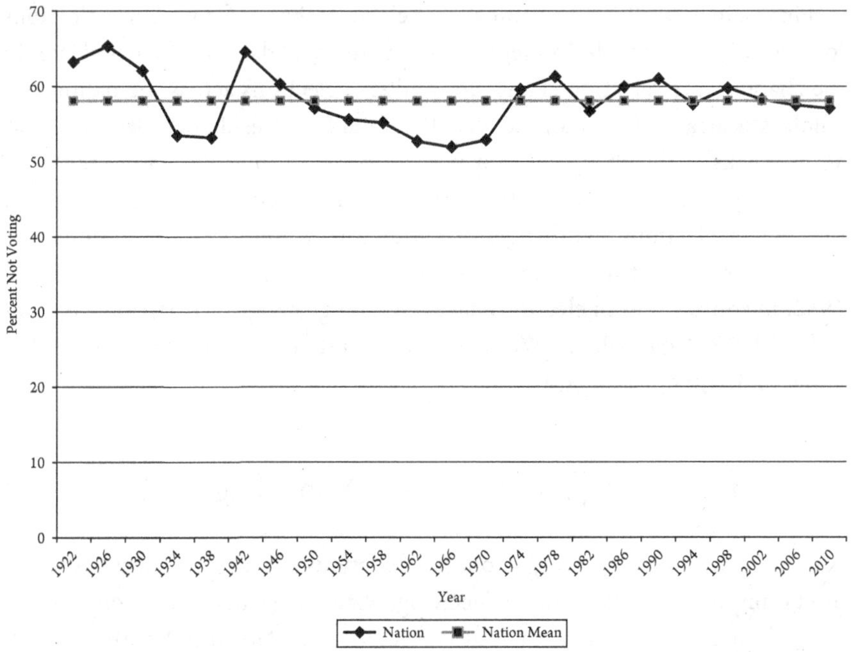

Figure 2.4 National Nonvoting in Midterm House Elections, 1922–2010

2010, no other midterm elections had lower nonvoting. Overall, no other series of elections had lower nonvoting than the six presidential and midterm House elections from 1960 through 1970. Since 1920, midterm nonvoting rates for the nation as a whole have never dropped below 50 percent.

Inter-Election Change

As seen in Figure 2.4, there is no evidence of a nationwide trend in midterm nonvoting. First, the slope of the national line in Figure 2.4 is flat at –.025, suggesting that, like presidential nonvoting rates, there has been no clear direction in midterm nonvoting since 1922. Second, we again estimate a simple time series model to examine the autocorrelation of the residuals. As with presidential elections, the autocorrelation of the residuals shows no trend in the midterm nonvoting. The pattern is stationary and random with a very low stationary R^2 of .00049.[35] In addition, like the presidential results, the best forecast of future nonvoting in midterm elections, based on current nonvoting patterns, is the mean nonvoting rate for the period of 58 percent.

[35] The Box-Ljung Q statistic is not statistically significant at the .05 level at lag 4, 5, or 6.

Finally, in Table 2.2 we examine inter-election change for midterm elections for the nation as a whole and regionally. The regional data are discussed later in the chapter. Inter-election change for midterm elections across the nation as a whole is as erratic, if not more so, than that found for presidential elections. This again speaks to the changing campaign context from one election to the next. Nationally, there are nine positive changes and 14 negative changes. And like presidential elections, the changes vary widely in magnitude: four elections post nonvoting change of at least a 5 percentage point change: 1934, 1942, 1974, and 1982. In contrast, seven elections have nonvoting change of 1 percentage point or less: 1938, 1958, 1966, 1970, 1990, 2006, and 2010. So there is no trend in either midterm or presidential races.

Regional Patterns in Nonvoting

Although knowing something about the directions of nonvoting at the national level is important, it can also be deceiving. National events and conditions and people's reactions to them play out differently from North to South, and federalism has a good deal to say about who votes and who does not.[36] Indeed, without understanding the role of region across time it is difficult to make any generalizations about the impact of the campaign context on nonvoting in American elections. This is not only because of the well-documented distinctiveness of southern politics.[37] It is also because claims about national patterns alone mask the degree of inter-state variation in any election result—whether turnout, nonvoting, vote totals, or party victories. Federalism makes it impossible to devise accurate statements about national aggregate outcomes without some consideration of what is happening at the state or regional level.

In the South

The national aggregate melds two very distinct regional pictures. Throughout the entire time period, southerners are less likely to vote than people in the rest of the country. As seen in Table 2.1, mean nonvoting in the South for presidential elections is 54 percent with a large standard deviation of 9 percentage points.

[36] See James Gimpel, *National Elections and the Autonomy of American State Party Systems* (Pittsburgh: University of Pittsburgh Press, 1996); Tari Renner, "Electoral Consequences and the Autonomy of American State Party Systems," *American Politics Research* 27 (January 1999): 122–132.

[37] E.g., V. O. Key, *Southern Politics in State and Nation* (New York: Alfred A. Knopf., 1950); J. Morgan Kouser, *The Shaping of Southern Politics* (New Haven: Yale University Press, 1974); Earl Black and Merle Black, *Politics and Society in the South* (Cambridge: Cambridge University Press, 1987).

This is fully 18 percentage points higher than the mean rate outside the South. Mean southern nonvoting in presidential elections is at its highest in 1924, when 70 percent of eligible voters did not vote, and at its lowest in 2008, when the southern nonvoting rate was 40 percent—the first time since 1888 that southern nonvoting dropped to 40 percent.[38]

As seen in Table 2.2, mean nonvoting in the South for midterm elections is 72 percent, with a standard deviation of 6 percentage points; this is 21 percentage points higher than the mean rate for the non-South. Midterm nonvoting in the South is at its highest level in 1942, when fully 85 percent of eligible voters did not go to the polls, and at its lowest in 2010 when 62 percent of eligible voters did not vote. Southern nonvoting last reached a lower level in 1894, when 53 percent of the eligible electorate did not vote.[39] Overall, in the recent presidential and midterm elections in the South, nonvoting has reached historic lows.

Yet, even with the promising indications from the most recent elections, southerners are still more likely not to vote than people in the rest of the country. This is clarified in Figures 2.5 and 2.6, which consider regional differences in nonvoting for presidential and midterm elections since 1920. There is at least a 4 percentage point gap between South and non-South in the last four presidential elections and at least a 7 percentage point gap in the last six midterm elections. The effect of the Voting Rights Act of 1965 is clear when the regional gap in nonvoting drops all but overnight—from 19 percentage points in 1964 to 11 percentage points in 1968, and from 28 percentage points in 1962 to 20 percentage points in 1966. But, nevertheless, a gap remains.

Inter-Election Change

Unlike the national time series, there is evidence of a trend in southern nonvoting in presidential elections, but the trend is downward rather than upward. The slope of the southern line in presidential elections is –.291, denoting a decline in nonvoting over time. A simple time series model for presidential nonvoting in the South shows that the autocorrelation function is significant at all lags, with a stationary R^2 of .702, indicative of a trend in the data.[40] There is also evidence of a decline in nonvoting in the South during midterm House elections, but it is less distinct than that found in presidential elections. The slope of the line indicates a slight trend downward in midterm nonvoting in the South (slope = –.200).

[38] See Rusk, 2001, 54.

[39] Ibid.

[40] The Box-Ljung Q statistic is significant at all lags. A first-difference model produces stationary and random residuals.

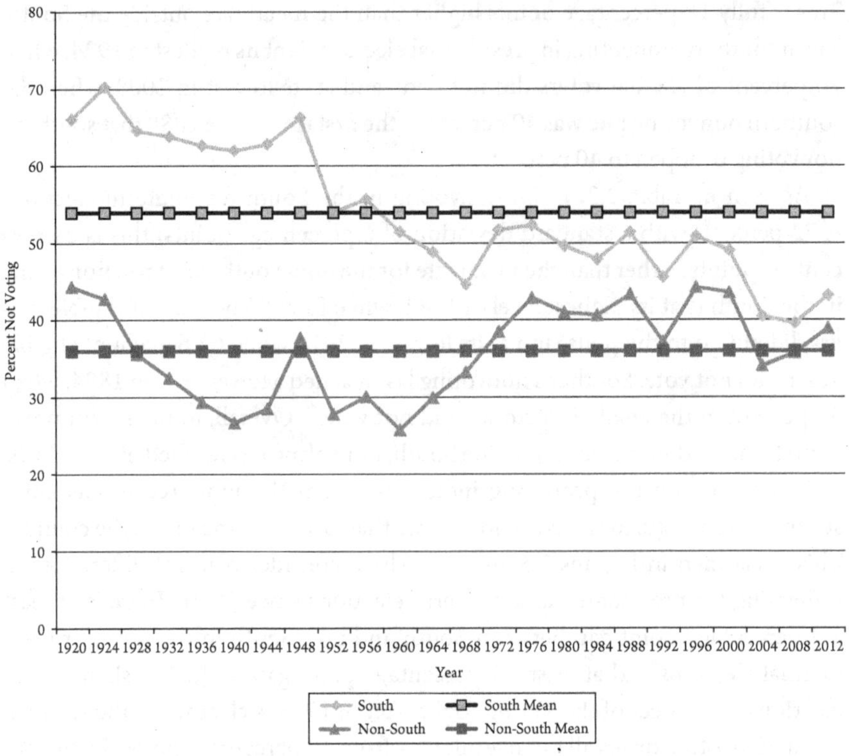

Figure 2.5 Regional Nonvoting in Presidential Elections, 1920–2012

A simple time series model also finds a significant autocorrelation function at all lags with a stationary R^2 of .697, again suggestive of a trend in the data.[41]

But even with the temporal decline, southern nonvoting remains dauntingly high. In presidential elections, southern nonvoting dropped below 50 percent for the first time in 1964 and continued to hover at or above the 50 percent mark in 1972, 1976, 1980, 1988, and 1996. In midterm elections the picture is bleaker still: southern nonvoting dropped to 66 percent for the first time in 1966. It has been remarkably stable since then, averaging 66.5 percent.

There is also considerable volatility between adjacent elections in both presidential and midterm years. Even with the decline in southern nonvoting, it has been anything but consistent. There are numerous election sequences in which a decrease in nonvoting in one election is followed by an increase in nonvoting in the next. As seen in Table 2.1, in presidential elections there

[41] The Box-Ljung Q is statistically significant at the .05 level at all lags and stationary R-squared is .733. With a first-difference model, the residuals are independent and stationary.

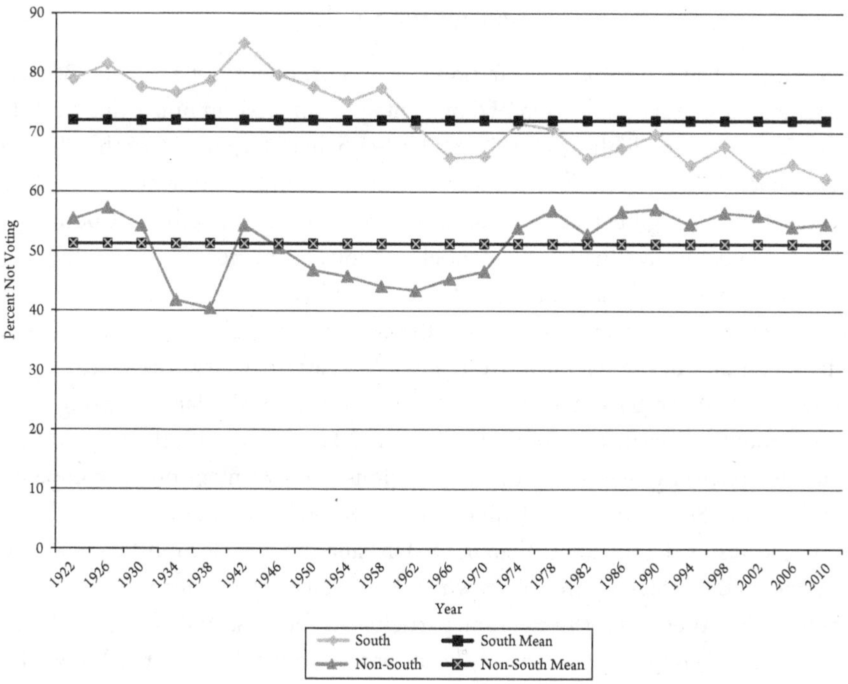

Figure 2.6 Regional Nonvoting in Midterm House Elections, 1922–2010

are 15 negative shifts and nine positive shifts. The magnitude of the shifts varies widely. There are six elections with inter-election change greater than 5 percentage points: 1928, 1952, 1992, and 2004 (negative shifts) and 1972, 1996 (positive shifts). But there are also six elections with shifts of 1 percentage point or less: 1932, 1936, 1940, and 2008 (negative shifts) and 1944, 1976 (positive shifts). There is only one 3-election sequence—1960, 1964, and 1968—in which nonvoting drops by significant amounts in successive elections.

As shown in Table 2.2, in midterm elections, there are 12 negative shifts and 11 positive shifts. The magnitude of inter-election change varies widely. There are eight elections in which inter-election change is greater than 5 percentage points—1942, 1946, 1962, 1966, 1974, 1982, 1994, and 2002. Three elections post change of one percentage point or less (1934, 1970, and 1978). As with presidential elections, there is a single 3-election sequence—1946, 1950, and 1954—when nonvoting declines in succession. Overall, the South remains consistently behind the non-South in getting people to the polls. Even though there has been a significant drop in nonvoting, especially after the Voting Rights Act of 1965, southern nonvoting rates remain substantial, especially at the midterm.

Outside the South

In states outside the South, mean nonvoting in presidential elections is 36 percent with a standard deviation of 6 percentage points. Mean nonvoting outside the South is at its highest in 1920 and 1996, when 44 percent of the eligible electorate did not vote. It is at its lowest in 1940 and 1960, when 27 and 26 percent of the eligible electorate did not vote, respectively. Table 2.1 permits a closer look at nonvoting in presidential elections in the non-South by dividing it into three sub-regions—the East, Midwest, and West. Although the South has long been distinct from other parts of the country, the politics, economics, and demographics of the East, Midwest, and West certainly vary. The table shows, however, that the East, Midwest, and West have fairly similar nonvoting rates throughout the entire time period.[42] From 1920 through 2012, the mean difference in nonvoting rates across the three regions is 3 percentage points compared with a mean South–non-South difference of 18 percentage points. Nonvoting in the Midwest is slightly lower than in the East and the West for most presidential elections. But generally the West, which has been depicted at times as lagging behind the other regions in electoral participation because of its fast growth and highly mobile populations, actually keeps pace with the East and the Midwest.

As seen in Table 2.2, mean nonvoting at the midterms in the non-South is 51 percent with a standard deviation of 5 percentage points. Nonvoting rates outside the South are at their highest in 1926, 1978, and 1990, when 57 percent of eligible voters stayed home, and at their lowest in 1934 (42 percent), 1938 (40 percent), and 1962 (43 percent). Nonvoting has remained stubbornly above 50 percent since 1974. The mean inter-election change for nonvoting outside the South from 1974 through 2010 is 1 percentage point. For nearly three decades, non-southern midterm House turnout has ranged narrowly from 54 percent to 57 percent. This may reflect the high success rate of House incumbents, whose repeated reelections minimize uncertainty and keep the number of people going to the polls relatively similar from one year to the next. As with presidential elections, nonvoting in the West, East, and Midwest are at comparable rates at the midterm across the time period. Indeed, there is less variation across the sub-regions for midterm elections than for presidential elections. The mean difference in nonvoting rates across the three regions is 2 percentage points, compared with a mean South–non-South difference of 21 percentage points.

[42] The East includes Connecticut, Delaware, the District of Columbia, Maine, Maryland, Massachusetts, New Hampshire, New Jersey, New York, Pennsylvania, Rhode Island, and Vermont. The Midwest comprises Illinois, Indiana, Iowa, Kansas, Michigan, Minnesota, Nebraska, North Dakota, Ohio, South Dakota, and Wisconsin. The West is made up of Alaska, Arizona, California, Colorado, Hawaii, Idaho, Montana, Nevada, New Mexico, Oregon, Utah, Washington, and Wyoming.

Inter-Election Change

There is no evidence of a trend in nonvoting in either presidential or midterm House elections for states outside the South. As seen in Table 2.1, in presidential years the slope in the non-South of .1 indicates no direction over time.[43] As depicted in Figure 2.4, in midterm years the slope in the non-South is again flat at .1, indicating that nonvoting is quite stable.[44] A simple time series model reveals no autocorrelation among the residuals in either presidential or midterm years, suggesting no evidence of a trend in either data set.[45]

As shown in Table 2.1, inter-election change between adjacent presidential elections in the non-South involves 12 negative shifts and 12 positive shifts. There are eight elections with inter-election change greater than 5 percentage points—1920, 1928, 1948, 1952, 1972, 1992, 1996, and 2004. The 1984 and 2000 elections are the only years in which inter-election change is 1 percentage point or less. There is a five-election sequence from 1924 through 1940 in which there are successive drops in the nonvoting rate for states outside the South. But thereafter, the variability to inter-election change is notable.

As shown in Table 2.2, in midterm elections there are 12 negative shifts and 11 positive shifts in inter-election change in the non-South. There are very large shifts from 1930 to 1934 of a nearly 13 percentage point shift downward in nonvoting and an even larger shift upward from 1938 to 1942 of 14 percentage points. But there are also very small inter-election shifts of 1 percentage point or less in seven elections: 1938, 1954, 1962, and 2002 (downward shifts) and 1970, 1990, and 2010 (upward shifts).

Conclusion

Part of the nonvoting dilemma, then, is actually a dilemma of analysis. Researchers have chosen various measures of turnout, often with little discussion of why one measure is preferred over another. In some cases they have employed measures that do not fully account for various people who are prohibited from voting. And many have chosen a starting point—1960—for examining the trend line,

[43] The autocorrelation function of the residuals shows a stationary, random pattern. The Box-Ljung Q statistic is not statistically significant at the .05 level at lag 4, 5, or 6. Stationary R-squared is .023.

[44] The autocorrelation of the residuals shows no overall trend in the data. The Box-Ljung Q statistic is not statistically significant at the .05 level at lags 3 through 9. In a simple model, the stationary R-squared is .045.

[45] There are low stationary R^2 in both cases: R^2 = .086 in presidential years and R^2 = .046 in midterm years.

which makes the nonvoting picture look worse. Properly measured, nonvoting has actually been steady over the 92 years of the study, moving up and down in a narrow band.

So, the answer to the question, "Has nonvoting increased?" is no. Selecting a proper time frame and a correct measure for the voting-eligible population shows there is no inexorable increase in nonvoting in presidential or midterm House elections. Nationally, there has been a tapering off of the low levels of nonvoting in the 1950s and 1960s, but not an upward march. Regional patterns drive the national results and illuminate different time periods. In the earliest elections, nonvoting drops rapidly outside the South and decreases somewhat in the South. In the unique period of the 1950s and 1960s, there is a trough in non-southern nonvoting combined with the near linear decrease in southern nonvoting. Then, non-southern nonvoting increases again but stabilizes, especially in midterm elections, while southern nonvoting declines modestly. In the most recent elections, nonvoting appears to be on the decline again in the South and the non-South. Indeed, in 2008 and 2010, southern nonvoting hit all-time lows.

Thus, this chapter has charted the course of nonvoting since 1920. But significant questions remain about why nonvoting has taken the various paths it has. While we know a considerable amount about the ups and downs of nonvoting, we do not yet know its relation to the national campaign context across the entire time period. We address this in the next chapter.

3

Campaign Context, Uncertainty, and Nonvoting

In 2012, Republican presidential candidate Mitt Romney was secretly videotaped as he spoke at a private $50,000 per plate fundraiser, lamenting "the 47 percent of people who will vote for the president (Obama), no matter what." In the tape, sent to *Mother Jones* magazine, Romney went on to say that this "47 percent who are with [the president], who are dependent on government, who believe they are victims, who believe the government has a responsibility to care for them . . . these are people who pay no income tax." A political firestorm ensued as Romney initially said his remarks could have been more eloquent and later commented "I was completely wrong."[1] While Democrats blamed Romney for insensitively characterizing half of the electorate, conservative commentators and Republican strategists accused the Romney campaign of ineptness—in former Reagan speechwriter Peggy Noonan's words, "a rolling calamity."[2] The video and the unscripted Romney message became the central topic of the campaign for several weeks. These were finally the true sentiments of a candidate, unfiltered by talking points or sound bites.

This incident is illustrative of uncertainty in the national campaign context that unfolds, in this case, with powerful mass communication technologies. A presidential candidate's private remarks at a fundraiser are no longer private; reporters are no longer required to break a story; instead, a bartender with a cell phone working at the fundraiser can create the story line as the video goes

[1] Emily Friedman, "Romney says he was completely wrong about the 47 percent remark," ABC News, October 5, 2012, found at http://abcnews.go.com/blogs/politics/2012/10/romney-says-he-was-completely-wrong-about-47-percent-comments/.

[2] Peggy Noonan, "Time for an Intervention," *Wall Street Journal,* September 18, 2012, found at http://blogs.wsj.com/peggynoonan/2012/09/18/time-for-an-intervention/; Stephanie Condon, "Noonan: Romney Campaign is a 'Rolling Calamity,'" CBS News, September 25, 2012, found at http://www.cbsnews.com/news/noonan-romney-campaign-is-a-rolling-calamity/.

viral. Mass communication now goes outside the boundaries of conventional journalism as it is possible that anyone can create a story at any time. This is the essence of uncertainty in the national campaign context as unique circumstances throw campaigners and the eligible electorate off guard.

Elements of the National Campaign Context

As spelled out in Chapter 1, varying levels of uncertainty in the national campaign context affect individual elections. This external uncertainty falls along a continuum from high to low; it is not a dichotomous condition that is either present or absent. Barry Burden wrote, "uncertainty arises from many sources, can take on multiple forms, and has a variety of consequences."[3] In short, as Robert Dahl offered, "uncertainty appears to be a characteristic of all political life."[4] Despite its ubiquity, uncertainty is a difficult construct to measure as a single process or phenomenon. Under uncertainty, even if an initial condition or starting point in a process is known, there are several (often infinitely many) directions in which the process may unfold over time. It cannot be captured in a simple mathematical formula like those for volume or circumference. As a matter of common sense, people know when they experience a high level of uncertainty. Yet, precisely because of the definitional indeterminacy of uncertainty, its parameters can at best be inferred. The most appropriate way to measure uncertainty is through what Nicholas Bloom has called "empirical proxies for uncertainty."[5] Economists use several measures including stock market volatility, newspaper articles that contain references to uncertainty, growth rate shocks, and technological innovations.

Thus, there is no perfect single empirical measure for uncertainty in the national campaign context. Instead, we examine four indicators of the level of uncertainty: economic change, innovations in mass communication technology, disruptions associated with major national events, and new federal legal requirements. These offer a range of empirical proxies for the uncertainty underlying the national campaign context. They are consistent with measures of uncertainty adopted in past studies including economic volatility, technological shocks, and world crises.[6] The four factors also provide multiple indicators of uncertainty

[3] Barry Burden, "Everything But Death and Taxes," in Barry Burden, ed. *Uncertainty in American Politics* (Cambridge: Cambridge University Press, 2003), 3.

[4] Robert Dahl, *Modern Political Analysis* (New York: Prentice-Hall, 1963), 10.

[5] Nicholas Bloom, "Fluctuations in Uncertainty," *Journal of Economic Perspectives* 28 (Spring 2014): 154.

[6] For a review, see Nicholas Bloom, "Fluctuations in Uncertainty," *Journal of Economic Perspectives* 28 (Spring 2014): 153–176.

that are plainly exogenous to the act of voting. In using these four indicators, we can thus incorporate uncertainty as a construct into the understanding of electoral participation. This chapter assesses how uncertainty in the national campaign context affects aggregate nonvoting in the American states during presidential and House midterm elections from 1920 through 2012. In the next chapter, we examine individual-level data to consider the impact of this uncertainty on citizens' decisions not to vote.

To clarify these uncertainty indicators, we specify four hypotheses that guide the aggregate analyses in this chapter and Chapters 5 through 8.

H1: Economic volatility—sharp increases or decreases in economic growth—decreases nonvoting.
H2: A technological shock—the introduction of a new form of political communication—decreases nonvoting.
H3: Dramatic national events decrease nonvoting.
$H3_1$: United States involvement in international conflict decreases nonvoting.
H4: Federal laws expanding the franchise—a shock to the political status quo—decrease nonvoting.

Economic volatility can produce drastic shifts in the national political outlook. Novelty emerges as the stock market soars or plummets, unemployment quickly worsens or improves, personal incomes rise or fall.[7] Surely, people are accustomed to some degree of economic change, because the economy is hardly ever purely stable. But when these shifts hit record highs or lows, become the central topic of news stories, and lead to government interventions of various kinds, uncertainty rises. As noted in Chapter 1, this economic volatility captures both downside uncertainty and upside uncertainty—when the economy drops precipitously or increases sharply. We hypothesize that uncertainty about future economic outcomes leads more people to vote. They "fear" what might happen next.[8] Looking back over the months before the election, people may feel that the party in power has failed to ensure national prosperity. It is in their best interest to go to the polls to show their disapproval and, more importantly, to avoid the reelection of the incumbent party. Under other economic conditions, people

[7] A common measure of economic uncertainty is the VIX index of 30-day implied volatility on the Standard and Poor's 500 stock market index. See Bloom, 2014; Geert Bekaert, Marie Hoerova, and Marco Lo Duca, "Risk, Uncertainty, and Monetary Policy," *Journal of Monetary Economics* 60 (October 2013): 771–788. As discussed below, we employ income change and unemployment change as measures of uncertainty since these are broader-based measures and have considerable relevance to political outcomes.

[8] Robert Whaley, "The Investor Fear Gauge," *Journal of Portfolio Management* 21 (Spring 2000): 12–17; Bekaert, Hoerova, and Lo Duca, 2013.

may observe that the economy is on a strong upward swing. They wish to ensure that the party in power remains in office to protect the good times but also worry that the prosperity may end. In periods of economic stability, however, there is less incentive to go to the polls. If there is little movement upward or downward in income and unemployment, then there is little uncertainty and less reason for people to vote. This is consistent with a large literature on retrospective voting, which suggests that voters look to past economic conditions to determine for which party they will vote.[9] It is also consistent with research that shows that rising unemployment increases turnout.[10]

High levels of uncertainty accompany a technology shock in which a new device is invented and becomes available to American households.[11] Technological advances in mass communication create political novelty as new messages are available from new forms of media. Innovations in radio, television, color television, cable broadcasting, the personal computer, and the Internet fundamentally alter the means by which candidates communicate with the public. This creates a technology shock which unmoors typical ways of disseminating and gathering political information. The level of uncertainty created by a new technology involves two dimensions: the technological advancement itself, and how it conveys political content. As we discuss in Chapter 5, technologically the major characteristic of radio was voice, while political content was conveyed across a small number of national broadcast networks which tend to follow the same stories. With the advent of television, analyzed in Chapter 6, visual content and images blended with voice technologically, while political content was conveyed in ways similar to that with radio—across a small number of broadcast networks which tended to follow the same stories. On the

[9] See Morris Fiorina, *Retrospective Voting in American National Elections* (New Haven: Yale University Press, 1981); David Lanoue, "Retrospective and Prospective Voting in Presidential-Year Elections," *Political Research Quarterly* 47 (March 1994): 193–205; Wayne Francis, Lawrence Kenny, Rebecca Morton, and Amy Schmidt, "Retrospective Voting and Political Mobility," *American Journal of Political Science* 38 (November 1994): 999–1024; Brad Gomez and Matthew Wilson, "Political Sophistication and Economic Voting in the American Electorate," *American Journal of Political Science* 45 (October 2001): 899–914; Jean-Francois Godbout and Eric Belanger, "Economic Voting and Political Sophistication in the United States: A Reassessment," *Political Research Quarterly* 60 (September 2007): 541–554; and William Mayer, "Retrospective Voting in Presidential Primaries," *Presidential Studies Quarterly* 40 (December 2010): 660–685.

[10] Barry Burden and Amber Wichowsky, "Economic Discontent as a Mobilizer: Unemployment and Turnout," *Journal of Politics* 76 (October 2014): 887–898.

[11] Michelle Alexopoulos and Jon Cohen, "Volumes of Evidence: Examining Technical Change in the Last Century through a New Lens," *The Canadian Journal of Economics* 44 (May 2011): 413–450; Michelle Alexopoulos and Jon Cohen, "The Media is the Measure: Technical Change and Employment, 1909–1949," Working Paper 351, University of Toronto, Department of Economics, February 23, 2009.

surface, the introduction of cable television was still television but, as discussed in Chapter 7, the technological advances of cable provided the opportunity to offer a multiplicity of channels that were not national broadcast networks. Cable then afforded viewers vastly more political content with all-news channels and vastly less political content with the availability of an array of channels with no political subject matter at all. Finally, the Internet disrupted both the technologies of the past and the forms of political content they offered. As detailed in Chapter 8, the Internet and the companion World Wide Web created an omnibus information space combining text, graphics, video, and audio content. Its introduction permitted people unprecedented access to political content—both fact and opinion—in real time.

Candidates are often uncertain how best to use the new forms of communication. A new technology adds risk to campaigns because no one knows whether embracing it rather than more established technologies is the right approach, either from the sheer power of the technology itself or the type and amount of political information it can convey. Some candidates may use an emerging technology to their advantage, while others may stumble and actually impede their campaign communication. Adjustments from a news cycle timed to the evening news to a news cycle that updates throughout the day vexed many campaigners as cable news gained strength in the 1980s. Too, as the Romney example above shows, candidates do not fully control the messages that may arise about them.

Similarly, the new technology is a source of novelty to the eligible electorate. The public receives political information in a new, possibly exciting way. This may create an environment in which eligible voters obtain more political information than they would otherwise.[12] In discussing the emergence of television, analyst Markus Prior stated "The popularity of television and the homogeneity of content of broadcast stations during the dinner hour led many Americans, even less educated, less interested, and less partisan, to watch the news."[13] As people obtain the technology, they can rely on a convenient source of information. Armed with this greater information, they are more likely to vote.

Yet, mass communication technologies also reach saturation points—they are found in virtually all American households and are used routinely for information gathering. So low levels of uncertainty occur with this technological saturation when everyone has a device, is comfortable with it, and takes this form of communication for granted. We hypothesize, then, that as the coverage of a

[12] Doris Graber, *Processing Politics: Learning from Television in the Internet Age* (Chicago: University of Chicago Press, 2001).

[13] Markus Prior, *Post-Broadcast Democracy* (Cambridge: Cambridge University Press, 2007), 15.

technology expands, nonvoting will decline.[14] However, when the technology reaches a saturation point, its use by politicians and the public becomes routine. We posit that when the technology is well established in the campaign context, it will have little effect on nonvoting.

Dramatic domestic and international events produce high levels of uncertainty in the political system.[15] They disrupt the existing political landscape with violence, invasions, natural disasters, scandals, and world-shattering government decisions. Novelty defines these circumstances: they have never happened before or happen rarely. By their nature, these major domestic and international events receive considerable news coverage because they define what news is supposed to be: timely, vivid, dramatic, and unpredictable. The events rivet public attention because the incidents are possibly life changing, their resolution is unclear, and there is a high degree of risk that things may end badly. When these unique, sometimes radical, circumstances occur in the months prior to an election, they disarm campaigners and the eligible electorate, preventing both of them from achieving good estimates of what will happen next. We hypothesize that the occurrence of such events will spur more people to go to the polls in an attempt to deal with the uncertainty. In contrast, if no such events occur during the months preceding an election, uncertainty in the campaign context is lessened. A quiet political setting is therefore likely to see nonvoting continue at past levels or perhaps even rise.

In Chapters 5 through 8, we consider US involvement in international conflicts as a subset of these major events. By its very nature war produces high levels of uncertainty and risk. There may be significant losses on the battlefield that trigger a national debate. There may be stunning victories that spur patriotism and celebration, but also discussions about when the war will end. We hypothesize that citizens will respond to these shifting levels of downside and upside uncertainty by going to the polls. Similar to the uncertainty of economic conditions, future international outcomes are unknowable. People are unsure what will happen next in the course of the war. If the war is going badly, it is in people's best interest to go to the polls to express their disapproval. If the war is going well, people participate to ensure the reelection of those winning the war.

[14] Work that finds an effect of political communication on electoral participation includes Bruce Bimber, *Information and American Democracy Technology in the Evolution of Political Power* (Cambridge: Cambridge University Press, 2003); Mijeong Baek, "A Comparative Analysis of Political Communication Systems and Voter Turnout," *American Journal of Political Science* 53 (April 2009): 376–393; and Felix Oberholzer-Gee and Joel Waldfogel, "Media Markets and Localism: Does Local News in Espanol Boost Hispanic Voter Turnout?" *The American Economics Review* 99 (December 2009): 2120–2128.

[15] Bloom, 2014, 156–157; Scott Baker, Nicholas Bloom, and Steven Davis, "Measuring Economic Policy Uncertainty," Working Paper 21633, National Bureau of Economic Research, October 2015.

Legal requirements that extend the franchise to new categories of people create uncertainty in the campaign context.[16] While political parties typically conduct major efforts to register the newly enfranchised, campaigners nevertheless struggle on how best to appeal to them. Campaigners must adopt strategies to engage the new potential voters without really knowing whether the strategies will work. The expansion of the franchise defines novelty for the newly eligible group of citizens: they have not voted before and now have their first opportunity to do so. We hypothesize that this novelty will push eligible voters to participate. Over time, however, the novelty will wear off as the new group establishes more consistent participation patterns. So, we would expect the extension of the franchise to have an initial effect on nonvoting in the years immediately after its introduction but not later on.

As noted in Chapter 1, elements of the campaign context are integrally linked to party competition. Competition does not simply emerge from the strengths of the two parties, the attractiveness of their candidates, or the skills and strategies they use in their campaigns. The campaign context also influences competition and provides opportunities for some candidates more than others. For the parties there is always ambiguity about how competitive they will be in any given election. Good times in the campaign context favor the party in power and diminish competition, while bad times favor the party out of power and increase competition. By definition, the more competitive a race is the more unclear its outcome. We hypothesize that the closer the race, the more likely people will vote. They do not wish to risk having the wrong party victorious. Conversely, when the eligible electorate sees little competition and understands the outcome well before the polls open, nonvoting increases. Even if some eligible voters fear the victory of the "wrong" party, there may be little they can do to prevent it by their votes.

Personal Resources, Social Connections, and Party Mobilization

The uncertainty in the campaign context, then, shapes the responses of the eligible electorate and the efforts parties can undertake to get people to the polls. At the same time, neither the electorate nor the parties come to the campaign context as blank slates. The eligible electorate is composed of various groups

[16] For research on legal changes and uncertainty, see Lubos Pastor and Pietro Veronesi, "Political Uncertainty and Risk Premia," Working Paper 17464, National Bureau of Economic Research, September 2011.

distinguished by key demographic characteristics and social connections. As discussed in Chapter 1, there are four primary models of nonvoting—psychological involvement, personal resources, social connections, and party mobilization. Since this chapter provides an aggregate analysis we cannot consider psychological involvement (but do so in Chapter 4), but we can devise measures for the other three sets of factors. The personal resources model considers the impact on nonvoting of a wide range of individual characteristics including demographic factors such as age, race, and education. In addition, those who study social connections argue that such factors as marital status, church attendance, and residential mobility lead to varying levels of social involvement, which affects how many people vote. While the personal resources and social connections models are specified at the individual level, they consider the impact of an individual characteristic or social connection to be similar across all people with that particular factor. As an example, it is not simply that a young person is less likely to vote than an older person, but rather that young people as a group are less like to vote than older people as a group. Similarly, young people as a group may see the uncertainty in the campaign context in a way that is different from older age groups. So, it becomes important to understand how the campaign context affects nonvoting relative to these demographic and social characteristics.

To that end, we consider two demographic characteristics—youth and education—and two social factors: marital status and church membership.[17] As noted above, there is considerable evidence that young people are less likely to vote than older people.[18] Steven Rosenstone and John Hansen viewed education as a personal resource, suggesting that lower levels of education are likely to provide insufficient resources for people to participate in politics.[19] Ruy Teixeira argued that marital status and church membership are elements of social connectedness which make people more likely to be involved in politics and their communities.[20]

[17] Of course, the various attitudinal measures used at the individual level cannot be examined at the aggregate level.

[18] We measure youth as the percentage of the adult population of a state that is from 21 through 25 years old (before 1972) and 18 through 25 years old (from 1972 onward).

[19] Steven Rosenstone and John Mark Hansen, *Mobilization, Participation and Democracy in America* (New York: Longman, 2003). Education is measured by the difference between the percentage of the population who completed college and the percentage of the population who only completed high school. Hence, a large positive difference means a more highly educated population; a large negative difference means a less highly educated population.

[20] Ruy Teixeira, *Why Americans Don't Vote: Turnout Decline in the United States 1960–1984* (Westport, CT: Greenwood Press, 1987). Marital status is measured as the percentage of the adult population who report being married. Church membership records the percent of the population who say they attend church.

In addition, party mobilization efforts may influence nonvoting. As discussed in Chapter 1, Rosenstone and Hansen maintained that parties attempt to get their message out to segments of the eligible electorate and they conduct get-out-the-vote campaigns to ultimately get these groups of eligible voters to the polls. While the uncertainty in the campaign context and the levels of party competition will help determine success, mobilization efforts may have an independent effect on nonvoting. This helps us disentangle party mobilization and party competition, which Rosenstone and Hansen treated interchangeably. Indeed, in one of their models they substitute party competition for a measure of party mobilization. But, as we discussed in Chapter 1, the two are interrelated but distinct. Parties may spend a good deal of money to devise a major get-out-the-vote drive but have a lopsided race. We measure mobilization in presidential years as the total campaign money spent by the parties. In House midterm elections, campaign spending cannot be used because no spending data exist before 1978. Instead, we adopt a measure of open seats as a proxy for party mobilization.[21] The more open House seats there are, the more likely both parties will invest in mobilization strategies to vie for those seats.

Finally, we know from existing research that past participation guides current participation.[22] People who have voted in the past often vote in the next election at high levels. The reverse is also true: eligible voters who have not voted in the past are more likely to not vote in the future. The association is not perfect, because we also know that people drop in and out of the electorate.[23] But to capture the dynamics of electoral participation, we employ a one-election lagged measure of nonvoting in the aggregate models in this and Chapters 5–8.[24]

[21] Money spent in presidential election campaigns is found in Lyn Ragsdale, *Vital Statistics on the Presidency*, rev. ed. (Washington, D.C.: CQ Press, 1998), 146, updated by the authors. Open seats in midterm elections is found in Harold Stanley and Richard Niemi, *Vital Statistics on American Politics 2013–2014* (Washington, D.C.: CQ Press, 2013), 43.

[22] Mark Franklin, *Voter Turnout and the Dynamics of Electoral Competition in Established Democracies since 1945* (Cambridge: Cambridge University Press, 2004); Donald Green and Ron Shachar, "Habit Formation and Political Behaviour: Evidence of Consuetude in Voter Turnout," *British Journal of Political Science* 30 (October 2000): 561–573; Eric Plutzer, "Becoming a Habitual Voter: Inertia, Resources, and Growth in Young Adulthood," *American Political Science Review* 96 (March 2002): 41–56.

[23] Lee Sigelman, Philip Roeder, Malcolm Jewell, and Michael Baer, "Voting and Non-Voting: A Multi-Election Perspective," *American Journal of Political Science* 29 (November 1985): 749–765.

[24] Luke Keele and Nathan Kelly underscore the appropriateness of using a lagged dependent variable when there is theoretical justification to do so, despite concerns by Christopher Achen that the lagged variable often leads to implausibly small values for the remaining substantive coefficients. Luke Keele and Nathan Kelly, "Dynamic Models for Dynamic Theories: The Ins and Outs of Lagged Dependent Variables," *Political Analysis* 14 (Spring 2006): 186–205; Christopher Achen, "Why Lagged Dependent Variables Can Suppress the Explanatory Power of Other Independent Variables,"

Testing a Baseline Model

We first provide an analysis of the effects on nonvoting of individual resources, social connections, and party mobilization to serve as a benchmark by which to better gauge the influence of the campaign context. The results are presented in Table 3.1 for the nation as a whole, the South, and the non-South across presidential elections from 1920 through 2012 and for midterm House elections from 1922 through 2010.[25] In presidential elections nationally, the only personal resource that is statistically significant is youth. The higher the percentage of young people in a state's electorate, the higher is the level of nonvoting. As shown in Table 3.1, the other personal and social connection variables—education, marital status, church membership—and mobilization have no statistical effects on nonvoting in presidential elections. In midterm House elections nationally, none of the resource, social connection, or mobilization variables have statistically significant effects on nonvoting. Overall, this model performs poorly at the national level.

Regional Results

Viewed at the regional level, the personal resources–social connections–mobilization model achieves slightly better results. In the South, education has a statistically significant effect on presidential and House midterm nonvoting. With a more educated population in a state, nonvoting rates fall. Consistent with Teixeira's concept of social connectedness, the higher the number of married people in the South in a given presidential election year, the lower is nonvoting.[26] But marital status does not significantly affect House midterm nonvoting. None of the other factors have a statistically significant influence on southern nonvoting, whether in presidential elections or House midterm elections. In the non-South, youth influences nonvoting in midterm House elections and mobilization affects nonvoting in presidential races, but no other variables have any statistical effect. In general, the model does not tell us a great deal about nonvoting

presented at the Annual Meeting of the Political Methodology Section of the American Political Science Association, Los Angeles, July, 2000.

[25] The nonvoting variable in this chapter is calculated as mean nonvoting across the states for a given election year. It is thus consistent with the data presented in Chapter 2. The independent variables are also measured as the mean across all states for the specific election year. We do this rather than a pooled time series analysis because we are most interested in the overall picture of nonvoting for a given election as it moves up and down nationally and regionally. Chapters 5 through 8 permit us to examine a cross section of the states for a given election year.

[26] Teixeira, 1987.

Table 3.1 **The Impact of Personal Resources and Party Mobilization on Nonvoting in Presidential and House Midterm Elections, 1920–2012**

Predictor	*Nation*				*South*				*Non-South*			
	President		*House*		*President*		*House*		*President*		*House*	
	Coefficient	*t-value*	*Coefficient*	*t-value*	*Coefficient*	*t-value*	*Coefficient*	*t-value*	*Coefficient*	*t-value*	*Coefficient*	*t-value*
Youth	1.105	2.697	0.650	1.565	0.342	0.772	−0.035	−0.085	1.001	1.215	0.919	1.736
Education	−0.058	−0.552	−0.001	−0.016	−0.417	−4.062	−0.171	−1.810	−0.137	−0.580	0.076	0.684
Marital Status	−0.273	−0.760	−0.281	−1.017	−0.449	−1.804	−0.385	−1.501	−0.514	−0.855	−0.220	−0.661
Church Membership	−0.207	−0.444	0.089	0.261	0.139	0.677	0.591	1.707	−1.333	−1.224	−0.112	−0.271
Mobilization	−0.00009	−1.176	−0.001	−0.009	0.000	−1.430	0.042	0.535	0.000	−1.821	−0.014	−0.142
Prior Nonvoting	0.024	0.092	0.244	1.122	0.123	0.576	0.110	0.415	−0.366	−1.254	0.307	1.470
Intercept	60.300	1.855	46.368	2.001	78.559	2.757	51.359	2.314	160.356	2.110	41.976	1.607
N	24		23		24		23		24		23	
R^2	0.474		0.409		0.868		0.837		0.391		0.585	
Adjusted R^2	0.277		0.187		0.822		0.776		0.176		0.429	
Durbin h statistic	0.459		0.802		0.273		0.143		1.180		0.795	

Note: Critical t-values are 1.771 at .10 probability; 2.160 at .05; 3.012 at .01. Mobilization is measured by campaign money in presidential elections and open seats in House elections. Critical Z-value for the Durbin h-statistic is 1.65 at .05 probability level.

across the country at the aggregate level. We will return to its predictive importance at the individual level in Chapter 4.

Investigating the National Campaign Context Model

This analysis of the model of personal resources, social connection, and party mobilization provides us with a baseline from which to explore the effects of uncertainty in the national campaign context—measured by economic change, communication technology shocks, dramatic major events, and legal shifts—on nonvoting. As controls, we include in the equation two personal resource variables—youth and education—which the analysis above showed had some influence on nonvoting and that previous research has consistently identified as important indicators of participation.[27] We also incorporate a measure for party competition (discussed in detail below) which, as noted in Chapter 1, is intertwined with elements of the campaign context. Lastly, we again include a measure of prior nonvoting to gauge the consistency of nonvoting from one election to the next.[28] Table 3.2 presents the presidential election results, while Table 3.3 depicts the midterm House findings.

Economic Change and Nonvoting

The theory of uncertainty in the national campaign context suggests that the greater the degree of economic change, the more eligible voters will go to the polls. Tables 3.4 and 3.5 depict economic change measured by personal income change and unemployment change for presidential elections and midterm elections.[29] The tables reveal that in a number of election years there was considerable

[27] We do not include marital status or mobilization in the model, even though they had sporadic effects in the results presented in Table 3.1. Preliminary tests revealed that neither variable had an effect on nonvoting in either presidential or midterm elections relative to campaign context factors.

[28] Because the equations contain a lagged dependent variable, tests for serial correlation were conducted using the Durbin h-statistic. The Durbin-Watson d statistic is inappropriate with lagged data. The h-statistic can be compared to the normal distribution. See John Johnston, *Econometric Methods* (New York: McGraw-Hill, 1972), 312–313; G. S. Maddala, *Introduction to Econometrics*, 3rd. ed. (New York: Wiley, 2001), 248–249. The critical Z = 1.65 at the .05 probability level.

[29] The income and unemployment change variables are calculated over a 4-year time frame from the previous presidential election in the case of presidential races and from the previous House midterm elections in the case of the House races. Income change is measured as the percentage change from time 1 to time 2. Unemployment change is measured as the absolute value of the change in the unemployment rate from time 1 to time 2. Since in most political debates and news coverage of unemployment it is the change in the rate, not the percentage change in the rate that is discussed,

Table 3.2 **The Influence of the National Campaign Context on Nonvoting in Presidential Elections, 1920–2012**

Predictor	*Nation*				*South*				*Non-South*			
	Coefficient	*t-value*	*Mean*	*Impact*	*Coefficient*	*t-value*	*Mean*	*Impact*	*Coefficient*	*t-value*	*Mean*	*Impact*
Income Change	−0.115	−2.887	20.921	−2.406	−0.118	−3.145	22.383	−2.641	−0.123	−2.487	20.213	−2.486
Unemployment Change	−0.240	−1.815	3.016	−0.724	−0.150	−2.173	3.290	−0.494	−0.283	−1.768	3.112	−0.881
Communication Technology	−0.053	−1.998	48.315	−2.561	−0.007	−0.286	42.472	−0.297	−0.065	−2.789	51.037	−3.317
Major Events	−0.932	−1.816	1.750	−1.631	−1.471	−2.590	1.750	−2.574	−0.623	−0.901	1.750	−1.090
Legal Requirements	−4.875	−1.408	n/a	n/a	−4.398	−2.403	n/a	n/a	−3.269	−0.784	n/a	n/a
Competition	0.166	1.399	2.840	0.471	0.029	0.303	−1.078	−0.031	−0.167	−1.082	4.804	−0.802
Youth	0.810	2.029	14.439	11.696	0.248	0.654	15.051	3.733	1.008	2.003	14.133	14.246
Education	0.002	0.049	39.759	0.080	−0.428	−4.416	34.236	−14.653	−0.122	−3.567	42.366	−5.169
Prior Nonvoting	−0.097	−0.434	42.657	−4.138	−0.007	−0.037	54.523	−0.382	0.059	0.233	38.605	2.278
Intercept	38.094	3.347			69.538	4.579			14.508	1.470		
N	24				24				24			
R^2	0.771				0.936				0.790			
Adjusted R^2	0.624				0.895				0.655			
Durbin h-statistic	0.271				1.580				1.570			

Note: Critical t-values are 1.771 at .10 probability; 2.160 at .05; 3.012 at .01. Critical Z-value for the Durbin h-statistic is 1.65 at .05 probability level. Because Legal Requirements is measured as a dummy variable, the mean impact measure is not calculated.

Table 3.3 **The Influence of the National Campaign Context on Nonvoting in Midterm House Elections, 1922–2010**

Predictor	*Nation*				*South*				*Non-South*			
	Coefficient	*t-value*	*Mean*	*Impact*	*Coefficient*	*t-value*	*Mean*	*Impact*	*Coefficient*	*t-value*	*Mean*	*Impact*
Income Change	–0.016	–0.374	22.387	–0.358	–0.022	–0.342	23.681	–0.521	–0.054	–1.047	21.530	–1.163
Unemployment Change	–0.509	–2.657	3.160	–1.608	–0.485	–1.958	3.244	–1.573	–0.489	–2.389	3.083	–1.508
Communication Technology	–0.047	–2.391	53.779	–2.528	–0.040	–1.750	49.326	–1.973	–0.048	–2.130	58.947	–2.829
Major Events	–0.610	–1.752	1.610	–0.982	–0.552	–1.356	1.610	–0.889	–0.654	–1.669	1.610	–1.053
Legal Requirements	–0.110	–0.078	n/a	n/a	–2.822	–1.767	n/a	n/a	1.759	1.086	n/a	n/a
Competition	0.071	0.549	0.076	0.005	–0.241	–1.832	3.033	–3.308	0.208	1.365	4.804	1.103
Youth	0.312	0.997	13.894	4.335	0.164	0.385	14.923	2.447	0.245	0.660	14.015	3.434
Education	–0.008	–0.281	39.269	–0.314	–0.244	–3.131	33.880	–8.267	–0.066	–1.672	41.787	–2.758
Prior Nonvoting	0.637	3.438	58.468	37.244	0.425	2.087	72.521	30.821	0.705	3.849	42.182	29.738
Intercept	18.137	3.185			50.692	2.502			9.263	1.025		
N	23				23				23			
R^2	0.857				0.925				0.916			
Adjusted R^2	0.757				0.873				0.857			
Durbin h-statistic	0.271				0.041				1.520			

Note: Critical t-values are 1.771 at .10 probability; 2.160 at .05; 3.012 at .01. Critical Z-value for the Durbin h-statistic is 1.65 at .05 probability level. Because Legal Requirements is measured as a dummy variable, the mean impact measure is not calculated.

Table 3.4 **Economic Change in Presidential Elections, 1920–2012 (from past presidential election)**

Year	*Income*	*Income Change*	*Income Percent Change*	*Unemployment Rate*	*Unemployment Rate Change*	*Unemployment Percent Change*
1916	497			1.40		
1920	489	–8	–1.62	5.20	3.80	271.43
1924	507	18	3.68	5.00	–0.20	–3.85
1928	697	190	37.42	3.20	–1.80	–36.00
1932	398	–299	–42.90	23.60	20.40	637.50
1936	535	137	34.42	16.90	–6.70	–28.39
1940	593	58	10.84	14.60	–2.30	–13.61
1944	1194	601	101.35	1.20	–13.40	–91.78
1948	1425	231	19.35	3.80	2.60	216.67
1952	1751	326	22.88	3.00	–0.80	–21.05
1956	2013	262	14.96	4.40	1.40	46.67
1960	2268	255	12.67	5.50	1.10	25.00
1964	2671	403	17.77	5.20	–0.30	–5.45
1968	3536	865	32.38	3.60	–1.60	–30.77
1972	4717	1181	33.40	5.60	2.00	55.56
1976	6754	2037	43.18	7.70	2.10	37.50
1980	10091	3337	49.41	7.50	–0.20	–1.10
1984	13807	3716	36.82	7.50	0.00	5.63
1988	17244	3437	24.89	5.50	–2.00	–26.67
1992	20799	3555	20.62	7.50	2.00	36.36
1996	24442	3643	17.52	5.40	–2.10	–28.00
2000	30318	5876	24.04	4.00	–1.40	–25.93
2004	32340	2022	6.67	5.50	1.50	37.50
2008	37642	5302	16.39	5.80	0.30	5.45
2012	38964	1322	3.50	8.10	2.30	39.66

Sources: Per capita income data from U.S. Department of Commerce, Bureau of Economic Analysis, Series SA-13, Personal Income and Population, found at http://www.bea.gov. Unemployment (1948–1966) National Bureau of Economic Research, NBER Macrohistory: VIII. Income and Employment, series M08292c, http://www.nber.org/databases/macrohistory/contents/chapter08.html (1966–2012) Bureau of Labor Statistics, found at http://www.bls.gov/lau/.

Table 3.5 **Economic Change in Midterm House Elections, 1922–2010 (from past midterm election)**

Year	*Income*	*Income Change*	*Income Percent Change*	*Unemployment Rate*	*Unemployment Rate Change*	*Unemployment Percent Change*
1918	552			1.70		
1922	440	−112	−20.31	6.70	5.00	294.12
1926	566	126	28.72	1.80	−4.90	−73.13
1930	618	52	9.19	8.70	6.90	383.33
1934	424	−194	−31.39	21.70	13.00	149.43
1938	526	102	24.06	19.00	−2.70	−12.44
1942	908	382	72.62	4.70	−14.30	−75.26
1946	1254	346	38.11	3.90	−0.80	−17.02
1950	1503	249	19.86	5.30	1.40	35.90
1954	1810	307	20.43	5.50	0.20	3.77
1958	2108	298	16.46	6.80	1.30	23.64
1962	2439	331	15.70	5.50	−1.30	−19.12
1966	3061	622	25.50	3.80	−1.70	−30.91
1970	4084	1023	33.42	4.90	1.10	28.95
1974	5708	1624	39.76	5.60	0.70	14.29
1978	8243	2535	44.41	6.10	0.50	8.93
1982	11901	3658	44.38	9.70	3.60	59.02
1986	15338	3437	28.88	7.00	−2.70	−27.84
1990	19354	4016	26.18	5.60	−1.40	−20.00
1994	22297	2943	15.21	6.10	0.50	8.93
1998	27258	4961	22.25	4.50	−1.60	−26.23
2002	29928	2670	9.79	5.80	1.30	28.89
2006	35768	5840	19.51	4.50	−1.30	−22.41
2010	39296	3528	9.86	9.60	5.10	101.13

Sources: Per capita income data from U.S. Department of Commerce, Bureau of Economic Analysis, Series SA-13, Personal Income and Population, found at http://www.bea.gov. Unemployment (1948–1966) National Bureau of Economic Research, NBER Macrohistory: VIII. Income and Employment, series M08292c, http://www.nber.org/databases/macrohistory/contents/chapter08.html (1966–2012) Bureau of Labor Statistics, found at http://www.bls.gov/lau/.

economic volatility from the previous election. In nine presidential elections and seven midterm elections, personal income shifted by 30 percent or more from the previous election. In only two of those elections (1932, 1934) was the shift negative. The volatility in unemployment change between elections is also apparent. There were 12 presidential elections and 9 midterm elections with a 2-point or greater change in the unemployment rate from the previous election.

Table 3.2 shows that income change and unemployment change significantly decrease presidential nonvoting, nationally and regionally. A 10 percentage point change in per capita income yields a 1 percentage point decrease in nonvoting for the nation, the South, and the non-South. A 4-point change in the unemployment rate prompts a roughly 1 percentage point decline in nonvoting for the nation and the non-South. Another appropriate way to analyze the economic and other effects is to consider not only the coefficients but their mean impact.[30] Impact measures provide an additional tool to understand the effect of the independent variables. For instance, the national mean inter-election change in per capita income over the period is 21 percent. Using this metric, mean income change prompts a decline of 2.4 percentage points in presidential nonvoting for the country as a whole. The corresponding regional impact measures are 2.6 percentage points in the South and 2.5 percentage points in the non-South. The impact of mean (absolute value) unemployment change is nearly a 1 percentage point drop in nonvoting for the country as a whole and for the non-South, and a 0.5 percentage point decline in nonvoting for the South.

Of course, there are also limits to these mean impact scores.[31] By definition, the mean impact score best captures election years in which extremes in economic change (or in any other independent variable) do not occur. Yet as noted above, there are elections in which income and unemployment changed substantially. To capture this, Table 3.6 presents nonvoting change at one and two standard deviations above and below the mean impact for income and unemployment change. For election years when income dramatically improves, nonvoting rates drop considerably. As one example, in presidential elections, income change of 40 percent—one standard deviation above the mean—is associated with a nearly 5 percentage point drop in nonvoting.

While income change does not influence midterm nonvoting, unemployment change has statistically significant negative effects on midterm nonvoting

we adopt this measure. These data were obtained from the National Bureau of Economic Research, *Macrohistory: VIII: Income and Employment*, found at http://www.nber.org/databases/macrohistory/contents/chapter08.html; U.S. Department of Labor, Bureau of Labor Statistics, at stats.bls.gov.

[30] Christopher Achen, *Interpreting and Using Regression* (Beverly Hills: Sage, 1982).

[31] The mean impact score is not useful in assessing the legal requirements variable which is a dummy variable and so is not presented.

Table 3.6 **Impact of Economic Change on Nonvoting at Various Levels of Change**

Nation		*South*		*Non-South*	
Income Change Values	*Nonvoting Change*	*Income Change Values*	*Nonvoting Change*	*Income Change Values*	*Nonvoting Change*
Presidential Elections					
−16.3	1.9	−17.8	2.1	−15.8	1.9
2.3	0.3	2.3	−0.3	2.2	−0.3
20.9	**−2.4**	**22.4**	**−2.6**	**20.2**	**−2.5**
39.5	−4.5	42.5	−5.0	38.2	−4.7
58.1	−6.7	62.6	−7.4	56.2	−6.9
Midterm Elections					
−18.4	2.1	−9.9	2.2	−10.4	1.6
−1.5	0.2	6.9	1.5	5.6	0.9
22.4	**−0.4**	**23.7**	**−0.5**	**21.5**	**−1.2**
42.8	−5.0	40.5	9.0	37.6	5.6
63.2	−7.3	57.3	12.7	53.6	8.3
Nation		***South***		***Non-South***	
Unemployment Change Values	*Nonvoting Change*	*Unemployment Change Values*	*Nonvoting Change*	*Unemployment Change Values*	*Nonvoting Change*
Presidential Elections					
−7.0	1.7	−8.0	1.2	−6.7	1.9
−1.9	0.5	−2.4	0.4	−1.8	0.5
3.0	**−0.7**	**3.2**	**−0.5**	**3.1**	**−0.9**
8.3	−1.9	8.8	−1.3	8.0	−2.2
13.4	−3.2	14.4	−2.2	12.9	−3.6
Midterm Elections					
−4.2	2.1	−11.6	5.7	−10.5	5.1
−0.5	0.3	−5.7	2.8	−5.2	2.5
3.2	**−1.6**	**3.2**	**−1.6**	**3.1**	**−1.5**
6.9	−3.5	6.1	−3.0	5.4	−2.6
10.6	−5.3	12.0	−5.9	10.7	−5.2

Note: Middle line (3) is the mean value. Other values are one and two standard deviations above/below the mean. Standard deviations for income are 18.6 (Nation), 20.1 (South), 18.0 (non-South). Income change does not have a statistically significant effect on nonvoting for the nation or the South in midterm elections, so is presented for illustrative purposes only. Standard deviations for unemployment are 5.64 (Nation), 6.51 (South), 5.53 (non-South).

nationally and regionally. At the mean (absolute value) of unemployment change, nonvoting declines by 1.6 percentage points for the nation and the South and 1.5 percentage points for the non-South. In examining Table 3.6, at one standard deviation above the mean, unemployment change yields a 4 percentage point drop in nonvoting. Overall, these results provide the first indication of the influence of economic conditions on nonvoting. In later chapters we find strong evidence of economic effects on aggregate nonvoting in individual elections. These effects are sizable in a variety of elections years when economic swings, both positive and negative, are present. Thus, downside and upside uncertainty (as discussed in Chapter 1) influence nonvoting.

Communication Technology and Nonvoting

The theory of uncertainty in the national campaign context suggests that the more pronounced a communication technology shock, the more likely eligible voters will go to the polls. To measure technological advances, we devise an indicator of mass media adoption in American households. Figure 3.1 examines how four forms of mass communication technology entered American homes—radio, television, cable television, and the Internet. Later chapters more fully explore the historic

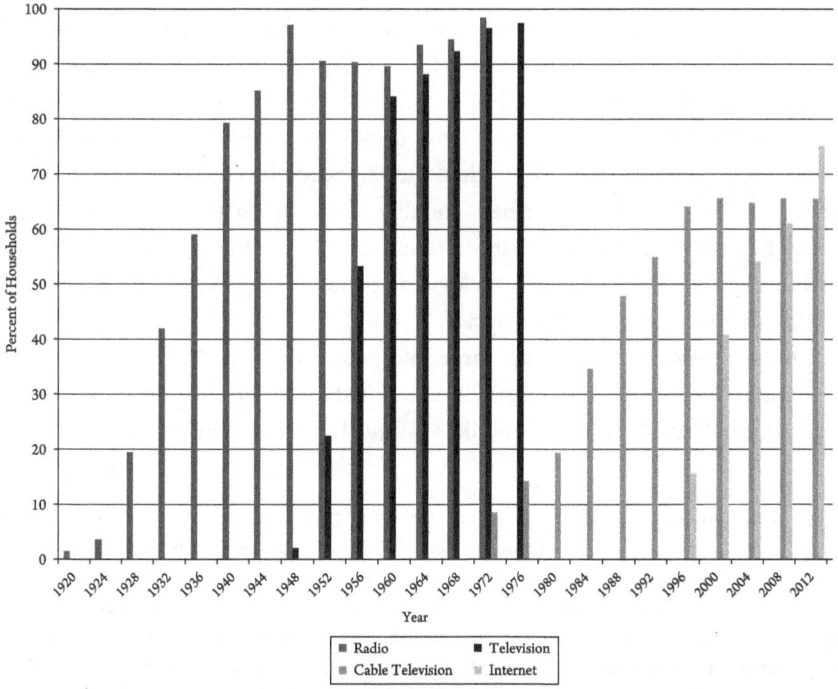

Figure 3.1 Households with Mass Communication Technology, 1920–2012

advances of these media and their influence on specific elections. This figure shows a similar pattern across the four technologies: initially, very few families have the communication form, but many acquire it soon thereafter, and then ultimately most families have the device. Just 2 percent of households owned radios in 1920, but by 1928 fully 20 percent of households did. As we discuss more fully in Chapter 5, 1928 was a pivotal year in the political use of radio and in establishing radio as the first mass communication technology. Sufficient numbers of households owned radios that it could not be ignored as a political communication device, even though, as we point out in Chapter 5, candidates were uncertain how best to exploit it. During the 1930s, even in the depths of the Great Depression, the number of radios in homes increased dramatically and reached a virtual saturation point immediately after World War II.

Similarly, with television's introduction in the late 1940s only 2 percent of homes had televisions in 1948. Regular television broadcasting had only begun on NBC in 1947 and on ABC and CBS in 1948.[32] This was certainly a medium that political campaigners could and did ignore. But by 1952, 23 percent of American households owned a television, and it began to eclipse radio as the most salient mode of communication. Cable television, launched in the mid-1960s, was found in just 9 percent of US households in 1972. But two decades later in 1992, 55 percent of households subscribed to it. While this mode of political communication still remained television-based, there was little similarity between the three major networks and the array of cable channels, including a fledgling 24-hour news network, CNN, launched in 1980. The expressly ideological channels, Fox News and MSNBC, both began in 1996. These channels dramatically changed the political news cycle, news content, and electoral politics. Cable television has not reached the saturation level of radio and network television, with cable subscribers roughly stable at 66 percent of American households since 2000. The cost of the subscriptions and the recent availability of Internet streaming services of television content clearly create a ceiling effect on the diffusion of this technology.

In the 1990s, Internet access came into people's homes. In 1996, 16 percent of households had Internet capabilities, but just four years later, in 2000, 42 percent did, and by 2012, 76 percent did. [33] While television remained an important

[32] The communication technology variable estimated in this and later chapters is derived from data found in the *Statistical Abstract of the United States* at http://www.census.gov/compendia/statab/ and the Census of Population and Housing at http://www.census.gov/prod/www/abs/decennial/. The variable is coded from 1920 through 1950, as the percentage of households with radios; from 1952 through 1970, as the percentage of households with televisions; from1972 through 1994, as the percentage of households with cable television subscriptions; and from 1996 through 2012, as the percentage of households with personal computer access to the Internet.

[33] U.S. Census, Current Population Survey, October 2009.

source of political communication, the Internet began to crowd it out as a primary source of political content. In 2012, 47 percent of Americans said they received most of their news from the Internet, up from 36 percent in 2008.[34] The growth of the Internet appears more closely aligned with that of radio and network television than with cable television. Internet use grew as quickly as did radio and continued even during the Great Recession, just as radio purchases increased during the Depression. If the current rate of growth continues, Internet use in American households is likely to reach a saturation point of more than 90 percent sometime in the next decade. This brief history shows that key communication innovations created technology shocks as a new medium came into American homes.

As shown in Tables 3.2 and 3.3, communication technology significantly decreases nonvoting in presidential and midterm elections for the nation as a whole and in the non-South and in midterm years in the South. The Impact columns of these tables reveal that during presidential elections and midterm elections, the mean level of households having a specific technology is associated with a decrease in nonvoting of roughly 3 percentage points in the nation and in the non-South. An increase in communication technology is associated with a 2 percentage point decrease in midterm nonvoting in the South. The fact that fewer households in the South acquired new technologies when radio, television, cable television, and the Internet became available likely explains the smaller communication technology effect in the South.[35] The results in later chapters reveal that the effect of communication technology on nonvoting is quite large in years in which the medium is in its infancy. Overall, uncertainty measured as a new technology creates more excitement about politics and brings more people to the polls.

Dramatic National Events

The theory of uncertainty in the national campaign context indicates that the more disruptive and dramatic major events are, the more likely people will

[34] Pew Research Center for the People and the Press "Section 4: News Sources, Election Night, and Views of Press Coverage," November 15, 2012, found at http://www.people-press.org/2012/11/15/section-4-news-sources-election-night-and-views-of-press-coverage/.

[35] Over the entire time period, there is an 8 percentage point gap between southern households with communication technology and non-southern households with this technology. The largest differences occurred during the Great Depression and World War II when the gap was on average 22 percentage points between the South and the non-South. For instance, in 1930 the number of southern households with radios was 27 percentage points lower than the number of non-southern households with radios.

vote. The novelty of these events creates uncertainty in the political system as people are unsure about their resolution. Forecasters and analysts have difficulty predicting what will happen next, as the spread of possible outcomes increases. When these dramatic events occur during an election period, they are likely to prompt more eligible voters to go to the polls in order to have some control over which party can best deal with the circumstances. We measure major events by identifying a group of novel, relatively long-lived, crisis-oriented happenings that are national or international in scope, with clear consequences for the country as a whole.[36] The novelty arises when nothing like the event has happened before, or it is at least significantly different from what has gone on before. Table 3.7 lists these major national events from 1920 through 2012. Since the typical news story receives only one day of coverage, the stories about these events are exceptional.[37] As displayed in the table, various dramatic events—including the entrance of China into the Korean War in 1950, the Cuban missile crisis in 1962, the Cambodian invasion in 1970, Ford's pardon of Nixon in 1974, and the world credit crisis in 2008—occurred in the months before Election Day.

As seen in Tables 3.2 and 3.3, major national events significantly decrease nonvoting in presidential elections nationally and in the South. Examining the coefficient column, with the presence of one dramatic event prior to a presidential election, nonvoting is reduced by 1 percentage point in the nation as a whole and slightly more than that in the South. The effect in the non-South is not statistically significant. Examining the Impact column, the mean number of major events in an election year (2 events) prompts presidential nonvoting to decline by nearly 2 percentage points in the nation and 3 percentage points in the South. The strong effect in the South may reflect major civil rights events, including the bus boycott in Montgomery Alabama in 1956, John Kennedy securing Martin Luther King, Jr.'s release from an Atlanta jail in 1960, and the murder of civil rights workers in Mississippi in 1964, all of which occurred in the midst of presidential campaigns. Major events have a statistically significant effect on nonvoting in midterm elections nationally, but not regionally. As shown in the Impact column, with the mean number of events (two events) in midterm elections, nonvoting decreases by 1 percentage point in the nation. Overall, the occurrence of these events is a catalyst for participation.

[36] The events were drawn from the "Year in the United States" found in the *Facts on File World News 2, the Digest.*

[37] The day count is taken from the *New York Times Index.*

Table 3.7 **Major National Events in Election Years, 1920–2012**

Year	*Date*	*Event*	*Days in News*
1920	January 16	Prohibition begins	15
1920	January 19	United States rejects participation in League of Nations	15
1920	August 18	Nineteenth Amendment (women's suffrage) receives final passage	5
1920	September 16	Italian separatists bomb Wall Street (38 killed, hundreds injured)	15
1922	April 14	*Wall Street Journal* uncovers Teapot Dome scandal—Secretary of Interior privately leases oil reserves without competitive bid to a friend.	4
1930	June 17	Smoot-Hawley Tariff Act becomes law	6
1932	June 17–July 28	President Hoover orders removal of Bonus Army Marchers from protest site in Washington, D.C.	16
1932	July 8	Dow Jones reaches lowest level	1
1934	April 14	Twenty major dust storms occur in the Great Plains on what becomes known as "Black Sunday"	1
1934	May 11	Another major dust storm hits the plains	4
1938	September 30	Britain supports Munich agreement transferring southern Czechoslovakia to Germany to appease Hitler	10
1940	June 22	France surrenders to Germany	3
1940	September 14	New peacetime draft begins under the Selective Service Act of 1940	28
1942	January 1–5	Battle of Bataan begins	7

(*continued*)

Table 3.7 **(Continued)**

Year	*Date*	*Event*	*Days in News*
1942	April 9	Battle of Bataan ends with the Philippines surrender to Japan; General Douglas MacArthur vows "I shall return."	14
1942	August 7	Battle of Guadalcanal begins	12
1944	February 3	United States captures the Marshall Islands	13
1944	August 19–24	Allied forces liberate Paris	4
1944	October 23–26	MacArthur returns to the Philippines in major naval victory at Battle of Leyte Gulf	10
1948	April 3	President Truman signs the Marshall Plan	4
1948	July 26	President Truman desegregates the military	2
1948	August 3	Whitaker Chambers testifies before a televised hearing of the House Un-American Activities Committee that Alger Hiss, a member of the State Department was a communist	14
1950	February	Sen. Joseph McCarthy announces that he has proof of hundreds of Communists in the State Department	10
1950	June 25	North Korea invades South Korea	29
1950	September 15	MacArthur lands at Inchon to begin counter-offensive against the North Koreans	4
1950	October 8	China enters Korean War	2
1952	April 8	President Truman seizes the steel mills	8
1952	June 2	Supreme Court orders Truman to return steel mills to owners	2
1954	April 22	Senate convenes Army-McCarthy hearings	25

Table 3.7 **(Continued)**

Year	*Date*	*Event*	*Days in News*
1956	Jan-Dec	Montgomery Alabama bus boycott	51
1960	February 1	African-American teenagers stage sit-in at Woolworth's lunch counter in Greensboro, NC.	2
1960	May 16	Soviet Premier Khrushchev demands apology for US U-2 spy flights over Soviet Union	4
1960	August 19	U-2 pilot Gary Powers' trial for espionage begins in Moscow	3
1960	July 25	Woolworths in Greensboro serves first African-American customer, ending sit-in.	1
1960	October 26	Robert Kennedy secures Martin Luther King's release from an Atlanta jail for a traffic ticket	2
1962	February 3	President Kennedy announces embargo against Cuba	2
1962	October 2	President Kennedy sends troops to help integration of University of Mississippi	4
1962	October 8–22	Cuban Missile Crisis	16
1964	June 21	3 civil rights workers are murdered in Philadelphia, Mississippi	15
1964	August 2	North Vietnamese attacks on US Navy vessels in the Gulf of Tonkin	9
1964	October 1	Massive student protest at University of California—Berkeley over free speech begins	1
1966	June 6	Civil rights activist James Meredith is shot in Mississippi	12
1966	July 18–23	Riots in Cleveland	16
1968	January 23	North Korea seizes USS Pueblo for violating its territorial waters	18

(continued)

Table 3.7 **(Continued)**

Year	*Date*	*Event*	*Days in News*
1968	February 1–17	North Vietnam launches Tet offensive, catches US by surprise	27
1968	March 31	President Johnson announces he will not run for reelection	2
1968	April 4	Dr. Martin Luther King, Jr. assassinated in Memphis	6
1968	April 5–14	Riots in major cities occur after King's death	11
1968	June 5	Robert Kennedy is shot; he dies the next day	4
1968	August 22–25	Anti-war protests at Democratic National Convention in Chicago	2
1970	April 29	United States invades Cambodia	25
1970	May 4	4 students killed at Kent State University during protest against the Vietnam war.	3
1972	June 17	Burglars connected to President Nixon's reelection campaign break-in to Democratic National Committee headquarters at the Watergate in Washington, D.C.	6
1974	May 9	House Judiciary Committee begins impeachment hearings against Nixon	16
1974	July 24	Supreme Court orders Nixon to turn over Watergate tapes to the House Judiciary Committee	5
1974	August 9	Nixon resigns	10
1974	September 8	Ford pardons Nixon	20
1978	September 17	Camp David Accords for Middle East Peace signed	3
1986	November 3	Lebanese magazine reports that the Reagan administration has been secretly selling missiles to Iran to secure release of several hostages.	26

Table 3.7 **(Continued)**

Year	*Date*	*Event*	*Days in News*
1990	August 2	Iraq invades Kuwait	25
1990	September 11	President G. H. W. Bush threatens use of force to remove Iraqi invaders from Kuwait	13
1998	January 17	Paula Jones accuses President Clinton of sexual harassment while governor of Arkansas.	4
1998	January 26	President Clinton denies having sexual relations with Monica Lewinsky	22
1998	August 7	Several US embassies bombed, linked to Osama bin Laden, an exile of Saudi Arabia	1
1998	August 19	Clinton admits having sexual relations with Lewinsky; preliminary impeachment proceedings begin	23
2002	September 12	Speaking before the UN, G. W. Bush says Iraq is a danger to the world	5
2002	October 16	Congressional resolution passed in support of Iraq War	7
2004	February 3	CIA admits there were no weapons of mass destruction in Iraq	3
2004	April 28	Abu Ghraib prison abuse against Iraqi prisoners is revealed.	21
2004	August 29	200,000 people protest G. W. Bush in advance of Republican National Convention	3
2008	January 21	Global stock markets plunge amid growing concerns of US-fueled worldwide recession	2
2008	February 5	US stock markets fall over 3 percent in single day amidst growing economic concerns.	2

(*continued*)

Table 3.7 **(Continued)**

Year	*Date*	*Event*	*Days in News*
2008	September 7	Worldwide credit crisis (Fannie Mae and Freddie Mac placed in federal conservatorship	7
2008	October 3	President G. W. Bush signs the Emergency Economic Stabilization Act to bail out failing banks	4
2010	March 23	President Obama signs Patient Protection and Affordable Care Act	43
2010	April 20	British Petroleum oil rig explodes in Gulf of Mexico, causing largest oil spill in history	85
2010	July 21	Obama signs Dodd-Frank Wall Street Reform and Consumer Protection Act	3
2012	June 28	Supreme Court upholds Affordable Care Act	28
2012	September 15	US Ambassador to Libya killed in raid of US consulate at Benghazi	21
2012	October 29	Superstorm Sandy hits New Jersey and New York	7

Legal Requirements

The theory of uncertainty in the national campaign context maintains that new laws expanding the electorate act as political shocks in much the same way that new communication devices are technological shocks. The laws disrupt the political status quo. They create novelty for campaigners who are unclear how best to reach the newly eligible voters and get them to the polls. They create novelty for the newly enfranchised citizens who now have an opportunity to participate that was previously blocked and this novelty will spur the newly eligible to vote. Over time, the uncertainty is likely to decline as people from the new group establish more consistent participation patterns. During this period of study, there were three changes in national voting laws that permitted the entrance of a large segment of citizens into the electorate: women's suffrage in the 19th Amendment ratified in August, 1920; the passage of the Voting Rights Act of 1965 which ended state restrictions on African-American voting; and 18-year-old enfranchisement in the 26th Amendment ratified in March, 1971.[38]

As shown in Tables 3.2 and 3.3, these legal requirements do not have an effect at the national level or the non-South in either presidential or midterm elections. However, they do have significant effects in diminishing nonvoting in the South in both presidential and midterm elections. The introduction of a voting rights measure decreases nonvoting in the South by 4 percentage points in presidential elections and by 3 percentage points in midterm elections.[39] For the South, this is presumably related to sharp increases in African-American voting after the implementation of the Voting Rights Act of 1965, which we explore more fully in Chapter 6.

Party Competition

The more competitive a race the more uncertainty about its outcome, and hence the more people will vote. Conversely, when the eligible electorate sees little competition and understands the outcome well before the polls open, uncertainty is reduced and nonvoting increases. While there are a variety of ways that party competition can be measured, we employ two indicators in our analyses. The first used in this chapter measures competition as the percent of the total vote received by the Democratic candidate subtracted from 50 percent. This indicator permits an assessment not only of the relative strength of the two parties but how close one is to claiming victory and also a majority. This measure also has merit in three-candidate races even when the victorious candidate may only win by a plurality, since it calculates how close the victorious candidate is to receiving a majority. Because this measure is based on when an election tips from one party to the other, depending on which one exceeds 50 percent, it is particularly effective in measuring competition across years. The second indicator, employed in Chapters 5 through 8, is a competitiveness index which measures the absolute value of the difference between the Democratic percent of the two-party vote and the Republican percent of the two-party vote subtracted from 100. So the closer the index value is to 100, the more competitive the race. Because this measure better captures a range of competitiveness, it is most effective in measuring competition across states in a given year (the focus of the analyses in Chapters 5–8).

Using the majority winner measure of competition, Figures 3.2 and 3.3 depict the level of competition in presidential and midterm elections during the period of study. Bars below the zero point indicate the strength of the Democratic Party; bars above the zero point indicate the strength of the Republican Party.

[38] They are measured as a dummy variable coded 1 in the presidential and midterm election years immediately following the act.

[39] Because the legal requirements variable is a dummy variable, the mean impact measure is not meaningful and therefore is not reported.

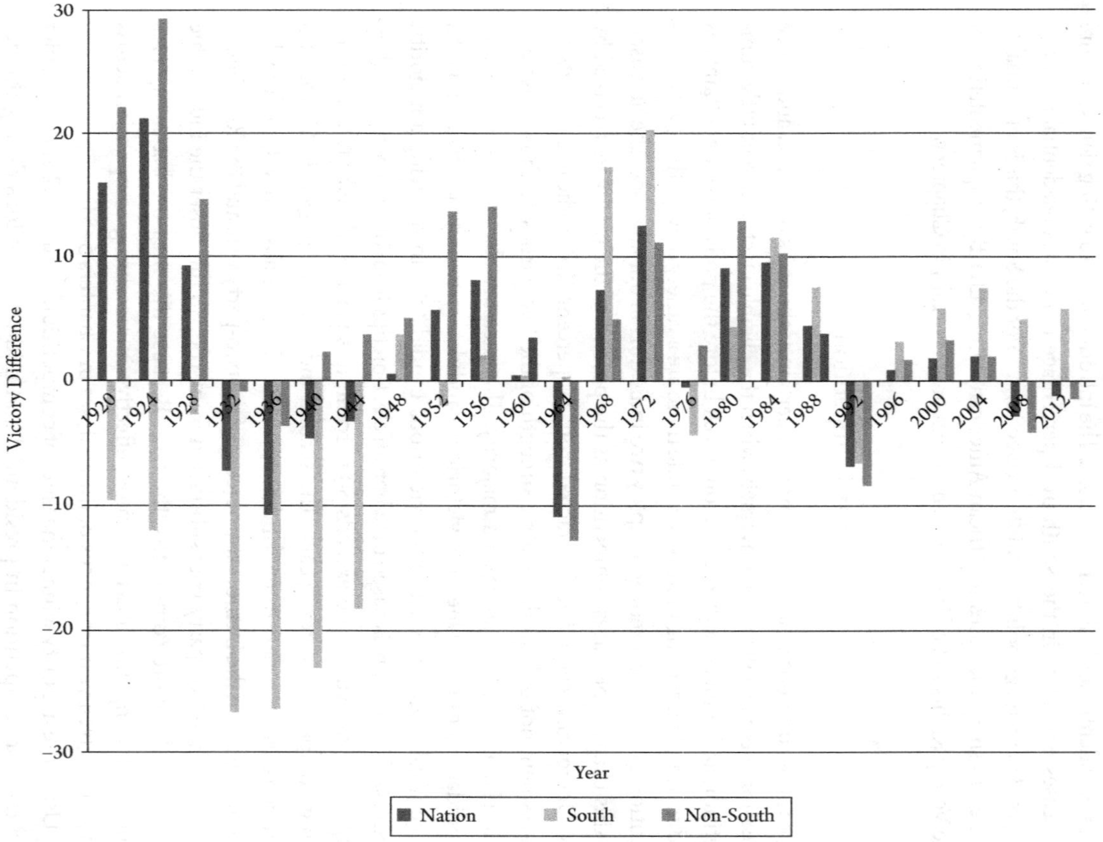

Figure 3.2 Party Competition in Presidential Elections, 1920–2012

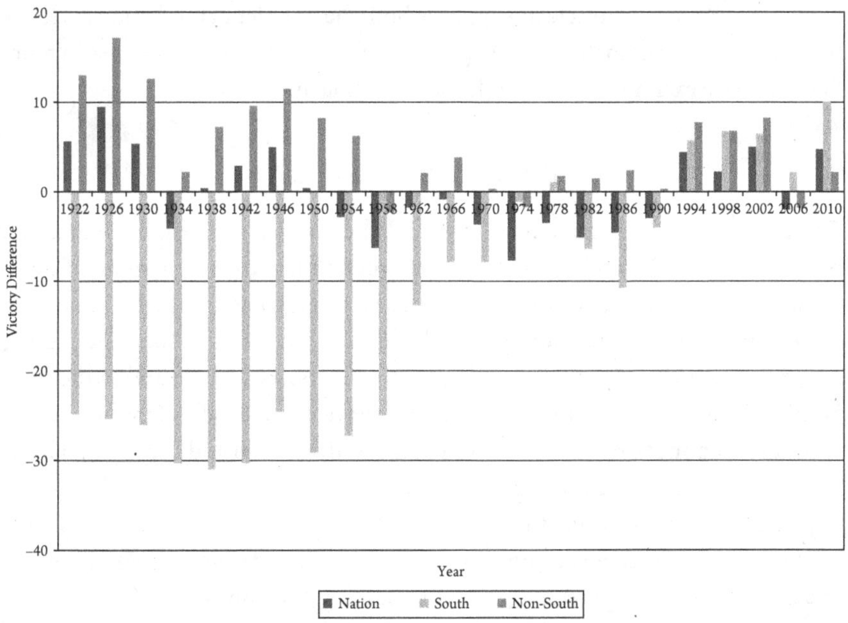

Figure 3.3 Party Competition in Midterm House Elections, 1922–2010

In other words, the longer the bar, the less competitive is the race; the shorter the bar, the more competitive is the race. The first observation is that competition can affect nonvoting only to the extent that there are actually competitive races. If there are large numbers of races in which the winner's victory margin is eye-catching, then competition will have little influence on nonvoting. Figure 3.2 clearly shows how distinctly uncompetitive many presidential elections have been. While it is most obvious among the Harding, Coolidge, and Roosevelt elections, it is also apparent in other races, including Eisenhower, Johnson, and Nixon in 1972. Considering the entire time period, there has been a distinct increase in the competitiveness of presidential elections since the Ford–Carter race in 1976. While the average victory margin was 8 percent in the period from 1920–1972, it dropped to 4 percent in the period from 1976 to 2012. Figure 3.3 also reveals how uncompetitive House races have been throughout most of the entire period of study. The figure shows the uncompetitiveness of the solid Democratic South from 1922 through 1970, a period of greater competitiveness from 1974 through 1990, and the emergence of Republican dominance in House races both in the South and the non-South after 1994.

As shown in Table 3.3, competition significantly affects midterm elections in the South but has no other effects. This southern effect undoubtedly reflects the shift over time depicted in Figure 3.3 from a one-party South dominated by Democratic members of Congress to a one-party South ultimately dominated by Republicans. In general, competition has limited influence on nonvoting examined longitudinally, because there are so many election years at both the presidential and midterm levels that are highly uncompetitive. This sporadic influence of competition is seen more fully when we examine individual elections starting in Chapter 5.

Personal Characteristics

To better gauge the relative importance of the national campaign context, the results in Tables 3.2 and 3.3 also estimate the influence on nonvoting of demographic characteristics of the electorate, measured by age and education. The more young people in the voting-eligible population, the more likely nonvoting rates increase in presidential elections for the nation as a whole and in the non-South, but not in the South. Youth does not have a statistically significant effect on midterm nonvoting. The effect of youth for the nation and the non-South is most telling when considering the impact measures. The mean level of youth population (14 percent for the nation and the non-South) is associated with a very sizable 12 percentage point increase in presidential nonvoting nationally and an even larger 14 percentage point increase in the non-South.

Education has considerable influence on nonvoting in the South and non-South in presidential election years, and in the South in midterm election years. As shown in the Impact column, for the South, the mean impact of education is associated with a 15 percentage point drop in nonvoting in presidential and an 8 percentage point drop in midterm elections. Education also decreases nonvoting in the non-South by 5 percentage points in presidential elections and 3 percentage points in midterm contests. In Chapters 5 through 8, the results for individual election years show that the effect of education is quite sizable in some election years but is absent in others.

Prior Nonvoting

Lastly, the results in the two tables show that prior nonvoting does not influence current nonvoting in presidential elections but does affect current nonvoting in midterm elections nationally and regionally. The absence of this effect at the presidential level reflects the inter-election swings discussed in Chapter 2. Across a lengthy time span, there is a somewhat erratic quality to presidential nonvoting as it moves up and down from one election to the next. This is distinct from the more stable nonvoting found in midterm elections.

The Certainty about Uncertainty in the Campaign Context

At a press briefing on February 12, 2002, then Secretary of Defense Donald Rumsfeld mused about uncertainty, "Reports that say that something hasn't happened are always interesting to me, because as we know, there are known knowns; there are things we know we know. We also know there are known unknowns; that is to say we know there are some things we do not know. But there are also unknown unknowns—the ones we don't know we don't know."[40] At the time, many commentators criticized Rumsfeld's comments, suggesting that he was trying to obfuscate the fact that no weapons of mass destruction had been found in Iraq. But the inherent logic of Rumsfeld's categorizations about certain and uncertain things is appealing and is applicable to campaign politics as much as to foreign policy. Although campaigners yearn for complete certainty about the campaign context and their political futures, there are many unknowns—both known and unknown. These unknowns are part of the uncertainty that permeates the national campaign context.

Within the uncertainty of the campaign context, economic volatility, technology shocks, disruptive major events, and new legal requirements have significant effects on nonvoting in presidential and midterm elections. Something novel interrupts the political commonplace, and fewer people remain on the sidelines. For each of these factors, this is not only the case in highly visible presidential elections but also holds true for the more obscure midterm House elections.

The uncertainty associated with economic change has a significant impact on nonvoting across presidential and midterm elections, nationally and regionally. This is especially clear in midterm elections in which gloomy unemployment news increases participation. In literally half of these House elections, the unemployment rate was greater than it had been four years earlier (see Table 3.5). And, more pointedly, the depths of several American recessions hit just before midterm elections in 1922, 1934, 1950, 1958, 1970, 1982, and most recently in 2010. Even though House races are more local in nature than presidential contests, they nonetheless are caught up in the national political environment, particularly at the midterm as voters often punish the president's party with a loss of seats.[41] Income change has greater influence on presidential elections as the degree of economic growth across the country becomes a typical campaign theme. "It's the Economy Stupid," the catchphrase of the Bill Clinton campaign of 1992, summarized the mottos of many presidential campaigns.

Generally, communication innovation has a somewhat greater impact than economic conditions in presidential and midterm elections, nationally and regionally. As we examine the results for individual elections in the chapters to come, the stronger influence of communication technology relative to economic conditions becomes even more apparent. A new device that brings entertainment and information into people's homes is initially a novelty but soon is

[40] http://www.defense.gov/transcripts/transcript.aspx?transcriptid=2636.

[41] From 1922 through 2010, the president's party has lost on average 24 seats in midterm elections (Rusk, 2001, as updated by the authors).

ubiquitous. One of the most important tasks of the campaign is to get information to potential voters. The information can surely come from old media, but the new medium provides a unique avenue to offer people information in a novel way. The influence of technology is particularly telling for the non-South. Since the 1920s, the non-South has consistently adopted a new technology faster than the South. For instance, in 1928, 25 percent of non-southern households had radios in their homes compared with just 9 percent of southern households. So, there is more opportunity in the non-South for the technology shock to spur more people to the polls.

Major crisis-oriented events that capture public attention near the time of the election also help to reduce nonvoting. In the South, events have a greater impact on presidential nonvoting than communication technology, as the civil rights movement upended southern politics. Also, as an additional gauge of the power of the civil rights movement in the South, legal requirements have the single largest effect of any variable in presidential years and a sizable effect in midterm races.

As control variables, youth and education temper the effects of the campaign context model in both presidential and midterm elections. Youth posts the largest impact value of any variable in the national and non-South models. Education has the strongest impact value of any variable on presidential and midterm nonvoting in the South model. Income change exceeds the effect of education on presidential and midterm nonvoting for the nation as a whole. The effect of education on nonvoting in the South is especially noteworthy. Electoral participation in the South was restricted through various election laws and the absence of party competition. But, education penetrated the structurally high levels of nonvoting in the South in proportionally greater ways than elsewhere. In the South, with education rates consistently below the rest of the country, education has a greater impact on getting people involved in politics. Results in the later chapters reveal that the effect of education on nonvoting in individual elections is more mixed. Nevertheless, it is important to keep in mind that our focus on the national campaign context is not designed to replace or repudiate earlier discussions of psychological, demographic, social, and campaign mobilizations facets of electoral participation. Instead, it is designed to properly measure the influence of these factors relative to economic conditions, communication technologies, and major events in the national political scene.

We now turn to an analysis of individual nonvoting and consider how the external uncertainty in the national campaign context influences the internal uncertainty of people in the eligible electorate. This will permit us to better assess how the generalizations revealed in this chapter remain relevant when considering individual nonvoters and voters.

4

Who Are Nonvoters?

Two questions surround American nonvoting: how many people do not vote, and who does not vote. The preceding chapter began to answer the first question, focusing on how the uncertainty of the national campaign context affects the number of people who do not vote across a long historical period. This chapter begins to answer the second question by considering how the uncertainty of the national campaign context affects individuals' decisions to vote or not. People pay attention to the campaign context to varying degrees, and this attention guides whether they will vote. The chapter proceeds in four parts. The first section delves more fully into the theory of uncertainty in connecting external uncertainty in the national campaign context to internal uncertainty among citizens about the candidates. The second section examines the differences between voters and nonvoters. The third analyzes the determinants of individual nonvoting. The fourth section explores differences among nonvoters, which are as important as differences between voters and nonvoters.

Unavoidable Politics

There are three central elements to our theory of the national campaign context at the individual level:

- *National campaign context awareness.* People have a general awareness of the national campaign context. The greater the degree of uncertainty in the national campaign context, the more people pay attention to it.
- *Candidate awareness.* American campaigns are candidate-based, and so people will also have some basic awareness of the candidates. The greater the degree of uncertainty in the national campaign context, the more likely candidates will focus their campaigns on that uncertainty and the more likely people will have information about the candidates.

- *External uncertainty drives internal uncertainty.* People are internally uncertain about which candidate will best handle the external uncertainty. If people are less internally uncertain about one candidate compared to another, they will vote. If people do not believe that any candidate adequately addresses the external uncertainty, individuals will not vote.

While the typical analysis of nonvoters suggests that they are apolitical and often lack the personal resources—education, income, residential stability—necessary to cast a vote, the discussion of the uncertainty of the national campaign context suggests that politics is often hard to ignore. As we discussed in the previous chapter, the level of external uncertainty prompted by a sharp turn in the economy, dramatic international involvements, and visible national events focuses people's attention on the campaign context as they assess what the future holds. Innovations in communication technology make it intriguing to follow the campaign. Changes in election laws encourage large segments of the population to understand politics. Thus, politics may be unavoidable to more people than is often assumed. This is not to say that nonvoters and voters are identical in their knowledge of the national campaign context, but it is to argue that nonvoters are not universally unaware of the political context. They are knowledgeable of prevailing economic conditions and dominant issues, inspired by new media communication techniques, and make reasonably good guesses about how competitive the election seems to be.

The core exercise of any campaign is for candidates to distinguish themselves from each other. And one central strategy is to describe how well they will handle the uncertainty of the national campaign context. The campaign affords a built-in comparison between the happenings in the national campaign context and the candidates' proposals.

Most generally, we maintain that the higher the level of uncertainty in the campaign context, the more citizens will know about the campaign context, the more distinct their views of the candidates and issues become, and hence the more likely they are to vote. This is consistent with research which has found that specific candidates in a race increase the likelihood of individuals voting; people's opinions of those candidates also influence participation.[1] If there is a candidate who is attractive in addressing people's concerns and alleviating

[1] Dean Lacy and Barry Burden, "The Vote-Stealing and Turnout Effects of Ross Perot in the 1992 U.S. Presidential Election," *American Journal of Political Science* 43 (January 1999): 233–255; Lyn Ragsdale and Jerrold Rusk, "Candidates, Issues, and Participation in Senate Elections," *Legislative Studies Quarterly* 20 (August 1995): 305–327; Mitchell Sanders, "Uncertainty and Turnout," *Political Analysis* 9 (Winter 2001): 45–57; Byron Shafer and Richard Spady, *The American Political Landscape* (Cambridge: Harvard University Press, 2014).

external uncertainty along many of the dimensions discussed in the preceding chapters, then people are more likely to vote. Thus, while the high levels of external uncertainty remain, people reduce their internal uncertainty about what will happen next by asserting their preference favoring one candidate over another.

At the same time, the theory suggests that there will be a group of citizens who know a fair amount about the campaign context and have distinct views about the candidates but do not feel that one or more candidates is adequately addressing the external uncertainty of the campaign context. If the candidates are unattractive—"tweedle-dum, tweedle-dee" candidates who do not seem distinct from one another, or the "lesser-of-two-evils" candidates who are similarly bad at addressing the national campaign context—then people will be less likely to vote. This is consistent with early formal theories which considered nonvoting as rational abstention that "depends upon the citizens' comparative evaluation of the candidates."[2] These theories posited two conditions of nonvoting: indifference (when citizens see little or no difference between the candidates) and alienation (when citizens dislike all candidates).[3] Also, with lower levels of external uncertainty in the campaign context, people will have less internal uncertainty. They will gather less information, have weaker or no opinions about the candidates, and hence will be less likely to vote. Thus, we build candidate evaluation into the campaign context theory of individual participation by reversing the order of the typical model of electoral participation: people decide for whom to vote before they decide whether to vote. If people know little about the candidates or feel that neither adequately addresses the prevailing conditions in the national campaign context, they will choose not to vote.

Internal Uncertainty

The juxtaposition between external uncertainty and candidates' promises creates internal uncertainty among citizens: which candidate will do a better job? The theory posits four additional premises about internal uncertainty:

1. *Uncertainty reduction.* Generally, people seek to reduce internal uncertainty whenever possible.

[2] Otto Davis, Melvin Hinich, and Peter Ordeshook, "An Expository Development of a Mathematical Model of the Electoral Process," *American Political Science Review* 64 (June 1970): 426–448.

[3] William Riker and Peter Ordeshook, "A Theory of the Calculus of Voting," *American Political Science Review* 62 (March 1968): 25–42.

2. *Uncertainty about choice.* Individuals are internally uncertain about the choice presented to them by the candidates. Even when individuals gather information and form opinions about the relative advantages and disadvantages of the candidates, they fear they could make a mistake.
3. *Uncertainty about consequences.* Individuals are internally uncertain about the consequences of the choice they ultimately make between candidates. If they make a mistake, what consequences follow for their lives or for the nation?
4. *Individual differences.* Individuals respond to internal uncertainty in unique ways based on their personal backgrounds and interests.

Considerable research points to reducing uncertainty as a consistent pattern of human behavior.[4] People prefer to avoid large unknowns and work in intuitive ways to reduce them, even when they recognize that these uncertainties cannot be fully eliminated. Applied to campaigns and candidates, people will make some attempt to find out what is going on in the national campaign context and who the candidates are, rather than leaving the election outcome to chance or to the decisions of others. People are unlikely to be completely oblivious to politics, because the external uncertainty in the national campaign context drives them to reduce their own internal uncertainty about what to do.

The second and third premises suggest that internal uncertainty takes two forms—uncertainty about the decisions or choices that an individual makes (specifically, whether to choose A over B) and uncertainty about the consequences of the decision itself (choosing A over B). With the second premise, individuals struggle to reduce the internal uncertainty of choice by finding the best mechanism to compare the candidates. These mechanisms may vary widely from one person to the next—determining the better candidate based on their personal styles, physical attributes, emotional appeals, specific issue positions, or broad ideological stances. Nevertheless, internal uncertainty is likely to remain about candidates' personal characteristics and issue positions.[5] The internal uncertainty about consequences noted in the third premise is unresolvable. What results from a decision about a candidate and participation are unknown and unknowable at the time the decision is made. While it may be

[4] See Claudio Cioffi-Revilla, *Politics and Uncertainty* (Cambridge: Cambridge University Press, 1998); Dennis Lindley, *Understanding Uncertainty* (Hoboken, NJ: Wiley-Interscience, 2007).

[5] Larry Bartels, "Issue Voting Under Uncertainty: An Empirical Test," *American Journal of Political Science* 30 (November 1986): 709–728; R. Michael Alvarez and Charles Franklin, "Uncertainty and Political Perceptions," *Journal of Politics* 56 (August 1994): 671–688; Garrett Glasgow and R. Michael Alvarez, "Uncertainty in Candidate Personality Traits," *American Politics Research* 28 (January 2000): 26–49; Mitchell Sanders, "Uncertainty and Turnout," *Political Analysis* 9 (Winter 2001): 45–57; Kathleen McGraw, Edward Hasecke, and Kimberly Conger, "Ambivalence, Uncertainty, and Processes of Candidate Evaluation," *Political Psychology* 24 (September 2003): 421–448.

factored in as guesswork when the decision is made, the uncertainty is in the future and unpredictable.

Finally, uncertainty is ultimately a personal matter that is subjective, not objective. It is *your* or *my* internal uncertainty. This means that people's life experiences, personal backgrounds, and social connections are likely to be important in defining how individuals perceive the external uncertainty of the national campaign context and how they handle the resulting internal uncertainty about candidates, electoral participation, and outcomes. This information-gathering process is not likely to be similar across people but instead may be highly specialized or even idiosyncratic.

This discussion of internal uncertainty adds to our understanding of why aggregate nonvoting rates go up and down across elections. As seen in Chapter 2, nonvoting rates change from one election to the next—not just between presidential and midterm elections but from one presidential year to the next and from one midterm to another.[6] As we first developed the theory of uncertainty in Chapter 3, high levels of uncertainty in the electoral setting push people off the sidelines, while low levels keep them at home. Individuals' decisions to skip one or more elections help account for these inter-election changes because people are not sufficiently concerned about the external uncertainty of the national campaign context, or they do not resolve their internal uncertainty about the candidates in favor of one candidate. In a 10–election year study, researchers Sigelman, Roeder, Jewell, and Baer found that the modal number of elections in which people voted was one or two elections. They concluded, "there was no hard-and-fast-distinction between voters and nonvoters . . . Rather there were only degrees of participation that shade into one another."[7] There is no uniform answer to the question "Who does not vote?"

Voters and Nonvoters

We consider nonvoting at the individual level using American National Election Study data in presidential elections from 1968 through 2012 and House midterm

[6] On average, there is a 16 percentage point increase in nonvoting between presidential and midterm years, a 4 percentage point change from one presidential election to the next, and a 6 percentage point change from one midterm election to the next.

[7] Lee Sigelman, Philip Roeder, Malcolm Jewell, and Michael Baer, "Voting and Nonvoting: A Multi-election Perspective," *American Journal of Political Science* 29 (November 1985): 752. See also formal models which indicate that people are inconsistent in going to the polls: Jonathan Bendor, Daniel Diermeier, and Michael Ting, "A Behavioral Model of Turnout," *American Political Science Review* 97 (May 2003): 261–280; James Fowler, "Habitual Voting and Behavioral Voting," *Journal of Politics* 68 (May 2006): 335–344.

elections from 1978 through 2002. [8] We measure nonvoters as those people who answer "no" to the question, "Did respondent vote in the November elections?" Studies of electoral participation have indicated that self-report survey data can overstate the number of people who vote.[9] Driven by a desire to appear civic-minded, survey respondents say they voted when in fact they did not. Our interest in nonvoting obviates the over-report issue, because there is no evidence in the vote validation literature that people say they did not vote when in fact they actually did. A few people may not remember whether they voted, but they do not actively misstate that they did not vote. To be sure, some inaccuracy occurs in the report of nonvoters from those people who say they voted when in fact they did not. But, in general, the measure of nonvoters is a conservative one which does capture those who truly did not vote. Moreover, the vote validation studies conducted as part of a select number of American National Election Studies in 1976, 1978, 1980, 1984, 1986, 1988, and 1990 show that across this set of elections, there is little over-reporting of voting or under-reporting of nonvoting. Among survey respondents, 62 percent reported they voted while 38 percent said they did not vote. The vote validation study found that 60 percent of these survey respondents actually voted while 40 percent did not. This small 2 percentage point discrepancy suggests that American National Election Study survey data present a valid measure for the nonvoting variable.

The results in Table 4.1 offer four generalizations about nonvoters and voters. First, nonvoters and voters know a fair amount about the national campaign context. This observation is counter to the more common portrayal of nonvoters as relatively removed from the political world. Yet, when we add uncertainty to that world and people's desires to minimize it, it becomes clearer that nonvoters will be more politically aware than existing research assumes. Table 4.1 shows nearly 84 percent of nonvoters pay attention to at least one form of media, while nearly all voters do. Nonvoters, like voters, are aware of major national problems, with 85 percent naming at least one, compared with 91 percent of voters. Nonvoters and voters judge national economic conditions

[8] The analysis begins in 1968 because candidate evaluation questions began in that year. House candidate questions began in 1978. No cross-sectional study was completed for the 2006 and 2010 elections.

[9] E.g., Paul Abramson and William Claggett, "Race-Related Differences in Self-Reported and Validated Turnout in 1984," *Journal of Politics* 48 (May 1986): 412–422; Brian Silver, Barbara Anderson, and Paul Abramson, "Who Overreports Voting?" *American Political Science Review* 80 (June 1986): 613–624; Jonathan Katz and Gabriel Katz, "Correcting for Survey Misreports Using Auxiliary Information with an Application to Estimating Turnout," *American Journal of Political Science* 54 (July 2010): 815–835; Stephen Ansolabehere and Eitan Hersh, "Validation: What Big Data Reveal about Survey Misreporting and the Real Electorate," *Political Analysis* 20 (Autumn 2012): 437–459.

Table 4.1 **Comparison of Nonvoters and Voters in Presidential and Midterm House Elections, 1968–2012 (percent of respondents)**

Awareness of the National Campaign Context	*Nonvoters*	*Voters*	*Candidate Evaluations*	*Nonvoters*	*Voters*	*Attention to Politics*	*Nonvoters*	*Voters*	*Background Characteristics and Social Connections*	*Nonvoters*	*Voters*
Watch Television Program on Election	72.1	87.6	*Compare the Candidates (President)*	81.8	91.4	*Interest in Public Affairs (President)*			*Age (mean)*	41.4	48.7
			Compare the Candidates (House)	48.5	77.0	Most of the time	13.9	34.7	*Education*		
Media Attention						Some of the time	29.9	39.3	Less than High School	12.0	6.2
Multiple forms of media	5.4	17.8	*Neutral Candidate Evaluations (President)*			Now and then	30.1	18.8	High School	55.1	37.4
Some forms of media	17.4	33.1	Both candidates	9.5	2.5	Hardly at all	26.1	7.1	Some College	21.7	27.5
Two forms of media	29.9	29.2	One candidate	24.5	16.5				College or Advanced Degree	11.2	28.9

(*continued*)

Table 4.1 **(Continued)**

Awareness of the National Campaign Context	Nonvoters	Voters	*Candidate Evaluations*	Nonvoters	Voters	*Attention to Politics*	Nonvoters	Voters	*Background Characteristics and Social Connections*	Nonvoters	Voters
One form of media	30.9	16.4	Neither candidate	66.0	81.0	*Interest in Public Affairs (House)*					
None	16.3	3.5	*Neutral Candidate Evaluations (House)*			Most of the time	14.8	37.6	*Income*		
			Both candidates	46.1	17.8	Some of the time	31.2	38.8	0–16 percentile	25.7	13.2
Aware of Major National Problem	84.9	90.7	One candidate	23.0	27.1	Now and then	29.9	17.4	17–33 percentile	20.5	15.4
			Neither candidate	30.9	55.1	Hardly at all	24.2	6.1	34–67 percentile	32.3	34.7
Economic Conditions									68–95 percentile	18.9	30.2

Much Worse than Before	24.2	23.8				*Interest in the Election (President)*			96–100 percentile	2.7	6.4
Somewhat Worse than Before	21.9	19.5	*Negative Candidate Evaluations (President)*			Very Much	14.1	33.6			
No Change	34.5	30.6	Both candidates	4.1	2.9	Somewhat	42.5	45.9			
Somewhat Better than Before	16.2	21.7	One candidate	43.4	59.5	Not very Much	43.5	20.4	Social Connections		
Much Better than Before	3.2	4.4	Neither candidate	52.0	37.6				*Married*	51.4	62.0
						Interest in the Election (Congress)			*Church attendance*	87.3	92.8
War Involvement			*Negative Candidate Evaluations (House)*			Very Much	9.3	34.7			
Should be involved	31.2	33.3	Both candidates	1.3	1.7	Somewhat	41.2	50.4			
Unsure, depends	9.9	8.0	One candidate	5.0	10.4	Not very Much	49.4	14.8			

(continued)

Table 4.1 **(Continued)**

Awareness of the National Campaign Context	***Nonvoters***	***Voters***	***Candidate Evaluations***	***Nonvoters***	***Voters***	***Attention to Politics***	***Nonvoters***	***Voters***	***Background Characteristics and Social Connections***	***Nonvoters***	***Voters***
Should not be involved	59.0	58.7	Neither candidate	93.7	87.9	*Closeness of Race (President)*			*Residential Stability*		
						Close	51.2	55.2	3 years or less	24.1	13.8
Concern about War			*Ideological Candidate Comparison (President)*			Not close/ Don't know	48.8	44.8	4 years or more	75.9	86.2
Very Worried	15.6	12.4	No Difference	39.1	19.8						
Somewhat Worried	43.0	42.7	Very Small Difference	13.0	10.1				*Unemployed*	27.0	18.8
Not Worried	40.2	44.4	Small Difference	15.9	16.5						
Unsure	1.2	0.5	Moderate Difference	24.2	39.8						
			Large Difference	5.6	11.0						

Care Who Wins (President)			Very Large Difference	2.2	2.7
Care a good deal	45.9	60.4	*Ideological Candidate Comparison (House)*		
Do not care very much	54.1	39.6	No Difference	28.1	15.4
Care Who Wins (House)			Very Small Difference	13.0	10.1
Care a good deal	35.8	69.9	Small Difference	15.9	16.5
Do not care very much	64.2	30.1	Moderate Difference	24.2	39.8
			Large Difference	5.6	11.0
			Very Large Difference	2.2	2.7

Source: American National Election Studies Cumulative File, found at http://www.electionstudies.org/.

in similar ways, although voters are more optimistic than nonvoters about the outlook of the economy. In addition, nonvoters' and voters' concerns about US involvement in war are very similar. Finally, nonvoters and voters are similarly aware of whether the presidential race is close, with 51 percent of nonvoters and 55 percent of voters judging the race to be close. Thus, there is an unavoidable quality to the uncertainty within the national campaign context to which both nonvoters and voters are exposed.

Second, nonvoters, like voters, have information and opinions about the candidates. Most nonvoters (82 percent) and nearly all voters (91 percent) make comparative judgments of the presidential candidates.[10] In addition, sizable numbers of nonvoters and voters see ideological differences between the candidates (61 percent of nonvoters and 80 percent of voters).[11] At the same time, there is considerable variation among nonvoters regarding what they know and how clear their opinions are. Among nonvoters, 48 percent have negative evaluations of at least one presidential candidate, while 34 percent have neutral evaluations of at least one.[12] While 39 percent of nonvoters see no ideological difference between the presidential candidates (compared to 20 percent of voters), 32 percent see at least a moderate ideological difference between the candidates (compared to 54 percent for voters). Table 4.1 clarifies that the level of candidate awareness is decidedly less for nonvoters approaching a midterm House election. Among nonvoters, 49 percent can make a comparative judgment about House candidates (in contrast to 77 percent of voters) and 54 percent make a concrete evaluation of one or both candidates.[13] In general, while

[10] Respondents are asked two feeling thermometer questions about their overall views of the candidates on a scale ranging from 0 (very unfavorable) to 100 (very favorable) with 50 as the neutral midpoint. The comparative candidate indicator is the absolute value of the difference between the overall rating of the Democratic candidate and the overall rating of the Republican candidate.

[11] Questions ask respondents to place the Democratic and Republican candidates on a 7-point liberal–conservative scale, which ranges from very liberal to very conservative. The ideological differences indicator calculates the absolute value of the difference between respondents' placement of one candidate on the scale and their placement of the other candidate.

[12] The negative evaluation variable is constructed as follows: If an individual rates both the Democratic and Republican candidates negatively (less than 50 degrees) on the feeling thermometer, the variable is scored 2. If the respondent rates only one candidate negatively, the variable is coded 1. If the individual rates both candidates at or above 50 degrees, the variable is coded 0. The neutral evaluation variable is constructed in a similar manner: If an individual rates both the Democratic and the Republican candidates neutrally (at 50 degrees) on the feeling thermometer, the variable is coded 2. If the respondent rates only one candidate neutrally, the variable is coded 1. If the individual rates neither candidate at 50 degrees, the variable is coded 0.

[13] Nonvoters see smaller comparative differences between the candidates than do voters—an 11 percentage point net difference compared with a 22 percentage point net difference.

nonvoters may not be as savvy as voters, they are by no means ignorant of what is going on in the national campaign context.

Third, in their attempts to lower internal uncertainty, nonvoters, like voters, have some interest in public affairs. In presidential elections, 44 percent of nonvoters suggest they are interested in public affairs at least some of the time and 57 percent reported being at least somewhat interested in the election itself. In midterm elections, political interest is lower but still 46 percent of nonvoters reported being interested in public affairs at least some of the time, and over half said they were at least somewhat interested in the outcome of the midterm elections. Moreover, not all voters are exceptionally interested in public affairs, with 26 percent saying they pay attention to politics only sporadically in presidential years and 24 percent reporting they pay minimal attention in midterm years. These three generalizations shed light on the unavoidable nature of politics.

Fourth, individual differences are apparent between nonvoters and voters, but also among nonvoters. The table confirms the long-observed differences between nonvoters and voters about their personal characteristics and social connections. Nonvoters are younger, less educated, and have lower incomes than voters.[14] They are also less likely to be married, attend church, be employed, and reside in the same place over an extended period of time. Still, the demarcations between nonvoters and voters are not as clear-cut as existing research has portrayed. While it is true that 56 percent of voters have some college education or better, 33 percent of nonvoters also have some college education. So there are a number of well-educated nonvoters in American elections. Nonvoters have lower incomes than voters, but 22 percent of nonvoters earn incomes in the top two brackets compared with 37 percent of voters. Similarly, many nonvoters are married (51 percent compared to 62 percent for voters), attend church (87 percent compared with 93 percent of voters), are employed (73 percent compared with 81 percent), and live in the same place for an extended period of time (76 percent of nonvoters live in the same place for four years or more compared to 86 percent of voters).[15] Thus, the stereotype of nonvoters who lack

[14] Age is measured as self-reported chronological age, which ranges from 17 to 99. Education is based on a response to the question, "What was the highest grade of school or year in college you completed?" measured on a 4-point scale from less than high school (coded as 0) to college or advanced degree (coded as 3). Income is measured by responses to the question, "About what do you think your total income will be this year for yourself and your immediate family?

[15] The married category includes people who say they are married and people who say they are living with a partner but not married. Church attendance is based on answers to the question "Would you say you go to church regularly, often, seldom, or never? The variable is calculated on a 4-point scale ranging from never (coded 0) to regularly (coded 4). Unemployment is based on individuals' self-reports of whether they are unemployed or temporarily laid off. The variable is coded as a

the personal resources and social networks to be political is overstated and does not explain the variability among nonvoters. In general, the results of Table 4.1 indicate that it is important to understand both the differences *between* nonvoters and voters and the variability *among* nonvoters.

Why People Do Not Vote

We now explore a multivariate model of individual nonvoting which tests the import of the national campaign context and impressions of the candidates relative to personal resources, social connections, psychological involvement in politics, campaign mobilization, and competition. To estimate the uncertainty in the national campaign context, we include indicators depicted in Table 4.1 of individuals' perceptions of economic issues, media attention, and awareness of a major national problem.[16] This parallels the economic conditions, mass communication technology, and national events that informed the aggregate model presented in Chapter 3. To capture the internal uncertainty people have about the candidates and how they will handle national circumstances, we include indicators of candidate comparison and ideological comparison referenced in Table 4.1. The more individuals can make comparative judgments between the candidates generally and about their ideological positions specifically, the more likely they will vote. We also adopt from Table 4.1 the indicator of how much an individual cares who wins. This is a crucial part of individuals' candidate comparisons and their internal uncertainty. To lower their internal uncertainty, people not only must see distinct differences between the candidates, but they must actively know which one they want to win.

To model individuals' personal resources, we include age and education to parallel the aggregate model in Chapter 3.[17] Indicators for marriage, residential stability, and unemployment measure people's social connections.[18] Individuals' interest in the current election serves as a measure of psychological involvement in politics. To measure campaign mobilization, we consider

dummy variable with 1=unemployed. Residential stability is the self-reported number of years the respondent has lived at his/her current address.

[16] The economic conditions variable is measured on a 5-point scale ranging from +2 ("the economy is much better than before") to –2 ("the economy is much worse than before"), with 0 denoting "no change." The media attention variable is measured on a 4-point scale where 4 = multiple forms of media, 3 = some forms of media, 2 = two forms of media, 1 = one form of media, and 0=no form of media. Issue awareness is measured as a dummy variable denoting whether a respondent was aware of a national issue (coded 1) or not (coded 0).

[17] These are the two most consistently available demographic indicators throughout the entire time period.

[18] In additional tests, we included a church membership variable which had no effect.

whether individuals received communication from any candidate's campaign.[19] Finally, as an indicator of competition, we employ people's assessment of the closeness of the election.[20] Table 4.2 presents the estimates of a panel probit model analyzing the effects of these variables on the likelihood that an individual does not vote in presidential elections from 1972 through 2004 and House midterm elections from 1978 through 2002.[21] In addition to the estimates, the final column for each set of elections assesses the difference in the probability of not voting between the highest and lowest values of the independent variable, holding all other independent variables at their means.[22]

Presidential Elections

The results show the importance of the external uncertainty of the national campaign context in individuals' decisions not to vote in presidential elections. Indistinct views about economic conditions, low media attention, and lack of awareness of a major national problem increase the likelihood that individuals will not vote in presidential elections. As an example, individuals who use only one form of media to track the campaign are nearly 18 percentage points less likely to vote than those who use multiple forms of media. (This number is found in the last column for president.) The results also show the influence of candidate comparisons on nonvoting decisions. People who make only limited candidate comparisons are 25 percentage points less likely to vote than those who see strong differences between the candidates. And those who see small

[19] Interest is measured on a 3-point scale with 1=not very much interest, 2=some interest, 3=very much interest. The contact variable is based on the question, "Did anyone from one of the major parties call you up or come by to talk to you about the campaign this year?"

[20] The closeness variable is based on the question, "How close do you think the current election will be?" It is coded 1 for "close" and 0 for "not close" or "don't know." It is not asked in midterm election years.

[21] Because of data availability and comparability issues, the 1968 and 2006 through 2012 elections are not considered. In 1968, the ideological comparison variable is unavailable; in 2008 and 2012, there is insufficient comparability in the questions asked to create the media exposure index. No survey was conducted in 2006 or 2010. Probit analysis yields probability estimates that are true probabilities lying in the range from 0 (a person votes) to 1 (a person does not vote). Because the variables themselves are not calculated in the same units, comparisons of the maximum likelihood estimates cannot be made. Thus the Z scores (ratio between the maximum likelihood estimates and their standard errors) provide appropriate interpretations of the results. Since probit estimates are based on a cumulative normal distribution function, the MLE/SE rations can be compared to the critical values of the Z distribution. Because this is a pooled cross-section data set, we initially estimated the model with election years as dummy variables. In neither the presidential nor the midterm models were election years statistically significant, so those indicators were dropped from the estimation.

[22] The high value of age is calculated as 65 years and older. The high value of residential stability is calculated as 40 years and above.

Table 4.2 **Effects of the National Campaign Context on Individual Nonvoting, 1972–2004 (Probit Maximum Likelihood Coefficients)**

Predictor	*Presidential Elections, 1972–2004*					*House Midterm Elections, 1978–1998*				
	Maximum Likelihood Estimate	*MLE/SE*		*Range of Value in the Variable*	*Change in Likelihood of the Variable*	*Maximum Likelihood Estimate*	*MLE/SE*		*Range of Value in the Variable*	*Change in Likelihood of the Variable*
National Campaign Context										
Economic conditions	–0.135	–9.073	***	–2, 2	0.158	–0.092	–4.910	***	–2, 2	0.236
Media attention	–0.134	–9.635	***	0, 4	0.177	–0.132	–4.326	***	0, 4	0.297
Issue awareness	–0.106	–3.374	***	0, 1	0.023	–0.102	–1.291		0, 1	0.051
Candidate Awareness										
Candidate comparison	–0.001	–1.904	*	0, 100	0.254	–0.008	–7.410	***	0, 100	0.432
Ideological comparison	–0.062	–6.756	***	1, 7	0.118	–0.056	–3.065	***	1, 7	0.100
Care who wins	–0.166	–10.675	***	–1, 1	0.071	–0.177	–9.209	***	–1, 1	0.256
Personal Characteristics										
Youth	0.013	15.196	***	17, 99	0.307	0.017	14.755	***	17, 99	0.285

Education	−0.302	−15.310	***	0, 3	0.256	−0.209	−8.831	***	0, 3	0.215
Social Connections										
Marriage	−0.090	−2.919	***	0, 1	0.040	−0.032	−0.787		0, 1	0.088
Residential stability	−0.002	−4.621	***	0, 99	0.087	−0.003	−5.628	***	0, 99	0.125
Unemployment	0.132	4.019	***	0, 1	0.028	0.128	2.903	***	0, 1	0.028
Psychological Involvement										
Campaign interest	−0.291	−13.070	***	1, 3	0.183	−0.485	−17.037	***	1, 3	0.258
Party Mobilization and Competition										
Campaign contact	−0.447	−12.040	***	0, 1	0.133	−0.156	−6.015	***	0, 2	0.233
Closeness of race	−0.104	−3.548	***	0, 1	0.010	n/a	n/a			
Intercept	1.796	23.462	***			2.755	22.536	***		
Number of Cases	9645					6316				

Note: SE = standard error. Significance levels of the maximum likelihood estimates: * .10 level, critical value Z = 1.65; **.05, critical value Z = 1.96; *** 01, critical value Z = 2.57.

ideological differences between the candidates are 12 percentage points less likely to vote than those who see sharp differences.[23] Thus, people who do not reduce their internal uncertainty about the candidates are less likely to vote than those who establish preferences about the candidates.

The findings of Table 4.2 also show the impact of individuals' personal backgrounds, social connections, and psychological involvement in politics. Consistent with the results in Chapter 3, age has the single largest effect on individual nonvoting. People who are younger are 31 percentage points less likely to vote than much older people. Education also affects the outcome—those who are less educated are 26 percentage points less likely to vote than those with college degrees or higher. The influence of social connections, including marriage, residential stability, and unemployment, is more limited. While the social variables have statistically significant effects on individual nonvoting, they have little influence on the change in the likelihood to vote. Residential stability has the largest effect—people who have not lived in a location very long are 9 percentage points less likely to vote than those who have lived in their community for a long time. Psychological involvement also has a substantial negative effect on nonvoting. Individuals who are not interested in the election are 18 percentage points less likely to vote than those who are highly interested. Lastly, campaign mobilization and closeness decrease individual nonvoting, with candidate contact having the much larger effect. People who have had no contact with a candidate's campaign are 13 percentage points less likely to vote than those who have had such contact.

The results tell a similar story for House midterm races. However, the effect of individuals' awareness of the national campaign context and their opinions about the candidates are proportionally greater in decisions at the midterm than in presidential years. Those who rely on only one media source are 30 percentage points less likely to vote than those who use multiple media sources. And those who make weak comparisons between the candidates are 43 percentage points less likely to vote than those who see very distinct differences between the candidates. Too, those who do not care who wins the election are 26 percentage points less likely to vote than those who do care. The effect of campaign interest is also somewhat greater in midterm elections than presidential years. This differential effect of knowledge and interest is consistent with midterm elections often being quiet, obscure affairs. Since it is more difficult for people to obtain information at the midterm amidst campaigns that are lackluster, having some information and interest is disproportionately valuable. Age and education again strongly influence the likelihood of someone not voting. Social connections

[23] This confirms Sanders, 2001, 50.

through residential stability and employment have smaller but statistically significant effects; marriage has no effect on individual nonvoting in midterm elections. Candidate contact also strongly influences individual nonvoting.

Levels of External Uncertainty

One of the central premises of our theory is that different levels of uncertainty in the national campaign context will help determine how much attention people pay to the campaign and to the candidates and, ultimately, whether they vote. To test this, we estimate the model presented in Table 4.2 for three different types of election years—those with low external uncertainty, moderate uncertainty, and high uncertainty. This categorization is derived from an additive index of the elements of the national campaign context during the election, drawn from the aggregate data set.[24] The results presented in Table 4.3 show variations in the importance of the national campaign context as uncertainty increases for presidential races. For example, when uncertainty is low, those who rely on only one media source are 17 percentage points less likely to vote than those who use multiple media sources; when uncertainty is high, the differential is 27 percentage points. Similarly, when external uncertainty is low, those who make weak comparisons between the candidates are only 5 percentage points less likely to vote than those who see very distinct differences between the candidates, but when external uncertainty is high, those who make weak candidate comparisons are 32 percentage points less likely to vote than others. Also, when uncertainty is low, people with little interest in the campaign are 16 percentage points less likely to vote than those with considerable campaign interest. Yet, when uncertainty is high, people with low interest in the campaign are 27 percentage points less likely to vote than those with high interest.

While the national campaign context and candidate indicators increase in their impact as we move from low-uncertainty to high-uncertainty elections, the same is not true for personal and social characteristics. Age and education have similar effects across the three levels of uncertainty. Marriage, residential stability, and unemployment status have very small effects across the three types of elections, with only residential stability having a consistent statistically

[24] The uncertainty variable is an index of unemployment change, personal income change, and mass communication technology change for a given election year. To categorize elections as high, medium, and low uncertainty elections, the mean of the index variable was calculated. Elections that are one standard deviation above the mean are coded as high-uncertainty elections; those that are one standard deviation below the mean are coded as low-uncertainty elections. All others are medium-uncertainty elections. The variable classifies elections as follows: High uncertainty: 1982, 1992, 1994, 2000; Moderate uncertainty, 1974, 1978, 1980, 1998, 2004; Low uncertainty: 1972, 1976, 1984, 1986, 1988, 1990, 1996, 2002.

Table 4.3 **Impact of Uncertainty on Individual Nonvoting in Presidential Elections, 1972–2004 (Probit Estimates)**

Predictor	*Low Uncertainty*					*Moderate Uncertainty*					*High Uncertainty*				
	Maximum Likelihood Estimate	*MLE/ SE*		*Range of Value in the Variable*	*Change in Likelihood of the Variable*	*Maximum Likelihood Estimate*	*MLE/ SE*		*Range of Value in the Variable*	*Change in Likelihood of the Variable*	*Maximum Likelihood Estimate*	*MLE/ SE*		*Range of Value in the Variable*	*Change in Likelihood of the Variable*
National Campaign Context															
Economic conditions	–0.141	–5.846	***	–2, 2	0.127	–0.107	–3.081	***	–2, 2	0.192	–0.140	–4.435	***	–2, 2	0.265
Media attention	–0.153	–6.631	***	0,4	0.167	–0.083	–2.646	***	0,4	0.229	–0.247	–4.608	***	0,4	0.270
Issue awareness	–0.103	–1.789	*	0,1	0.002	–0.170	–2.169	**	0,1	0.007	0.027	0.395		0,1	0.009
Candidate Awareness															
Candidate comparison	–0.002	–1.664	*	0,100	0.045	–0.002	–2.062	**	0,100	0.242	–0.002	–2.761	***	0,100	0.318
Ideological comparison	–0.038	–2.464	**	1,6	0.064	–0.090	–4.074	***	1,6	0.070	–0.083	–4.234	***	1,6	0.095
Care who wins	–0.108	–4.211	***	–1,1	0.071	–0.169	–4.757	***	–1,1	0.059	–0.201	–5.936	***	–1,1	0.084
Personal Characteristics															
Youth	–0.012	–8.390	***	17,99	0.231	–0.015	–7.112	***	17,99	0.222	–0.013	–6.954	***	17,99	0.251

Education	−0.222	−6.885	***	0,3	0.242	−0.326	−6.998	***	0,3	0.262	−0.335	−7.908	***	0,3	0.296
Social Connections															
Marriage	−0.057	−1.158		0,1	0.051	−0.175	−2.420	**	0,1	0.032	−0.173	−2.593	***	0,1	0.015
Residential stability	−0.002	−2.256	**	0,99	0.101	−0.003	−2.699	***	0,99	0.119	−0.003	−3.140	***	0,99	0.126
Unemployment	0.083	1.592		0,1	0.024	0.244	3.061	***	0,1	0.050	0.187	2.759	***	0,1	0.015
Psychological Involvement															
Campaign interest	−0.246	−6.860	***	1,3	0.163	−0.393	−7.381	***	1,3	0.228	−0.256	−5.492	***	1,3	0.272
Party Mobilization and Competition															
Campaign contact	−0.395	−6.914	***	0,1	0.138	−0.338	−3.804	***	0,1	0.129	−0.547	−6.405	***	0,1	0.132
Closeness of race	−0.093	−1.975	**	0,1	0.009	0.092	1.339		0,1	0.001	−0.201	−3.033	***	0,1	0.038
Intercept	1.547	12.164	***			1.749	9.770	***			2.059	12.492	***		
Number of Cases	4281					2439					2925				

Note: SE = standard error. Significance levels of the maximum likelihood estimates: * .10 level, critical value Z = 1.65; **.05, critical value Z = 1.96; *** 01, critical value Z = 2.57.

Table 4.4 **Impact of Uncertainty on Individual Nonvoting in House Midterm Elections, 1978–2002 (Probit Estimates)**

Predictor	*Low Uncertainty*					*Moderate Uncertainty*					*High Uncertainty*				
	Maximum Likelihood Estimate	*MLE/ SE*		*Range of Value in the Variable*	*Change in Likelihood of the Variable*	*Maximum Likelihood Estimate*	*MLE/ SE*		*Range of Value in the Variable*	*Change in Likelihood of the Variable*	*Maximum Likelihood Estimate*	*MLE/ SE*		*Range of Value in the Variable*	*Change in Likelihood of the Variable*
National Campaign Context															
Economic conditions	–0.168	–3.889	***	–2, 2	0.110	–0.080	–2.226	**	–2, 2	0.291	–0.078	–2.518	**	–2, 2	0.300
Media attention	–0.012	–0.690		0,4	0.184	–0.109	–3.026	***	0,4	0.229	–0.136	–2.730	***	0,4	0.270
Issue awareness	0.058	0.564		0,1	0.061	0.029	0.856		0,1	0.086	–0.020	–0.076		0,1	0.100
Candidate Awareness															
Candidate comparison	–0.008	–3.245	***	0,100	0.123	–0.008	–3.917	***	0,100	0.482	–0.016	–4.940	***	0,100	0.734
Ideological comparison	–0.019	–0.488		1,7	0.047	–0.043	–1.011		1,7	0.119	–0.064	–1.122		1,7	0.051
Care who wins	–0.179	–4.066	***	–1,1	0.253	–0.123	–3.098	***	–1,1	0.258	–0.212	–4.139	***	–1,1	0.289
Personal Characteristics															
Youth	–0.021	–8.353	***	17,99	0.257	–0.018	–7.673	***	17,99	0.298	–0.016	–5.255	***	17,99	0.321
Education	–0.238	–4.539	***	0,3	0.353	–0.202	–4.215	***	0,3	0.338	–0.215	–3.227	***	0,3	0.390

Social Connections															
Marriage	−0.097	−1.083		0,1	0.004	0.303	0.369		0,1	0.082	−0.188	−1.668	*	0,1	0.010
Residential stability	−0.004	−2.837	***	0,99	0.052	−0.001	−1.261		0,99	0.109	−0.007	−4.238	***	0,99	0.125
Unemployment	0.216	2.020	**	0,1	0.079	0.190	2.295	**	0,1	0.146	0.127	1.115		0,1	0.069
Psychological Involvement															
Campaign interest	−0.536	−8.166	***	1,3	0.321	−0.442	−7.361	***	1,3	0.295	−0.491	−6.096	***	1,3	0.432
Party Mobilization and Competition															
Campaign contact	−0.226	−3.406	***	0,1	0.258	−0.093	−1.802	*	0,1	0.276	−0.195	−2.840	***	0,1	0.232
Intercept	3.523	13.022	***			2.357	9.929	***			3.012	8.381	***		
Number of Cases	2693					1547					2366				

Note: SE = standard error. Significance levels of the maximum likelihood estimates: * .10 level, critical value Z = 1.65; **.05, critical value Z = 1.96; *** 01, critical value Z = 2.57.

significant effect. Campaign contact also has similar effects across the three levels of uncertainty. Thus, the level of uncertainty in the campaign context accentuates the import of the political variables in individual nonvoting but not the impact of the personal, social, and candidate contact variables. Since personal characteristics are often quite stable from one election to the other, they would not be affected by different levels of uncertainty. Candidate contact has similar influence across levels of uncertainty, too. This suggests that the value of contact for a candidate's campaign does not vary with the level of uncertainty and intensity of the race. It is the sheer act of contact that is crucial, not the political environment within which the contact occurs.

A similar pattern emerges in House midterm elections: the results in Table 4.4 show that the importance of the national campaign context and candidate comparisons increases from election years with low external uncertainty to those with high external uncertainty. As an example, people who make weak candidate comparisons are 12 percentage points less likely to vote during low-uncertainty election years but 73 percentage points less likely during high-uncertainty years. The demographic and social characteristics do not show this variability across the election types. Age, education, and residential stability have roughly the same effects across the three election types.

Profiles of the American Nonvoter

We anticipate that the connection between external and internal uncertainty will provide different paths for nonvoters in why they fail to vote, depending on their assessments of the external uncertainty in a given election year and their evaluations of how well candidates will handle that external uncertainty. We conceptualize citizens' decisions about which (if any) candidate to support as resulting from one of four decision scenarios, each of which involves a different level of attention to the campaign context and the candidates. These scenarios describe conditions for nonvoting: political ignorance (people who know little about the campaign context or candidates), indifference (people who know something about the campaign context but who do not make clear comparisons between the candidates), dissatisfaction (people who know something about the campaign context but who view one or both candidates negatively), and personal hardship (people who know something about the campaign context, can compare the candidates, but who are unemployed). Thus, there are four distinct types of American nonvoters.[25]

[25] Our initial treatment of this subject can be found on Senate elections in Lyn Ragsdale and Jerrold Rusk, "Who Are Nonvoters? Profiles from the 1990 Senate Elections," *American Journal of Political Science* 37 (August 1993): 721–746. The results were similar to those presented here.

Political Ignorance. Some individuals pay little attention to the national campaign context or the candidates' campaigns. They gather little specific information about the campaign context and the candidates and therefore form few concrete judgments about the candidates. With little basis upon which to evaluate the candidates, these individuals are unable to decide for whom to vote, and as a result, usually do not vote. These people face little internal uncertainty about which candidate would be best because their knowledge of the national campaign context does not rise to a level sufficient to acquire candidate opinions. This scenario describes a condition of political ignorance, and it comes closest to the typical characterization of nonvoters found in existing research.

Indifference. Other individuals gather some information about the national campaign context and the candidates but are unable to make clear comparisons between the candidates. Unlike the politically ignorant who do not form opinions about the candidates, the indifferent are more likely to have impressions about the candidates but see little difference between them. Positive and negative information about one candidate offsets the positive and negative information about the other. For the indifferent there is a genuine inability to choose between the candidates, even though they are aware of key elements of the national campaign context and the uncertainty within it. Their internal uncertainty remains unresolved, so there is no reason to vote.

Dissatisfaction. Still other individuals may pay a good deal of attention to the uncertainty in the national campaign context, gather considerable information about the candidates, but one or more of the candidates are evaluated negatively. This scenario illustrates a condition of dissatisfaction in which individuals do not vote because they dislike the candidates for whatever reasons. Rather than vote for the candidate they dislike the least, individuals stay home. These people are aware of the external uncertainty in the campaign context, but they are unable to alleviate the internal uncertainty because neither candidate is perceived as able to handle the task.

Personal Hardship. Finally, some individuals do not participate in elections because they face key personal challenges that make it difficult to vote. They may have some information about the national campaign context and have opinions about the candidates, but the personal hardship prevents them from voting. One such group of people is the unemployed. This challenge prevents them from getting to the voting booth, but it does not prevent them from paying attention to the campaign context and the candidates. Indeed, they may be unemployed because the economy has suffered a downturn. So this final group of nonvoters has a direct personal interest in following politics, even if they ultimately do not vote.

Individual Differences. These four conditions for nonvoting are associated with individuals' personal characteristics, social connections, political interest, and contact with the candidates. Individual demographics are likely to be highly variable across nonvoters. Generalizations distinguishing voters from nonvoters can easily create the impression that all nonvoters are alike. But, the results shown in Table 4.1 suggest that individual demographics are quite different among nonvoters. Many nonvoters are older and well-educated, despite the fact that in comparison with voters they are on average younger and less well educated. Demographics and social connections augment or minimize the four conditions. They do not, per se, reveal why individuals do not vote. For instance, very few low-income individuals do not vote literally because they have too little money to get to the polls. Instead, difficulties associated with low incomes may prevent individuals from paying attention to the campaign. The combination of low income and political ignorance creates the situation for nonvoting. Similarly, individuals' political interest will vary widely among nonvoters. Scholars often assume that nonvoters as a lot are politically disinterested. But, again in examining Table 4.1, it is clear that there are various levels of political interest among nonvoters. Thus, political interest may heighten or mute the four conditions for nonvoting. Individual characteristics, social connections, political interest, and candidate contact combine with each of the four conditions to prompt an individual not to vote.

Nonvoter Profiles in Presidential Elections

To identify several profiles of nonvoters, we performed a cluster analysis on nonvoters in presidential and House midterm elections. Cluster analysis is a search technique for locating groups of individuals who have similar scores on a series of variables. In the present case, this results in relatively homogeneous groups of nonvoters. The characteristics that the members of one group share can be compared to those characteristics that make them different from the other groups. Because we have a pooled time series data set, several steps were taken to complete the cluster analysis. First, the analysis is conducted on presidential elections from 1972 to 2004 and midterm elections from 1978 to 1998. The other elections are not included because of data availability and comparability issues. Second, a random sample of each of the included election years was taken in order to obtain equal sample sizes for each election year. This then creates a data set of identical variables and equal cases per election year. This is necessary because when one series does not have values on a variable, the data set is ill-defined.

The cluster centers presented in Table 4.5 are the standardized mean values of the variables for cases in the cluster. Since the variables are in standard form (with mean 0 and standard deviation 1) it is easy to judge how far above or below

Table 4.5 **Cluster Analysis of Nonvoters in Presidential and House Midterm Elections**

	Presidential Elections, 1972–2004				*House Elections, 1978–1998*			
	Cluster[a]				***Cluster***[a]			
	1	*2*	*3*	*4*	*1*	*2*	*3*	*4*
National Campaign Context								
Economic Conditions	−0.512	0.033	−0.023	−1.224	0.418	−0.223	−0.048	−0.614
Media Attention	−1.025	−0.186	−0.491	−0.496	−0.439	−0.286	−0.500	−0.692
Issue Awareness	0.186	0.494	0.248	0.204	0.861	0.865	0.798	0.751
Candidate Awareness								
Candidate comparison	−0.902	−0.837	0.139	−0.006	−0.542	0.454	0.124	−0.405
Negative evaluation	−0.945	−1.022	0.839	−0.196	−0.249	0.055	3.924	−0.249
Neutral evaluation	1.889	−0.059	−0.387	−0.101	0.985	−0.170	−0.330	−0.237
Ideological comparison	−0.892	−0.485	−0.211	−0.663	−0.366	1.063	−0.209	−0.529
Care who wins	−0.688	0.120	−0.050	0.187	−0.627	0.383	−0.584	−0.687
Personal Characteristics								
Youth	−0.482	−0.577	−0.778	0.697	−0.751	−0.515	−0.434	−0.125
Education	−0.474	−0.008	0.003	−0.835	0.303	0.125	−0.011	−0.509
Social Connections								
Marriage	−0.161	−0.150	−0.073	−0.541	0.193	−0.264	0.077	−0.251
Residential stability	−0.716	−0.777	−0.858	−0.448	−0.786	−0.582	−0.564	−0.493
Unemployment	0.263	−0.189	−0.147	0.994	−0.319	−0.135	0.013	0.474
Psychological Involvement								
Campaign interest	−0.902	−0.038	−0.295	−0.239	−0.572	0.144	−0.511	−0.724

(continued)

Table 4.5 **(Continued)**

	Presidential Elections, 1972–2004				*House Elections, 1978–1998*			
	Cluster[a]				***Cluster***[a]			
	1	*2*	*3*	*4*	*1*	*2*	*3*	*4*
Party Mobilization and Competition								
Campaign contact	−0.495	−0.328	−0.399	−0.328	−0.022	0.424	−0.059	−0.632
Closeness of race	0.681	1.137	0.710	0.460	n/a	n/a	n/a	n/a
Uncertainty	0.322	0.191	0.308	0.244	−0.129	−0.092	0.239	0.175
Cases	535	509	578	405	928	514	131	317
Percentage of total cases	26.4	25.1	28.5	20.0	49.1	27.2	6.9	16.8

Note: Entries are standardized mean values for cases in the cluster.

[a] Cluster 1: Political Ignorance; Cluster 2: Indifference; Cluster 3: Dissatisfaction; Cluster 4: Personal Hardship.

the mean a cluster of individuals is on a given variable.[26] To clarify these profiles, Table 4.6 presents a comparison of unstandardized means for all variables across nonvoters and voters. Once the cluster analysis has categorized individuals into one of the clusters, it is appropriate to obtain unstandardized mean scores for each of the clusters. This then permits an analysis of how subsets of nonvoters differ from voters. Included in the cluster analysis are the variables employed in the multivariate analysis presented in Table 4.2. In addition, to better delineate the conditions of political ignorance, ambivalence, and dissatisfaction, we add

[26] While factor analysis reveals patterns across variables, cluster analysis reveals patterns across cases—in this instance, individuals. To determine the clusters, Euclidean distances between cases based on standardized variables are calculated. The variables are standardized because Euclidean distance depends on the units of measurement of the variables. If unstandardized scores are used, variables that are measured in larger numbers will contribute more to the distance than variables that are recorded in smaller units. Euclidean distance sets the distance between two individuals as the square root of the sum of the squared differences in values for reach variable. We adopted a k-means method of clustering, which handles a large number of cases. We tested several solutions with 3, 4, and 5 clusters in order to determine the homogeneity of the clusters. The 4-cluster solution created the sharpest contrast across the clusters. In other tests, we added election years to the analysis to ensure that the results were not being driven by specific election years. No election-specific effects were found.

Table 4.6 **Comparison of Means across Nonvoters and Voters, Presidential and Midterm House Elections (Unstandardized Entries)**

	Presidential Elections, 1972–2004						*House Midterm Elections, 1978–1998*					
	Voter Mean	***Nonvoter Grand Mean***	***Nonvoter Clusters***[a]				***Voter Mean***	***Nonvoter Grand Mean***	***Nonvoter Clusters***[a]			
			1	2	3	4			*1*	2	3	4
National Campaign Context												
Economic conditions	3.051	2.447	2.617	3.151	2.117	1.580	3.018	2.828	2.791	2.667	2.646	1.146
Media attention	2.435	1.626	1.215	2.073	1.850	1.349	2.496	1.482	1.256	1.400	1.604	1.578
Issue awareness	0.652	0.654	0.612	0.787	0.544	0.644	0.542	0.967	0.923	0.921	0.917	0.946
Candidate Awareness												
Candidate comparison	38.436	28.468	14.659	19.496	49.278	21.243	22.466	12.104	5.863	7.203	25.607	21.369
Negative evaluation	0.610	0.467	0.123	0.691	0.877	0.208	0.160	0.084	0.000	0.000	1.209	0.000
Neutral evaluation	0.233	0.456	1.067	0.114	0.064	0.519	0.669	0.817	1.305	0.067	0.000	0.053
Ideological comparison	2.203	1.371	1.062	1.592	2.341	0.642	2.064	1.247	0.390	0.289	1.202	1.049
Care who wins	0.547	−0.006	−0.418	0.065	0.674	0.250	0.398	−0.342	−0.572	−0.631	−0.187	0.284
Personal Characteristics												
Youth	47.543	40.870	34.213	31.930	47.923	55.151	48.342	38.698	40.676	34.755	38.425	44.668

(*continued*)

Table 4.6 **(Continued)**

	Presidential Elections, 1972–2004						*House Midterm Elections, 1978–1998*					
	Voter Mean	***Nonvoter Grand Mean***	***Nonvoter Clusters***[a]				***Voter Mean***	***Nonvoter Grand Mean***	***Nonvoter Clusters***[a]			
			1	2	3	*4*			*1*	2	3	*4*
Education	1.758	1.215	1.288	1.502	1.723	0.665	1.678	1.407	1.384	1.394	1.485	1.425
Social Connections												
Marriage	0.618	0.492	0.484	0.767	0.326	0.500	0.647	0.552	0.722	0.340	0.548	0.716
Residential Stability	28.773	26.470	24.752	17.602	29.053	30.118	53.104	26.725	25.762	28.100	28.531	24.374
Unemployment	0.176	0.279	0.150	0.294	0.150	0.580	0.207	0.226	0.241	0.151	0.261	0.420
Psychological Involvement												
Campaign interest	2.267	1.700	1.431	1.924	1.947	1.505	2.144	1.586	1.464	1.447	1.672	1.892
Party Mobilization and Competition												
Campaign contact	0.341	0.122	0.101	0.121	0.154	0.118	0.715	0.540	0.490	0.491	0.572	0.645
Closeness of race	0.682	0.637	0.737	0.581	0.731	0.443	n/a	n/a	n/a	n/a	n/a	n/a
Uncertainty	1.682	1.579	1.961	1.465	1.859	1.600	2.056	1.771	1.49	1.905	1.849	1.681
Cases	6711	2027	535	509	578	405	3356	1890	928	514	131	317
Percentage of total cases			26.4	25.1	28.5	20.0			49.1	27.2	6.9	16.8

[a] Cluster 1: Political Ignorance; Cluster 2: Indifference; Cluster 3: Dissatisfaction; Cluster 4: Personal Hardship.

two variables—neutral and negative candidate evaluations.[27] Summary results for the cluster analysis presented in the two tables reveal four distinct profiles of nonvoters in presidential elections.

Political ignorance (paying little attention to the national campaign context and the candidates) characterizes the profile of nonvoters found in cluster 1. Individuals in this cluster have limited information about the national campaign context and the candidates. Relative to nonvoters in the other clusters, the politically ignorant nonvoters pay little attention to the media, are less aware of a major issue, but view the economy positively. The most telling aspect of their profile is that they evaluate the candidates neutrally and are not able to make strong ideological or overall candidate comparisons. As one example shown in Table 4.6, the politically ignorant see only a 15 percentage point difference in their overall evaluation of presidential candidates, compared to an average of a 28 percentage point difference for nonvoters as a whole and a 38 percentage point difference for voters. The results also reveal the individual backgrounds of these politically ignorant nonvoters. They are younger (mean age=34), with a high school education, who have resided in their community for a moderately long time (mean=25 years), but who have low campaign interest and no interest in who wins the election.

Indifference (paying attention to the national campaign context but not making strong comparisons between the candidates) defines the next profile of nonvoters found in cluster 2. Unlike the politically ignorant, these nonvoters have some awareness of the national campaign context and the candidates. They actually use more media sources than any of the other nonvoters (mean=2.1 media sources), which is close to that of voters (mean=2.4 media sources). Among nonvoters, they are most likely to evaluate the economy positively and pay attention to a major issue during the campaign. Thus, these nonvoters are fairly well aware of the uncertainty in the national campaign context. However, the indifferent nonvoters do not make sharp general comparisons between the candidates (a 19 percentage point difference in their overall evaluation of presidential candidates), even though their comparisons are somewhat more defined than those provided by the politically ignorant nonvoters. These nonvoters are roughly the same age as the politically ignorant (mean age=32) but have some

[27] The neutral evaluation indicator is constructed as follows: If an individual rates both the Democratic and Republican candidates neutrally (at 50 degrees) on the feeling thermometer, the variable is coded 2. If the respondent rates one candidate at 50 degrees, the variable is coded 1. If the individual rates neither candidate at 50 degrees the variable is coded 0. The negative evaluation variable is constructed as follows: If an individual rates both the Democratic and Republican candidates negatively (less than 50 degrees) on the feeling thermometer, the variable is coded 2. If the respondent rates only one candidate negatively, the variable is coded 1. If the individual rates both candidates at or above 50 degrees, the variable is coded 0.

college education. They are likely to reside in their community for a shorter time than the politically ignorant (mean=18 years).

Dissatisfaction (paying attention to the national campaign context but seeing one or both candidates negatively) identifies the profile of the nonvoters in cluster 3. Like indifferent nonvoters they use, on average, two media sources to obtain political information. They are likely to see the economy less positively than either politically ignorant or indifferent nonvoters. Most tellingly, they have strongly held opinions about the candidates. They make sharper comparative evaluations of the candidates than do voters (49 percentage point differences compared with 38 percentage point differences for voters). They also see strong ideological differences between the candidates that are equivalent to those seen by voters. The key, though, is that they view one or more candidates negatively and these views are more negative than those held by voters and the other groups of nonvoters. The dissatisfied nonvoters are older (mean age = 48), with some college education, and have resided in their community for an average of 29 years.

Finally, personal hardship (paying attention to the national campaign context, knowing the candidates, but being unemployed) characterizes the fourth cluster of nonvoters. These nonvoters are aware of the national campaign context. They are as aware of major issues confronting the nation as are voters. They use slightly more than one media source (mean = 1.3) and view the economy more negatively than the other groups of nonvoters. There is good reason for this: these individuals are more likely to be unemployed than any of the other nonvoters. They are older (mean age = 55), with limited education, and have lived in their community for an extended period of time (mean = 30 years). These individuals can make clear candidate comparisons (21 percentage point difference) but see no ideological differences between the candidates. They have some interest in the campaign but care little about who wins. The hardship nonvoters do resolve the internal uncertainty about the candidates, but fail to vote because of their own personal circumstances, which short-circuit their interest in the campaign and who will win.

Nonvoter Profiles in House Midterm Elections

The patterns across the four types of nonvoters also exist in midterm elections. In midterm elections, the politically ignorant are identified in cluster 1. As conveyed in Table 4.6, these nonvoters have some awareness of the national campaign context—they have opinions about the economy, are aware of a major issue, and follow media sources about the campaign. However, their ability to make comparisons between the candidates is minimal (a small 6 percentage point difference in their overall evaluation of House candidates) and they see the candidates neutrally. Unlike their presidential-year counterparts, the politically ignorant midterm nonvoters are middle-aged (mean age = 41). But like their presidential-year comparators, they have a high school education and have lived in their communities for moderately long time periods (mean = 26 years compared with mean = 25 years for presidential years).

The indifferent nonvoters are found in cluster 2. They are aware of the national campaign context in ways similar to voters. They share a positive economic outlook with voters, are somewhat more aware of a major national problem than are voters, and, like voters, use on average two media sources to gain political information. But, they make weak comparisons between the candidates (7 percentage point difference in their overall evaluation of House candidates), do not see ideological distinctions between the candidates, and do not care who wins. They are young, like their presidential counterparts (mean age = 35), with a high school education. They have resided in their community for longer than other nonvoters (mean = 28 years).

Dissatisfied nonvoters are observed in cluster 3. These nonvoters are aware of the national campaign context and the candidates. They use on average two media sources during the campaign, are aware of a major national problem, and view the economy favorably. They are able to make comparisons between the candidates at a level that approaches that of voters, primarily because they see at least one candidate quite negatively. They are able to make more distinct comparisons between the candidates than any other group, including voters (26 percentage point difference in their overall evaluation of House candidates compared with 22 percentage points for voters). These nonvoters are middle-aged (mean age = 38), with some college education. They are likely to be married and have lived in the same place for roughly the same time as other nonvoters at the midterm (mean = 29 years).

Finally, hardship nonvoters are featured in cluster 4. They are more likely to be unemployed than the other groups of nonvoters. They view economic conditions more unfavorably than other nonvoters or voters and pay some attention to the media. They are more aware of major issues than are voters. Like their presidential comparators, they are able to make strong general comparisons between the candidates that rival those made by voters. They also make strong ideological comparisons between the candidates. However, they are more likely to be unemployed than other nonvoters. They are older than the other groups (mean age = 45), with education just past high school. They are married and have lived in the same residence for an average of 24 years.

Revising the American Nonvoter Stereotype

Who are nonvoters? Conventional wisdom characterizes nonvoters as a decidedly downcast lot. They are depicted as insufficiently motivated to participate in politics or oblivious to the campaign and so are better off staying away from the polls. The findings of the cluster analysis, in particular, reveal that no such stereotypic nonvoters exist. The politically ignorant nonvoters of cluster 1 come closest to the typecast. They screen out most information about the candidates, but even they know something about the campaign context. Still, they only represent one-quarter of presidential nonvoters and one-half of midterm nonvoters.

Beyond the politically ignorant nonvoters, there are three other types of nonvoters who do not fit the stereotype of being uninterested and uninvolved. They are aware of the external uncertainty in the national campaign context and in varying degrees make overall candidate comparisons and ideological comparisons. Indeed, many of these nonvoters actually have more campaign knowledge and sharper candidate views than do voters. Indifferent nonvoters pay almost as much attention to the media as do voters in presidential elections and are more aware of major issues than voters in both presidential and midterm races. Their views of the economy are similar to those of voters in both presidential and midterm election years. Thus, while they falter in making direct candidate comparisons, they are keenly aware of the national campaign context and are interested in the campaign. Dissatisfied nonvoters stand out as people who rival voters in their ability to judge the candidates. In both presidential and midterm races, dissatisfied nonvoters actually develop stronger candidate comparisons than do voters. In the presidential context, these nonvoters also make stronger ideological comparisons between the candidates and care more about who will win than do voters. The dissatisfied nonvoters are roughly as educated, about the same age, and have resided in their community about the same length of time as voters. They represent 29 percent of nonvoters in presidential elections, although a much smaller 7 percent in midterm elections. Personal hardship nonvoters also form distinct opinions about the candidates and pay as much attention to the issues as do voters in both presidential and midterm elections. They too represent a sizable group of nonvoters—20 percent of nonvoters in presidential years and 17 percent in midterm years.

These results pose a central irony about voters and nonvoters. Many voters actually go to the polls with less information about the campaign context and less well developed comparisons about the candidates than do a significant group of nonvoters. Yet, the former group chooses to vote and the latter stays home. Thus, it is important to reflect on the four distinct paths that individuals take to decide they will not vote. While the outcome is the same in each case—the individual does not vote—the ways in which they get to that decision are vastly dissimilar. There are stark differences among nonvoters in how they obtain and organize the information and opinions they have about the campaign context and the candidates. These differences hinge on how nonvoters weigh internal uncertainty about the candidates as they assess the external uncertainty of the national campaign context. When their views of the candidates are either indistinct or distinctly negative, they fail to resolve the internal uncertainty about the candidates and do not vote. Thus, the psychological mechanisms of information processing and preference ordering that researchers have found so important in understanding how voters make up their minds in the voting booth are equally central to how nonvoters make up their minds to stay out of the voting booth.

The individual-level analysis allows us to more fully understand the relative impact of the collective environment and individuals' own personal experiences and preferences. The answer to the question, "Why do individuals not vote?" lies in the mix among the campaign context and candidate preferences as well as individuals' own backgrounds, mobility, political interest, and campaign contact.

5

Searching the Past

The 1920 election occurred almost two years to the day after World War I ended with the signing of the armistice on November 11, 1918 at Compiegne, France. Despite the victory, there was deep frustration in its aftermath, long debates about American participation in the League of Nations, hundreds of thousands of soldiers dead, and tens of thousands of veterans suffering from what was then called "shell shock." Unlike the enthusiasm and optimism that emerged at the close of World War II, there was disenchantment and pessimism at the end of the Great War as people asked how this could be the "war to end all wars." A deeply unpopular Woodrow Wilson was the central opponent in the 1920 presidential campaign, even though he was not running. As the wartime economic boom capsized into recession, fanned by labor strikes in meatpacking and steel, race riots over jobs and housing, and the first of many Red scares over fears of Bolshevism, Warren Harding's campaign slogan, "A Return to Normalcy," made for an appealing antidote.[1]

Individual elections take place at a particular moment in history. As noted in Chapter 2, each election has unique features that immediately distinguish it from the election before and the election after. The very nature of uncertainty in the national campaign context varies from one election to the next. Yet, elections are also part of a much larger ongoing political history. As much as they reflect the politics of the moment, they also reflect patterns, conditions, and innovations that emerge, sometimes quite slowly, over a series of elections. There may be economic, technological, political, and legal markers within the campaign context that are similar across a series of elections. These similarities may create broad historic eras. The 1960 and 1964 elections were quite different—the closest race of the twentieth century between two centrist candidates followed by a lopsided battle between a popular incumbent and a candidate out of the mainstream. But they also took place during a time when the campaign context

[1] David Pietrusza, *1920: The Year of the Six Presidents* (New York: Basic Books, 2008).

had distinctive features of strong economic growth, increasing US involvement in Vietnam, and historic civil rights protests, with these national milestones captured nightly on the evening news.

Midterm contests also are part of the ongoing, longer-term historical currents that encompass the presidential elections adjacent to them. The 1962, 1966, and 1970 midterm elections carried the same economic, international, and domestic markers as did the presidential elections. Indeed, it is an accident of history that all of the midterms during this period were preceded, in some cases in mere weeks, by major dramatic national events, all captured by the ubiquity of television: the Cuban Missile Crisis and Kennedy's order of federal troops to assist desegregation at the University of Mississippi (1962), the escalation of the Vietnam war and riots in major American cities (1966), and the Cambodian invasion, ensuing campus protests, and student killings at Kent State University (1970).

Chapter 3 provided a summary perspective about the influence of the uncertainty of the national campaign context on nonvoting across the entire sweep of elections from 1920 to 2012. This chapter and the three that follow trace the impact of this uncertainty on nonvoting during individual election years. It also permits an assessment of sets of individual elections within broad historic eras. What defined the campaign context in the 1920s was not relevant in the 1950s, and nonvoting patterns shifted accordingly.

Political Periods in America

Is there such a thing as a political period? Analysts have loosely referred to historical time frames as eras, epochs, periods, phases, cycles, or years. In American political history, these are often terms of convenience using presidents as their primary labels, as authors discuss the Roosevelt era, the Eisenhower period, or the Reagan years. As Silbey, Bogue, and Flanigan wrote, "historians generally considered themselves particularly qualified to deal with problems of periodization and the analysis of social processes occurring through extended periods of time, but most of them navigated the seas of American political history using charts in which presidential administrations or presidential incumbencies provided the historical equivalent of longitude."[2]

Here the conception of political period is the summation of economic conditions, technological advances in mass communication, major national and

[2] Joel Silbey, Allan Bogue, and William Flanigan, eds. *The History of American Electoral Behavior* (Princeton: Princeton University Press, 1978), 31.

international events, legal shifts, demographic changes, and key national policy directions that are central to a particular set of years. Thus the term "period" is, per se, an aggregate concept that summarizes defining elements of the national campaign context over a series of years. As discussed in Chapter 1, uncertainty, novelty, and risk define the national campaign context. Uncertainty involves politicians' and citizens' inability to know what will happen next, and this impedes their ability to make decisions. Much of this uncertainty arises from novelty, when something new, unique, or unexpected happens in the political environment. The novelty fosters risk because, faced with a novel occurrence, there is considerable risk of an unsatisfactory outcome. For the eligible electorate this unacceptable result is, ultimately, the wrong candidate winning.

A political period thus begins and ends with shifts in the type and degree of uncertainty, novelty, and risk. This means that the demarcations between periods may be sharp or fuzzy. A period may begin when one or more novel events abruptly alter the national campaign context: a war begins, a war ends, and the degree of uncertainty in the American political landscape is drastically altered. But there may also be periods that blur into one another when conditions shift subtly but inexorably: fast-paced economic growth gives way to sluggish growth. The novelty does not occur overnight, but conditions shift in noticeable ways so it is clear that the inflation rate that was on no one's mind is now in everyone's view. Political periods are also about more than politics. They are as much driven by novel circumstances in economic markets and technological innovations as they are by party politics. The Internet radically changed politics over a period of years beginning in the 1990s and so transformed elections by 2008 that communication tools used then bore little resemblance to those used in campaigns just two decades earlier. Thus, the concept of political period is somewhat elastic and imprecise, but it is more formal and definitive than the notion that history, unstructured, is one event after the other.

The national campaign context across a series of years creates a participation environment in which people do and do not go to the polls. Thus, although presidential and midterm elections are typically viewed separately, in considering the influence of the campaign context and the presence of historical eras it is important to analyze adjacent presidential and midterm elections, which are similar to each other across a sequence of elections and distinct from those elections which take place years earlier or later.

These periods, while viewed as aggregate national phenomena, nevertheless play out in distinct ways from one region of the country to another. States and locales respond to the various facets of national development in different ways and at different paces. The strong Republican era of the 1920s was neither strong nor Republican in the states of the former Confederacy. The tightly competitive period of the early twenty-first century was decidedly uncompetitive in what was by then the Republican-dominant South. The summary tendencies in a political period are ultimately shaped in greater and lesser degrees in states from particular regions of the country with specific economic bases, cultural backgrounds, and demographic characteristics. These facets of the states are exceedingly important in mapping how the central leitmotif of a given time period does or does not unfold.

The National Campaign Context of Individual Elections

We begin with a simple analysis that permits us to chart the overall effect of the national campaign context on nonvoting in individual elections and how it shapes broader historic periods. Nonvoting in each state in an election year may be considered as the sum of three components: an election-specific component reflecting the shifts in national election forces, an idiosyncratic component involving sub-national factors within a given state, and a continuity component which reflects the consistency in nonvoting from the prior election. This captures the impact of habitual voters and nonvoters. The model is:

$$NV_{st} = \alpha_t + \beta_{1t} NV_{st-1} + \in_{st}$$

where NV represents nonvoting in state s in election year t and $NV_{st-1,}$ represents nonvoting in that state in the immediate past election. This approach follows Larry Bartels, who devised the model for partisan voting.[3] We have also used the model to examine the effects of the national context on participation, as distinct from nonvoting.[4] The intercept α_t measures the shift in nonvoting from the previous election that is attributable to national forces in a given election. The parameter β_{1t} estimates the effect of lagged state nonvoting on current-year nonvoting, reflecting continuity. The parameter $\in_{st}$ is a stochastic term pertaining to state-specific idiosyncratic factors in election year t. The model assumes that this standard error term $\in_{st}$ is drawn from a probability distribution with mean zero and election-specific variance σ_n^2. Hence, the stochastic variance parameter σ_n^2 measures the magnitude of current-year state forces in a given election. The intercept α_t is an appropriate summary measure of the various factors that make up the national campaign context, and the standard error term $\in_{st}$ encapsulates state

[3] Larry Bartels, "Electoral Continuity and Change, 1868–1996," *Electoral Studies* 17 (1988): 301–326.

[4] Lyn Ragsdale and Jerrold Rusk, "Casting Votes: The National Campaign Context and State Turnout, 1920–2008," *Political Research Quarterly* 64 (December 2011): 840–857.

differences. While the measures cannot assess specific factors—communication technology, the economy, suffrage laws, political competition, or the composition of the adult population, which we explore as the chapter progresses—they offer a consistent composite across time and election types.

Table 5.1 presents the estimates for the effect of the national campaign context on nonvoting for each presidential and midterm House election year since 1920 for the nation as a whole, the South, and the non-South. The results can be assessed along three dimensions: whether the national campaign context increases or decreases nonvoting, how the South and non-South differ, and the relative impact of national and state factors. To better understand the state dimension, the net effect columns in the table record the percentage of the variance explained by national relative to state factors. Negative entries denote elections with greater state effects relative to national effects, namely, net state effects, with the maximum being –100 (total state effects). Positive entries denote elections with net national effects, with the maximum being 100 (total national effects).[5]

This table along with Tables 2.1 and 2.2 reveal three key breakpoints in the data when there are changes in the direction of nonvoting up or down and shifts in the relative balance between national and state effects: between 1944 and 1946, 1972 and 1974, and 1990 and 1992. Prior to 1946, there was a period of moderate levels of nonvoting (see also Tables 2.1 and 2.2) and the presence of both national and state effects. Beginning with 1946, there is a period of declining nonvoting and strong national effects with little evidence of state influences. Another breakpoint occurs in 1974 when the overall decline in nonvoting throughout the 1950s and 1960s stops, and nonvoting begins to edge up, reaching a plateau in the 1980s. In addition, strong national effects, which had contributed to declining nonvoting, now contribute to increasing nonvoting. The final breakpoint occurs in 1992 when nonvoting begins to decline again. National factors that increased nonvoting from 1974 through 1990 now decrease nonvoting beginning in 1992. In addition, some state effects return—not as pronounced as in the earliest elections of the 1920s and 1930s, but more prevalent than in the years from the 1940s through the 1980s. There are also distinct differences in net national effects between the South and the non-South which did not exist in the previous years. As we discuss in detail

[5] Entries in the net effect columns are determined as follows: (1) National variance (the square of the national forces coefficient α_t) and state variance (the square of the state forces term σ_n) are calculated. (2) The proportion of the variance explained by national forces is then calculated as the ratio of national variance to national variance plus state variance. (3) Similarly, the magnitude of state factors is calculated as the ratio of state variance to national variance plus state variance. (4) Net national or state effects are determined by the difference between the national proportion of the variance explained and the state proportion of the variance explained of turnout in a given election.

Table 5.1 **National Effects on Nonvoting for the Nation and Regions in Presidential and Midterm Elections, 1920–2012**

Year	*Nation*		*Net Effect (Percent)*	*South*		*Net Effect (Percent)*	*Non-South*		*Net Effect (Percent)*
1920	17.17	***	83.21	14.44	***	86.96	23.74	***	89.82
1922	14.38	***	53.62	23.23	***	83.89	26.18	***	84.41
1924	–1.07		–93.42	8.74	**	43.69	8.22	*	51.23
1926	2.31		–54.92	1.87		–79.23	6.95	*	57.40
1928	–6.32	***	19.36	–5.34		13.36	–4.63		–9.26
1930	–3.84		–26.57	–8.20	*	61.22	–5.57		0.65
1932	–3.48	**	–22.24	–1.67		–49.06	–3.13	*	28.58
1934	–15.44	***	52.57	–2.36		–67.77	–8.00		23.72
1936	–3.77	***	–6.44	–3.27		–12.92	–4.25		10.70
1938	0.18		–99.77	6.99	**	77.86	–15.08	***	79.29
1940	–2.21	**	–39.77	1.75		–60.04	–3.87	*	33.21
1942	22.54	***	92.37	26.41	***	98.70	20.01	***	86.85
1944	3.37	***	–13.81	6.97	***	70.72	0.40		–98.24
1946	–1.86		86.97	–16.58	**	88.96	–7.06		33.63
1948	14.54	***	88.47	13.96	***	95.81	19.42	***	91.90

(continued)

Table 5.1 **(Continued)**

Year	*Nation*		*Net Effect (Percent)*	*South*		*Net Effect (Percent)*	*Non-South*		*Net Effect (Percent)*
1950	–2.34		–64.52	–0.12		–99.89	11.93	**	76.04
1952	–7.03	***	68.92	–9.31	**	76.55	–4.33		39.09
1954	–4.44	**	12.10	–13.15	**	83.77	–10.50	**	78.85
1956	3.53	***	35.76	4.77	*	45.08	4.75	**	64.73
1958	–5.03	**	14.87	–0.85		–94.89	6.98	*	66.34
1960	–3.50	***	24.21	–2.73		26.09	–1.06		–76.30
1962	–7.04	***	51.74	–12.18	*	74.02	–6.26		78.08
1964	11.58	***	91.10	14.91	***	92.30	9.26	***	89.51
1966	–18.83	***	85.21	–46.99	***	95.80	–16.50	***	93.24
1968	–12.90	***	87.22	–21.38	***	95.67	–2.98	*	33.40
1970	–6.91	**	38.10	–22.85	*	87.72	–13.04	**	84.15
1972	3.29	*	16.64	3.62		27.22	7.52	***	82.35
1974	15.69	***	87.73	34.58	***	97.56	20.82	***	93.46
1976	12.31	***	87.54	17.69	***	98.19	7.49	**	64.30
1978	16.39	***	83.38	20.98		86.53	20.20	**	67.43
1980	1.98		–33.97	5.05		69.11	1.65		–56.54
1982	–1.91		–56.12	13.73		85.58	0.18		42.48

1984	7.35	***	79.76	0.91		−59.50	8.72	***	82.31
1986	27.01	***	87.86	31.82	**	91.28	2.72		−55.34
1988	6.27	***	82.48	6.49	***	93.98	9.23	***	90.78
1990	12.11	***	43.29	30.72	**	94.32	15.56	***	79.22
1992	−4.24	*	44.78	0.84		−72.99	−3.30		15.16
1994	−11.97	***	87.99	−52.87	***	97.87	0.79		60.54
1996	13.05	***	93.16	12.95	***	95.83	11.97	***	90.26
1998	17.54	***	65.51	55.02	***	97.94	16.94	***	88.20
2000	−1.36		−66.95	−12.30	*	94.79	−1.33		−73.49
2002	−17.98	***	95.78	−34.85	***	97.51	−11.21	*	74.20
2004	−4.94	**	65.19	−10.23	*	94.17	−4.34		50.29
2006	−3.12		−63.59	−24.09		91.57	−9.28		−92.48
2008	−8.73	***	82.07	−3.53		69.79	−9.35	***	85.11
2010	−28.91	***	95.39	−31.17	***	97.34	−34.04	***	96.46
2012	2.03		−30.94	−3.52		47.80	3.60		15.76

Note: *Coefficient significant at .10 level; **Coefficient significant at .05 level; ***Coefficient significant at .01 level. Net effect is measured in percent and ranges from −100 (only state effects) to 100 (only national effects)

in Chapter 8, this is evidence of the growing political polarization during the final period. Thus, the results suggest four historic time periods: 1920–1944, 1946–1972, 1974–1990, and 1992–2012. To further understand the distinctiveness of the four periods, Table 5.2 provides summary measures including mean, standard deviation, slope, inter-election change, and mean net national or state effects. As we outline in this and the next chapters, the breakpoints are not just electoral in nature. There are fundamental shifts in national campaign context that occur across economic, communication, legal, and international dimensions. These facets of the national campaign context influence elections during one period in ways that are distinct from their influence in an earlier or later period.

Outline of Four Historic Periods

The central feature of the first set of elections encompassing the inter-war years and World War II is the cross-currents of national and state influences on nonvoting. As seen in Table 5.1, the national campaign context has strong but mixed effects: national factors initially prompt increases in nonvoting rates in presidential and midterm elections in 1920 and 1922. Then, beginning in 1928 and throughout the 1930s, national factors generally push nonvoting rates downward. With the outbreak of World War II, national factors again push nonvoting rates higher, presumably as large numbers of people became involved in the war effort. Despite these national effects, the net effect column of the table shows that state factors influence nonvoting more during this period than at any other time, especially in the South. As seen in Table 5.2, the era is also characterized by stronger national effects in the non-South than in the South. This table shows that the regional gap in nonvoting is at its largest during this period, with nonvoting in the non-South at its lowest levels and nonvoting in the South at its highest.

The second period, beginning after World War II and continuing through the early 1970s, is marked by the most consistent national effects on nonvoting rates for any period, both nationally and regionally. National effects decrease nonvoting rates throughout the period, as the rates hit historic lows in both presidential and midterm elections. As the net effect columns clarify, regional differences are less substantial than any time before or since, and the impact of state factors is smaller than any time before or since. Table 5.2 shows that in presidential elections mean nonvoting is at its lowest point—34 percent compared with 44 percent mean nonvoting for the elections from 1920 through 1944. In midterm elections, mean nonvoting also reaches its lowest point—55 percent compared with 60 percent mean nonvoting in the elections from the prior period.

Table 5.2 **Historic Periods of Nonvoting, 1920–2012**

	Presidential Nonvoting						*House Midterm Nonvoting*					
	Nation	***South***	***Non-South***	***West***	***Midwest***	***East***	***Nation***	***South***	***Non-South***	***West***	***Midwest***	***East***
1920–1944												
Mean	44.3	64.6	34.2	36.6	32.0	34.1	60.3	79.7	50.6	50.5	50.5	50.7
Standard Deviation	5.1	2.6	6.4	6.1	6.1	7.6	5.1	2.8	6.8	5.7	7.5	7.6
Slope	–0.6	–0.3	–0.8	–0.7	–0.7	–0.9	–0.3	0.1	–0.5	–0.3	–0.6	–0.6
Inter-election Change	–1.9	–0.5	–2.6	–2.3	–2.5	–3.2	0.8	1.7	0.4	–1.7	1.0	0.2
Mean Net Effects[1]	9.8	20.6	33.9									
1946–1972												
Mean	33.9	53.2	31.8	33.7	30.6	31.0	55.1	73.2	46.1	46.2	46.6	45.5
Standard Deviation	4.2	6.3	4.5	4.0	4.4	5.1	2.7	5.3	2.2	2.4	2.2	2.2
Slope	–0.1	–0.6	0.1	0.2	1.0	0.7	–0.3	–0.6	–0.2	–0.2	–0.2	–0.1
Inter-election Change	–0.5	–3.0	0.8	0.7	0.8	0.8	–1.7	–2.7	–1.1	–1.3	–1.0	–1.0
Mean Net Effects[1]	45.5	49.6	59.6									

(*continued*)

Table 5.2 **(Continued)**

	Presidential Nonvoting						*House Midterm Nonvoting*					
	Nation	***South***	***Non-South***	***West***	***Midwest***	***East***	***Nation***	***South***	***Non-South***	***West***	***Midwest***	***East***
1974–1990												
Mean	44.2	50.6	41.2	43.2	38.0	42.2	59.7	68.9	55.5	54.8	54.2	57.9
Standard Deviation	1.4	1.6	1.7	2.3	1.5	1.8	1.6	2.2	1.8	1.9	1.7	2.5
Slope	0.1	−0.1	0.2	0.1	0.2	0.2	0.0	−0.2	0.2	0.1	0.1	0.3
Inter-election Change	1.4	0.6	1.8	1.6	1.6	2.2	1.6	0.7	2.1	1.9	2.0	2.5
Mean Net Effects[1]	51.3	73.0	45.3									
1992–2012												
Mean	40.7	44.8	38.9	41.7	37.4	38.4	58.0	64.4	55.2	55.0	54.2	56.5
Standard Deviation	3.8	4.2	3.8	4.2	4.8	3.9	0.9	1.9	0.9	1.3	0.8	2.7
Slope	−0.2	−0.4	−0.2	0.1	−0.2	−0.3	−0.1	−0.2	−0.1	0.1	0.0	−0.3
Inter-election Change	−0.9	−1.4	−0.7	0.5	−0.7	−1.1	−0.8	−1.5	−0.5	−0.5	−0.4	−0.8
Mean Net Effects[1]	41.0	73.8	37.3									

[1] Mean net effects calculated from Table 5.1 based on both presidential and midterm elections in the period.

The third political period, unfolding during the 1970s and 1980s, is all but the mirror opposite of the second period. As shown in Table 5.1, during no other set of years does the national campaign context consistently increase nonvoting. Nonvoting rises in the 1970s and then plateaus during the 1980s, both nationally and regionally (see Tables 2.1 and 2.2). As seen in Table 5.2, national nonvoting rates in the third period return to levels seen in the first period in both presidential and midterm House elections. During presidential elections from 1976 through 1988, mean nonvoting is at the same level as that seen in the first period—44 percent when it was 34 percent in the second period. Similarly, during the midterms from 1974 through 1990, nonvoting rates hover at 60 percent, again returning to levels found in the first period and 5 percentage points above those found in the second period. Another difference between the two periods is that the inter-election change in nonvoting rates during the second period (seen in Table 5.2) shows a downward trend in nonvoting, while the inter-election change during the third period shows an upward trend.

The fourth period, which emerges in the early 1990s and continues, reverses the increase in nonvoting seen in the third period. As shown in Table 5.1, during these most recent years, national effects more consistently decrease nonvoting. Table 5.2 indicates that for presidential elections, mean nonvoting declines to 41 percent, 3 percentage points below the mean for the prior period; for midterm elections, mean nonvoting is 58 percent, 2 percentage points below the prior mean and with a very small standard deviation of 1 percentage point. Although these recent midterm rates are not as low as those in 1962, 1966, and 1970, they do rival those found throughout the 1950s: mean midterm nonvoting from 1950 to 1958 was 56 percent, and mean nonvoting from 1994 through 2010 was 58 percent. Table 5.2 also shows regional differences as nonvoting in the South continues to decrease, dropping some 6 percentage points from the third period and hitting historic lows in 2008 and 2010 (see Tables 2.1 and 2.2). Nonvoting outside the South drops 2 percentage points from the prior period, but it remains higher than that found in the first or second periods. The tables indicate that in the fourth period, national campaign effects prevail in the South to a greater extent than in the non-South: mean net national effects of 74 percent of the variance explained in the South as compared to 37 percent of the variance explained in the non-South.

This brief accounting of four historical periods permits us to examine each one in greater depth in this and upcoming chapters. We discuss how the periods are distinct from each other across economic, technological, international, and political dimensions of uncertainty in the national campaign context. To best understand how the national campaign context unfolds across these four periods, we interweave three forms of analysis. First, we offer a historical analysis that describes the political uncertainty and economic, technological, legal, and international milestones taking place across these years. Second, we offer the empirical results of a multivariate aggregate model of state nonvoting for each election from 1920 through 2012. Third, beginning with Chapter 6, we reintroduce the individual-level analysis as data become available from 1968 onward to understand how external and internal uncertainty influence individuals' decisions not to vote in the latter three time periods.

This multivariate model differs from that presented in Chapter 3 in two important respects. Initially, because our analysis has now moved from the national to the state level, we no longer have the ability to assess the impact of individual national events on state nonvoting. When major national events occur, there is no consistent way to test their differential influence on individual states. However, we can test for the effect of a relevant subset of national events, specifically American involvement in major wars—World War II, the Korean War, the Vietnam War, the Persian Gulf War, and the Iraq War—using state casualty and public attitude data.

Also, we add a measure for state residency requirements for elections from 1920 through 1970. Although US election history at the federal level is a story of the expansion of voting rights for women, African Americans, and young people, the story at the state level is one of restrictions and barriers to voting, especially aimed at blocking African Americans' participation in the South through poll taxes, literacy tests, and residency requirements.[6] "The legal-institutional properties of the electoral system—ballot and registration systems, voting systems, suffrage requirements, and the like—have important effects in influencing and shaping voting behavior; in essence, they define the conditions and boundaries of decision-making at the polls."[7] Because residency requirements ranging from 3 month to 2 years were present in all states, not just in the South, we employ this measure to gauge the extent to which state laws affected participation.[8] The Voting Rights Act of 1970 stopped lengthy residency requirements for presidential elections, and the Supreme Court applied the new standard to all elections in *Dunn v. Blumstein* in 1972.

[6] Jerrold Rusk, *A Statistical History of the American Electorate* (Washington, D.C.: CQ Press, 2001).

[7] Jerrold Rusk, "Comment: The American Electoral Universe: Speculation and Evidence," *American Political Science Review* 64 (September 1974): 1044. See also Erik Engstrom and Samuel Kernell, *Party Ballots, Reform, and the Transformation of America's Political System* (New York: Cambridge University Press, 2014).

[8] Melanie Springer provides an exhaustive analysis of all state laws in their effects on turnout. Because our primary interest is in the effect of national factors on state participation levels, a consideration of all state laws is outside the scope of the current study. See Melanie Springer, *How the States Shaped the Nation: American Electoral Institutions and Voter Turnout, 1920–2000* (Chicago: University of Chicago Press, 2014).

Taken separately, the historical analysis and the quantitative models tell only one part of the story about the effects of the national campaign context on nonvoting. When the two analyses are brought together we can more fully understand the differences across the four time periods and how uncertainty shifts from one election to the next. For the sake of clarity, we label these periods based on the characteristics and events that most define the novelty and uncertainty of the era: the government expansion period (1920–1944), the post-war period (1946–1972), the government reassessment period (1974–1990), and the Internet technology period (1992–2012). The periods could all carry many tags and markers, but these are indicative of the complexity faced by the eligible electorate in the national campaign context.

Government Expansion Period: 1920–1944

Despite Warren Harding's assurances of a "return to normalcy," an interrelated series of national episodes unfolded after World War I, among them the postwar recession, the "Roaring 20s" by mid-decade, the Great Depression, the New Deal, and World War II. The swiftness with which one set of events and circumstances cascaded into another pointed to an unusually uncertain national landscape. The sharp changes were made all the more prominent by the emergence of radio as the principal, and ultimately ubiquitous, form of news media. While these factors worked differently on each election, they typified the period with large problems, national solutions, and nationwide communication. The role of the national government in offering programs and solutions became the central focus of the period as expectations about what government should accomplish expanded. During the 1920s, the prevailing view of government was as a sponsor for business. Yet, with the stock market crash in 1929 people recognized that the very narrowness of this approach helped precipitate the problem. Proposals for public construction plans to ease unemployment, direct relief to the unemployed, and federal government loans to states and businesses circulated well before the New Deal, which continued in this vein.[9] Hence, we refer to these years as the government expansion period.

The impact of the national campaign context begins with increases in nonvoting in 1920 and 1922. Nonvoting rose 12 percentage points from 1916 to 1920 and also increased 4 percentage points in the midterm elections from 1918 to 1922 (see Tables 2.1 and 2.2). As Table 5.1 shows, the national campaign context sharply increases nonvoting by 17 percentage points in 1920

[9] Arthur Schlesinger, Jr., *The Crisis of the Old Order* (Boston: Houghton Mifflin, 1957).

(α_t = 17.17) and 14 percentage points in 1922 (α_t = 14.38) for the nation as a whole. These positive effects also occur regionally in 1924 and in the non-South in 1926. As we discuss below, women entering the electorate for the first time in 1920 did not vote in large numbers, and this increased nonvoting rates. But starting in 1928, national factors have consistent negative effects on non-voting nationally, except in 1938 and in the war years of 1942 and 1944. As the period unfolded, there were four major changes within the national campaign context which defined uncertainty and altered nonvoting rates: the juxtaposition between economic expansion in the 1920s and collapse in the 1930s, radio as the first truly mass medium, women's suffrage, and America's entrance into World War II.

Bad Times and Good Times

During the two decades from 1920 through 1944, the US economy moved from bad times to good times and back again. While the 1920s are often depicted as universally prosperous and heady, the early 1920s were caught in the middle of a post-war economic downturn. Five million veterans, returning from the war, searched for jobs as unemployment soared from 1.4 percent in 1919 to 5.2 percent in 1920 and 7 percent by 1922.[10] Gross national product fell by 4 percent between 1919 and 1920 and by another 9 percent between 1920 and 1921.[11] This nearly 13 percent decline in two years was almost twice the drop during the previous downturn in the four years of the Panic of 1893. Indeed, the 1920s "roared" for only five short years from 1925 through 1929. By 1925 and into 1926, the US economy was in full expansion aided by national government shifts in tax and regulatory codes. Calvin Coolidge remarked, "The federal government justified itself only as it served business."[12] US businesses, notably automobiles, iron, steel, telephones and electricity, entered record-breaking years in production and profits. Gross national product increased sharply by 8 percent between 1924 and 1925 and another 6 percent between 1925 and 1926.[13]

[10] See Tables 3.4 and 3.5.

[11] US Department of Commerce, "Gross National Product, Total, and Per Capita, in Current and 1958 Prices: 1869 to 1970," *Historical Statistics of the United States, Colonial Times to 1970,* Part 1, p. 224.

[12] Calvin Coolidge, *Autobiography,* (New York: Cosmopolitan Book Corporation, 1929), 196.

[13] US Department of Commerce, "Gross National Product, Total, and Per Capita, in Current and 1958 Prices: 1869 to 1970," *Historical Statistics of the United States, Colonial Times to 1970,* Part 1, p. 224.

Yet, what appeared to be, according to Irving Fisher, a noted economist at the time, a "permanently high plateau" was transformed in a matter of weeks in October and November 1929 when the stock market lost nearly half of its value, from its high of 381.17 on September 3, 1929 to its year low of 198.60 on November 13, 1929.[14] Unemployment, which had been at 3 percent in the 1928 election, tripled to 9 percent by 1930 and nearly tripled again to 24 percent by 1932. Personal income fell by more than 43 percent between 1928 and 1932.[15] As early as December 1929, President Herbert Hoover observed the effects of a "depression with widespread unemployment and suffering."[16] A year later in his December 1930 State of the Union Address, Hoover wrote paradoxically that "the fundamental strength of the Nation's economic life is unimpaired," yet "during the past 12 months we have suffered with other Nations from economic depression."[17]

The theory of uncertainty in the national campaign context states that economic volatility will bring more people to the polls. They participate to end the bad times or protect the good times. As a first test of this model on individual elections, Table 5.3 investigates the effects of this economic volatility relative to the influence of radio in American households and women's suffrage for the period from 1920 through 1928. The percent of adult women in a state's population serves as the measure of women's suffrage.[18] Also included in the model are indicators of party competition, age, education, and state residency requirements.[19] Table 5.4 tests the model for the years from 1930 through 1944 and includes a variable for American involvement in World War

[14] Quoted in Edward Teach, "The Bright Side of Bubbles," *CFO Magazine*, May 1, 2007, found at http://www.cfo.com/article.cfm/9059304/c_9064230.

[15] See Tables 3.4 and 3.5.

[16] Herbert Hoover, "Annual Message to the Congress on the State of the Union," *Public Papers of the Presidents, 1929*, December 3, 1929. Found at American Presidency Project, http://www.presidency.ucsb.edu.

[17] From *Public Papers of the Presidents, Herbert Hoover, 1930* found at http://www.presidency.ucsb.edu/ws/index.php?pid=22458.

[18] We also tested the raw number of eligible adult women in the electorate as an indicator for women's suffrage. It performs less well than the percent measure. In order to capture as much of the effect of women's suffrage as possible, we use the percent measure. In later chapters, when considering the entrance of African-American voters into the electorate after the passage of the Voting Rights Act of 1965 and the entrance of 18-year-olds into the electorate after the ratification of the 26th Amendment in 1972, we employ the raw number measures.

[19] Party competition is measured by the absolute value of the difference between Democratic and Republican percentages of the vote subtracted from 100. This measure differs from the competition measure used in Chapter 3 and is discussed in the text below. State residency requirements are measured on an ordinal scale coded 0 for states with no requirement, 1 for 3 months, 2 for 4 months, 3 for 6 months, 4 for 12 months, and 5 for 24 months. For the requirements of individual states over time, see Rusk, 2001, 26.

Table 5.3 **Effects of the National Campaign Context on Nonvoting, 1920–1928**

Predictor	*1920*				*1922*				*1924*
	Coefficient	*t-value*	*Mean*	*Impact*	*Coefficient*	*t-value*	*Mean*	*Impact*	*Coefficient*
Income Change	0.008	0.096	−39.528	−0.316	0.011	0.431	−129.701	−1.427	−0.207
Unemployment Change	7.090	0.296	0.119	0.844	−0.295	−0.569	6.042	−1.782	−2.892
Communication Technology									
Women	0.512	1.937	47.348	24.242	1.221	4.032	47.587	58.104	−0.103
Competition	−0.098	−2.221	66.629	−6.530	−0.197	−4.563	68.688	−13.532	−0.082
Youth	0.727	1.031	15.459	11.239	−1.445	−2.069	15.489	−22.382	−0.962
Education	−0.178	−1.350	21.354	−3.801	−0.374	−2.387	20.666	−7.729	−0.344
State Residency	0.133	0.265	0.479	0.064	0.565	1.008	0.479	0.271	0.191
Prior Nonvoting	0.846	14.473	39.104	33.082	0.512	6.084	5.621	2.878	1.016
Intercept	15.257	0.758			21.189	1.014			26.143
Number of Cases	48				48				48
R^2	0.937				0.911				0.94
Adjusted R^2	0.924				0.893				0.928
Durbin h-statistic	0.022				0.023				1.183

II in 1942 and 1944.[20] The tables reveal that economic change reduces nonvoting rates throughout the era. Table 5.3 reveals how economic growth reduces nonvoting rates during the late 1920s. Table 5.4 amplifies this for the period from 1930 through 1944: changes in income and unemployment decrease nonvoting rates during the Great Depression and the wartime boom.

Table 5.3 reveals how rising per capita income—a 29 percent increase from 1922 to 1926 and a 37 percent increase in per capita income from 1924 to

[20] American war involvement is measured by state casualty counts in the year of the election. These data are available from the Department of Defense, Defense Manpower Data Center, Statistical Information Analysis Division, found at http://siadapp.dmdc.osd.mil/personnel/CASUALTY/castop.htm.

			1926[a]				1928			
t-value	*Mean*	*Impact*	*Coefficient*	*t-value*	*Mean*	*Impact*	*Coefficient*	*t-value*	*Mean*	*Impact*
−1.403	20.588	−4.262	−0.041	−2.079	102.938	−4.220	−0.033	−1.781	102.938	−3.397
−0.239	0.232	−0.671	−0.475	−1.128	5.586	−2.653	−1.663	−0.535	0.918	−1.527
			−0.528	−1.611	11.345	−5.990	−0.662	−3.400	20.091	−13.300
−0.344	47.124	−4.854	0.390	1.316	46.429	18.107	0.466	1.347	46.295	21.573
−1.973	59.288	−4.862	−0.072	−2.272	63.425	−4.567	0.017	0.338	77.404	1.316
−1.756	15.535	−14.945	0.0004	1.027	212388	84.955	0.024	0.085	15.705	0.377
−2.151	19.978	−6.872	−0.139	−0.968	19.290	−2.681	−0.239	−1.268	18.602	−4.446
0.361	0.479	0.091	0.949	2.212	0.479	0.455	1.008	2.001	0.479	0.483
14.050	51.549	52.374	0.795	10.098	59.529	47.326	0.850	14.933	51.549	43.817
1.398			2.144	0.146			34.435	1.754		
			48				48			
			0.954				0.952			
			0.943				0.940			
			0.006				0.781			

Note: Critical t-values are 1.679 at .10 probability; 2.009 at .05; 2.700 at .01. Critical value for Durbin h-statistic at .05 probability = 1.695.

[a] Total youth in the state population, rather than percent youth in the state population, used to estimate the model. See note 36.

1928—decreases nonvoting in the 1926 midterm and 1928 presidential contests. The impact of income change is evident: mean income change is associated with nearly a 4 percentage point drop in nonvoting in 1926 and a 3 percentage point drop in 1928. Republicans, taking credit for the good times, also suggested economic cataclysm if the Democrats gained office: "Is your bread buttered? Remember hard times when we had a Democrat President! You can't eat promises. Play safe! Vote a straight Republican ticket!"[21] The campaign context thus fueled uncertainty about what would happen if the good times suddenly stopped.

[21] Lawrence Fuchs, "The Election of 1928," in Arthur Schlesinger, Jr. ed., *The History of American Presidential Elections*, vol. III 1900–1936 (New York: Chelsea House, 1971), 2607.

Table 5.4 **Effects of the National Campaign Context on Nonvoting, 1930–1944**

Predictor	*1930*				*1932*			
	Coefficient	*t-value*	*Mean*	*Impact*	*Coefficient*	*t-value*	*Mean*	*Impact*
Income Change	−0.044	−0.579	43.390	−1.909	0.014	1.530	−263.438	−3.688
Unemployment Change	−0.009	−2.284	480.289	−4.323	−0.007	−1.710	574.929	−4.025
Communication Technology	−0.087	−1.102	34.792	−3.027	−0.244	−3.798	43.728	−10.670
Competition	−0.065	−1.746	65.683	−4.269	0.044	0.986	70.042	3.082
Youth	0.079	0.380	15.872	1.254	0.219	1.100	15.423	3.378
Education	−0.033	−0.188	17.914	−0.591	−0.440	−3.974	18.432	−8.110
State Residency	0.444	0.720	0.375	0.167	−0.293	−0.759	0.375	−0.110
Prior Nonvoting	0.937	10.168	62.061	58.151	1.096	17.981	45.213	49.553
Intercept	19.055	2.014			−12.667	−1.619		
N	48				48			
R^2	0.931				0.980			
Adjusted R^2	0.916				0.976			
Durbin h-statistic	0.791				0.726			

Predictor	**1938**				**1940**			
	Coefficient	**t-value**	**Mean**	**Impact**	**Coefficient**	**t-value**	**Mean**	**Impact**
Income Change	−0.012	−0.395	100.063	−1.201	−0.064	−2.402	52.317	−3.348
Unemployment Change	−0.232	−1.952	16.462	−3.819	−0.108	−2.855	35.581	−3.843
Communication Technology	−0.214	−1.699	70.537	−15.095	−0.181	−2.748	79.473	−14.385
International Involvement								
Competition	−0.111	−1.781	68.129	−7.562	−0.008	−0.151	77.946	−0.624
Youth	−1.828	−2.128	14.532	−26.564	0.067	0.145	14.305	0.958
Education	−0.475	−1.888	19.984	−9.492	−0.082	−0.628	20.502	−1.681
State Residency	0.990	1.143	0.271	0.268	0.088	0.203	1.188	0.105
Prior Nonvoting	0.694	7.517	53.501	37.130	0.853	16.767	40.440	34.495
Intercept	11.045	0.495			15.727	1.290		
N	48				48			
R^2	0.935				0.984			
Adjusted R^2	0.922				0.981			
Durbin h-statistic	0.699				0.126			

1934				*1936*			
Coefficient	*t-value*	*Mean*	*Impact*	*Coefficient*	*t-value*	*Mean*	*Impact*
−0.129	−2.030	−24.238	−3.127	−0.030	−1.008	133.250	−3.998
−0.254	−3.590	139.525	−35.439	0.022	0.225	28.465	0.626
−0.319	−2.803	52.664	−16.800	−0.173	−2.464	61.600	−10.657
−0.114	−2.088	69.733	−7.950	−0.085	−1.736	66.421	−5.646
0.620	1.207	15.075	9.347	0.325	0.806	14.785	4.805
−0.007	−0.033	18.949	−0.133	0.099	0.721	19.467	1.927
0.278	0.353	0.271	0.075	−1.426	−1.840	0.271	−0.386
0.836	9.148	62.061	51.883	0.892	15.958	42.953	38.314
46.524	2.753			27.965	2.389		
48				48			
0.944				0.980			
0.932				0.976			
1.549				0.782			

1942				**1944**			
Coefficient	**t-value**	**Mean**	**Impact**	**Coefficient**	**t-value**	**Mean**	**Impact**
−0.070	−2.198	356.729	−24.971	−0.012	−1.911	545.775	−6.549
0.140	0.849	77.663	10.873	0.014	0.002	91.840	1.286
−0.107	−0.803	82.506	−8.828	−0.279	−2.205	85.540	−23.866
−0.002	−1.746	773.339	−1.547	−0.001	−1.700	10017	−10.017
−0.060	−1.458	68.163	−4.090	−0.020	−0.021	81.408	−1.628
0.051	0.080	14.607	0.745	−0.672	−1.656	14.611	−9.819
0.057	0.259	22.057	1.257	−0.109	−0.030	23.612	−2.574
1.294	1.796	0.271	0.351	0.234	0.012	0.271	0.063
0.640	8.969	53.111	33.991	0.848	13.035	39.694	33.661
64.015	2.734			12.641	0.079		
48				48			
0.936				0.975			
0.921				0.969			
0.386				0.136			

Note: Critical t-values are 1.679 at .10 probability; 2.009 at .05; 2.700 at .01. Critical value for Durbin h-statistic at .05 probability = 1.695.

And, indeed, they did stop. The triumphs of the Republicans at the polls in 1928 were short-lived, as the stock market crashed less than one year later in October 1929 and the economy slid from downturn into freefall. For a dozen years, Americans suffered high unemployment, low personal income, and shaky corporate profits. As Table 5.1 shows, the national campaign context decreases nonvoting for the country as a whole in elections from 1932 through 1940, except 1938. National factors pushed nonvoting downward by 3 percentage points in 1932, 15 percentage points in 1934, 4 percentage points in 1936, and 2 percentage points in 1940. Although, as shown in Table 2.1, the drop in nonvoting was not as dramatic as it had been in 1928, nevertheless, it decreased by at least 2 percentage points each year for the three presidential elections from 1932 through 1940.

As revealed in Table 5.4, the dramatic rise in unemployment drives nonvoting downward. The 24 percent unemployment rate in 1932, noted above, was a historic high and was only slightly lower in 1934 at 22 percent. Unemployment dropped in 1936, although it remained high at 17 percent, and it increased to 19 percent in 1938 during what was nicknamed the "Roosevelt Recession" as federal spending was reduced, taxes were increased, and the money supply was tightened in a series of decisions in the summer of 1937. By 1940, unemployment declined but was still high, hovering at 15 percent (see Tables 3.4 and 3.5). During each of these six election cycles from the 1930 midterms through the 1940 presidential election, except 1936, change in the unemployment rate decreases nonvoting, with the largest effect in 1934, when mean unemployment change prompts a 35 percentage point decline in nonvoting (see the Impact column in Table 5.4).

During the two elections that took place during World War II, income change, not unemployment change, influences nonvoting. Although unemployment dropped sharply between 1938 and 1942 and even more dramatically between 1940 and 1944, personal income was expanding at even faster rates in all states, and among all sectors personal income expanded by over 73 percent from 1938 to 1942 and by 101 percent from 1940 to 1944.[22]

The central generalization about the first period that can be drawn from the interplay between the economy and electoral participation is that economic uncertainty in the national campaign context pushes nonvoting rates downward. With the high unemployment rates of the 1930s, people went to the polls. When the economy improved, yet uncertainty remained about how long prosperity would last, people went to the polls. With large increases in personal income in

[22] It dropped by 14.3 percentage points between 1938 and 1942 and by 13.4 percentage points between 1940 and 1944. The unemployment measure is the absolute value of change from the previous presidential or House election.

the 1920s and again in the 1940s, the number of people participating in electoral politics increased. When economic conditions were more stationary, there was no effect on participation. With unemployment roughly stable in 1924 and 1928 and returned to pre-Depression rates in 1942 and 1944, it has no influence on nonvoting.

On the Air

Despite the economic challenges of much of the first era, radio began to fundamentally reshape how people approached information-seeking, entertainment, and their connections to politics. Although considered a luxury in the early 1920s, a radio was a household necessity even in the toughest of times by the 1930s. The first radio station in the United States, KDKA of Pittsburgh, broadcast the returns of the 1920 elections to no more than 2,000 people. Announcers read the results from telegraph tickers as they came in. By 1924, only 1,500 sets were produced and a scant 3 percent of American households owned radios. Yet major companies including AT&T and Westinghouse, smaller local firms, and even individuals raced to set up radio stations. There was no coast-to-coast network, but 530 stations operated in cities across the country in 1924.[23] Campaign coverage took two forms—live broadcast from the floor of presidential conventions, and paid political party broadcasts that blended entertainment and politics. Radio rallies were conceived, which included a "Midnight Theatrical Revue" from 11:30 pm to 2:00 am that mixed political speeches and entertainment by vaudeville entertainers Al Jolson and Elsie Ferguson, and other programs with music from the Metropolitan Opera House in New York. President Calvin Coolidge finished his reelection campaign with a radio speech: "To my father, who is listening in my old home in Vermont, and to my other invisible audience, I say 'good night.' "[24]

The 1928 presidential election, often lost in the footnotes of longer discussions of the 1932 election, was actually a watershed year in US electoral history. It was the *first* mass media election. Radio was a truly novel element of the

[23] US Department of Commerce, Bureau of the Census, "Radio and Television Stations, Sets Produced, and Households with Sets: 1921–1970," Series R 93-105, *Historical Statistics of the United States, Colonial Times to 1970*, Vol. 2, p. 796. Found at http://www2.census.gov/prod2/statcomp/documents/CT1970p2-05.pdf.

[24] David Clark, "Radio in Presidential Campaigns: The Early Years, 1924–1932," *Journal of Broadcasting and Electronic Media* 6 (Spring 1962): 229–238; Don Moore, "The 1924 Radio Election," 1992, found at http://www.pateplumaradio.com/genbroad/elec1924.html.

campaign, and campaigners encountered considerable risk in choosing how to best handle the mass aspect of this new medium. Nothing in the use of newspapers in prior campaigns provided guideposts. While radio was a factor in the 1924 election, it dominated the presidential campaign in 1928. Networking had reached the West Coast in 1927 when the National Broadcasting Company, NBC, connected its stations in New York and Washington, D.C. with its station in San Francisco. The Columbia Broadcasting System, CBS, soon followed. Among American households, 20 percent owned radios in 1928. Even during the depths of the Depression, the number of radios in homes grew successively larger from 35 percent in 1930 to 71 percent by 1938, but the level of uncertainty about how to capitalize on radio was never greater than it was in 1928.

Republican and Democratic strategists relied on guesswork in determining how best to appeal to Coolidge's invisible audience. The radio's political usefulness and its entertainment value for American households blended in 1928. With little strictly entertainment programming on the air, people avidly followed coverage of the Republican and Democratic national party conventions and eagerly tuned into the paid political broadcasts and campaign speeches of Herbert Hoover and Al Smith. The single largest item of party campaign budgets was for radio. The Republicans allocated $400,000 for their radio broadcast budget, although they actually spent $436,000, while the Democrats allotted $530,000, with the average price of one hour of radio time at $7500.[25] Smith had the better radio voice. As one radio critic wrote, "Radio transmits Smith's magnetic personality whereas it even further chills Hoover's delivery of cold facts." Still, there was no hiding Smith's heavy New York accent as he pronounced radio "raddio."[26] Republicans warned this meant that Smith was not from Main Street and, according to Hoover, "Main Street [is] the principal thoroughfare of the nation." Both parties began mastering radio as a medium for attack: Smith accused Hoover of distorting facts when Hoover promised "a chicken in every pot." Smith railed "A man who invents a lie like that, what must be his estimation of the average intelligence of the American people?" For his part, Hoover accused Smith of needlessly enlarging the scope of government and "turning to state socialism as a solution."[27] The campaign was so popular with listeners that radio industry analysts estimated 3 million new sets were purchased just during the campaign period.[28]

[25] Douglas Craig, *Fireside Politics: Radio and Political Culture in the United States, 1920–1940* (Baltimore: Johns Hopkins University Press, 2000), 147; Clark, 1962, 232–233.

[26] Craig, 2000, 149.

[27] Clark, 1962, 232–233.

[28] Anthony Rudel, *Hello Everybody: The Dawn of American Radio* (New York: Houghton Mifflin Harcourt, 2008). Rudel considers in detail how politicians beginning with Coolidge began to adapt to the new medium.

The theory of uncertainty in the national campaign context suggests that radio as a technological shock decreases nonvoting. Its novelty creates a new and unexpected source of information that draws people into the political realm. Results in Table 5.3 show that in 1926 and 1928, with a one percent increase in households with radios, nonvoting decreases by nearly one percentage point. As shown in Table 5.4, radio continues to have powerful effects in the 1930s and 1940s, as it consistently decreases nonvoting in all elections except 1930 and 1942. Thus, during the first period, uncertainty measured by radio as a technology shock is evident not just in presidential elections but also in midterm House races. The effect of this uncertainty is most aptly captured in the impact measures in Tables 5.3 and 5.4. Given that presidential campaigns beginning in 1928 started to be built around radio, its importance in major nationwide presidential races is both substantial and unsurprising. In 1928, an average of 20 percent of American households with radios is associated with a 13 percentage point drop in nonvoting. The impact remains sizable throughout the 1930s and 1940s, with the smallest effect still extensive in 1936 when 61 percent of American households with radios is associated with an 11 percentage point drop in nonvoting.

But it is in midterm House elections— small local affairs with little money spent, little newspaper coverage, and little interest from even the most informed members of the public—where radio has its largest impact. The 1926 election marked the first time radio influenced midterm races. Although not as well developed as in the 1928 presidential campaign, in the 1926 midterm an average of 11 percent of households across the states with radios is associated with a 6 percentage point decline in nonvoting. Not only did local radio stations cover the races, but they also offered airtime to candidates for political advertisement. For example, "in upstate New York, local stations in 1940 offered candidates one-minute spots for between $5 and $10 dollars when sold in a group of 70."[29] This impact of radio remains sizable in midterm elections during the period, increasing to 17 percentage points in 1934, 15 percentage points in 1938, although not statistically significant in the 1942 midterm elections.

Women's Suffrage

The theory of uncertainty in the national campaign context suggests that a new franchise law disrupts the political status quo, and its novelty spurs the

[29] Craig, 2000, 130.

now-eligible group to vote. As seen in Table 5.3, we find the opposite to be true with women entering the electorate. Women increase nonvoting rates in 1920 and 1922, and they have no effect thereafter.

While the economy and mass communication technology reduce nonvoting, women entering the electorate increases nonvoting. Seventy years in the making, the women's suffrage movement began in earnest after the Civil War and succeeded in gaining women's right to vote after World War I despite the opposition of many prominent men, typified by Elihu Root of New York, secretary of war and secretary of state under William McKinley and Theodore Roosevelt, who feared that women were "distinctly inferior" to men in engaging in the "functions implied in suffrage."[30] But, once the suffrage battle was won, women did not uniformly vote.

While both parties sought to attract women voters to the polls, they were unclear on how to approach them. Tammany Hall leaders in New York City lamented that while they could tell men for whom to vote, the bosses could not cajole women in the same way.[31] The effect is particularly striking during the 1922 midterm: a one percent increase in women in a state's population yields almost a two percentage point increase in state nonvoting. By 1924, however, the effect of women's suffrage is gone for the balance of the period.[32] Economic and technological factors within the national campaign context outrun the effect of women in the population.

Thus, the uncertainty in the national campaign context model does not fully account for the introduction of women into the electorate. The model, as spelled out in Chapter 1, posits that higher uncertainty prompts lower nonvoting as members of the eligible electorate do not wish to risk unsatisfactory electoral outcomes. In the case of a legal change affording a new group entrance into the eligible electorate, uncertainty involves not only this risk but also how to convince the newly enfranchised to actually participate. A fair number of women did vote in the early elections, but it was not a rush to the polls that many suffragettes had desired and many men had feared. It took several elections before women were effectively socialized into the new role as voters. This is consistent with work by Rusk and Stucker, who found that in initial elections after women received the right to vote, participation fell, but it increased

[30] "Nugent Quotes Root in War on Suffrage," *New York Times*, July 12, 1915, found at http://query.nytimes.com/gst/abstract.html?res=F40F12F83B5C13738DDDAB0994DF405B858DF1D3.

[31] Ernest Havier, "Tammany Puzzled by Women Voters," *New York Times*, October 17, 1920, E7.

[32] There is no effect of women in the adult population on nonvoting from 1928 onward. The variable is not presented in the results for 1930–1944 in Table 5.4.

in later elections.[33] Thus women were initially uncertain about voting, rather than uncertain about the risks of not voting.

Table 5.5 examines in greater detail the effect of women's suffrage through an ecological inference analysis.[34] The table presents women's and men's nonvoting levels in elections from 1920 through 1952. Among eligible women, 80 percent did not vote in 1920 and 91 percent did not in 1922. The dilemma was most striking in the South. While 66 percent of eligible women failed to vote in the non-South in 1920, 83 percent of eligible women did not vote in the South. In contrast, among eligible men only 34 percent did not vote in 1920 and 47 percent did not vote in 1922. Among men, nonvoting actually declined by 5 percentage points in 1920 from 1916 (from 39 percent to 34 percent) and dropped by fully 13 percentage points in 1922 from 1918 (from 60 percent to 47 percent).

The table also shows that it was not until 1940 that women's nonvoting rate dropped below that of men in presidential years and remained consistently below it through 1952. This began much earlier for women in the non-South, who had very low rates of nonvoting from 1934 onward. Southern women had strikingly high nonvoting rates until 1952. While women began to participate in higher numbers in presidential election years, their participation in midterm House elections remained low. And this was true regardless of region. While only 27 percent of women did not vote in the 1940 election, 84 percent did not vote in 1942. Similarly, a large gap between presidential and midterm years occurs between 1944 and 1946 (47 percentage point difference) and 1948 and 1950 (43 percentage point difference). This is especially notable among women in the non-South, who had nonvoting rates far below those of men for all presidential elections from 1936 to 1952. But, generally women failed to go to the polls at the midterm. So there were ultimately two gender gaps by 1940: the first in presidential elections as women voted more than men; the second in midterm House elections, as men voted more than women.

At War Again

The theory of uncertainty in the national campaign context states that war by its very nature is highly unpredictable and changeable. This uncertainty prompts more people to go to the polls, as they are unsure of future outcomes of victory or

[33] Jerrold G. Rusk and John Stucker, "Legal-Institutional Factors and Voting Participation: The Impact of Women's Suffrage on Voter Turnout," in William Crotty, ed., *Political Participation and American Democracy* (New York: Greenwood Press, 1991), 113–138.

[34] Gary King, *A Solution to the Ecological Inference Problem* (Princeton: Princeton University Press, 1997).

Table 5.5 **Women and Men Nonvoting, 1916–1952**

Year	*National Nonvoting*	*Men Nonvoting*	*Women Nonvoting*	*South Women Nonvoting*	*Non-South Women Nonvoting*
1916	39.10	39.10	—	—	—
1918	59.53	59.53	—	—	—
1920	51.55	33.76	79.90	83.29	66.07
1922	63.23	47.00	90.83	91.40	42.82
1924	51.88	32.77	71.58	71.12	33.16
1926	65.32	50.46	91.15	83.39	94.56
1928	45.21	34.71	64.33	65.97	56.93
1930	62.06	40.74	88.17	88.48	77.10
1932	42.95	30.76	57.63	63.47	58.19
1934	53.40	39.75	72.21	80.06	32.15
1936	40.44	27.81	52.31	62.86	21.60
1938	53.11	34.26	65.63	71.38	31.82
1940	38.44	49.03	27.28	62.96	19.05
1942	64.55	40.39	83.83	96.02	63.18
1944	39.93	53.70	26.83	62.04	10.97
1946	60.26	35.73	73.88	75.34	72.01
1948	47.19	65.34	30.48	63.71	14.84
1950	57.09	32.91	73.96	73.18	73.61
1952	36.50	44.67	28.78	51.92	12.63

Note: Data entries in Column 1 for 1916 and 1918 are from Rusk, 2001; for 1920 onward, data are from Table 2.1 Remaining columns are results from an ecological inference analysis following King (1997).

defeat. The level of uncertainty in the national campaign context, which surely had been high during the Great Depression, was no less high after Japan attacked Pearl Harbor in December 1941. In 1940, there were only a half-million active duty personnel across the US military, but this climbed by 1942 to 3.9 million people and skyrocketed by 1944 to 11 million. The war's effect on nonvoting was complex. During the two war elections, nonvoting across the country increased by 11 percentage points in 1942 and 2 percentage points in 1944 (see Tables 2.1 and 2.2). These increases likely resulted from large numbers of servicemen not voting.

But as displayed in Table 5.4, state-level casualties in the war actually lower nonvoting. In examining the impact measures in 1942 and 1944, mean war deaths across the states decrease nonvoting by 2 percentage points in 1942 and by 10 percentage points in 1944. This nonvoting decline likely reflects people's uncertainty about victory in the war. In general, the uncertainty of the war, like uncertainty about the economy and technology, decreases nonvoting.

Party Competition

As noted in Chapter 1, party competition and uncertainty in the campaign context are inextricably linked. Uncertainty in the national campaign context helps define how many resources a party brings to a race, the attractiveness of the candidates who are racing, and how close the final vote will be. Based simply on election victories, the post–World War I period is very much a one-party period—first dominated by the Republicans in the 1920s, then dominated by the Democrats through the end of World War II. But this would miss the competition that did exist during the period. Even though the outcomes of many races were foregone conclusions, nevertheless the losing party did not disappear from American politics and was able to successfully mount regional, if not national, campaigns. And even when a party looked dominant in a presidential year, it nevertheless managed to consistently lose ground in the next midterm House elections, except in 1934.

Tables 5.6 and 5.7 examine the competitiveness of the two parties, the Democratic percent of the two-party vote, and the Democratic vote margin nationally and regionally for presidential elections from 1920 through 2012, and in midterm elections from 1922 through 2010.[35] During the first period, competition was generally at its lowest for both presidential and midterm races in the 1920s and at its highest in the 1940s.

As shown in Tables 5.3 and 5.4, the degree of competition strongly reduces nonvoting in the first period, except in four lopsided presidential elections—Hoover's victory in 1928, Roosevelt's election in 1932 and his reelections in 1940 and 1944—and one midterm in 1942. Indeed, what particularly stands out is the effect of competition on midterm nonvoting. As seen in Table 5.7, the mean competition index score for the midterms does not exceed

[35] As introduced in Chapter 3, the competitive index measures the absolute value of the difference between the Democratic percent of the two-party vote and the Republican percent of the two-party vote subtracted from 100. The closer the index value is to 100, the more competitive the race.

Table 5.6 **Levels of Competition by Region in Presidential Elections, 1920–2012**

Year	*Nation*			*South*			*Non-South*	
	Competition Index	*Democratic Percent of 2-Party Vote*	*Democratic Vote Margin*	*Competition Index*	*Democratic Percent of 2-Party Vote*	*Democratic Vote Margin*	*Competition Index*	*Democratic Percent of 2-Party Vote*
1920	66.63	41.92	–14.81	71.28	61.46	22.23	64.31	32.15
1924	59.29	40.84	–11.59	65.23	68.19	30.75	56.32	28.16
1928	77.40	43.65	–12.57	76.44	52.96	5.94	77.89	38.99
1932	70.04	64.14	27.82	45.14	77.43	54.48	82.49	57.49
1936	66.42	66.21	31.81	46.34	76.83	53.48	76.46	60.91
1940	77.95	59.45	18.84	53.09	73.46	46.81	90.38	52.44
1944	81.41	57.12	13.93	60.91	69.54	38.16	91.66	50.91
Mean	**71.31**	**53.33**	**7.63**	**59.77**	**68.55**	**35.98**	**77.07**	**45.86**
1948	83.88	53.96	6.03	65.38	60.98	17.46	93.13	50.45
1952	83.05	44.04	–11.86	89.20	52.15	4.30	79.98	39.99
1956	81.00	43.19	–13.89	85.25	50.68	0.48	78.88	39.44
1960	91.28	49.42	–1.46	90.14	52.37	3.86	91.82	48.03
1964	73.83	58.87	18.30	73.69	49.79	1.48	73.89	63.03
1968	86.97	48.65	–2.36	89.45	48.66	–2.85	85.84	48.65
1972	71.04	36.81	–25.81	60.50	30.25	–38.84	75.85	38.81
Mean	**81.58**	**47.85**	**–4.44**	**79.09**	**49.27**	**–2.02**	**82.77**	**46.91**
1976	89.77	50.55	1.15	89.55	55.06	10.03	89.87	48.91
1980	82.94	43.66	–11.47	92.63	47.78	–4.24	78.50	41.79
1984	76.62	39.73	-20.35	77.49	38.74	–22.37	76.22	40.18
1988	85.97	45.66	–8.60	85.06	42.83	–14.21	86.39	46.95
Mean	**83.83**	**44.90**	**–9.82**	**86.18**	**46.10**	**–7.70**	**82.75**	**44.46**
1992	88.00	52.49	4.34	91.81	50.92	1.59	86.26	53.21
1996	85.29	53.69	6.60	92.21	51.29	2.28	82.12	54.78
2000	83.98	48.17	-3.61	88.48	45.29	-9.93	81.93	49.43
2004	83.73	47.10	-5.74	84.31	42.98	-13.95	83.46	48.99
2008	82.06	52.16	4.27	86.72	45.57	-8.76	79.93	55.17
2012	81.05	50.34	0.70	83.87	44.99	-9.89	79.97	52.78
Mean	**84.02**	**50.66**	**1.09**	**87.90**	**46.84**	**-6.44**	**82.28**	**52.39**

	West			Midwest			East		
)emocratic 'ote 1argin	*Competition Index*	*Democratic Percent of 2-Party Vote*	*Democratic Vote Margin*	*Competition Index*	*Democratic Percent of 2-Party Vote*	*Democratic Vote Margin*	*Competition Index*	*Democratic Percent of 2-Party Vote*	*Democratic Vote Margin*
−33.33	72.40	36.20	−25.35	56.13	28.06	−40.46	64.40	32.20	−34.26
−32.76	60.85	30.43	−26.72	48.36	24.18	−35.77	60.08	30.04	−36.09
−21.83	76.40	38.20	−23.36	76.13	38.06	−26.65	81.46	40.89	−18.13
14.49	75.96	62.02	23.21	79.66	60.17	19.77	92.80	49.56	−0.92
20.98	64.69	67.66	34.43	79.16	60.42	19.58	86.44	54.02	7.71
4.86	85.04	57.25	14.42	93.33	47.79	4.40	93.00	52.28	4.52
1.81	89.95	54.19	8.35	92.18	47.00	−5.95	92.93	51.60	3.16
−6.54	**75.04**	**49.42**	**0.71**	**74.99**	**43.67**	**−9.30**	**81.59**	**44.37**	**−10.57**
0.80	93.33	53.01	5.00	94.51	49.64	−0.71	91.40	48.52	−2.65
−19.94	80.80	40.40	−19.12	75.20	37.60	−24.69	84.32	42.16	−15.61
−21.08	82.60	41.30	−17.35	82.60	41.30	−20.50	74.14	37.07	−25.80
−4.05	95.08	47.78	−4.78	89.93	45.29	−9.40	89.66	51.37	2.72
25.99	81.02	59.49	20.05	79.74	60.05	18.95	81.02	59.49	40.05
−2.13	86.65	45.14	−8.67	87.16	45.47	−8.29	83.56	55.98	11.75
−19.85	72.66	36.33	−26.24	78.47	39.24	−21.25	77.00	44.48	−10.91
−5.75	**84.59**	**46.21**	**−7.30**	**83.94**	**45.51**	**−9.41**	**83.01**	**48.44**	**−0.06**
−2.90	88.54	44.47	−10.65	93.85	48.31	−3.35	87.47	53.43	6.72
−14.78	71.42	35.88	−25.19	80.56	40.68	−17.05	84.84	49.87	−0.20
−19.43	71.40	35.70	−28.18	79.45	39.75	−20.37	78.69	45.91	−8.15
−6.03	85.37	43.92	−11.92	89.42	46.62	−6.70	84.56	50.86	1.59
−10.79	**79.18**	**39.99**	**−18.99**	**85.82**	**43.84**	**−11.87**	**83.89**	**50.02**	**−0.01**
5.59	88.31	50.43	1.16	89.56	49.98	0.13	80.53	59.74	16.29
8.58	87.32	49.69	−0.40	87.07	51.08	1.92	71.02	64.49	25.86
−1.01	80.94	43.48	−12.16	86.78	45.32	−9.01	78.25	60.76	20.17
−1.99	82.88	43.78	−12.15	86.32	44.78	−10.30	81.28	59.36	18.34
10.23	79.74	50.80	1.65	88.08	51.51	2.98	72.01	63.99	27.42
5.55	78.45	48.29	−3.22	86.83	48.02	−3.78	74.27	62.86	25.24
4.49	**82.94**	**47.75**	**−4.19**	**87.44**	**48.45**	**−3.01**	**76.23**	**61.87**	**22.22**

Table 5.7 **Levels of Competition by Region in Midterm Elections, 1922–2010**

	Nation			*South*			*Non-South*		
Year	*Competition Index*	*Democratic Percent of 2-Party Vote*	*Democratic Vote Margin*	*Competition Index*	*Democratic Percent of 2-Party Vote*	*Democratic Vote Margin*	*Competition Index*	*Democratic Percent of 2-Party Vote*	*Democratic Vote Margin*
1922	68.69	52.94	6.90	49.60	75.20	50.29	78.23	41.82	−14.80
1926	63.43	49.43	−0.07	48.74	75.42	50.83	70.77	36.43	−25.52
1930	65.68	53.09	6.99	47.65	76.18	52.26	74.70	41.55	−15.64
1934	69.73	63.64	27.01	37.60	81.20	61.77	85.80	54.86	9.63
1938	68.10	59.19	18.91	36.63	81.69	62.88	83.88	47.93	−3.08
1942	68.16	56.92	14.06	37.90	80.81	61.19	83.29	44.98	−9.51
Mean	**67.30**	**55.87**	**12.30**	**43.02**	**78.42**	**56.54**	**79.45**	**44.60**	**−9.82**
1946	70.33	53.50	6.76	47.39	75.61	50.26	81.81	42.44	−14.99
1950	71.71	57.14	14.24	41.18	79.39	58.55	86.98	46.02	−7.91
1954	75.07	57.83	15.61	45.14	77.43	54.76	90.03	48.02	−3.96
1958	74.42	61.98	25.39	39.35	80.33	62.84	89.90	53.89	7.76
1962	81.67	54.98	10.60	65.00	67.50	35.39	89.02	49.46	−1.07
1966	83.02	52.29	4.41	74.73	62.63	24.73	86.68	47.73	−4.56
1970	79.63	56.16	13.23	65.96	67.02	34.03	85.26	51.69	3.45
Mean	**76.55**	**56.27**	**12.89**	**52.75**	**72.84**	**45.79**	**87.10**	**48.46**	**−3.04**
1974	79.45	56.80	14.69	70.98	63.77	28.77	83.44	54.14	8.06
1978	80.19	53.06	8.19	74.81	58.95	23.22	82.73	50.64	1.11
1982	80.16	53.86	7.54	77.64	60.70	21.18	81.20	50.84	1.51
1986	79.48	52.91	6.83	77.30	61.35	23.24	80.37	49.43	−0.90
1990	83.54	54.08	8.79	79.83	58.81	16.17	85.28	52.00	5.31
Mean	**80.56**	**54.14**	**9.21**	**76.11**	**60.72**	**22.52**	**82.60**	**51.41**	**3.02**
1994	82.63	45.42	−7.91	86.34	46.86	−6.48	83.84	44.83	−8.59
1998	78.19	46.65	−4.71	82.57	48.76	−1.86	76.51	45.84	−6.05
2002	76.69	44.93	−8.49	82.71	44.94	−9.47	73.95	44.93	−8.04
2006	83.70	53.58	6.46	87.88	48.88	−2.12	81.79	55.79	10.50
2010	79.95	45.30	−9.03	76.83	39.93	−19.40	81.37	47.82	−4.15
Mean	**80.23**	**47.17**	**−4.74**	**83.27**	**45.87**	**−7.87**	**79.49**	**47.84**	**−3.27**

West			*Midwest*			*East*		
Competition Index	*Democratic Percent of 2-Party Vote*	*Democratic Vote Margin*	*Competition Index*	*Democratic Percent of 2-Party Vote*	*Democratic Vote Margin*	*Competition Index*	*Democratic Percent of 2-Party Vote*	*Democratic Vote Margin*
76.67	44.54	−9.38	69.84	34.92	−27.19	89.18	46.41	−7.12
73.20	39.53	−20.13	63.55	31.90	−32.54	76.04	38.02	−23.74
70.29	45.42	−8.95	70.96	36.70	−23.18	83.66	42.63	−14.70
75.84	61.70	23.05	90.16	51.28	2.83	91.96	51.26	2.36
81.46	57.15	14.28	81.75	41.16	−14.68	88.90	45.25	−9.42
88.29	52.35	4.64	76.44	38.22	−21.97	85.34	44.31	−11.36
77.62	**50.11**	**0.59**	**75.45**	**39.03**	**−19.46**	**85.85**	**44.65**	**−10.66**
86.58	46.91	−6.19	70.33	53.50	−23.58	82.76	42.32	−15.21
90.11	50.25	0.56	84.65	42.33	−15.33	86.08	45.42	−9.08
90.89	49.92	−0.17	87.85	44.82	−10.35	91.48	49.46	−1.08
83.71	56.93	13.83	95.69	51.61	3.21	91.58	52.43	4.89
87.18	51.48	2.97	90.09	45.43	−9.12	90.24	51.26	2.52
86.98	49.69	−0.61	86.82	43.41	−13.16	86.14	49.93	−0.23
82.57	55.33	10.68	91.07	48.75	−2.30	82.38	50.17	0.37
86.86	**51.50**	**3.01**	**86.65**	**47.12**	**−10.09**	**87.24**	**48.71**	**−2.55**
85.94	55.37	10.50	87.09	51.55	3.03	76.16	55.40	10.43
80.69	54.93	9.26	87.22	46.35	7.24	80.44	49.76	−0.31
78.43	49.58	−1.40	83.44	52.45	4.80	82.34	50.71	1.68
84.95	47.26	−5.45	84.25	52.93	5.81	70.14	48.41	−2.36
87.28	51.38	2.56	88.05	55.06	10.10	79.64	49.44	3.62
83.46	**51.70**	**3.09**	**86.01**	**51.67**	**6.20**	**77.74**	**50.74**	**2.61**
82.91	45.25	−9.17	84.69	45.40	−9.19	74.80	43.64	−7.16
78.92	45.26	−8.68	80.82	42.97	−13.77	68.64	49.74	5.87
76.40	44.36	−10.59	83.33	42.73	−13.69	61.67	48.07	1.51
85.39	51.64	3.34	87.16	53.79	7.48	72.16	63.39	23.12
81.06	44.60	−10.14	86.33	43.70	−12.13	76.77	56.55	12.42
80.94	**46.22**	**−7.05**	**84.46**	**45.72**	**−8.26**	**70.81**	**52.28**	**7.15**

67 percent nationally. This indicates that while competition was not overly high throughout the period, there were nevertheless a number of House seats in play. Indeed, some of the largest seat swings between the two parties ever occurred during this period, including the Democrats wresting 77 seats from the Republicans in 1922 and 52 seats in 1930 and the Republicans capturing 72 seats from the Democrats in 1938 and 45 seats in 1942. Competitiveness had a substantial dampening effect on nonvoting, ranging from a 4 percentage point impact in 1930 to a 14 percentage point impact in 1922. The key generalization from the first period is that competition matters when competition exists.

Personal Characteristics and Nonvoting

We weigh the effect of the national campaign context relative to indicators for key personal factors, youth and education. As revealed in Tables 5.3 and 5.4, youth and education have sporadic effects on nonvoting. The number of young people in a state lowers nonvoting in four of the 13 elections during the period: 1922, 1924, 1938, and 1944.[36] As seen in the Impact column, these effects are substantial. This suggests that in the first period, youth may have been more inclined to engage politically, at least in some elections, than they were later on. Still, we do not wish to make too much of this finding because there is no influence of youth on nonvoting in any of the other nine election years. These results also help clarify the robust effect of youth observed in the overall aggregate analysis presented in Chapter 3. When examining individual elections, the effect of youth is more muted.

Education also influences nonvoting in 4 of 13 elections—1922, 1924, 1932, and 1938. When present, the effects are sizable, the largest in 1938 when mean education prompts a 9 percentage point drop in nonvoting. This mixed effect occurs despite the steady increase in education depicted in Table 5.8 at both the high school and college levels. Even in the midst of the Depression, the number of people completing high school and college degrees increased. Nor did this slow down during World War II. These strides in education occurred both in the South and outside of the South. Although during the period education rates were decidedly lower in the South than in the non-South, nevertheless southerners increased high school completion by 11 percentage points and college by 3 percentage points.

[36] In 1926, we estimated the model with a variable for number of youth in the population rather than the variable for percent of youth in the population used in the other election years. This provided for more robust estimates and the absence of autocorrelation among the error terms.

Overall, it appears that the influence of personal characteristics of a state's population is election-specific. It depends on the extent to which economic and technological factors also influence participation in a given year.

State Influences and Prior Nonvoting

In addition to the dramatic changes within the national campaign context during the period, state boundaries were not simply geographic lines. As depicted in Table 5.1, strong net state effects occurred for the country as a whole in much of this period in both presidential and midterm elections, most notably in 1924, 1926, and 1938. And even with the strong national campaign context in 1932, 1936, 1940, and 1944, net state effects occurred for the country as a whole during these years (compare the first and second columns of Table 5.1). Perhaps most telling was net state effects of 22 percent of the variance explained in the 1932 elections. Only the 1934 and 1942 midterms stand out as elections with strong national effects and little evidence of state influences. Otherwise, even in the midst of the Great Depression and World War II, state effects continued to influence nonvoting.

In the South

These net state effects were more evident in the South than in the non-South. As seen in Table 5.1, this is especially true in the 1920 and 1924 presidential elections and the 1922 and 1938 midterm elections. This is consistent with the South's greater insularity from the rest of the country during these years, politically, economically, and technologically.[37]

Politically, as shown in Table 5.2, the nonvoting rate in the South was 30 percentage points higher than in the non-South. Poll tax, literacy tests, and other laws across the South hampered many African Americans and poor whites from voting. These laws stood as crucial elements of control as states invested in and enforced legal trap doors to prevent large contingents of people from voting.[38] The region also was isolated from the rest of the country in its party politics, as Democrats maintained the "Solid South." Figure 5.1 considers

[37] V. O. Key, *Southern Politics* (New York: Alfred Knopf, 1949); Morgan Kousser, *The Shaping of Southern Politics* (New Haven: Yale University Press, 1974).

[38] Jerrold G. Rusk and John Stucker, "The Effect of the Southern System of Election Laws on Voting Participation," in Joel Silbey, Allan Bogue, and William Flanigan, eds., *The History of American Voting Behavior* (Princeton: Princeton University Press, 1978), 198–250.

Table 5.8 **Education Rates by Region, 1920–2012 (percent who graduated)**

Year	*Nation*			*South*			*Non-South*		
	High School	*College*	*Difference*	*High School*	*College*	*Difference*	*High School*	*College*	*Difference*
1920	23.49	2.14	21.35	11.58	1.37	10.21	29.45	2.52	26.93
1922	22.94	2.27	20.67	12.10	1.49	10.61	28.35	2.66	25.69
1924	22.38	2.40	19.98	12.62	1.60	11.02	27.26	2.80	24.46
1926	21.83	2.54	19.29	13.14	1.72	11.42	26.17	2.95	23.22
1928	21.27	2.67	18.60	13.66	1.83	11.83	25.08	3.09	21.99
1930	20.72	2.80	17.92	14.18	1.94	12.24	23.99	3.23	20.76
1932	21.30	3.12	18.18	15.24	2.32	12.92	24.24	3.51	20.73
1934	22.31	3.50	18.81	16.31	2.69	13.62	25.21	3.89	21.32
1936	23.31	3.88	19.43	17.37	3.06	14.31	26.19	4.27	21.92
1938	24.32	4.25	20.07	18.44	3.44	15.00	27.17	4.65	22.52
1940	25.32	4.63	20.69	19.50	3.81	15.69	28.15	5.02	23.13
1942	27.18	4.93	22.25	20.76	4.07	16.69	30.29	5.35	24.94
1944	29.03	5.23	23.80	22.03	4.33	17.70	32.43	5.67	26.76
Mean	**23.49**	**3.41**	**20.08**	**15.92**	**2.59**	**13.33**	**27.23**	**3.82**	**23.41**
Percentage Difference t_2–t_1	**23.58**	**144.91**	**11.44**	**90.24**	**214.83**	**73.46**	**10.11**	**125.28**	**–0.65**
1946	30.88	5.54	25.34	23.29	4.58	18.71	34.56	6.00	28.56
1948	32.74	5.84	26.90	24.55	4.84	19.71	36.70	6.32	30.38
1950	34.59	6.14	28.45	25.82	5.10	20.72	38.84	6.65	32.19
1952	34.95	6.25	28.70	27.43	5.40	22.03	38.40	6.64	31.76
1954	36.68	6.60	30.08	29.03	5.69	23.34	40.17	7.01	33.16
1956	38.40	6.95	31.45	30.64	5.99	24.65	41.94	7.39	34.55
1958	40.12	7.30	32.82	32.25	6.29	25.96	43.72	7.76	35.96
1960	41.84	7.65	34.19	33.86	6.59	27.27	45.49	8.14	37.35
1962	44.10	8.26	35.84	35.88	7.10	28.78	47.86	8.79	39.07
1964	46.36	8.87	37.49	37.91	7.62	30.29	50.23	9.44	40.79
1966	48.63	9.48	39.15	39.93	8.13	31.80	52.60	10.09	42.51
1968	50.89	10.09	40.80	41.96	8.65	33.31	54.97	10.75	44.22
1970	53.15	10.70	42.45	43.98	9.16	34.82	57.34	11.40	45.94
1972	56.01	11.82	44.19	46.98	10.14	36.84	60.14	12.59	47.55
Mean	**42.10**	**7.96**	**34.14**	**33.82**	**6.81**	**27.01**	**45.93**	**8.50**	**37.43**
Percentage Difference t_2–t_1	**81.37**	**113.51**	**74.35**	**101.69**	**121.18**	**96.92**	**74.00**	**109.89**	**66.46**

Table 5.8 **(Continued)**

Year	*Nation*			*South*			*Non-South*		
	High School	*College*	*Difference*	*High School*	*College*	*Difference*	*High School*	*College*	*Difference*
1974	58.87	12.94	45.93	49.97	11.12	38.85	62.94	13.78	49.16
1976	61.74	14.07	47.67	52.97	12.10	40.87	65.75	14.97	50.78
1978	64.60	15.19	49.41	55.96	13.07	42.89	68.55	16.16	52.39
1980	67.46	16.32	51.14	58.96	14.05	44.91	71.35	17.35	54.00
1982	69.21	17.06	52.15	61.18	14.74	46.44	72.89	18.11	54.78
1984	70.97	17.80	53.17	63.41	15.44	47.97	74.42	18.88	55.54
1986	72.72	18.54	54.18	65.63	16.13	49.50	75.96	19.64	56.32
1988	74.47	19.28	55.19	67.86	16.82	51.04	77.49	20.41	57.08
1990	76.22	20.02	56.20	70.08	17.51	52.57	79.03	21.17	57.86
Mean	**67.23**	**16.30**	**50.93**	**59.30**	**14.11**	**45.19**	**70.85**	**17.31**	**53.54**
Percentage Difference t_2–t_1	**29.47**	**54.68**	**22.36**	**40.24**	**57.52**	**35.30**	**25.56**	**53.63**	**17.69**
1992	78.42	21.09	57.33	72.72	18.49	54.23	81.02	22.27	58.75
1994	78.86	21.30	57.56	73.25	18.68	54.57	81.42	22.50	58.93
1996	82.81	23.21	59.60	77.99	20.43	57.56	85.01	24.49	60.52
1998	83.96	24.02	59.95	79.86	21.58	58.28	85.84	25.13	60.71
2000	81.87	24.07	57.80	77.46	21.15	56.31	83.89	25.41	58.48
2002	85.52	26.36	59.16	81.83	24.06	57.77	87.21	27.41	59.80
2004	85.26	26.68	58.58	81.43	23.61	57.82	87.01	28.09	58.92
2006	85.47	26.81	58.66	81.85	27.53	54.32	87.12	26.49	60.63
2008	86.58	27.44	59.14	83.31	28.08	55.23	88.08	27.15	60.93
2010	86.90	27.60	59.30	83.68	24.37	59.31	88.34	29.06	59.28
2012	89.34	31.43	57.91	87.11	27.44	59.67	90.36	33.25	57.11
Mean	**84.09**	**25.46**	**58.63**	**80.04**	**23.22**	**56.82**	**85.94**	**26.48**	**59.46**
Percentage Difference t_2–t_1	**13.93**	**49.06**	**1.01**	**19.78**	**48.46**	**10.01**	**11.53**	**49.29**	**–2.79**

Source: Compiled from the American State Election Data Set as taken from successive volumes of the *Statistical Abstract of the United States*.

differences between the South and the Non-South on three measures: annual per capita income, households with radios, and people who graduated from high school.

Economically, the boom and bust of the 1920s were less pronounced in the South than in the Non-South, because the South's far more agrarian, rural,

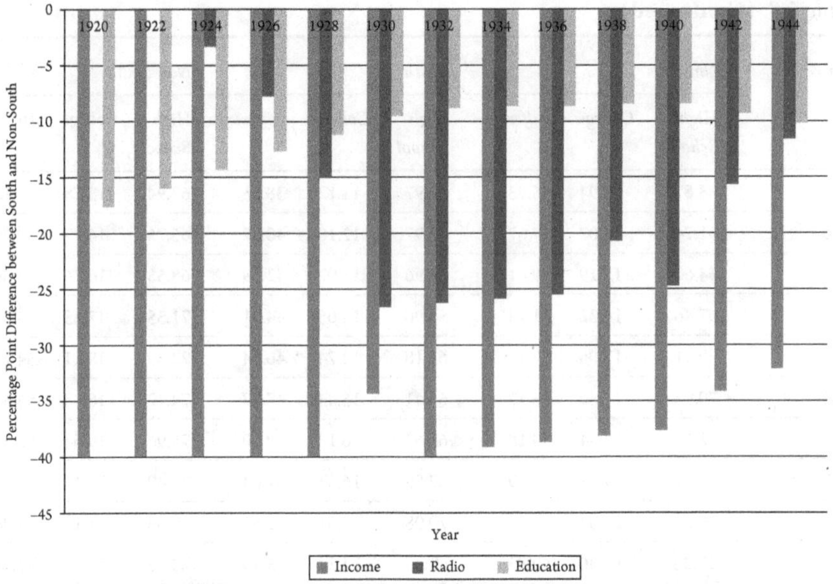

Figure 5.1 Regional Differences in Income, Radio, and Education, 1920–1944

and poor economy had much less to gain and, therefore, less to lose. Figure 5.1 shows the far smaller mean income among southerners than among northerners. During the recession after World War I between 1920 and 1924, per capita personal income declined by 14 percent in the Non-South, but only 6 percent in the South. As the Roaring 20s took hold between the 1924 and 1928 elections, per capita personal income grew by 40 percent in the Non-South, but only by 30 percent in the South. Then, when the crash occurred it did so more harshly in the Non-South, with a 15 percent decline in per capital income until World War II but only a ten percent drop in the South.

Technologically, the South was also a much less connected region, both within state boundaries and to a national outlook. In 1920 the South had only 66 telephones per 1000 in population, while the non-South had more than double that—131 phones per 1,000. Even by 1944, southerners had less than 100 telephones per 1,000 in population while those in the rest of the country had 175 phones per 1,000.[39] As seen in Figure 5.1, southern households consistently lagged behind non-southern households in having radios: even as late as 1944, southern households had 12 percentage points fewer radios. The figure also shows the education gap between the South and the non-South. Fewer

[39] *Statistical Abstract of the United States, 1946,* telephone data found at http://www2.census.gov/prod2/statcomp/documents/1946-07.pdf.

southerners attained high school diplomas than non-southerners—a gap of 11 percentage points across the period.

It is also important to recognize that despite the isolation from the national campaign context, the South was not totally removed from national politics. As shown in Table 5.1, during key elections in 1930, 1942, and 1944 the South actually had stronger national effects than the non-South. The pivotal economic and international conditions that dominated these elections seemingly affected the South more intensely than the rest of the country.

State Laws

Throughout American history, states actively legislated who should be allowed to vote. Some states sought to entice people westward with alien voting laws that immediately offered immigrants the right to vote before achieving US citizenship. Other states sought to directly restrict the franchise through poll taxes and literacy tests. Although literacy tests are almost always associated with the South, all told 20 states—seven states in the South and 13 states outside the South—had some form of literacy test until they were struck down in the 1965 Voting Rights Act.[40] Writing about the benefits of the literacy test, the *New Orleans Daily Picayune* suggested in an editorial that it was a good idea to exclude "every unworthy white man and every unworthy Negro" from the franchise.[41] Outside of the South, some states passed literacy laws that reflected anti-immigrant sentiment while others adopted them as progressive reforms that demanded voters be informed and responsible. Surely people who were illiterate could be neither.

As seen in Table 5.9, all states except New Hampshire adopted residency requirements, ranging from three months to two years, which remained in force until the Voting Rights Act of 1970 that restricted residency requirements to no longer than 30 days for presidential elections.[42] Many residency requirements were just one part of a combination of requirements at the state, county, and city or even precinct level. In a typical case, to be an eligible voter an individual needed to reside in a state for a year, but then also reside in a

[40] Literacy tests were found in seven confederate states (Alabama, Georgia, Louisiana, Mississippi, North Carolina, South Carolina, and Virginia) and thirteen northern states (Alaska, Arizona, California, Connecticut, Delaware, Hawaii, Maine, Massachusetts, New Hampshire, New York, Oregon, Washington, and Wyoming). The Voting Rights Act of 1965 banned these tests.

[41] Kousser, 1974, 70; see also Rusk and Stucker, 1978.

[42] In 1972, the Supreme Court applied the new standard to other elections in a Supreme Court decision *Dunn v. Blumstein*.

Table 5.9 **State Residency Requirements for Voting, 1920–1970**

State	*Number of Months*
Alabama	24
Alaska	12
Arizona	12
Arkansas	12
California	12
Colorado	12
Connecticut	12
Delaware	12
Florida	12
Georgia	12
Hawaii	12
Idaho	6
Illinois	6
Indiana	12
Iowa	6
Kansas	6
Kentucky	24
Louisiana	24[a]
Maine	3[b]
Maryland	12
Massachusetts	12
Michigan	6
Minnesota	6
Mississippi	24[c]
Missouri	12
Montana	12
Nebraska	6
Nevada	6
New Hampshire	0
New Jersey	12[d]
New Mexico	12
New York	12

Table 5.9 **(Continued)**

State	*Number of Months*
North Carolina	24
North Dakota	12
Ohio	12
Oklahoma	12[e]
Oregon	6
Pennsylvania	12
Rhode Island	24[f]
South Carolina	24[g]
South Dakota	6
Tennessee	12
Texas	12
Utah	12
Vermont	12
Virginia	24
Washington	12
West Virginia	12
Wisconsin	12
Wyoming	12

Source: Jerrold G. Rusk, A Statistical History of the American Electorate (Washington, D.C.: CQ Press, 2001), 26.

[a]Reduced to 12 months in 1960.
[b]Increased to 6 months in 1935.
[c]Reduced to 12 months in 1968.
[d]Reduced to 6 months in 1957.
[e]Reduced to 6 months in 1964.
[f]Reduced to 12 months in 1952.
[g]Reduced to 12 months in 1963.

county for at least six months and then in a city in that county for a similar length of time.[43]

Tables 5.3 and 5.4 reveal that state residency laws influence nonvoting only sporadically throughout the period, specifically in 1926, 1928, 1936, and 1942. In 1926, 1928, and 1942, a one-unit shift in the stringency of the residency

[43] Rusk, 2001, 26–30.

requirement prompts a one percentage point increase in nonvoting. In 1936, residency laws actually decrease nonvoting by a similar amount. But in general, state laws are less consistent in their influence than the national campaign context or party competition.[44] State residency requirements did not keep as many people away from the polls as some states might have preferred. This is true even in the South. We tested a simple two-variable model of nonvoting with state residency and prior nonvoting as the independent variables. Only in 1930 does state residency have a statistically significant effect on nonvoting in the South, but, ironically, the effect is negative.[45] These results help clarify Springer's findings about the impact of residency requirements on turnout.[46] Considering the period from 1920 through 2000 as a whole, she observes that residency requirements influence voting in the South in presidential election years but not in non-presidential election years. Our examination of individual election years reveals that the effects of these state requirements are muted in the elections of this first period.

In contrast to the sporadic effects of state residency requirements on nonvoting, there is little doubt that past levels of nonvoting in a state strongly predict current levels of nonvoting. As seen in Tables 5.3 and 5.4, prior nonvoting has a sizable impact on current nonvoting. This indicates the limits to the effects of the national campaign context on nonvoting. In a given year, the number of people who do not vote is directly related to the number of people who have not voted in the past. This political inertia is present even as nonvoting rates declined during the period.

American Political Periods Revisited

It might seem that a period encompassing the 1920s, 1930s, and 1940s is only in the loosest sense a single political period. But in fact in four ways these decades were closely linked. First, the sheer extent of the uncertainty that defined these years was extraordinary. Bookmarked by the ends of two world wars, these were years when the unthinkable was commonplace. The integrity of the period as an identifiable block of time rests on uncertainty measured across economic, technological, legal, and international elements of the national campaign context. Economically, no years before or since had seen an economic downturn of such

[44] See also Jason Mycoff, Michael Wagner, and David Wilson, "The Empirical Effects of Voter-ID Laws: Present or Absent," *PS: Political Science and Politics* 42 (January 2009): 121–126.

[45] The absence of this effect is also likely due to the fact that these laws were designed to target smaller sub-populations in a state, while the dependent variable in the study is nonvoting for the entire state.

[46] Springer, 2014, 97–112.

depth and length. It was not only that the risk of collapse encircled the investment strategies of the 1920s, but the risk of permanently high unemployment and inadequate living standards jeopardized Americans' ways of life in the 1930s. Technologically, radio was strikingly novel both as an innovation and in its popularity as an everyday feature of American households. As World War I ended, no one would have dreamed that just a decade later listening to nationwide political broadcasts and evening entertainment shows would define a new family activity around the radio. And the communication device had nothing whatever in common with the newspaper. Legally, uncertainty enveloped women obtaining the right to vote, when just years before the idea had been considered laughable and out of the question. Overnight the size of the eligible electorate doubled and women began to go to the polls, if slowly. Internationally, the lack of success in mobilizing a structure for peace after World War I combined with global economic upheaval to produce a highly uncertain world setting which America never left, despite desires in some corners for isolation and inward-looking approaches. World War II was an amalgam of incalculable novelty and risk, as German troops made their way through the streets of Paris, Japan attacked Pearl Harbor, and American nuclear bombs decimated Hiroshima and Nagasaki.

Second, this high degree of uncertainty brought people to the polls; it did not keep them from the polls. Perhaps the most telling evidence of this is that nonvoting did not increase in the elections held during the Depression when many Americans lost income and jobs and worried about their family finances. Significant personal obstacles to voting did not prevent voting.

Third, regionalism was a defining feature of the period. During these three decades, the South was notably more isolated from the rest of the country than it ever was again. It was not only its distinctiveness as an area dominated by the Democratic Party but also its slower economic growth, more limited reach of communication technology, and aggressive restrictions on voting rights that defined barriers between the South and the non-South.

Fourth, even with this regionalism, the pace of nationalism in American politics accelerated. The excesses of capitalism in the 1920s led to a wholly new role for the national government in creating stability in the economy through federal regulations and social welfare programs. This also created a new set of issues around which elections were fought. The new role of the national government in domestic affairs was combined with an enlarged profile for the national government in international affairs, as America shed its isolationist profile. Radio made American politics more inclusive as people knotted around the radio to hear news reports, presidential speeches, and party broadcasts, all at the same time as a single audience. Nothing more compressed the geographic breadth of the country.

The novelty and risk in these four dimensions changed with the end of World War II. Radio was no longer novel but instead, by 1947, television sets began to be found in a few American living rooms. Women routinely voted, and much more attention was emerging about African-American voting rights, partly because of their pivotal fighting role in the war. Economic growth replaced economic upheaval. An us-versus-them game between the United States and the Soviet Union replaced international cataclysm. Republican candidates began to conduct credible campaigns in the South. As this second post-war period emerged, nonvoting responded to these changes in the uncertainty in the national campaign context.

6

The Post-War Period: 1946–1972

The uncertainty after World War II was distinct from that before and during the war. While the uncertainty might have been less intense because the war was won, it was a complicated victory achieved at the cost of 60 million dead and, ultimately, through the use of a weapon that people feared should never be used again as they rushed to build more. The victors carved up territory in ways that could not have been envisioned when the original declarations of war went out in 1938. Poland—the initial impetus for French and English declarations of war on Germany—was now, despite English attempts to secure free Polish elections, given to the Soviet Union in the partition of land. As Harry Truman wrote in his notes at the Potsdam Conference among Great Britain, the Soviet Union, and the United States in July 1945, "Russia helped herself to a slice of Poland . . ."[1] If the uncertainty after the war was less intense, it was not absent, and the risks and novelty of decisions and circumstances in the post-war period were manifest.

The uncertainty of the post-war context was defined by a series of interrelated transitions from a government defined by Roosevelt to one without him, from a wartime economy to a peacetime economy, and from a world where the United States had reluctantly engaged in international interventions to one where it was an unabashed world power. The combined effect of Roosevelt's death and the end of the war within months of each other put a full stop to the first period. The novelty of this breakpoint cannot be underestimated. For seven election cycles, Roosevelt had either been on the ballot or worked to elect New Deal Democrats in midterm races. This was now over.

Much like the 1920 elections, the 1946 elections were caught in the dismantling of a wartime economy, with numerous labor strikes and many seeking work. But unlike the 1920 election, the shift to a peacetime economy was not as disruptive as it had been at the end of World War I. Strikes against auto,

[1] "Notes by Harry S. Truman on the Potsdam Conference, July 15, 1945, President's Secretary File, Truman Papers, Harry S. Truman Library, found at http://www.trumanlibrary.org/whistlestop/study_collections/bomb/large/documents/pdfs/63.pdf#zoom=100.

coal, rail, steel, power, sugar, and tobacco were numerous and long in 1946, but they lessened thereafter, whether because of the Taft-Hartley Act of 1947, which restricted strikes, or the general improvement of the economy. Unemployment, a negligible 1.2 percent at the time of the 1944 election, rose to 3.9 percent in 1946 but hardly surged. Average unemployment during the period was 4.7 percent. Only once, in 1958, did unemployment rise above 5.5 percent, when it hit 6.8 percent. Indeed, unemployment was lower during this post-war era than during any of the other three time periods. And except for a slowdown in 1948, personal income rose throughout the period.

But despite the good times, many people still had vivid memories of the Depression and were uncertain how long this prosperity would last. Throughout the late 1940s and 1950s, public opinion polls showed considerable concern among Americans that another depression was likely.

- In January 1946, 56 percent of respondents to a Roper Poll believed that a new depression was likely in the next year or so.
- In May 1947, a Gallup poll found that 52 percent of Americans said another depression was likely in the next 10 years.
- In June 1949, a *Foreign Affairs* poll observed that 41 percent of Americans thought there would be a depression within two years.
- In April 1953, 33 percent of respondents to a Gallup Poll felt that a depression was likely within the next two years if the Korean War ended.
- In March 1958, a Gallup Poll found that 32 percent of Americans felt the economic slowdown then was a depression.[2]

After World War I, there was ambiguity in the international setting about what the war had settled. After World War II, there was considerable clarity about a new role for the United States in what Henry Luce, editor of *Life* magazine, had coined "The American Century." [3] Writing prophetically before the war began, Luce claimed that the opportunity and the challenge for America was to "accept wholeheartedly our duty and our opportunity as the most powerful and vital nation in the world and in consequence to exert upon the world the full impact of our influence, for such purposes as we see fit and by such means as we see fit."[4] This new role was matched by an increasingly aggressive posture of the Soviet Union in expanding its sphere of influence. In preparation for the Potsdam Conference, Winston Churchill sent a telegram to Harry Truman

[2] Query using the key word "depression" from the I-Poll, Roper Center for Public Opinion Research Archives, found at http://www.ropercenter.uconn.edu.

[3] Henry Luce, "The American Century," *Life*, February 17, 1941, 61–65.

[4] Luce, 1941, 63.

on May 12, 1945 describing "'[an] iron curtain' drawn down upon their front. We do not know what is going on behind."[5] This was a confrontational world, within which the United States, as one emerging superpower, controlled and was controlled by the other, the Soviet Union. Truman, writing in his diary at the Potsdam Conference on July 17, 1945, sized up his first (and by his own later admission, naïve) impression of Soviet leader Joseph Stalin: "I can deal with Stalin. He is honest but smart as hell."[6] Truman later wrote that he was "an innocent idealist" in his early dealings with Stalin.[7]

Post-War National Influence on Nonvoting

In five ways, these and other factors made the post-war period decidedly different than the previous period in terms of the relative influence of national and state factors on nonvoting. First, as referenced in Table 5.1, in eight of the 14 elections during the post-war era, national factors have large, significant, negative effects on nonvoting for the country as a whole. These effects are present for both presidential and midterm elections and exceed those found in the first period when national factors significantly decreased nonvoting in just five of the 13 elections. Moreover, as revealed in Table 5.2, mean net national effects are over four times greater in the second period than in the first, tallying 46 percentage points in the second period compared with 10 percentage points in the first period.[8] These large national effects help account for declining nonvoting rates during the period (discussed in greater detail in Chapter 2). From the first to the second period, nonvoting rates in presidential elections declined by 10 percentage points for the country as a whole, 11 percentage points in the South, and 2 percentage points in the non-South. In addition, nonvoting rates in midterm

[5] Winston Churchill, *The Second World War, Triumph and Tragedy*, Book 2 (New York: Bantam, 1962), 489. Churchill sent a second cable on June 4 reiterating the warning (Churchill, 1962, 514). Ironically, the term was used earlier by the Nazis in reference to the Soviets. In an article entitled "Das Jahr 2000" published on February 25, 1945 in *Das Reich*, the weekly Nazi newspaper, Joseph Goebbels—striking out against Stalin's intentions after the Yalta agreement among Britain, the United States, and the Soviet Union—wrote: "An iron curtain would fall over this enormous territory controlled by the Soviet Union, behind which nations would be slaughtered." German Propaganda Archive, Calvin College, found at http://www.calvin.edu/academic/cas/gpa/goeb49.htm.

[6] "Notes by Harry S. Truman on the Potsdam Conference, July 17, 1945," President's Secretary File, Truman Papers, Harry S. Truman Library, found at http://www.trumanlibrary.org/whistlestop/study_collections/bomb/large/documents/pdfs/63.pdf#zoom=100.

[7] Harry Truman, *Memoirs*, 2 volumes (New York: Doubleday, 1956), vol. 2, 21.

[8] The results are based on the net difference between national effects and state effects. A number closer to 0 means there are greater state effects.

elections posted a 5 percentage point drop across the period nationally, 7 percentage points in the South, and 5 percentage points in the non-South.

Second, as revealed in Table 5.1, while national factors decrease nonvoting throughout the period, the effects are most sizable in the 1960s. National effects that are no greater than 7 percentage points in 1952 are nearly 19 percentage points in 1966 and 13 percentage points in 1968. The 1960s were a decade with Americans transfixed on a highly uncertain national context, including the construction of the Berlin Wall, the Cuban missile crisis, space missions, the civil rights movement, assassinations, urban riots, the Vietnam War, and massive war protests.[9] These national events, then, seemingly had strong effects on decreasing nonvoting nationally and regionally. As one simple measure of this, the bivariate correlation between events and nonvoting was –.298 from 1946 through 1958 but –.806 between 1960 through 1972. The uncertainty of the 1960s was all but crammed into a short span of six years from 1962 through 1968, when many thought America had come unspooled.

Third, Table 5.1 also shows for the first time how the non-South and the South act in unison as national forces have significant effects with the same signs in both regions. During the first period, statistically significant national effects are found only sporadically in one or both regions. But in the second period, these effects occur in 10 of the 14 elections in the South and the non-South. Mean net effects are also somewhat more similar between the South and the non-South in the second period than during the first period. A 10 percentage point difference in net effects between the South and the non-South in the second period compares with a 13 percentage point difference in the first period.

Fourth, as shown in Figure 6.1, except in 1950, 1958, and 1960 no state effects of any kind are present. The distinctiveness of states, so in evidence during the 1920s and the Great Depression, was far less apparent after World War II. States were in general much more similar demographically than they were during the first period: more urban than rural, more suburban than urban, more children in school, and more families with higher incomes than just a decade before. Thus, inter-state differences diminished and national effects increased.

Finally, economic growth, television, civil rights, and American involvement in the Korean and Vietnam wars defined the post–World War II period. The robustness of the post-war economy left few on the sidelines. Communication technology continued to bring politics into American homes but now with images, not just voices, as television supplanted radio. The social fabric of the

[9] Michael Flamm and David Steigerwald, *Debating the 1960s: Liberal, Conservative, and Radical Perspectives* (New York: Rowman and Littlefield, 2007).

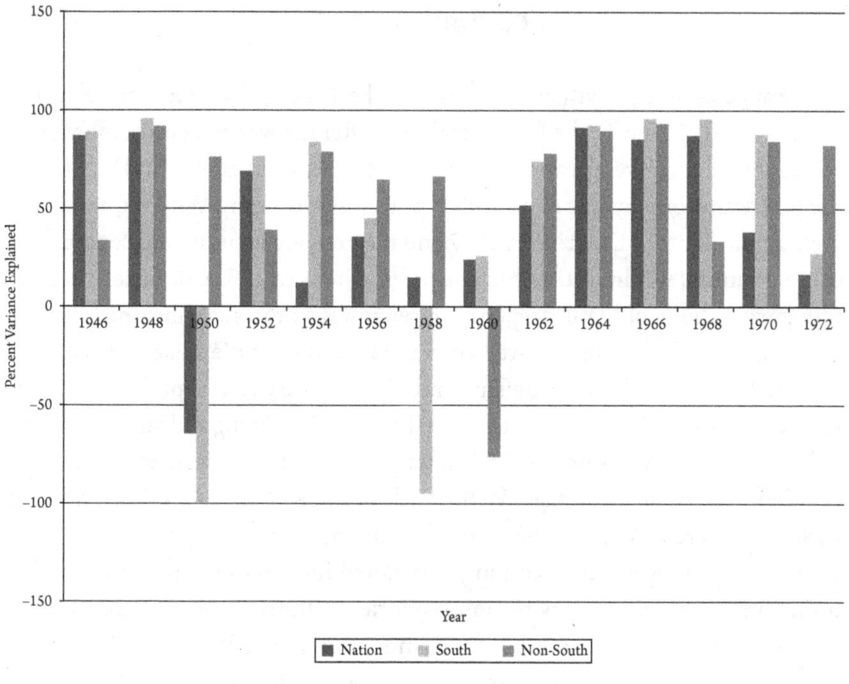

Figure 6.1 Net National and State Effects on Nonvoting, 1946–1972

country was altered along its racial axis in ways that would have seemed inconceivable prior to the war. As much as women's suffrage defined the early years of the previous era, African-American efforts at desegregation and gaining voting rights characterized the post-war period.[10] The international objective of the United States to contain communism led to a large number of high-stakes military interventions in places where the United States had not ventured before—Korea, Cuba, Vietnam, Cambodia, Laos, and the Dominican Republic. For 50 years the Soviets and the Americans never directly fought each other, but battled proxy wars under the Truman Doctrine. According to Truman, "This is nothing more than a frank recognition that totalitarian regimes imposed on free peoples, by direct or indirect aggression, undermine the foundations of international peace and, hence, the security of the United States."[11] Successive presidents saw little need to change the text.

[10] We use the number of eligible African-American voters in a state as an indicator to monitor the effect of the Voting Rights Act of 1965 on state voting. These data are taken from successive years of the *Statistical Abstract of the United States* and *Current Population Reports.*

[11] "Address to the Congress Recommending Assistance to Greece and Turkey," March 12, 1947, *Public Papers of the Presidents, Harry S. Truman, 1947.*

Economic Growth

Post-war economic growth exceeded that of the Roaring 20s and occurred over a longer period of time. In the first several years after the war, the disassembly of the war economy had several features that were not in evidence after World War I. First, the post-war economy was never truly a peacetime economy. With the announcement of the Truman Doctrine in 1947 and the growing focus on the containment of communism, war industries became defense industries. The defense infrastructure grew as the Cold War deepened. Eisenhower's protest against the "military-industrial complex" in his farewell address in 1960 did little to stop its advance. A pivotal government goal of defense and a key industry goal of profit were joined for the long term, not just for a war effort that had a beginning and an end.[12]

Second, in the years immediately after the war the American economy had a decided worldwide advantage. With much of the rest of the world devastated, with food scarce, houses gone, and governments not functioning, it was little wonder that the American economy accounted for half of the world's manufacturing and 40 percent of its income. American efforts to help rebuild Europe with $13 billion in loans and products under the Marshall Plan heightened the advantage, aiding US manufacturing industries, energy companies, and agriculture over the four years of the plan from 1947 through 1951.[13] Although many Americans may have felt that post-war economic growth was justly a part of Luce's American Century, it was in no small measure due to the wreckage left by the war everywhere else.

Third, consumerism expanded at a pace faster than that seen in the 1920s. During this period, automobile purchases increased some 80 percent in just three years from 1952 to 1955; home construction increased by over 40 percent over the same years; and, to outfit these homes, Americans purchased an array of electric appliances that no one had previously owned. People bought newly devised electric kitchen appliances including blenders, dishwashers, skillets, and automatic coffee makers that began hitting the market in 1950.[14]

And, lastly, the boom continued. While the 1920s saw only five years of unfettered prosperity, the 1950s and 1960s were two decades of such growth as personal income nearly doubled from the beginning to the end of the era. With the

[12] James Ledbetter, *Unwarranted Influence: Dwight Eisenhower and the Military-Industrial Complex* (New Haven: Yale University Press, 2011).

[13] Michael Hogan, *The Marshall Plan: America, Britain, and the Reconstruction of Western Europe, 1947–1952* (Cambridge: Cambridge University Press, 1987).

[14] *Statistical Abstract of the United States*, various years: Value of New Construction Put in Place, 1929–1959; Motor-Vehicle Factory Sales and Registrations, Manufacturers' Sales of Home Appliances, 1940 to 1959; found at http://www.census.gov/prod/www/abs/statab1951-1994.htm.

exception of the 1958 recession, the economy moved forward consistently with low unemployment and steady income growth.

The theory of uncertainty in the national campaign context suggests that this upside uncertainty about how long the prosperity will last is a key feature of the national campaign context: as people see growth increasing, they participate to protect the growth. Table 6.1 examines the effects of this uncertainty associated with economic change relative to other elements of the national campaign context—youth, education, party competition, state residency requirements, and prior nonvoting on nonvoting in individual elections from 1946 through 1958—while Table 6.2 considers these effects from 1960 through 1972. The tables show that income change decreases nonvoting in eight of the 14 elections. For presidential elections, the effect of income change on nonvoting is present in all years except 1948 and 1972. Income has its greatest impact in 1952 and 1964, when mean personal income change decreases nonvoting by 20 percentage points and 18 percentage points, respectively (see the last column of data entries labeled "Impact"). The effect of income change on nonvoting is more muted in midterm elections. There are no effects in four midterms—1946, 1950, 1954, and 1966. Income change has its greatest impact in the 1958 and 1962 midterm elections, when mean personal income change prompts a decline in nonvoting of 25 percentage points and 24 percentage points, respectively. In general, income growth diminishes nonvoting in the post-war era, just as it did during the Roaring 20s and the war years.

The influence of unemployment change on nonvoting is substantially less than the effect of income change. Unemployment change decreases nonvoting in just two of the seven presidential elections—1968 and 1972. Its impact is far less than that of income change. Unemployment has no impact on midterm elections. Since unemployment was low and stable during these years, changing less than .3 percent across the period and with little inter-state variation, unemployment contributed little to the uncertainty in the national campaign context and had correspondingly little effect on participation.

Television Images

Like the pivotal use of radio in the 1928 election, television defined the 1952 presidential election. The medium was barely used in the 1948 campaign when only 2 percent of households owned sets. Both the Truman and Dewey campaigns relied on short news-reel campaign films that were shown in movie theaters in the final weeks of the campaign.[15] Four years later, television became

[15] David McCullough, *Truman* (New York: Simon and Schuster, 1992), 684.

Table 6.1 **Effects of the National Campaign Context on Nonvoting, 1946–1958**

Predictor	*1946*				*1948*				*1950*				*1952*			
	Coefficient	*t-value*	*Mean*	*Impact*	*Coefficient*	*t-value*	*Mean*	*Impact*	*Coefficient*	*t-value*	*Mean*	*Impact*	*Coefficient*	*t-value*	*Mean*	*Impact*
Income Change	−0.012	−1.245	291.451	−3.497	−0.020	−1.506	244.776	−4.896	−0.001	−0.063	250.837	−0.251	−0.053	−1.719	377.118	−19.987
Unemployment Change	−6.721	−1.649	0.790	−5.310	−1.401	−1.399	2.549	−3.571	−0.064	−0.108	0.531	−0.034	−0.321	−0.307	1.890	−0.607
Communication Technology	−0.151	−0.823	88.573	−13.375	0.057	0.276	91.606	5.222	−0.081	−0.241	94.640	−7.666	−0.160	−1.662	22.927	−3.668
African Americans	−0.0002	−0.334	167891	−33.578	0.0001	2.802	173155	17.316	0.0001	1.850	178418	17.842	0.0006	1.056	183682	110.209
International Involvement									−0.001	−0.024	444.507	−0.445	0.023	1.080	46.547	1.071
Competition	−0.127	−3.140	70.333	−8.932	−0.001	−0.010	83.879	−0.084	0.005	0.092	71.708	0.359	−0.130	−2.531	83.050	−10.797
Youth	0.184	0.335	13.743	2.529	−0.220	−0.488	12.706	−2.795	0.598	0.879	12.363	7.393	0.721	1.556	11.972	8.632
Education	0.150	0.922	25.168	3.775	0.002	0.015	26.723	0.053	−0.150	−0.827	28.279	−4.242	−0.191	−1.435	28.704	−5.482
State Residency	0.030	0.047	0.271	0.008	−0.352	−0.749	0.271	−0.095	0.873	1.297	0.271	0.236	0.091	0.183	0.271	0.025
Prior Nonvoting	0.778	9.779	64.552	50.221	0.721	11.428	38.437	27.713	0.809	8.460	60.264	48.753	0.669	12.912	47.193	31.572
Intercept	28.014	1.176			24.639	0.979			10.694	0.280			11.331	1.225		
N	48				48				48				48			
R^2	0.953				0.971				0.946				0.966			
Adjusted R^2	0.942				0.964				0.932				0.957			
Durbin h-statistic	1.544				1.255				1.053				0.635			

Predictor	*1954*				*1956*				*1958*			
	Coefficient	*t-value*	*Mean*	*Impact*	*Coefficient*	*t-value*	*Mean*	*Impact*	*Coefficient*	*t-value*	*Mean*	*Impact*
Income Change	−0.025	−1.486	262.333	−6.558	−0.027	−2.286	200.059	−5.402	−0.088	−2.388	282.765	−24.883
Unemployment Change	−12.747	−1.014	0.163	−2.078	−0.459	−1.252	1.625	−0.746	−0.534	−1.115	0.646	−0.345
Communication Technology	−0.193	−1.644	38.491	−7.429	−0.288	−2.919	54.030	−15.561	−0.390	−2.150	69.771	−27.211
African Americans	0.0001	2.552	188945	18.895	0.0005	2.131	194208	97.104	0.0003	0.695	199463	59.839
International Involvement												
Competition	−0.044	−1.168	75.067	−3.303	−0.053	−1.274	81.004	−4.293	−0.111	−2.477	74.443	−8.263
Youth	0.203	0.406	11.526	2.340	1.330	3.774	11.101	14.764	0.331	0.562	10.735	3.553
Education	−0.025	−0.181	30.533	−0.763	−0.031	−0.473	42.972	−1.332	−0.306	−1.914	32.997	−10.097
State Residency	0.300	0.531	0.271	0.081	0.311	0.872	0.271	0.084	−0.409	−0.706	0.277	−0.113
Prior Nonvoting	0.727	10.591	60.264	43.812	0.749	15.363	36.500	27.338	0.686	9.160	55.198	37.866
Intercept	22.189	2.559			22.886	16.676			46.300	2.629		
N	48				48				48			
R^2	0.961				0.979				0.960			
Adjusted R^2	0.952				0.974				0.950			
Durbin h-statistic	0.540				0.251				0.454			

Note: Critical t-values are 1.679 at .10 probability; 2.009 at .05; 2.700 at .01. Critical value for Durbin h-statistic at .05 probability = 1.695.

Table 6.2 **Effects of the National Campaign Context on Nonvoting, 1960–1972**

Predictor	*1960*				*1962*				*1964*				*1966*[a]			
	Coefficient	*t-value*	*Mean*	*Impact*	*Coefficient*	*t-value*	*Mean*	*Impact*	*Coefficient*	*t-value*	*Mean*	*Impact*	*Coefficient*	*t-value*	*Mean*	*Impact*
Income Change	−0.051	−1.944	126.156	−6.434	−0.053	−3.377	455.889	−24.162	−0.028	−2.408	652.912	−18.282	0.011	1.199	654.049	7.195
Unemployment Change	−0.031	−0.374	0.828	−0.026	0.167	0.387	0.033	0.006	−0.246	−0.261	0.010	−0.002	0.103	0.129	1.465	0.151
Communication Technology	−0.281	−2.991	84.490	−23.742	−0.197	−1.078	87.309	−17.200	0.057	0.219	88.616	5.051	−0.110	−0.610	90.794	−9.987
African Americans	0.0002	3.022	196706	39.341	0.0007	2.178	212667	148.867	0.0007	2.224	210988	147.691	−0.0008	−1.717	218882	−175.106
International Involvement													0.073	1.676	126.358	9.224
Competition	−0.048	−2.147	91.280	−4.381	−0.119	−3.109	81.660	−9.717	−0.010	−0.270	74.724	−0.747	−0.042	−0.935	83.024	−3.487
Youth	0.234	1.239	15.423	3.609	0.558	1.247	11.264	6.285	−0.906	−2.280	12.260	−11.108	−0.0002	−1.164	283232	−56.646
Education	−0.337	−2.935	34.204	−11.527	−0.176	−1.775	42.609	−7.499	−0.302	−2.098	37.544	−11.338	−0.318	−1.896	39.411	−12.533
State Residency	−0.401	−1.104	0.260	−0.104	0.702	1.405	0.277	0.194	1.239	1.964	0.260	0.322	−0.396	−0.607	0.265	−0.105
Prior Nonvoting	0.910	16.906	41.043	37.349	0.762	11.847	55.198	42.061	0.518	6.709	41.043	21.260	0.628	7.451	51.616	32.415
Intercept	11.839	1.520			15.556	0.956			49.272	2.112			37.361	1.801		
N	50				50				51				50			
R^2	0.983				0.954				0.873				0.890			
Adjusted R^2	0.979				0.946				0.844				0.861			
Durbin h-statistic	0.289				1.071				0.813				1.231			

Predictor	*1968*				*1970*				*1972*			
	Coefficient	*t-value*	*Mean*	*Impact*	*Coefficient*	*t-value*	*Mean*	*Impact*	*Coefficient*	*t-value*	*Mean*	*Impact*
Income Change	−0.017	−2.252	652.912	−11.100	−0.017	−1.718	653.125	−11.103	−0.005	−1.032	1416.832	−7.084
Unemployment Change	−1.501	−1.969	1.196	−1.795	−0.061	−0.076	1.058	−0.065	−0.560	−1.677	1.555	−0.871
Communication Technology	−0.193	−1.024	92.743	−17.899	−0.608	−1.892	94.856	−57.673	0.916	1.063	96.702	88.579
African Americans	−0.0002	−2.621	225269	−45.054	−0.0001	−1.957	227448	−22.745	0.0002	0.212	246052	49.210
International Involvement	0.001	0.518	343.198	0.343	0.023	1.778	123.415	2.839	−0.002	−0.034	12.626	−0.025
Competition	−0.135	−1.791	87.984	−11.878	−0.076	−1.990	79.633	−6.052	−0.104	−2.472	71.592	−7.446
Youth	−0.038	−0.193	13.491	−0.513	−0.546	−1.386	12.950	−7.071	0.160	0.880	17.890	2.862
Education	−0.116	−1.091	40.884	−4.743	−0.504	−3.005	42.754	−21.548	−0.163	−1.772	44.318	−7.224
State Residency	1.065	2.594	0.260	0.277								
Prior Nonvoting	0.644	8.809	36.305	23.380	0.512	6.454	51.211	26.220	0.924	13.809	36.855	34.054
Intercept	13.513	0.678			16.986	2.921			17.117	2.562		
N	51				50				51			
R^2	0.899				0.856				0.940			
Adjusted R^2	0.873				0.822				0.927			
Durbin h-statistic	1.487				0.985				0.112			

Note: Critical t-values are 1.679 at .10 probability; 2.009 at .05; 2.700 at .01. Critical value for Durbin h-statistic at .05 probability = 1.695.

[a]Total youth in the state population, rather than percent youth in the state population, used to estimate the model. See note 34.

the centerpiece of presidential campaign strategy. Across American households, 23 percent owned a television and countless more routinely visited friends who had one. As Murray Edelman asserted, "The television screen presenting a live performance creates not close contact but a semblance of close contact, and the distinction is crucial . . . instead of a channel of information, we have an instrument for influencing opinion and response."[16]

In 1952, both the Eisenhower and the Stevenson campaigns recognized television as that instrument for influence, but were uncertain how best to use the latest novel medium of political communication. The Republicans mastered it more effectively than did the Democrats by hiring the first-ever media consultants. Eisenhower worked on his television performances with actor Robert Montgomery, who showed the general how to look into a camera and appear natural. The campaign also enlisted Madison Avenue advertising executive Rosser Reeves, who had created commercials for M&M candies—"they melt in your mouth, not in your hand." Through Reeves, the campaign unveiled the first television political commercials with a catchy jingle "You like Ike, I like Ike, Everybody likes Ike for President." The Democrats countered with their own near-carbon-copy commercial "I love the Guv" for their nominee Illinois Governor Adlai Stevenson. But the Democrats' primary approach to television consisted of 30-minute shows that aired on Tuesday and Thursday nights from 10:00–10:30 pm. Their goal was to capitalize on Stevenson's oratorical abilities, but instead, the lateness of the time slot drew small, already committed audiences. Eisenhower, by contrast, presented short 20-second spots that were placed before and after popular TV programs such as *I Love Lucy*. The commercials were cheaper and attracted more viewers than the longer, stand-alone shows. The candidate was treated like a sellable product for the first time.[17] Although Stevenson complained that "The idea that you can merchandise candidates for high office like breakfast cereal is the ultimate indignity to the democratic process," the idea worked, and no campaign after 1952 could afford other thoughts.[18]

The theory of uncertainty in the national campaign context indicates that the introduction of television, like radio, presents a novel, live source of political information that makes politics relatively unavoidable. The uncertainty created by this technology shock reduces nonvoting. Tables 6.1 and 6.2 display the effect of the technology shock of television on electoral politics. In the elections of 1946, 1948,

[16] Murray Edelman, *The Symbolic Uses of Politics* (Urbana, IL: University of Illinois Press, 1964), 101.

[17] http://www.livingroomcandidate.org/commercials/1952.

[18] Background material and Stevenson quotation, "Introduction," *The Living Room Candidate Presidential Campaign Commercials, 1952–2016*, Museum of the Moving Image, found at http://www.livingroomcandidate.org/.

and 1950, radio has no effect on nonvoting. During these elections the technology had reached a saturation point as virtually all households in all states owned radios, and campaign techniques to reach these households were well established. In contrast, beginning in 1952 and continuing through 1960, television significantly decreases nonvoting with successively larger effects. Television has its largest impact in 1960 when mean household television use prompts a decline in nonvoting of 24 percentage points. Undoubtedly, the introduction of the televised debates between John Kennedy and Richard Nixon made television a catalyst for electoral interest. Except in 1970 there is no effect of television on nonvoting from 1962 through 1972, as the percentage of households owning televisions reaches saturation levels—87 percent of households in 1962 and 97 percent of households in 1972.[19] So, the saturation of television marked low uncertainty in the national campaign context. This is not to suggest, however, that all campaign strategies related to television had been exhausted. Efforts to package candidates and negative campaign commercials evolved in ever more sophisticated ways.[20] Overall, though, the pattern for television is similar to that for radio observed in Chapter 5: when the medium is novel, its effect on dampening nonvoting is substantial; when it reaches a saturation point, its electoral effect is gone.

The Civil Rights Movement

During the post-war period, legal-institutional change as an indicator of uncertainty in the national campaign context was captured in the civil rights movement. While the movement's impact extended far beyond electoral participation, the passage of the Civil Rights Act of 1964 and the Voting Rights Act of 1965 had a large effect on voting. It is hard to imagine an amendment to the Constitution with less effect than the 15th Amendment from the time of its ratification in 1870 to the early 1960s. The amendment assured that "The right of citizens of the United States to vote shall not be denied or abridged by the United States or by any State on account of race, color, or previous condition of servitude." Yet, throughout the South, few if any African Americans were registered to vote because an array of literacy tests, poll taxes, and residency requirements blocked them from doing so.[21] Federal remedies were limited and

[19] There are no data available for the number of households with color televisions by state, so it is impossible to determine whether the introduction of color television had an effect on nonvoting beginning in the mid-1960s.

[20] Joe McGinnis, *Selling of the President* (New York: Penguin Books, 1969); David Mark, *Going Dirty: The Art of Negative Campaigning* (New York: Rowman and Littlefield, 2006).

[21] Jerrold G. Rusk and John Stucker, "The Effect of the Southern System of Election Laws on Voting Participation," in Joel Silbey, Allan Bogue, and William Flanigan, eds., *The History of American Voting Behavior* (Princeton: Princeton University Press, 1978), 198–250.

difficult to enforce under the existing Civil Rights Acts of 1957 and 1960 passed during the Eisenhower administration. Even though the 1957 law created a new Civil Rights Division in the Justice Department and the 1960 law provided for federal inspection of local registration rolls and penalties for obstructing someone's attempt to register or vote, the laws were structured reactively, permitting the Justice Department to enjoin injustices after they had been committed, one registrar, sheriff, and county at a time. The Civil Rights Act of 1964 toughened language against the unequal application of voter registration requirements but still offered no direct enforcement mechanisms against voter intimidation.

This meant that the problem of African-American voter registration was vast. Table 6.3 compares voter registration in southern states before and after the passage of the Voting Rights Act of 1965. The pre-passage entries are taken from the 1964 elections, with the exceptions of Arkansas (October 1963) and Georgia (December 1962). So even with the many registration efforts that began in 1961 and continued through the 1964 elections, voter registration among African Americans in the South remained very low, with Tennessee being the only state where African-American registration was similar to white registration. As one example, under Alabama law, prospective voters had to fill out a complicated form, answer a 20-page questionnaire on constitutional topics, and have a registered voter sponsor them. Little wonder that in Lowndes County Alabama in 1965, with an African-American adult population of 12,000 and a white adult population of 3,000, no African Americans were registered to vote, while three-quarters of whites were. Commented one of the members of the Board of Registrars, "I don't know of any Negro registration here, but there is a better relationship between whites and niggers here than any place I know of."[22]

These numbers only partly illuminate the depth of the problems facing African Americans in the South. Long-standing patterns of discrimination, harassment, and violence intensified as efforts increased to register more voters. This clash between civil rights efforts and white resistance lunged into the national context during "Freedom Summer" 1964, when the Student Nonviolent Coordinating Committee organized more than 1,000 volunteers, mostly white, northern college students, to register African-American voters in Mississippi.[23] Violence hit the effort almost as soon as it started in June, when members of the Ku Klux Klan, aided by a deputy sheriff, murdered three volunteers and hid their bodies. The 6-week-long FBI hunt for the remains became a national fixation made

[22] John Herbers, "Black Belt of Alabama is a Stronghold of 19th Century Racism," *New York Times*, February 14, 1965, 70.

[23] Doug McAdam, *Freedom Summer* (Oxford: Oxford University Press, 1990).

Table 6.3 **Voter Registration by Race, Before and After the Passage of the Voting Rights Act of 1965**

State	*Pre-Act Registration*	*Post-Act Registration*	*Pre-Act Percent Registered*	*Post-Act Percent Registered*
Alabama				
African American	92,737	248,432	19.3	51.6
White	935,695	1,212,317	69.2	89.6
Arkansas				
African American	77,714	121,000	40.4	62.8
White	555,944	616,000	65.5	72.4
Florida				
African American	240,616	299,033	51.2	63.6
White	1,938,499	2,131,105	74.8	81.4
Georgia				
African American	167,663	332,496	27.4	52.6
White	1,124,415	1,443,730	62.6	80.3
Louisiana				
African American	164,601	303,148	31.6	58.9
White	1,037,184	1,200,517	80.5	93.1
Mississippi				
African American	28,500	263,754	6.7	59.8
White	525,000	665,176	69.9	91.5
North Carolina				
African American	258,000	277,404	46.8	51.3
White	1,942,000	1,602,980	96.8	83.0

(*continued*)

Table 6.3 **(Continued)**

State	*Pre-Act Registration*	*Post-Act Registration*	*Pre-Act Percent Registered*	*Post-Act Percent Registered*
South Carolina				
African American	138,544	190,017	37.3	51.2
White	677,914	731,096	75.7	81.7
Tennessee				
African American	218,000	225,000	69.5	71.7
White	1,297,000	1,434,000	72.9	80.6
Texas				
African American	NA	400,000	NA	61.6
White	NA	2,600,000	NA	53.3
Virginia				
African American	144,259	243,000	38.3	55.6
White	1,070,168	1,190,000	61.1	63.4

Source: United States Commission on Civil Rights, Political Participation: A Study of the *Participation by Negroes in the Electoral and Political Processes in 10 Southern States since Passage of the Voting Rights Act of 1965, May 1968, pp. 12–13.*

more complicated by FBI Director J. Edgar Hoover's foot-dragging and by overt objections to civil rights advances. As President Lyndon Johnson ruefully observed, "There's three sovereignties involved—there's the United States and there's the State of Mississippi and there's J. Edgar Hoover."[24]

In the first three months of 1965, voter registration efforts, southern resistance to them, and government interventions at the national and state levels progressed in rapid succession. On January 2, 1965, Martin Luther King, Jr. pledged, "we will march by the hundreds. We will show the nation we are determined to vote," and launched a major registration effort in Selma, Alabama.[25] Selma, a city

[24] Transcript, Burke Marshall Oral History Interview I, 10/28/68, by T. H. Baker, Internet copy, Lyndon B. Johnson Library, found at http://www.lbjlib.utexas.edu/johnson/archives.hom/oralhistory.hom/MARSHA-B/marsha-b.asp.

[25] "Dr. King Will Lead Selma Rights Test," *New York Times*, January 15, 1965, 14.

of 28,000 and the county seat of Dallas County, was widely viewed as "the city that has had the most oppressive history against Negroes in the South."[26] This description of the city was borne out in the ensuing month as over 3,300 African Americans were arrested, protesting their inability to register, even after a federal judge ordered that the registration process be accelerated. At the center of white resistance in Selma was segregationist Dallas County Sheriff Jim Clark, who instructed prospective African-American registrants to enter the courthouse through the back door, while whites were assembled in line going through the front door, thus preventing African-American applicants from ever reaching the registration window. Clark then arrested African-American applicants who lined up two-by-two seeking entrance to the front of the building. "You can't make a playhouse out of the corridors of this courthouse," Clark insisted as he and deputies used nightsticks to push away applicants from the front door. "Some of you think you can make it a Disneyland."[27]

As the protests and the arrests became a near daily occurrence, President Lyndon Johnson, in a January 15 telephone conversation, advised King on political strategy as the Justice Department worked on voting rights legislation that Johnson had promised during his State of the Union message on January 4:

> I think one of the worst I ever heard of is the president of the school at Tuskegee or the head of the government department there or something being denied the right to cast a vote and if you just take that one illustration and get it on radio, get it on television, get it on—in the pulpits, get it in the meetings, get it everyplace you can. Pretty soon the fellow that didn't do anything but drive a tractor will say, "Well, that's not right, that's not fair," and then that will help us on what we're going to shove through in the end.[28]

In the weeks after the phone call between Johnson and King, a series of bloody clashes occurred between civil rights participants and sheriffs' officers and volunteer posses. On February 18, in Marion, a town near Selma, police killed a protestor taking refuge in a café and injured numerous others, including an NBC reporter and two UPI photographers covering the protest.[29] In response,

[26] Paul Good, "Dr. King to Open 1965 Rights Drive with Speech in Selma, Al. Today," *The Washington Post*, January 2, 1965, A-2.

[27] John Herbers, "Negro Teachers Protest in Selma," *New York Times*, January 23, 1965, 18.

[28] Mary Jo Murphy, "Phone Call into History," *New York Times*, January 27, 2008, found at http://www.nytimes.com/2008/01/27/weekinreview/27tapes.html.

[29] John Herbers, "Two Inquires Open on Racial Clash in Alabama Town," *New York Times*, February 20, 1965, 1.

on Sunday March 7, civil rights organizers began a march from Selma to the state capitol in Montgomery some 50 miles away, to press Governor George Wallace for an explanation for the police attack. As 600 marchers crossed the Edmund Pettus Bridge on the outskirts of Selma, national network reporters and film crews captured the police beating and using tear gas on the marchers in what became known as "Bloody Sunday." Millions of Americans saw the event that evening on the Sunday night news. King, not present at the first march, led a group of 2,800 in a second protest on March 9 but obeyed a court order seeking to protect the participants by ending the march at the bridge and turning around.[30] In an incident later that evening, three white ministers who had participated in the march were beaten, and one, a Unitarian minister from Boston, died two days later.

Four days after the deaths, Johnson introduced the Voting Rights Act of 1965 to a joint session of Congress, stating, "And we shall overcome." Civil rights protestors finally completed their third attempt at a march to Montgomery on March 25, as President Johnson called out federal troops to protect the marchers along the route.[31] The legislation became law on August 6, 1965, mandating direct federal action to enable African Americans to register and vote without reliance on the protracted case-by-case litigation available as remedy in prior civil rights laws.

Tables 6.1 and 6.2 provide evidence of the impact of legal-institutional change in the form of the Voting Rights Act of 1965 on African-American nonvoting. The theory of uncertainty in the national campaign context hypothesizes that the uncertainty of the legal reforms will decrease nonvoting since they disrupt the status quo, and their novelty encourages those who previously have been blocked from voting to exercise the franchise. The tables show that there is a clear pre–post effect surrounding the law's introduction. In elections prior to its passage—1948, 1950, 1954, 1956, and 1960, 1962, and 1964—the more eligible African-American voters in a state, the higher is nonvoting. However, in the 1966, 1968, and 1970 elections after the passage of the Act, African-American eligible voters significantly decrease nonvoting. Unlike women, who did not immediately enter the voting

[30] John Herbers, "Dr. King Leads 2800 in 3 Alabama Vote Marches," *New York Times*, February 16, 1965, 18.

[31] In a meeting at the White House on March 18, Governor Wallace agreed to Johnson's request that the governor call out the Alabama National Guard to secure the route. However, Wallace then betrayed Johnson after leaving the White House, telling reporters, "the federal government has created this matter and they can help protect them." Johnson, livid at Wallace, described him as "a very treacherous guy, and . . . a no good son of a bitch," and ordered federal troops to Alabama. See transcript of telephone conversation between Lyndon Johnson and Buford Ellington, March 18, 1965, found at the Miller Center at the University of Virginia, http://millercenter.org/presidentialclassroom/exhibits/lbj-governor-wallace-and-buford-ellington-in-selma-alabama.

booth in large numbers, African Americans did. Thus, the high uncertainty surrounding the voting laws and their enforcement in the states prompted African Americans to vote.

Figures 6.2 and 6.3 continue this examination by considering the difference between African-American nonvoting and white nonvoting in midterm and presidential elections from 1966 through 2012 in the South and outside the South. The figures show that in the early elections there are substantially more African-American nonvoters than white nonvoters, especially in the South, but the number of African-American nonvoters rapidly declines, hitting low points in the 1982 midterms and the 1984 presidential race. Figure 6.4 makes clearer this decrease in nonvoting among African-Americans in the South by displaying the difference between African-American and white nonvoting across time. However, beginning in 1990 a key pattern emerges in which African-American nonvoting in the South is consistently lower than that in the non-South. This is true for each of the twelve elections through 2012. Overall, the rate of African-American nonvoting in the South continues to be lower than it is outside the South (Figures 6.2 and 6.3). Indeed, white southern nonvoting exceeds

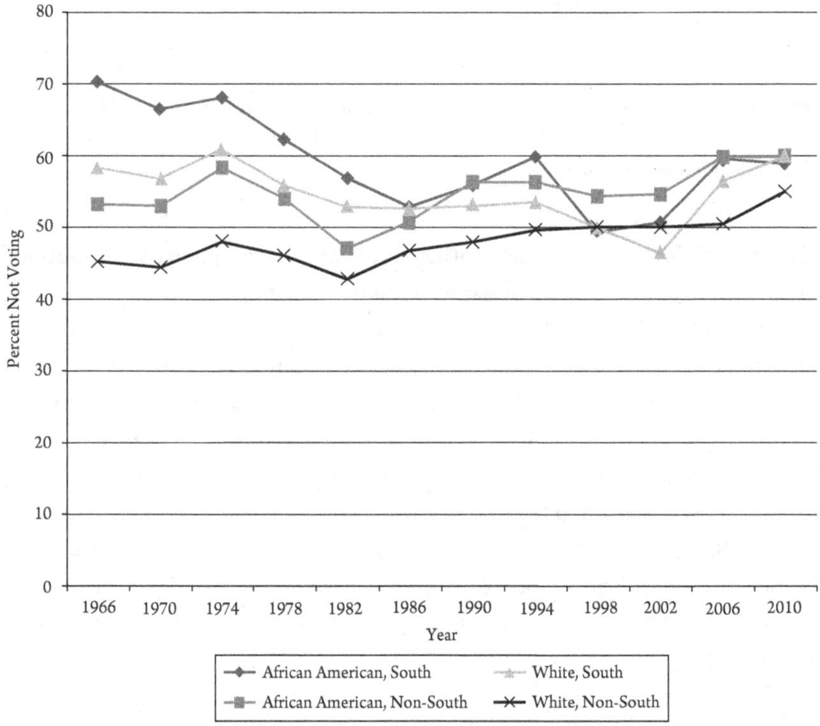

Figure 6.2 Nonvoting by Race and Region in Midterm Elections, 1966–2010
Source: U.S. Census, Voting and Registration, Report P-20 found at http://www.census.gov/hhes/www/socdemo/voting/publications/p20/

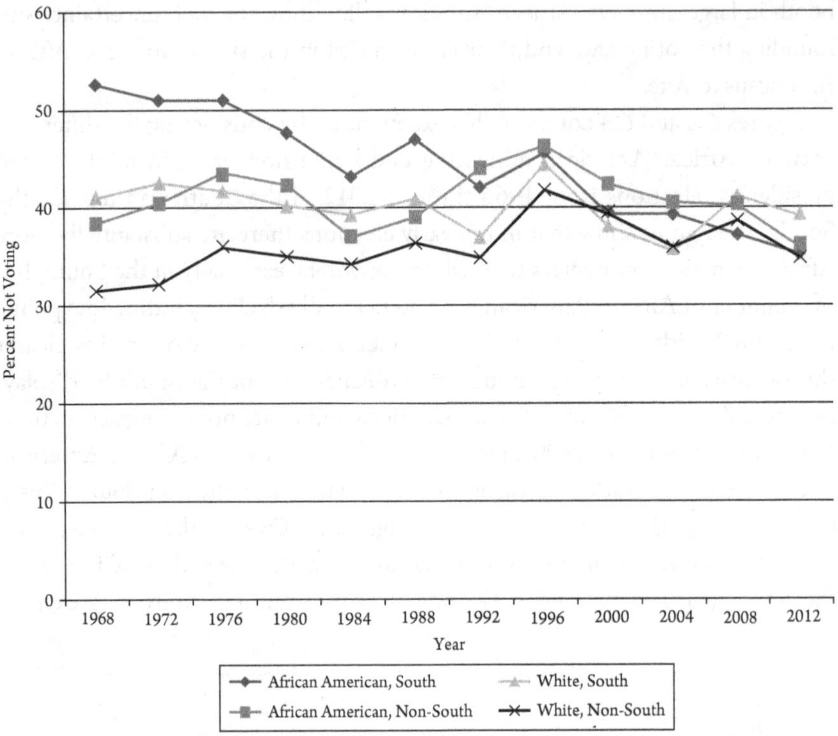

Figure 6.3 Nonvoting by Race and Region in Presidential Elections, 1968–2012
Source: U.S. Census, Voting and Registration, Report P-20 found at http://www.census.gov/hhes/www/socdemo/voting/publications/p20/

African-American southern nonvoting from 2008 through 2012, undoubtedly a reflection of the candidacy of Barack Obama (Figure 6.3).

Figure 6.5 elaborates on the differences between African-American and white nonvoting with a breakdown by sex. African-American men are much more likely to be nonvoters than African-American women.[32] Indeed, in every election from 1964 through 2012, more African-American men fail to vote than do African-American women. Beginning in 1982, African-American women and white women fail to participate at similar levels. Indeed, from 2008 through 2012, white women exceed African-American women as nonvoters. Overall, the long-term impact of the Voting Rights Act of 1965 has been as profound as were the earlier opposing efforts to leave the 15th Amendment unenforced.

[32] The relationship is also generational. In data not shown, older African-American men are much more likely not to vote than younger African-American men.

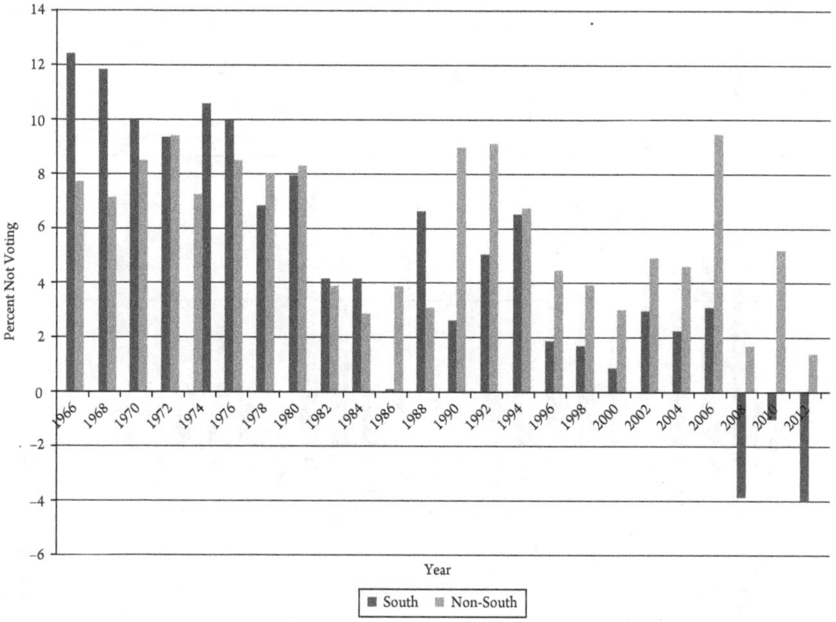

Figure 6.4 Difference between African-American and White Nonvoting, 1966–2012
Note: Bars above zero indicate higher African-American nonvoting; bars below zero indicate higher White nonvoting.

The Youth Vote

We further test our hypothesis about legal change as a measure of uncertainty in the national campaign context with an examination of the expansion of youth suffrage. Many students protesting the Vietnam War and the draft argued that if they were old enough to fight and die for their country, they should be old enough to vote. Many members of Congress from both parties agreed that the voting age should be lowered to alleviate youth alienation by giving them more direct access to the political system. Indeed, conservative Republican Senator Barry Goldwater of Arizona and liberal Democratic Senator Edward Kennedy of Massachusetts jointly proposed that the voting age be lowered by statute rather than by constitutional amendment.[33] Unlike the decades of struggle women and African-Americans undertook to secure the right to vote, the youth effort happened very quickly. Discussions throughout 1969 culminated in a provision in the 1970 extension of the Voting Rights Act of 1965, mandating an 18-year-old voting age in all federal, state, and local elections. Richard Nixon, who had called for an end to the draft and lowering the voting age during the 1968 campaign,

[33] "Political Foes Urge Lower Voting Age," *New York Times*, March 10, 1970, 16.

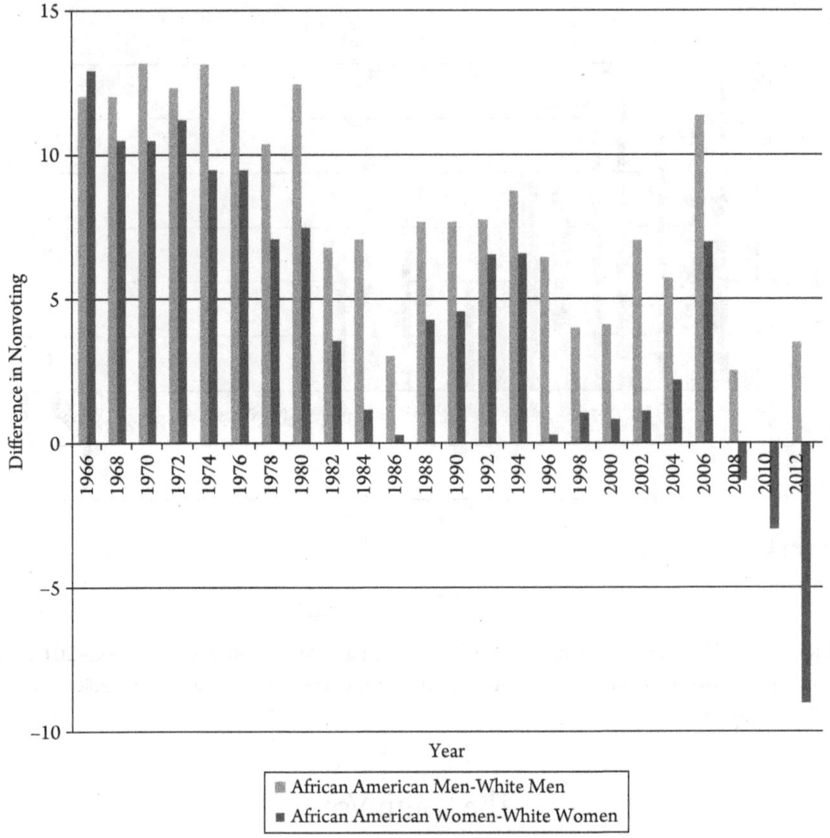

Figure 6.5 Difference in Nonvoting by Race and Sex, 1966–2012
Note: Bars above zero indicate higher African-American nonvoting; bars below zero indicate greater White nonvoting.

signed the bill into law. In his signing statement, however, Nixon objected to the constitutionality of the 18-year-old provision, suggesting that a constitutional amendment was required. In December 1970 the Supreme Court agreed in *Oregon v. Mitchell* that federal law could not set age requirements for voting in state and local elections. In response to the Court's decision, Congress passed the 26th Amendment to the Constitution mandating the 18-year-old age requirement for all elections. The states then ratified the amendment faster than any other constitutional amendment, and it formally took effect on July 5, 1971.

Tables 6.1 and 6.2 reveal that, prior to the passage of the 26th Amendment, youth has no effect on nonvoting, except in 1956 when the percentage of young people in a state increases nonvoting, and in 1964 when youth in the state decreases nonvoting.[34] It also shows that in 1972, the first election in which those

[34] In 1966 we estimated the model with youth in the population rather than percent youth in the population. This provided for more robust estimates and the absence of autocorrelation among the error terms.

18–20 year olds became eligible to vote, the number of young people in the electorate has no effect on nonvoting. So, unlike the initial entrance of African Americans into the electorate, the entrance of young people did not influence nonvoting. As we will see in the next chapter, a negative effect is present in the 1974 elections, but there is no other effect through 1990. Thus these findings, like those for women, point to the limits of the legal change hypothesis. The uncertainty and novelty of national legal changes do not universally motivate newly enfranchised groups. For women, social norms discouraged many of them initially from voting in large numbers. For 18-to-20-year-olds, the much quieter, shorter, and consensual quest for the vote brought proportionally fewer young people to the polls. Moreover, the high rate of mobility among the young dampens routine participation.

Proxy Wars

A new American role in international affairs defined the post-war period as the cold peace blurred into the Cold War. The emerging bipolar world was both highly novel and uncertain. The post-war uncertainty hinged on two key guesses made by American presidents, beginning with Truman, about the intentions of the Soviet Union. The first was the domino theory. The communist threat was perceived to be geographically boundless. Although Truman's immediate concern in announcing the Truman Doctrine was a feared Soviet expansion toward Greece and Turkey, the threat was seen as insidious: if one country was threatened, it seemed likely that all countries in the region would fall, one by one. "Like apples in a barrel infected by one rotten one," wrote Truman's secretary of state Dean Acheson, "the corruption of Greece would infect Iran and all to the east. It would also carry infection to Africa through Asia Minor and Egypt and to Europe through Italy and France . . ."[35] Later the metaphor would change, and Acheson's "apples" became "dominoes," but the logic held. Eisenhower spoke of the domino theory or the "falling domino principle. You have a row of dominoes set up, you knock over the first one, and what will happen to the last one is the certainty that it will go over very quickly. So you could have a beginning of a disintegration that would have the most profound influences."[36] The dominoes were countries with weak economies and little strategic importance, but with the invocation of the Truman Doctrine all such countries took on national security dimensions. But, there was considerable uncertainty about whether the

[35] Dean Acheson, *Present at the Creation: My Years in the State Department* (New York: Norton, 1969), 219.

[36] News Conference, April 7, 1954, *Public Papers of the Presidents, Dwight Eisenhower, 1954* (Washington, D.C.: US Government Printing Office, 1955), 382–383.

domino theory would actually be borne out. No one knew for sure whether Iran would fall if communists took over Greece.

The second guess was that American military intervention was necessary to prevent the dominoes from falling and also prevent the prospect of a third World War. There was substantial novelty and risk as the United States began to assert American military involvement in countries it knew little about. As the Soviets helped North Koreans build up equipment, planes, and advisors in its invasion of South Korea, Stalin sent a telegram to Czech President Klement Gottwald, writing, "America became entangled in a military intervention in Korea and is now squandering its military prestige and moral authority."[37] The application of the domino theory meant that the United States would be involved in critical areas of the world in aiding Berlin and blockading Cuba, but would also take on much more ambiguous battlefronts in Korea and Vietnam. As with the first guess, no one really knew whether US involvement in small, less than strategic countries was the right approach to withstand communism.

As noted in the previous chapter, while a number of studies have examined the impact of foreign policy decisions on candidate preferences and vote choice, there has been no examination of the influence of foreign policy efforts on nonvoting. The central hypothesis states that international conflict as an indicator of uncertainty decreases nonvoting, as people are unsure of the outcome of the war. Tables 6.1 and 6.2 show how the Korean and Vietnam Wars had different effects on electoral participation. Korean War casualties had no effect on nonvoting in the 1950 and 1952 elections. In 1950, China had entered the war in October of that year and American casualties were high. In 1952, Korea was a central issue, even with casualties much lower, in that year's Eisenhower campaign as he announced "I shall go to Korea."[38] Yet, public support for the war dropped precipitously after the Chinese advance, from 66 percent to 39 percent, and remained stable at 40 percent throughout the 2-year period from October 1950 through October 1952.[39] This stability of opinion about the war may then have obviated the uncertainty surrounding the war on the battlefield. From the very beginning there was little doubt among Americans that the Korean War was a bad idea. Perhaps because of this consistently negative national outlook, the uncertainty surrounding the conduct of the war had no effect on nonvoting.

[37] Telegram from Joseph Stalin to Klement Gottwald, August 27, 1950, the North Korean Documentation Project, Woodrow Wilson International Center for Scholars, found at http://www.wilsoncenter.org/publication/did-stalin-lure-the-united-states-the-korean-war-new-evidence-the-origins-the-korean-war.

[38] Eisenhower speech on October 25, 1952, found at https://www.eisenhower.archives.gov/education/bsa/citizenship_merit_badge/speeches_national_historical_importance/i_shall_go_to_korea.pdf.

[39] John Mueller, *Wars, Presidents and Public Opinion* (New York: John Wiley, 1973), 45–46.

By contrast, Vietnam War casualties had statistically significant positive effects on nonvoting during the 1966 and 1970 midterms although not during the 1968 or 1972 presidential elections. Casualties were modest in these years, except in 1972 when casualties were quite low. But support for the war eroded steadily during the Johnson administration from 61 percent approval in 1965 to 52 percent approval in 1966 to 48 percent approval in 1967 to 39 percent approval in 1968. The news was little different for President Nixon as the 1970 elections approached, with 36 percent approval of the war in 1969 and 34 percent in 1970.[40] Massive war protests throughout the Vietnam War years magnified these negative public views. Thus, although public approval of the Korea War was low, it did not prompt the demonstrations and disillusionment over government legitimacy that accompanied the Vietnam War. This mistrust about the Vietnam War led to an increase in nonvoting.[41] These results, then, fail to confirm the international conflict hypothesis and are distinct from those observed during World War II as seen in Chapter 5. Although uncertainty surrounds war, it appears that the level and intensity of public opinion about the war is distinct from the uncertainty itself. It is those public attitudes that more directly influence participation.

In School

The social fabric of the country was altered not just by advances in civil rights but also by strides in education. During the post-war period, the expansion of education and the federal role in education defined a pivotal aspect of American society in ways that did not occur in any other time period. Referring back to Table 5.8, after World War II high school education skyrocketed, increasing by over 81 percent across the period. By 1968 over half of Americans had graduated from high school, when only 31 percent had done so immediately after the war. College graduates doubled across the same period, from 6 percent of the adult population in 1946 to 12 percent in 1972. These increases were also true regionally. Even though the South lagged behind the non-South, it too saw a doubling of the people who graduated from high school and college during the period. The overall expansion of education and the pace of that growth during the post-war period exceeded that of any of the other time periods.

Federal support of education helped fuel this growth through a series of policy measures to expand educational opportunities. This began in 1944 with the "GI

[40] Mueller, 1973, 54–55.
[41] See Mueller, 1973.

Bill," which provided for post-secondary education assistance to veterans, some 8 million of whom attended college under the law. In 1958 Congress passed the National Defense Education Act, in response to the Soviet's launch of Sputnik, to improve science, math, and foreign language instruction from elementary school through graduate training. But by far the largest national investment in education came in the form of the Elementary and Secondary Education Act of 1965 which provided, among other items, federal aid to disadvantaged children, teacher training and preparation funds, and new library resources. The Higher Education Act of the same year provided for financial assistance to college students and was amplified by amendments in 1972 that created the Pell Grant program, grants to college-bound students in need that did not require repayment.[42] So although, as discussed in earlier chapters, we treat education as a personal resource in order to be consistent with previous studies, it should be kept in mind that during the post-war period education policy had a lot to do with who was able to claim this resource. The rising number of educated people was inextricably tied to the expanded federal role in education.

Tables 6.1 and 6.2 clarify the effect of education on nonvoting. In the immediate post-war years, education has no effect on nonvoting. It was not until 1958 that the first significant effect emerges. Education significantly decreases nonvoting in each election thereafter, except 1968. The effects are strong in both midterm and presidential elections, most notably in 1960, 1964, 1966, 1970, and 1972. In examining the impact column, education's relative impact is typically less than that of income, technology, and most especially number of African Americans in the population. But, in general, the more educated a state's population the more nonvoting diminishes.

The Effects of Declining Regionalism

Another central feature of the post-war era was a gradual decrease in regional differences. This is not to suggest that regionalism, so apparent in the first period, disappeared. The discussion above of the civil rights movement immediately suggests otherwise. But, in contrast to the first period when regional differences were at their most stark, in the second period the South and the non-South move together in pivotal ways. Figure 6.6 shows that throughout the second period, the gaps lessened between the South and the non-South regarding income, technology, and education. The regional income gap is cut in half from 1946 to 1972;

[42] "Overview: The Federal Role in Education," U.S. Department of Education, found at http://www2.ed.gov/about/overview/fed/role.html.

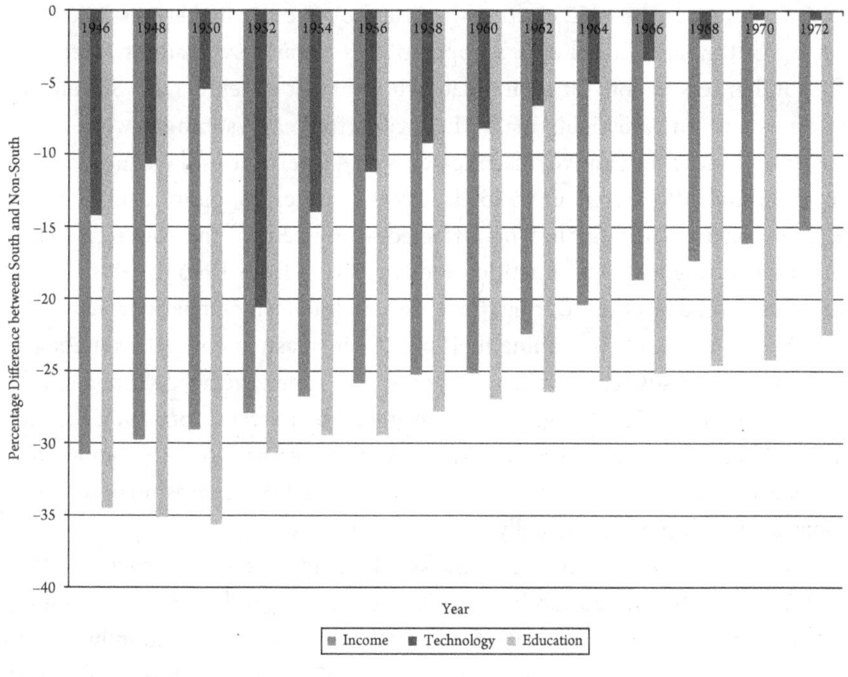

Figure 6.6 Regional Differences in Income, Technology, and Education, 1946–1972

the technology gap is non-existent by 1970, when every household, no matter where, owned at least one television set; and the education gap, while more pronounced than the income gap, nevertheless declines by 10 percentage points across the period. As the 1970s started, then, the two regions looked much more alike than in the immediate aftermath of World War II.

Party Competition

A similar phenomenon occurred in party politics. It had been unthinkable in the first era that Republicans would make permanent inroads into the once solidly Democratic South. During the first period, Herbert Hoover did remarkably well in the South against Al Smith of New York, winning 48 percent of the southern vote in 1928. But this was an anomaly and due more to southern opposition to Smith than southern support of Hoover. In all other elections of the first period, Republicans never gained more than 27 percent of the southern vote, which occurred in 1948 with Thomas Dewey.[43]

[43] Jerrold G. Rusk, *A Statistical History of the American Electorate* (Washington, D.C.: CQ Press, 2001), 139.

By contrast, in the 1952 election the Eisenhower campaign expressly focused on the South, and Eisenhower's popularity as a war hero made it acceptable for southerners to vote for a candidate who was not a Democrat.[44] Stevenson's strong stand on civil rights made the switch for many southern whites even easier and more imperative. Eisenhower won 48 percent of the southern vote in 1952 and 49 percent in 1956. In 1960, southern support continued for Republican Richard Nixon, who attracted 46 percent of the southern vote.[45] Figure 6.7 presents the competition index measure from 1946 to 1972.[46] In all the presidential elections during the period, Republican competitiveness in the South is in evidence. Beginning in 1962, the increase in competitiveness also emerges in House races. While the competitive index averaged 43 percent for midterms from 1946 through 1958, it averaged 69 percent from 1962 through 1970. Although Lyndon Johnson lamented that "we have lost the South for a generation" upon signing the Voting Rights Act of 1965, the erosion of southern Democratic support had actually started much earlier.

As seen in Tables 6.1 and 6.2, in the keenly fought presidential races of 1952, 1960, and 1968 competition has considerable effect on decreasing nonvoting. In the more lopsided races in 1956 and 1964, competition has no influence on participation, although anomalously it does in 1972. In the midterm elections of 1946, 1958, 1962, and 1970, competition also decreases nonvoting. This midterm effect is especially noteworthy given the high number of incumbent members of Congress winning re-election during this period.[47]

But Tables 6.1 and 6.2 also reveal that in both presidential and midterm elections, the effect of competition on nonvoting is less than the effects of television and civil rights. As shown in the "Impact" columns of the two tables, the impact of television is typically at least twice that of competition. The impact of African Americans is, in turn, considerably more than television. This is also true in the first period when the impact of competition is less than the impact of radio or of women entering the electorate. Thus, even when races are not highly competitive, nonvoting declines amidst the uncertainty of the technology shocks and

[44] Barton Bernstein, "Election of 1952" in A. Schlesinger, ed. *History of American Presidential Elections, 1789–1968*, vol. IV (New York: Chelsea House, 1971), 3215–3266; James Sundquist, *Dynamics of the Party System: Alignment and Realignment of Political Parties in the United States*, 2nd ed. (Washington, D.C.: Brookings Institution, 1983).

[45] Rusk, 2001, 140.

[46] The index introduced in Table 5.6 is the difference between the Democratic and Republican percentages of the 2-party vote subtracted from 100, with scores closest to 100 being most competitive.

[47] Harold Stanley and Richard Niemi, *Vital Statistics on American Politics*, 2009–2010 (Washington, D.C.: CQ Press), 43–44.

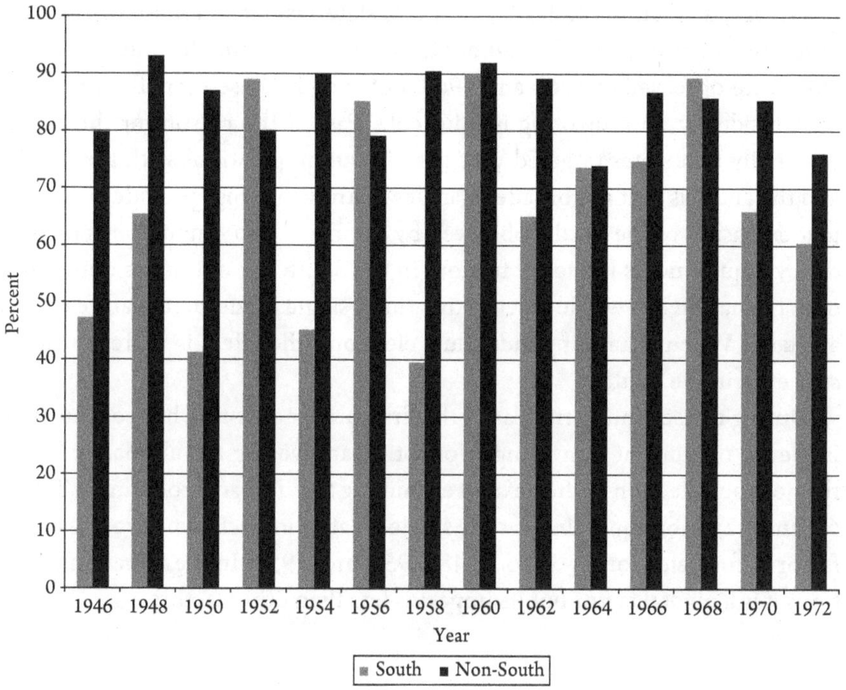

Figure 6.7 Party Competition Index by Region, 1946–1972

election law changes. It is important to keep in mind that key features of the national campaign context diminish nonvoting levels more than does the actual competition in the race.

State Residency Requirements and Prior Nonvoting

During the post-war period, states continued to enforce residency requirements that differed between the South and the non-South, with many southern states requiring that people reside in the state for two years to attain voter eligibility and most other states requiring one year or less (see Table 5.9). Residency requirements were finally reduced and made uniform in the Voting Rights Act of 1970, which imposed a 30-day-only residency requirement for presidential elections. A subsequent Supreme Court decision in *Dunn v. Blumstein* in 1972 invoked a similar residency requirement limit for other elections, making all elections across all states roughly uniform.[48]

[48] See the discussion in Rusk, 2001, 15. As we did in Chapter 5, we tested a simple two-variable model of nonvoting with state residency and prior nonvoting as the independent variables. State

Overall, as seen in Tables 6.1 and 6.2, state residency requirements have little effect on nonvoting throughout the post-war period. The only significant effects are observed in 1964 and 1968, but even in these years the impact of state residency on nonvoting is miniscule. Part of the reason for this is undoubtedly that states targeted very specific sub-populations with these laws, and the analysis is at the broader state level. These findings provide an important extension of the results observed by Springer, who found that state residency requirements influence turnout in the South but not in the non-South or in the nation as a whole when estimating a single model across all years and all states. When examining individual elections, the effect is more restricted still, even in the South.[49]

During the second period, as in the first, prior nonvoting has considerable influence on current nonvoting. Nonvoting and voting are ultimately habits that join one election to the next. In examining the "Impact" columns of Tables 6.1 and 6.2, prior nonvoting has the single greatest impact on nonvoting of any factor in four elections—1946, 1948, 1950, and 1954. In the remaining elections it is a pivotal factor but its impact is less than other factors.

Individual Nonvoters

The historical analysis of aggregate nonvoting provides a backdrop for a study of the effect of the national campaign context at the individual level. This refines the omnibus discussion in Chapter 4. Recall that the theory of uncertainty in the national campaign context suggests that high levels of external uncertainty increase people's awareness of politics and push them to reduce their internal uncertainty about which candidate is the best at handling the unpredictable external situation. In Table 6.4 we present a probit analysis of individual nonvoting in the 1968 and 1972 elections when data from the American National Election studies begin to be available. The two elections were starkly different in specific elements of external uncertainty and individuals' ways of handling the resulting internal uncertainty. The election period of 1968 was a time in which politics was all but unavoidable. The months prior to the election were rife with a succession of highly uncertain events vividly captured on the nightly news (see Table 3.7).

residency has no statistically significant effect on nonvoting in the South during the elections of the period.

[49] Melanie Springer, *How the States Shaped the Nation* (Chicago: University of Chicago Press, 2014), 97–100.

On January 30 the North Vietnamese launched the Tet offensive, catching the United States and South Vietnamese by surprise and prompting major losses of lives and territory. The week ending February 18, 1968 posted the single largest number of casualties of any week during the war. The following month, on March 31 President Johnson announced before a nationwide audience that "I will not seek nor will I accept my party's nomination to be your president." Just five days later on April 4, Martin Luther King Jr. was slain outside his motel room in Memphis. Riots broke out across the country in Baltimore, Washington, D.C., Chicago, and Kansas City. In June, Robert Kennedy, who had entered the race for the Democratic nomination for president just two weeks before Johnson's exit, was slain in Los Angeles after winning the California primary. And in August, violence broke out at the Democratic National Convention as Chicago mayor Richard Daley sent in the Chicago police to arrest thousands of anti-war protestors.

The 1972 election period could not have been more different. Nixon was a popular incumbent who touted strong economic growth and the virtual end of US involvement in Vietnam. His opponent George McGovern ran on an anti-war platform and trailed badly throughout the campaign. Although the election later became infamous because of the break-in at the Democratic National Committee offices at the Watergate complex in Washington, D.C. in June 1972, little was known about the break-in or any White House connection to it on Election Day. Despite McGovern's plea that the White House was undertaking a "whitewash" to "spare them embarrassment in an election year," only half of Americans had heard of Watergate by election time, and in early 1973 only 3 percent believed Nixon had anything to do with it.[50]

This juxtaposition is evident in the results in Table 6.4. We expand the analysis from Chapter 4 to include two factors within the national campaign context that were specific to these elections—people's perceptions of the Vietnam War and the civil rights movement.[51] We also include the candidacy of George Wallace

[50] Douglas Kneeland, "McGovern Accuses Nixon of Whitewash on Break-in." *New York Times*, September 17, 1972, 1, found at www.nytimes.com. Survey results obtained from iPoll Databank provided by the Roper Center for Public Opinion Research, University of Connecticut: "Have you heard or read about the Watergate situation?", Gallup Poll, September 1972, and "Who do you think put these men up to the break-in bugging attempt at the Democratic National Committee headquarters?", Opinion Research Corporation poll, February 13, 1973, found at http://www.ropercenter.uconn.edu.

[51] The Vietnam indicator asks respondents to assess available options regarding US involvement in Vietnam with immediate withdrawal coded -1, work for peace settlement coded 0, and taking a stronger stand coded 1. The civil rights indicator is based on a feeling thermometer question about African Americans as a group. The indicator was coded 1 for people who rated African Americans as

Table 6.4 **Effects of the National Campaign Context on Individual Nonvoting, 1968 and 1972 (Probit Maximum Likelihood Coefficients)**

Predictor	*1968*					*1972*				
	Maximum Likelihood Estimate	*MLE/SE*		*Range of Value in the Variable*	*Change in Likelihood of the Variable*	*Maximum Likelihood Estimate*	*MLE/SE*		*Range of Value in the Variable*	*Change in Likelihood of the Variable*
National Campaign Context										
Economic conditions	–0.275	–5.576	***	0, 2	0.646	–0.076	–1.722	*	0,2	0.318
Media attention	–0.202	–4.163	***	0,4	0.538	–0.091	–2.105	**	0,4	0.298
Vietnam war	0.114	1.226		–1,1	0.139	0.014	0.165		–1,1	0.005
Civil rights	0.121	1.340		–1,1	0.095	0.157	1.942	*	–1,1	0.156
Candidate Awareness										
Candidate comparison	–0.003	–1.652	*	0,100	0.279	0.001	0.866		0,100	0.047
Ideological comparison	n/a	n/a				–0.099	–3.701	***	1,7	0.176
Care who wins	–0.082	–1.741	*	–1,1	0.161	–0.179	–4.091	***	–1,1	0.348
George Wallace candidacy	0.002	1.540		0,100	0.169	n/a	n/a			

Personal Characteristics										
Youth	0.014	4.625	***	17,99	0.212	0.008	3.046	***	17,99	0.595
Education	–0.116	–1.865	*	0,3	0.136	–0.265	–4.476	***	0,3	0.328
Social Connections										
Marriage	–0.132	–1.250		0,1	0.089	–0.158	–1.692	*	0,1	0.191
Residential stability	–0.006	–3.806	***	0,99	0.324	–0.003	–1.934	*	0,99	0.306
Unemployment	0.038	0.386		0,1	0.023	–0.050	–0.597		0,1	0.056
Psychological Involvement										
Campaign interest	–0.303	–4.468	***	1,3	0.662	–0.096	–1.552		1,3	0.169
Party Mobilization and Competition										
Campaign contact	–0.298	–2.611	***	0,1	0.299	–0.393	–3.958	***	0,2	0.397
Closeness of race	0.044	0.483		0,1	0.062	–0.137	–1.553		0,1	0.152
Intercept	2.095	7.232	***			0.64	2.768	***		
Number of Cases	1193					1036				

Note: SE=standard error. Significance levels of the maximum likelihood estimates: * .10 level, critical value Z=1.65; **.05, critical value Z =1.96; *** 01, critical value Z=2.57.

in 1968.[52] Within the national campaign context, perceived economic volatility and media attention have statistically significant effects on individual nonvoting in both election years. However, as seen in the "Change" column, the influence of the two indicators is more than double in 1968 compared with 1972. In 1968, people who see the economy as stable are 65 percentage points more likely to be nonvoters that those who see the economy as moving in highly positive or negative directions. The difference in 1972 is 32 percentage points. This is consistent with the greater impact of income change in 1968 compared with 1972, seen in Table 6.2, and the higher level of inflation in 1968 compared with 1972.[53] Although a mix of economic growth and inflation dominated both elections, the combination was greater in 1968 than 1972.

Media attention is also more important in 1968 than in 1972. In 1968, people who rely on only one source of media for information are 54 percentage points less likely to vote than those who gather information from multiple sources among radio, television, newspapers, and magazines. The specific events of 1968 including the Vietnam war, civil rights, and the Wallace candidacy do not have independent effects on nonvoting separate from the large media effect. In 1972, people who rely on only one source of media are 30 percentage points less likely to vote than those who have considerable media attention. While this is still a sizable effect of media attention on nonvoting, it is not as large as that observed in 1968. The numerous disruptive events of 1968 stood in contrast to a quieter media environment in 1972, framed by a strong incumbent and a weak challenger. Presumably, people sought more information from more sources in 1968 than they did in 1972 in order to alleviate uniquely high levels of external uncertainty.[54]

a group at 70 or above on the 100-point feeling thermometer, -1 for people who rated them at 30 or below, and 0 for all other ratings.

[52] This indicator is the feeling thermometer rating for Wallace on a 100-point scale from highly unfavorable to highly favorable.

[53] The inflation rate was 4.7 percent in November 1968 compared with 3.7 percent in November 1972. "Historical Inflation Rates, 1914–2015" found at http://www.usinflationcalculator.com/inflation/historical-inflation-rates/.

[54] In 1968, 87 percent of voters and 62.8 percent of nonvoters sought information from two sources or more, while in 1972, 79 percent of voters and 56.3 percent of nonvoters did so. There should be no confusion about the absence of the media effect at the aggregate level in 1968 and 1972 (shown in Table 6.2) and its presence at the individual level. These are two distinct measures—the aggregate one measures the percentage of American households who own a particular form of media; the individual one is an index of media attention which combines people's use of up to four sources. The fact that most American households owned television sets in 1968 and 1972 would suggest that television was one of the primary sources of individuals' political information.

People's assessments of the candidates are also important to individual nonvoting. As discussed in Chapter 4, people seek information and develop opinions about the candidates to resolve their internal uncertainty on which candidate will best handle circumstances in the national campaign context. As seen in Table 6.4, in 1968, people who see little difference between the candidates are 28 percentage points less likely to vote than those who see large differences between the candidates. Although some people criticized Nixon and Humphrey as "tweedle-dum and tweedle-dee" candidates with few differences between them, there were apparently enough differences that actually helped people resolve internal uncertainty about the two candidates and ultimately decide to vote.[55] In 1972, while general candidate comparisons do not influence nonvoting, people who see no ideological differences between the candidates are 18 percentage points less likely to vote than those who see ideological differences. This may be the result of Republicans spending much of the campaign portraying McGovern as a left-wing radical. In both elections, those who do not care who wins the election are much more likely to be nonvoters. To resolve their internal uncertainty about the candidates, individuals must ultimately care who wins the race—not simply develop opinions about them.

As noted in Chapter 4, people's personal backgrounds and political interest are also central to why individuals do not vote. The table results show that age and education have strong effects on nonvoting in both years, although the effect of age is dramatically higher in 1972 than in 1968. In 1972, people under the age of 25 are 60 percentage points more likely not to vote than people over the age of 50. In 1968 this difference is 21 percentage points. This effect on individual nonvoting and the absence of an aggregate effect in 1972 may be the result of a lopsided race between a strong incumbent and a weak challenger in which young people were less interested. It also represents the first year of implementation of the 26th Amendment granting 18-year-olds the right to vote, during which many young people were not yet socialized to exercise the new right.

This table also shows the important of people's psychological involvement in politics in nonvoting. Campaign interest as an indicator of psychological involvement has among the strongest effects of any indicator in the model. In 1968, people who are not interested in the campaign are 66 percentage points less likely to vote than those who are interested. In contrast, in 1972 campaign

[55] Philip Converse, Warren Miller, Jerrold G. Rusk, and Arthur Wolfe, "Continuity and Change in American Politics: Parties and Issues in the 1968 Election," *American Political Science Review* 63 (December 1969): 1063–1105.

interest does not have a statistically significant effect on individual nonvoting. This may well be indicative of a lopsided race in which many people do not pay as much attention as they would when candidate competition is more clear-cut, as it was in 1968.

Social connections have more modest effects on nonvoting in both years, with residential stability being key. In 1968, people who lived in their community for four years or less are roughly 32 percentage points more likely to be nonvoters than those who lived in their communities longer; in 1972, the difference is 31 percentage points. Unemployment, which was quite low during both elections, is not a factor in individual nonvoting.

Finally, the table shows the impact of campaigners' efforts to get their messages out by directly contacting individuals. In both races, people who had no personal contact with at least one of the campaigns are much more likely not to vote than those who did receive some form of personal contact—30 percentage points less likely in 1968 and 40 percentage points less likely in 1972. Campaigners are typically quite uncertain what activities they undertake during the campaign actually pay off, and so they tend to engage in all activities for which they have money. This empirical result shows that direct personal contacts with eligible voters, which can take various forms including door-to-door canvassing, phone calls, and mailings, have significant mobilization effects.

Thus, the influence of the national campaign context is apparent in both state aggregate nonvoting patterns and individual nonvoting. Individuals understand what is occurring in the national campaign context as they evaluate the economy and pay attention to various forms of media. They also gather information and form opinions about the candidates. Their views of the uncertainty of the national campaign context and their internal uncertainty about the candidates inform their participation decisions. People's life experiences, interest in politics, and campaigners' efforts also shape these choices.

Conclusion: The 1950s and 1960s

The 1950s and 1960s are often juxtaposed as mirror opposites, but they were inextricably linked in the post-war campaign context. Many look nostalgically back at the 1950s as a prosperous, safe, simple period and see the 1960s as a disruptive, anxiety-prone time overrun with startling events that simply seemed to happen. To be sure the 1950s were prosperous, but so were the 1960s. The 1950s were neither safe nor placid, instead reflecting the involvement of the United States in an unwinnable war in Asia as American troops landed in Korea less than five years after the end of World War II. The uncertainty of the 1950s was further heightened by the Soviets launching the first intercontinental ballistic missile in August 1957, and then in October sending the first satellite, Sputnik, into orbit. Just months apart, the arms race and the space race began. The 1960s were similarly dominated by an unwinnable war in Asia with America's bigger, longer military effort in Vietnam, nuclear arms proliferation, and space missions that Apollo astronaut Frank Borman asserted were "just a battle in the cold war."[56] Struggles against discrimination and for civil rights perplexed many party politicians in the 1950s who were afraid of "going too fast." Politicians in the 1960s realized that going less fast was not an option, as the struggles for civil rights peaked.

In addition, most of these post-war politicians throughout the period embraced major government programs in ways consistent with the New Deal. While Eisenhower's highway program was not social security, it was nevertheless a large national government allocation that transformed millions of Americans' lives as they now took long road trips across the country. And centrist politics on the Republican and Democratic sides dominated this post-war period. As an example, in the early development of the rebuilding of Europe, former president Herbert Hoover toured the region and returned with the idea that a strong Germany was necessary for a strong Europe. While many saw this as inappropriate in the immediate aftermath of the war, nevertheless the Truman administration agreed with Hoover's assessment, and this was one of the earliest seeds for the Marshall Plan. Such bipartisan agreement on such a radical idea seems unthinkable in more recent times.

These two decades and the broader post–World War II period were both similar to but distinct from the first period after World War I. In each period, a single election—defined by considerable novelty—stands out as the most pivotal election for electoral participation. In the first period, the 1928 election combined strong economic growth with the introduction of radio into American politics. In the second period, the 1952 election joined even more dramatic economic expansion with the inaugural use of television in the campaign. The lessons about communication technology from those two elections could not have been clearer for politicians and citizens alike: politicians who use the medium skillfully win; those who do not, lose. People with access to the new medium are more likely to vote; those without it are less likely to do so.

Yet, the periods are characterized by more than these pivotal elections. Throughout both eras, the uncertainty of the national campaign context drew people to politics rather than away from politics. In both periods, economic change and technological shocks brought people to the polls. However, the

[56] Quoted in Michael Klesius, "To Boldly Go," *Air and Space Magazine*, Smithsonian Institution, December 19, 2008, found at http://www.airspacemag.com/space-exploration/To-Boldly-Go.html.

impact of economic change on nonvoting was consistently greater in the second period than in the first. Particularly during the economic expansion of the 1960s, the impact of income growth exceeded the impact of income decline in the 1930s. The impact of television on nonvoting in the second period was also more sizable than the impact of radio in the first period. By the early 1960s, television had on average twice the impact that radio had in the 1930s. Distinct from the first period, a major change in legal requirements for voting prompted proportionally more African Americans to enter the electorate more quickly beginning in 1966 than did women in 1920 or young people in 1972.

The first two periods differed in the degree of regionalism apparent in American politics. During the second period, regionalism became less apparent. Southerners had progressively better incomes and education and observed more competitive political races. Thus, while the first period after World War I was a time in which politics became more nationally focused, the second period after World War II was a time in which politics was largely nationally focused.

Aspects of the national campaign context began to shift and end in the 1970s. Income growth slowed, and the economy grew stagnant. Everyone owned a television and there was less novelty about how it influenced politics. The escalation of the Vietnam War stopped, and the so-called "Vietnamization" of the war began. These factors showed evolutionary changes that were nevertheless distinct from what had happened in earlier years and were suggestive of a demarcation between one time period and another. Yet, if there was any doubt that the second period was ending, the resignation of Richard Nixon in August 1974 stopped those questions. Nixon symbolized the end of the second period. He had stood as a tough, hardened cold warrior during the height of his political career in the 1950s, but Americans watched Nixon in 1972 lead the opening of American relations with the People's Republic of China and sign the first of several strategic arms limitation treaties with the Soviet Union. He had widened the Vietnam War with invasions of neighboring Cambodia and Laos and had called the Vietnam War protestors "bums," only to lead the withdrawal of tens of thousands of American troops from the country without an American victory. Nixon's unsurprising landslide victory in 1972 masked a series of surprising incidents of obstruction of justice, as Nixon himself ordered aides in June 1972 to block the FBI's investigation of the break-in of the Democratic National Committee offices at the Watergate complex in Washington, D.C. and pay hush money to the burglars.

As much as the 1946 election was pivotal in starting this period of heightened national influence, Nixon's resignation was equally crucial in bringing it to a close. Like the first period, which came to a readily identifiable close with the end of World War II, the second period ended noisily with Richard Nixon's helicopter farewell in August 1974. The "American Century" had lasted less than three decades, and American electoral participation going into the third period shifted in reflection of this.

7

A Period of Government Reassessment: 1974–1990

"We were sure that ours was a nation of the ballot, not the bullet, until the murders of John Kennedy and Robert Kennedy and Martin Luther King, Jr. We were taught that our armies were always invincible and our causes were always just, only to suffer the agony of Vietnam. We respected the Presidency as a place of honor until the shock of Watergate. We remember when the phrase 'sound as a dollar' was an expression of absolute dependability, until 10 years of inflation began to shrink our dollar and our savings. We believed that our Nation's resources were limitless until 1973, when we had to face a growing dependence on foreign oil." In a major address to the nation on July 15, 1979, President Jimmy Carter captured the essence of uncertainty in the late 1970s. The speech became known as the "great malaise" speech, even though Carter never actually used those words.[1] As much as Carter attempted to look back at problems others had created in the second period, he was saddled with their aftermath in the third period amidst a "crisis of confidence . . . threatening to destroy the social and the political fabric of America." Carter concluded "This is not a message of happiness or reassurance, but it is the truth and it is a warning."[2]

The term *post-war* cannot be assigned to a period of time indefinitely. As in Carter's depiction, the emergence of the third era hinged on subtle and not so subtle shifts away from the aftermath of World War II. By the 1970s, the Cold War had become rigidified and familiar. While in the 1950s people worried about a third World War with the use of nuclear missiles, by the 1970s people counted on the tit-for-tat arms race and parity between the superpowers as the

[1] Frances X. Clines wrote a column in the *New York Times* several weeks later referencing Carter's "cross-of-malaise speech" and other journalists picked up the phrase. Francis X. Clines, "About Chautauqua: The Circuit is Gone but not the Oratory," *New York Times*, August 2, 1979, B4.

[2] "Address to the Nation on Energy and National Goals," *Public Papers of the Presidents, Jimmy Carter*, July 15, 1979, found at www.presidency.ucsb.edu.

insurance the world needed against the missiles' use. The economic growth that had been taken for granted in the 1950s and 1960s slowed and became more muddled by the 1970s as inflation and unemployment began to move upward in tandem. The civil rights movement, which defined American society in the 1950s and 1960s, struggled to regain its footing after Martin Luther King's assassination in 1968. The post-war period ended in loud, decisive ways too. In January 1973, American involvement in the Vietnam War formally ended and, with it, more than two decades of debate about America's efforts to protect the world from communism in Southeast Asia. And, in August 1974, Richard Nixon resigned the presidency over his involvement in the Watergate scandal. Vietnam and Watergate, as entangled constitutional crises and their aftermaths, confirmed that Americans no longer lived in the big time defined by the victory of World War II.

As discussed in Chapter 1, external uncertainty rides on a continuum from high to low. When conditions in the national campaign context incite fast changes or novel disruptive events, uncertainty is high and nonvoting is likely to decrease. When changes in the national campaign context are more incremental or cumulative, uncertainty is lower. This does not suggest that uncertainty is absent, but rather less glaring. Under conditions of low or moderate uncertainty, nonvoting is likely to increase because there is less incentive for eligible voters to protect against the worst possible outcomes, given that the severity of outcomes seems less well defined. Not only does uncertainty fall along a continuum from high to low, it also occurs in a temporal sequence. Uncertainty at time t compares to uncertainty at time t–1 and time t+1.

Distinct levels of uncertainty distinguish the third period from the second period. Compared to the fast-paced changes in the 1950s and 1960s, there were fewer dramatic, even shocking, events after American disengagement from the Vietnam War and Nixon's resignation. In the middle and late 1970s, "WIN" buttons announcing that the Ford administration would "whip inflation now" and the Carter administration efforts to tax "gas-guzzling" cars replaced revelations of imperial presidential power in the administrations of Presidents Johnson and Nixon. In the 1980s, dry congressional debates about the increasing budget deficit and its possible effect on the economy replaced Senate hearings divulging tape-recorded conversations with President Nixon urging the payment of hush money to the Watergate burglars: "You could get a million dollars. And you could get it in cash. I know where it could be gotten."[3] The intensity and uncertainty of events in the 1960s and early 1970s—war, corruption, the civil

[3] Richard Nixon to John Dean, March 21, 1973, 10:12 AM, Miller Center Presidential Recordings Project, found at http://whitehousetapes.net/transcript/nixon/you-could-get-million-dollars.

rights movement, the women's movement, assassinations, riots, and campus protests—abated.

This is not to suggest that "nothing happened" in the mid-1970s through the 1980s, but the problems encountered were less shattering. What had been radical changes were now more incremental adjustments. What had been touted as the "American Century" of growth, success, and international prowess was replaced by a more ordinary and gray plane of sluggish economic performance and cautious international steps. We refer to this period as the government reassessment period because it was typified by questions about the scope and direction of the national government and its elected officials. Much of this reassessment initially focused on preventing any future constitutional and political crises of the kind that had engulfed the American presidency. But it also extended to the broader mission of the national government itself, both domestically and internationally. For example, in public opinion polls in 1976, 40 percent of Americans favored cutting back on government programs and 41 percent indicated that the United States should not maintain its dominant position in the world if it meant going to war.[4] The idea of limits to federal government size and reach, largely absent during the post-war period, became the primary theme of the Reagan administration.

During the government reassessment period, four dimensions defined the uncertainty of the national campaign context. First, unlike the economic volatility of the first period and the unabashed prosperity of the second period, economic stagnation characterized much of the third period. One of the central questions associated with the upside uncertainty in the economy during the second period was, "When will the good times end?" Economic stagnation—a harsh combination of high unemployment, high inflation, and slow growth—answered this question. Unemployment, which had averaged 5 percent in the 1950s and 1960s, crept slowly upward, averaging 7 percent in the 1970s and 1980s. The unemployment rate never fell below 6 percent for nearly two decades. In the 1970s and 1980s, inflation grew on average by more than 6 percent annually. Growth in real per capita income, which had increased 5 percent in the second period, was much more stable during the third period, slowing to just 2 percent.

Second, unlike the national quality of radio and television for political communication in the first and second periods, the emergence of cable television began to dismantle broadcasting and replace it with more personalized narrowcasting as people chose what they wanted to watch when they wanted to

[4] Government programs reference from a *Time* magazine poll, January 21–28, 1976; war reference from Gallup poll, June 1976, found at http://www.ropercenter.uconn.edu/.

watch it. Cable subscriptions grew steadily from 10 percent of American households in 1975 to 50 percent by 1990. J. C. R. Licklider, Massachusetts Institute of Technology computer science pioneer and public broadcasting advocate, first adopted the term "narrowcasting." In a 1967 report, when cable was only in its infancy, Licklider predicted a multiplicity of television networks aimed at smaller, specialized audiences. He wrote, "I should like to coin the term 'narrowcasting,' using it to emphasize the rejection or dissolution of the constraints imposed by commitment to a monolithic, mass-appeal broadcast approach."[5]

Third, major social movements to increase voting rights for more Americans were no longer bringing large numbers of new voters into the electorate. The hard-fought battles by women and African Americans in the two earlier periods had led to significant numbers of new voters. As we discuss below, the expansion of the electorate to 18–20-year-olds created little fanfare even among those granted the franchise. Thus, the absence of uncertainty surrounding historic voting rights efforts in the third period was as important as the presence of uncertainty had been in the first and second periods.

Fourth, American international involvements were purposely more constrained and less risky than those in the previous periods. With the victory of North Vietnam over South Vietnam in 1975, America remained a superpower but one reluctant to enter into other big fights. What were once military efforts became diplomatic initiatives. The Iranian hostage crisis, in which militant students held hostage 52 Americans at the US Embassy in Tehran, roiled the Carter administration for 14 months as a diplomatic crisis, not a military one. Carter pursued negotiations with the Iranian government for five months before attempting a helicopter rescue of the hostages. After the rescue mission failed, Carter returned to nine more months of diplomacy. The Reagan administration's secret effort to sell arms to Iran to buy the release of other American hostages was perhaps the most unique form of diplomacy aimed at an enemy.

In the third period, what were once protracted military engagements became quick interventions and exits. Even with Reagan's emphasis on military strength and bellicosity, calling the Soviet Union the "evil empire," the administration largely protected rather than projected American power abroad. It conducted a short mission to Grenada, the bombing of Libya, and pulled troops out of Lebanon well before a self-imposed deadline.[6] During the Persian Gulf War, the George H. W. Bush administration invoked a strategy

[5] Patrick Parsons, "The Evolution of Cable-Satellite Distribution System," *Journal of Broadcasting and Electronic Media* 47(1) (2003): 5.

[6] Reagan first used the term "evil empire" in a speech in 1983: "Remarks at the Annual Convention of the National Association of Evangelicals, Orlando Florida," *Public Papers of the Presidents, Ronald Reagan,* March 8, 1983, found at http://www.presidency.ucsb.edu.

that was expressly the opposite of that used in Vietnam. It eschewed both an incremental military build-up and a lengthy time horizon. As Colin Powell, chair of the Joint Chiefs of Staff, emphasized "We've gotta take the initiative out of the enemy's hands if we're going to go to war. We've got to make sure that . . . there'll be no guessing as to, you know, we're going to be successful with this plan."[7] A rapid build-up of over a half-million troops in the region over a 6-month period stood in stark contrast to the slow build-up of a similar number of troops that had taken place in Vietnam over a 6-year period. Combined with a sophisticated air campaign, Operation Desert Storm took just five weeks.

The National Campaign Context after Nixon

The relative normalcy within the national campaign context had a profound effect on nonvoting. Referring back to Table 5.1, it shows that for the first time the national campaign context consistently increases nonvoting. During seven of the nine elections in the government reassessment period, the national campaign context has sizable positive effects on nonvoting for the country as a whole (see the "Nation" column in Table 5.1). This is especially true of the 1970s elections, when national factors increase nonvoting by more than 12 percentage points for the country as a whole. Indeed, the positive effect of national factors in the 1970s is the mirror opposite of the negative effect of national factors in the 1960s, when national factors decreased nonvoting for the country as a whole from 4 percentage points in 1960 to 19 percentage points in 1966. In addition, as seen in Figure 7.1, while there are sporadic state effects during the 1980s, in general national effects dominate the period. Indeed, there are somewhat larger net national effects during this period than in the second period. Returning to Table 5.2, the mean net national effect for the third period was 51 percentage points as compared with 46 percentage points for the second period. Thus, the national quality of politics did not erode from the second period. Politics after Vietnam and Watergate was no less national in nature than it was during these events. In the government reassessment period, these large positive national effects help account for increasing nonvoting rates. At the national level, presidential nonvoting surged from 34 percent in the second period to 44 percent in the third, while midterm nonvoting increased from 55 percent in the second

[7] Colin Powell, Oral History of the Gulf War, *Frontline,* found at http://www.pbs.org/wgbh/pages/frontline/gulf/oral/powell/1.html.

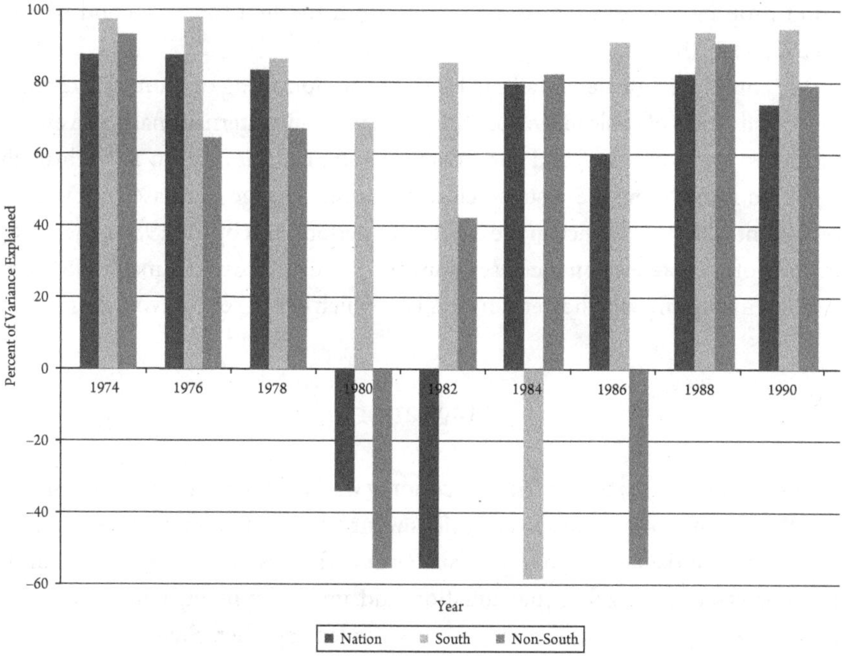

Figure 7.1 Net National and State Effects on Nonvoting, 1974–1990

period to 60 percent in the third (see Table 5.2). Once this increase occurred in the mid-1970s, nonvoting rates plateaued with only small movements up or down throughout the 1980s.

Figure 7.1 also shows that the national factors dominate state factors in their influence on regional nonvoting. The national effects are greater in the South than in the non-South and, as Table 5.1 depicts, these effects are positive. In the South, national factors increase nonvoting by 6 percentage points or more in five out of nine elections. The decline in southern nonvoting that had taken place since 1948 all but stopped during the 1970s and 1980s. What had been a 11 percentage point drop in southern nonvoting during presidential elections in the second period became a 2 percentage point decline in the presidential races of the third period (see Table 5.2). The 7 percentage point drop in southern nonvoting in midterm elections in the second period became a 4 percentage point drop in midterms of the third period (see Table 5.2). In the non-South, national factors increase nonvoting by 7 percentage points or more in six of the nine elections. These positive effects are associated with increases in nonvoting from the second period in the non-South of 9 percentage points in both presidential and midterm House elections (see Table 5.2). This compares with a 2 percentage point decline in presidential nonvoting and a 5 percentage point drop in midterm House nonvoting from the first to the second period (see Table 5.2).

We consider in greater detail the influence on nonvoting of economic change, the introduction of cable television, the youth vote, and international involvement relative to age, education, and party competition in elections from 1974 through 1990. To foreshadow the results below, economic change decreases nonvoting, consistent with its influence in the earlier two periods. But by the 1980s, the introduction of cable television increases nonvoting. We also consider major US international involvement in the Persian Gulf War which decreased nonvoting in 1990.[8]

Stagflation

By the middle 1970s, the American economy was no longer a post-war economy and the boom that had defined it. Prices went up, unemployment was comparatively high, and a new term *stagflation* became the descriptor for the economy. Economists were puzzled that inflation and unemployment, which had typically moved in opposite directions, now moved together. Figure 7.2 displays unemployment rates and the percent change in inflation from 1920 through 2012. As seen in the figure, the inflation rate had actually begun to rise slowly and unnoticed beginning in 1960 and continued to climb through 1980. In the 1970s and 1980s, inflation grew rapidly and spiked in 1974 and 1975 and then again in 1979, 1980, and 1981. Unemployment, which had been below 4 percent from 1966 through 1969, began creeping upward first to 5 percent in 1970, then 6 percent in 1971 and 1972, and 8 percent by 1975. As Figure 7.2 also makes clear, the larger of the two problems in historic terms was inflation. Unemployment during the third period was by no means at an all-time high. With the addition of many women and young people in the job market, there appeared to be a new, higher floor for the jobless rate, with some economists pegging the "natural rate of unemployment" at 6 percent.[9] By contrast, inflation

[8] We do not consider other international initiatives during the period primarily because they do not fall within an election year or data are lacking. These include Carter's dealings with the Iran hostage crisis in 1979 and 1980, Reagan sending troops to Lebanon (September 1983) and removing them (February 1984), the invasion of Grenada (October 1983), the bombing of Libya in April 1986, and the Iran-Contra scandal (revealed 2 days after the 1986 midterm elections). The Iran hostage crisis, removal of troops from Lebanon, and the Libyan bombings did occur within an election year cycle, but state-level data are inadequate.

[9] Robert Barsky and Lutz Kilian, "Oil and the Macroeconomy since the 1970s," *The Journal of Economic Perspectives*," 18 (Autumn 2004): 132; Stephen Turnovskly and Mark Wohar, "Alternative Modes of Deficit Financing and Endogeneous Monetary and Fiscal Policy in the U.S.A. 1923–1982," *Journal of Applied Econometrics* 2 (January 1987): 1–25.

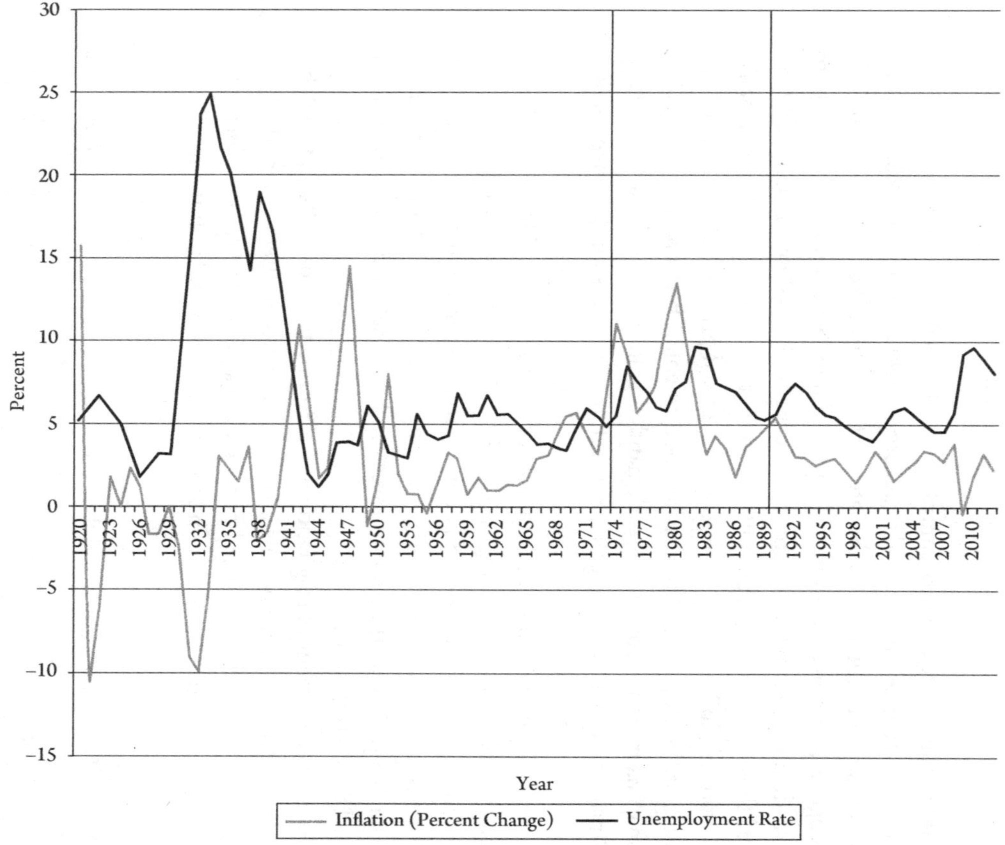

Figure 7.2 Unemployment Rate and Inflation Change, 1920–2012

had last been this worrisome during World War I. So by the middle 1970s, inflation and unemployment rates were drifting upward in unison but with inflation rising on a steeper slope.[10] Arthur Burns, then Chairman of the Federal Reserve Board, lamented "the rules are not working the way they used to."[11] Burns' comments encapsulated the economic uncertainty of the third period.

Causes of Stagflation

A series of interrelated factors contributed to the economic conundrum. First, the origins of stagflation appeared in the breakdown of the Bretton Woods world monetary system beginning in the late 1960s. Bretton Woods, a post-war fixed exchange rate system devised in 1944, pegged member countries' currencies to the US dollar. Separately, to instill confidence in the system the United States backed the dollar with gold, permitting member governments and central banks to convert the dollars they held into gold at a fixed price of $35 per ounce. This meant that the dollar was literally "as good as gold." Bretton Woods began to fall apart as member governments demanded gold for their dollars at the low fixed price and then sold the gold for much higher prices on the open market. In an effort to stop the rush for gold and the massive outflow of dollars from the United States, which heated up world markets, Richard Nixon unilaterally closed the gold window on August 15, 1971. This ended the convertability of dollars into gold and stopped, in Nixon's words, "international money speculators."[12] Nixon also ordered a 90-day wage and price freeze and a 10 percent import surcharge, but world attention was on the monetary decision, which was dubbed the "Nixon shock."[13]

The second element of stagflation was US monetary policy itself, which became more expansionary and unstable in the absence of Bretton Woods.[14] The discipline of Bretton Woods' fixed-rate regime was as much a restraint on the US Federal Reserve Board as it was on foreign central banks. With the new "more

[10] Wallace Peterson, "Stagflation and the Crisis of Capitalism," *Review of Social Economy* 38 (December 1980): 278.

[11] Arthur Burns, *Reflections of an Economic Policy Maker. Speeches and Congressional Statements: 1969–1978* (Washington, D.C.: American Enterprise Institute, 1978), 118.

[12] Richard Nixon, "Address to the Nation Outlining a New Economic Policy: The Challenge of Peace," *Public Papers of the Presidents, Richard Nixon, 1971*, found at the American Presidency Project, www.presidency.ucsb.edu.

[13] A. H. Raskin, "Dr. Nixon Prescribes Shock Therapy," *New York Times*, August 22, 1971, E1; Herman Kahn, "Thinking More Unthinkable Thoughts: I," *New York Times*, September 13, 1971, 37; Max Frankel, "'Japan Inc.' and 'Nixon Shocks,'" *New York Times*, November 25, 1971, 2

[14] Robert Barsky and Lutz Kilian, "Do We Really Know that Oil Caused the Great Stagflation? A Monetary Alternative," *NBER Macroeconomics Annual* 16 (2001): 137–183.

or less managed float" for the dollar, the Federal Reserve had much greater flexibility in manipulating the money supply.[15] The Fed initially did so with an expansionist policy that increased the money supply by 12 percent in 1971 and another 12 percent in 1972.[16] Economists Robert Barsky and Lutz Kilian showed that this expansion of the money supply and resulting worldwide liquidity led directly to peaks in the US inflation rate.[17] With inflation rising, the Fed then contracted the money supply in 1973 and 1974, beginning before the first oil shock in late 1973 but tightening the money supply still further during the oil crisis, only to expand it again in 1975, 1976, and 1977. Thus, partly in response to its own policy decisions, the Federal Reserve practiced a "go-stop monetary policy" and triggered an inflation trap.[18]

Third, there were significant price increases for commodities, including both industrial raw materials and staple food, much of it imported.[19] Between 1971 and 1974, the price of raw materials jumped 31 percent.[20] Prices remained at this new level until the end of the decade. Most fundamentally, these price increases occurred well before the oil shocks in late 1973 and were "consistent with a picture of increased demand driven by the sharp increase in global liquidity" fueled by the Federal Reserve's expansion of the money supply.[21]

Finally, stagflation worsened with oil shocks in late 1973 and 1979. Oil prices, something Americans had never worried about before, became one of the defining features of the economy. Until the late 1960s the US oil companies not only had sufficient capacity to meet domestic demand, but used excess capacity to regulate world oil markets by threatening to flood them to keep oil prices low. However, in March 1971, US oil production reached 100 percent of capacity for the first time. In response, the Organization of Petroleum Exporting Countries (OPEC) increased its production. Initially, prices stayed fairly stable because many oil delivery contracts were locked in long-term agreements. But, beginning in late 1972 and continuing throughout 1973, oil prices rose. In October 1973, OPEC invoked an embargo against the United States for its support of Israel during the Yom Kippur War against Egypt and Syria. The embargo, which

[15] Michael Bruno, "Import Prices and Stagflation in the Industrial Countries: A Cross-Section Analysis," *The Economic Journal* 90 (September 1980): 488.

[16] M2 money supply found at the St. Louis Federal Reserve, http://research.stlouisfed.org/fred2/data/M2SL.txt.

[17] Barsky and Kilian, 2001.

[18] Barsky and Kilian, 2001, 149.

[19] Michael Bruno, 1980, 479–492.

[20] Robert Barsky and Lutz Kilian, "Raw Materials, Profits, and the Productivity Slowdown," *Quarterly Journal of Economics* 99 (February 1984): 10–11; D. Grubb, R. Jackman, and R. Layard, "Causes of the Current Stagflation," *The Review of Economic Studies* 49 (Special Issue, 1982): 707–730.

[21] Barsky and Kilian, 2001, 153.

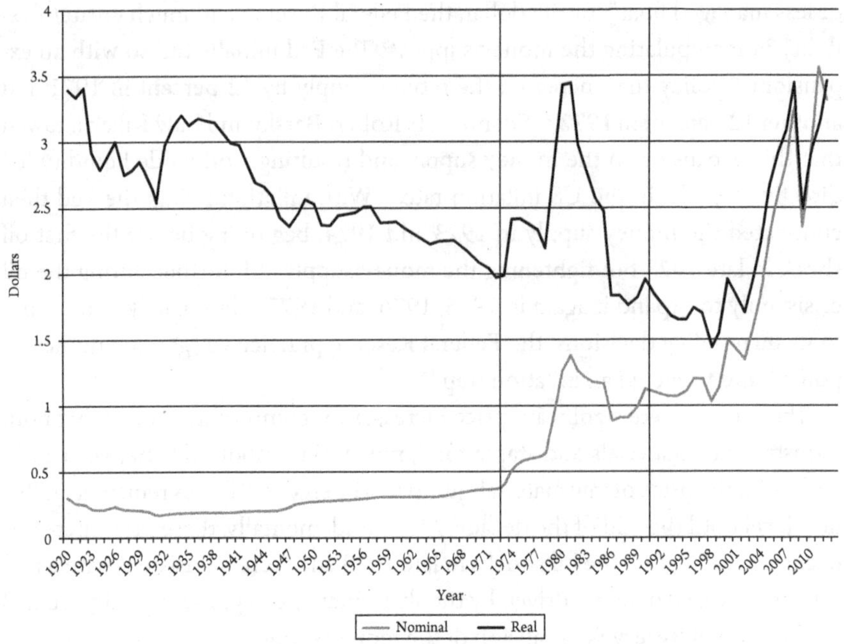

Figure 7.3 Gasoline Prices at the Pump, 1920–2012
Source: U.S. Energy Information Administration, "Short-Term Energy Outlook, January 2012" and "Annual Energy Outlook, 2012," found at http://www.eia.gov/

continued through April 1974, heightened oil price increases; it did not start them.[22] As the embargo went on, OPEC abandoned its contractual agreements with oil companies and turned to the spot market. The price of oil more than doubled from $2 a barrel in 1972 to $5 a barrel in 1974. As shown in Figure 7.3, for the American consumer prices at the gasoline pump rose from 36 cents per gallon in 1971 and 1972 to 52 cents per gallon in 1974.[23] Moreover, as noted above, as oil prices rose the Federal Reserve contracted the money supply, producing more stagflation. As economists Ben Bernanke, Mark Gertler, and Mark Watson stated, "The majority of the impact of an oil price shock on the real economy is attributable to the central bank's response to the inflationary pressures engendered by the shock." [24]

[22] Barsky and Kilian (1984, 174) find that the embargo was responsible for only 50% of the increases in oil prices, while the balance of the oil prices increases occurred before the embargo.

[23] Data are from the US Energy Information Administration http://www.eia.gov/forecasts/steo/realprices/.

[24] Ben Bernanke, Mark Gertler, and Mark Watson, "Systematic Monetary Policy and the Effects of Oil Price Shocks," *Brookings Papers on Economic Activity*, 1997: 122.

A second oil crisis unfolded in January 1979 in the wake of the Iranian Revolution which deposed the Shah of Iran and instated the Ayatollah Khomeini. Oil prices, at $13 a barrel before the crisis, soon moved to $16 in March after the revolution and eventually $24 a barrel by December. This second shock was fundamentally different from the first crisis. The increase in prices far exceeded inflation, and monetary expansion was less responsible for the increase.[25] President Jimmy Carter's dual decisions of banning the importation of Iranian oil and the deregulation of American oil prices in April 1979 had the effect of lowering oil imports but increasing domestic oil prices. The price increases also reflected that OPEC, now a much stronger cartel, was able to sustain prices even when demand declined. OPEC was thus most influential not in the initial outsized price increases, but rather in keeping prices from falling after the crises ended. Gasoline prices rose from 63 cents per gallon in 1978 to 86 cents per gallon in 1979 and then, breaking through the dollar per gallon mark, increased to $1.25 per gallon in 1980.

In general, then, this combination of factors—the end of Bretton Woods, "go-and-stop" monetary policy, commodity price increases, and the 1973 and 1979 oil shocks—created neither a boom nor a bust economy but rather a stalled economy through the 1970s. Uncertainty rose as the economy moved in previously uncharted directions. While personal income grew, the price of goods and services outpaced income growth. The stagflation continued with record inflation that peaked at 13.5 percent in 1980, numbers that were higher only in 1920. Unemployment continued to nudge upward to 7 percent in 1980. In his 1979 address to the nation, President Carter observed an economy of "paralysis and stagnation and drift."

Stagflation and Nonvoting

The theory of uncertainty in the national campaign context suggests that stagflation, as a truly perplexing economic condition, defined economic uncertainty in the government reassessment period. Unsure of future economic outcomes, people are less likely to remain on the political sidelines. Instead they participate in an attempt to improve the odds of better economic fortunes. Table 7.1 examines the effects of economic uncertainty relative to other aspects of the national campaign context on aggregate nonvoting from 1974 through 1980. In 1974, with unemployment low and inflation relatively flat, economic factors do not influence nonvoting. However, as stagflation becomes more worrisome, mean personal income change has a sizable negative impact on nonvoting in 1978 and

[25] Barsky and Kilian (2001) find that only 33 percent of the rise in oil prices can be attributed to monetary policies.

Table 7.1 **Effects of the National Campaign Context on Nonvoting, 1974–1980**

Predictor	1974				1976				1978				1980			
	Coefficient	*t-value*	*Mean*	*Impact*	*Coefficient*	*t-value*	*Mean*	*Impact*	*Coefficient*	*t-value*	*Mean*	*Impact*	*Coefficient*	*t-value*	*Mean*	*Impact*
Income Change	0.003	0.464	2180.752	6.542	–0.001	–0.040	2137.992	–2.138	–0.007	–1.712	2535.611	–17.749	–0.010	–2.142	2180.752	–21.808
Unemployment Change	0.429	0.544	0.638	0.274	–0.764	–1.754	1.762	–1.346	–1.635	–2.235	0.124	–0.203	–0.418	–0.677	0.238	–0.099
Communication Technology	–0.178	–0.125	97.961	–17.437	–0.020	–0.028	97.981	–1.960	–0.746	–0.636	97.961	–73.079	1.410	2.389	19.808	27.929
Competition	–0.043	–0.676	79.451	–3.416	0.001	0.006	89.773	0.090	0.004	0.605	80.195	0.321	–0.011	–1.677	83.988	–0.924
Youth	–0.627	–1.739	17.428	–10.927	–0.071	–0.223	18.420	–1.308	0.282	0.605	18.731	5.282	0.015	0.238	18.020	0.270
Education	–0.346	–1.849	46.083	–15.945	–0.280	–2.513	47.668	–13.347	–0.324	–1.673	49.612	–16.074	–0.272	–2.622	51.376	–13.974
Prior Nonvoting	0.662	7.584	52.838	34.979	0.882	12.710	42.593	37.567	0.554	5.563	60.349	33.433	0.829	15.053	45.445	37.674
Intercept	50.389	4.009			–4.326	–0.405			45.254	2.992			14.816	1.809		
N	50				51				50				51			
R^2	0.828				0.859				0.734				0.910			
Adjusted R^2	0.799				0.836				0.690				0.895			
Durbin h-statistic	0.502				0.531				0.851				0.942			

Note: Critical t-values are 1.679 at .10 probability; 2.009 at .05; 2.700 at .01. Critical value for Durbin h-statistic at .05 probability = 1.695.

1980. Unemployment also has a negative effect on nonvoting in 1976 and 1978. The uncertainty created by the stagnant economic conditions brought people to the polls in ways similar to the association between the economy and nonvoting in the earlier two periods.

"Go-and-stop" monetary policy continued in the 1980s as the Federal Reserve constricted the money supply and raised interest rates to record levels in order to bring down inflation. The prime rate topped out at 21.5 percent in December 1980, a rate never before seen since the Federal Reserve was created in 1913. The Fed's austere contraction of the money supply triggered a recession in 1980 that continued through 1982. Unemployment rose to nearly 8 percent in 1981 and was at its worst in November and December of 1982, reaching 10.4 percent.[26] But the unfamiliar link between high unemployment and high inflation was broken as inflation fell to 6 percent in 1982 and then 3 percent in 1983. A sharp drop in oil prices in 1982 also helped end inflation as a worldwide oil glut sent prices plummeting. Prices at the gas pump declined from $1.26 per gallon in 1982 to 88 cents a gallon in 1986. For the next four years, gasoline prices generally stayed below a dollar per gallon.

The claim made during Reagan's 1984 reelection that it was "morning again in America" was relative to tougher years during the Ford and Carter administrations and, indeed, Reagan's first term. Examined in a broader time frame, economic growth was modest throughout the 1980s with only 1984 showing an annual increase in real per capita income of 5 percent that rivaled income gains in the 1960s. In all other years from 1981 through 1988, income growth averaged 2 percent, compared to 1 percent growth from 1974 through 1980.[27] Unemployment, at nearly 10 percent in 1982 and 1983, dipped below 7 percent only beginning in 1987.

This slow growth persisted with the collapse of the savings and loan industry, which began in 1986 as the Federal Savings and Loan Insurance Corporation went insolvent, unable to cover the mounting losses from thrift failures. The problem intensified through 1995 as 1,043 savings and loans with assets of $519 billion were closed.[28] The strain on the financial sector contributed to an economic slowdown in 1990 and 1991. While the recession seemed to catch the George H. W. Bush administration by surprise in the aftermath of the Persian Gulf War victory, it was consistent with limited growth in the years before.

[26] These monthly data are taken from the Bureau of Labor Statistics at www.bls.gov.

[27] These annual data are taken from the U.S. Department of Commerce, Bureau of Economic Analysis at www.bea.gov.

[28] Timothy Curry and Lynn Shibut, "The Cost of the Savings and Loan Crisis: Truth and Consequences," *FDIC Banking Review* 13 (December 2000), found at http://www.fdic.gov/bank/analytical/banking/2000dec/brv13n2_2.pdf.

Economist Olivier Blanchard showed that consumption had begun to decline as early as the second quarter of 1989, and this continued through the third quarter of 1992. Some of this was surely prompted by the increase in oil prices set off by Iraq's invasion of Kuwait. The tightening of credit and financial regulations after the savings and loan debacle also contributed to the problem. Blanchard observed that negative shocks to investment in housing began in the third quarter of 1990.[29] Economists also indicated that the recession-like behavior among businesses and consumers lasted after the official end to the recession. This was especially telling in the labor market, as employment declines were heaviest in construction and the financial sector and continued through 1993.[30]

Table 7.2 displays the effects on nonvoting of economic change and other factors in the national campaign context for the latter part of the period from 1982 through 1990. In each election year, income change, unemployment change, or both significantly decrease nonvoting, except in 1986. Thus, even though stagflation was lessened by the middle 1980s, a recession ensued with high levels of unemployment that rode above 7 percent even in 1986. And by 1987, the savings and loan crisis precipitated slowdowns in housing and the financial sector which led to a recession in 1990. So throughout the period, economic uncertainty roiling from stagflation to recession decreased nonvoting levels.

Cable Television and Narrowcasting

Cable television was a technological shock in sharp contrast to the shocks offered by radio and broadcast television. It tapered and stylized political information rather than expanding it in the way radio and broadcast television had done. While the novelty of radio and television news made politics all but unavoidable, the personal selections available through cable made politics quite avoidable. Early cable television was heavily regulated in order to protect local television channels and was designed to serve viewers living in mountainous and remote rural locations.[31] But two changes ended this limited reach. First, in 1972 the Federal Communications Commission lifted restrictions on the

[29] Olivier Blanchard, "Consumption and the Recession of 1990–1991," *American Economics Review* 83 (May 1993): 272.

[30] Jennifer Gardner, "The 1990–91 Recession: How bad was the labor market?" *Monthly Labor Review* 117 (June 1994): 3–11.

[31] For an historical account of the advance of cable and satellite, see Patrick Parsons, "The Evolution of the Cable-Satellite Distribution System," *Journal of Broadcasting and Electronic Media* 47(1) (2003): 1–17.

ability of cable television companies to operate in large cities. Second, in 1975 RCA launched SATCOM1, a commercial communication satellite with greater capacity than earlier satellites, which led to a reduction in the cost of transmission. In 1976 a fledgling network, the Home Box Office (HBO) became the first cable network to deliver programming nationwide through satellite transmission when it carried the "'Thrilla in Manila" heavyweight boxing match between Joe Frazier and Muhammad Ali. This was quickly followed in 1977 by Ted Turner's Turner Broadcasting System (TBS) superstation from Atlanta and evangelist Pat Robertson's Christian Broadcasting Network (CBN). In 1980 Turner launched Cable News Network (CNN), the nation's first 24-hour news network, promising:

> We won't be signing off until the world ends. We'll be on, and we will cover the end of the world live, and that will be our last event . . . and when the end of the world comes, we'll play "Nearer My God, to Thee" before we sign off.[32]

Unlike the introduction of television itself, the growth of cable was slower, but steady. The number of Americans who had cable television subscriptions was no more than 2 percent in the 1960s but grew to 9 percent in 1972 and 20 percent in 1980. By 1990, 50 percent of American households had cable television subscriptions. As noted in Chapter 3, cable television subscriptions topped out at roughly two-thirds of American households in 1996 and so—unlike radio, television, and the Internet—the effect of cable broadcast is over a smaller but still sizable subset of the American population.

With cable television and the expansion of the 24-hour format, television changed in two fundamental ways. First, as cable television grew it allowed people to pick and choose what they wanted to watch in ways that were not available to them with network television. Political scientist Markus Prior discussed viewers' "relative entertainment preference" based on the number of hours of entertainment relative to news they watch. He found that "cable access increases news exposure for some people—those with a high appreciation of news—but lowers it for those who watch television primarily to be entertained."[33] Second, it allowed people to do so 24 hours a day. In the immediate term, the former was more important than the latter. By being able to pick MTV over CNN, people could avoid politics of any kind. As cable

[32] Antonina Jedrzejczak, "Here Are the Greatest Moments in CNN History," *Business Insider*, June 1, 2010, found at http://www.businessinsider.com/here-are-some-of-the-greatest-moments-in-cnn-history-2010-6?op=1.

[33] Markus Prior, *Post-Broadcast Democracy* (Cambridge: Cambridge University Press, 2007), 110.

Table 7.2 **Effects of the National Campaign Context on Nonvoting, 1982–1990**

Predictor	*1982*				*1984*				*1986*			
	Coefficient	*t-value*	*Mean*	*Impact*	*Coefficient*	*t-value*	*Mean*	*Impact*	*Coefficient*	*t-value*	*Mean*	*Impact*
Income Change	–0.004	–2.220	3440.500	–13.762	–0.001	–0.036	4378.529	–4.379	0.001	0.147	3196.979	3.197
Unemployment Change	0.091	0.276	3.585	0.326	–0.820	–3.109	0.460	–0.377	–0.667	–1.367	2.321	–1.548
Communication Technology	0.942	2.530	25.039	23.587	0.222	2.232	35.126	7.798	0.221	1.746	42.265	9.341
Competition	–0.002	–0.056	80.163	–0.160	0.018	0.553	76.620	1.379	0.056	1.520	79.475	4.451
Youth	–0.031	–0.061	18.020	–0.559	–0.265	–1.147	16.998	–4.504	0.884	1.179	15.889	14.046
Education	–0.288	–2.114	52.546	–15.133	0.100	1.040	53.168	5.317	–0.300	–1.472	54.588	–16.376
Prior Nonvoting	0.802	9.831	60.897	48.839	–0.820	–3.109	43.650	–35.793	0.786	7.687	56.467	44.383
Intercept	14.672	1.014			9.525	1.054			1.904	0.086		
N	50				51				50			
R^2	0.868				0.909				0.809			
Adjusted R^2	0.845				0.894				0.776			
Durbin h-statistic	1.063				0.812				1.486			

Predictor	*1988*				*1990* [a]			
	Coefficient	*t-value*	*Mean*	*Impact*	*Coefficient*	*t-value*	*Mean*	*Impact*
Income Change	–0.002	–5.239	3118.196	–5.560	–0.005	–1.963	3799.520	–18.998
Unemployment Change	–0.676	–3.948	1.812	–1.225	–2.197	–2.949	1.517	–3.333
Communication Technology	0.150	3.360	48.317	7.248	0.190	1.253	53.115	10.092
International Involvement					–4.021	–2.021	2.663	–10.708
Competition	0.019	0.888	85.973	1.633	0.049	1.013	83.536	4.093
Youth	–0.020	–0.084	14.814	–0.296	0.0005	0.310	513354.167	256.677
Education	–0.185	–3.354	55.191	–10.210	–0.850	–3.019	56.530	–48.051
Prior Nonvoting	0.924	22.924	42.878	39.619	0.516	4.266	59.911	30.914
Intercept	12.196	1.767			83.333	3.056		
N	51				50			
R^2	0.954				0.743			
Adjusted R^2	0.947				0.690			
Durbin h-statistic	0.048				0.211			

Note: Critical t-values are 1.679 at .10 probability; 2.009 at .05; 2.700 at .01. Critical value for Durbin h-statistic at .05 probability = 1.695.

[a] Total youth in the state population, rather than percent youth in the state population, used to estimate the model. See note 34.

television expanded during this period, the tastes of viewers began to drive media content from broadcasting to narrowcasting—tailoring content to very specific audiences and explicitly excluding others. In the longer term, the 24-hour clock also had tremendous implications because it changed the political news cycle from one pegged to how things would appear on the nightly news to one that involved real-time coverage of an event as it happened at any time of the day or night.

Tables 7.1 and 7.2 monitor the effects of the technological shift from broadcast television to cable television. We compare the effect of broadcast television from 1974 through 1978 with the effect of cable beginning in the 1980 election, when 20 percent of American households had cable subscriptions. Television ownership had no effect on nonvoting in 1974, 1976, and 1978 as it reached saturation points of nearly 98 percent of American families. This is consistent with results observed in Chapter 6 for elections in the 1960s and 1970s when most Americans had access to television. However, beginning in 1980 cable television consistently increases nonvoting in each election except in 1990. The "Impact" column reveals that at the mean level of cable households, the increase in nonvoting in a state ranges from 7 percentage points in 1988 to 28 percentage points in 1980. These positive effects are similar in magnitude to the negative effects of radio and network television in the early periods. In addition, the impact of cable television in the 1980s typically exceeds that of other national campaign factors, notably economic conditions even at the height of stagflation in 1980.

In a fundamental way, the ability of cable television subscribers to pick and choose what they want to watch and when creates a kind of personal certainty as a new element of the campaign context. Cable television offers people an array of entertainment channels that expressly do not cover the news or focus on politics. It is not simply that media matters in political participation—but, amplifying Prior's conclusion about entertainment preferences, the growth of cable suggests that some people who may not be interested in politics opt out with their cable channel choices, and consequently nonvoting increases. Thus, this creates an important exception to the central hypothesis that technological shocks decrease nonvoting.

Youth Nonvoting Revisited

As discussed in the last chapter, we hypothesized that uncertainty associated with federal legal changes to the franchise would decrease nonvoting. Specifically, the novelty of being able to vote will decrease nonvoting. Yet, despite the efforts of 18-year-olds to obtain the right to vote in 1971 with the 26th Amendment to the

Constitution, the 18- to 24-year-old age group has been the least likely of any age group to vote. As seen in Figures 7.4 and 7.5, this is true for all election years, whether in presidential or midterm House races. In a few presidential years—1992, 2004, and 2008—youth nonvoting declines, but it does not drop to the level of older age groups. In midterm House election years, youth nonvoting has actually increased over time from 76 percent nonvoting in 1974 to 82 percent nonvoting in 2010. This helps ensure the stubbornly high nonvoting rates in the more local and less interesting midterm elections.

The question arises, then, about the effect of youth on nonvoting relative to other elements of the national campaign context. As observed in Chapter 6, youth did not influence nonvoting in the 1972 election—the first election in which 18- to- 20-year-olds were eligible to vote. However, as seen in Table 7.2, youth does decrease nonvoting in the 1974 midterms. Just months after Nixon's resignation and Ford's pardon of Nixon, the 1974 elections were unusually high-visibility midterms, and the uncertainty surrounding the election in the wake of Nixon's departure likely motivated young people to vote. However, thereafter youth has no other effects during the period.[34] Thus, like the results observed in the first and second periods, youth has little influence on nonvoting in the third period. This is an important finding in sharp contrast to the results found in Chapter 3 for the entire time frame as a whole, which showed a strong effect of youth on increasing nonvoting from 1920 through 2012. When considering individual elections the uncertainty of the national campaign context, party competition, and education negate the overall effect of youth observed earlier. Even though young people vote less frequently than other age groups, the consistently high nonvoting rate among the young with little variation from one election to the next helps clarify why youth does not have an impact on individual elections.

The entrance of young people into the electorate currently marks the end of historic voter registration efforts to expand participation. At the national level, the only substantial effort to ease voter registration since then came in 1993 with the passage of the National Voter Registration Act, otherwise known as "motor voter." The law requires states to provide voter registration at drivers' license and social service offices. Evidence suggests that the law has had some effect on increasing turnout.[35] If attention to federal immigration reform continues, a

[34] In 1990 we estimated the model with a variable measuring youth in the population rather than one tapping percent youth in the population. This provided for more robust estimates and the absence of autocorrelation among the error terms.

[35] Benjamin Highton and Raymond Wolfinger, "Estimating the Effects of the National Voter Registration Act of 1993," *Political Behavior* 30 (June 1998): 79–104; Stephen Knack, "Does 'Motor Voter' Work? Evidence from State-Level Data," *Journal of Politics* 57 (August 1995): 796–811;

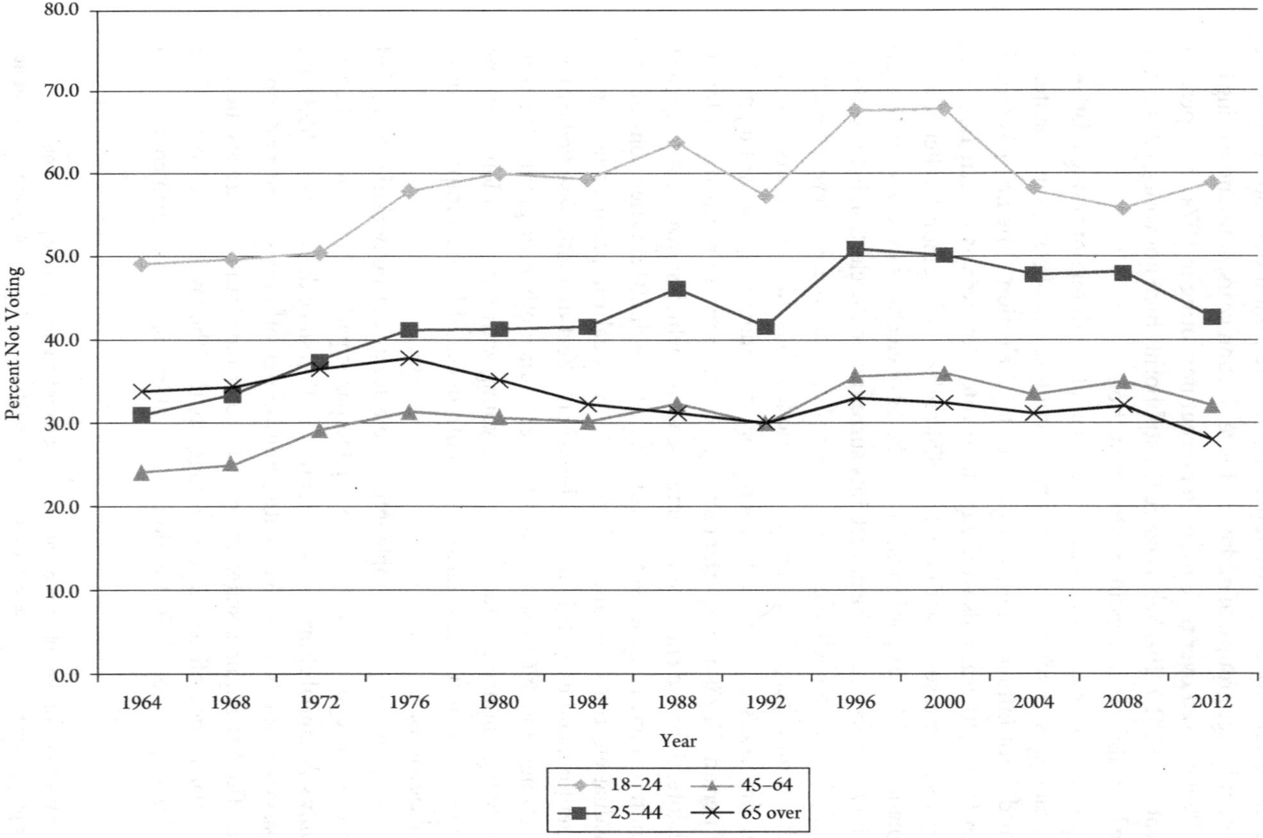

Figure 7.4 Nonvoting Among Age Groups in Presidential Elections, 1964–2012

Source: U.S. Census, "Voting and Registration in the Election of November 2012" found at http://www.census.gov/hhes/www/socdemo/voting/publications/p20/2012/tables.html

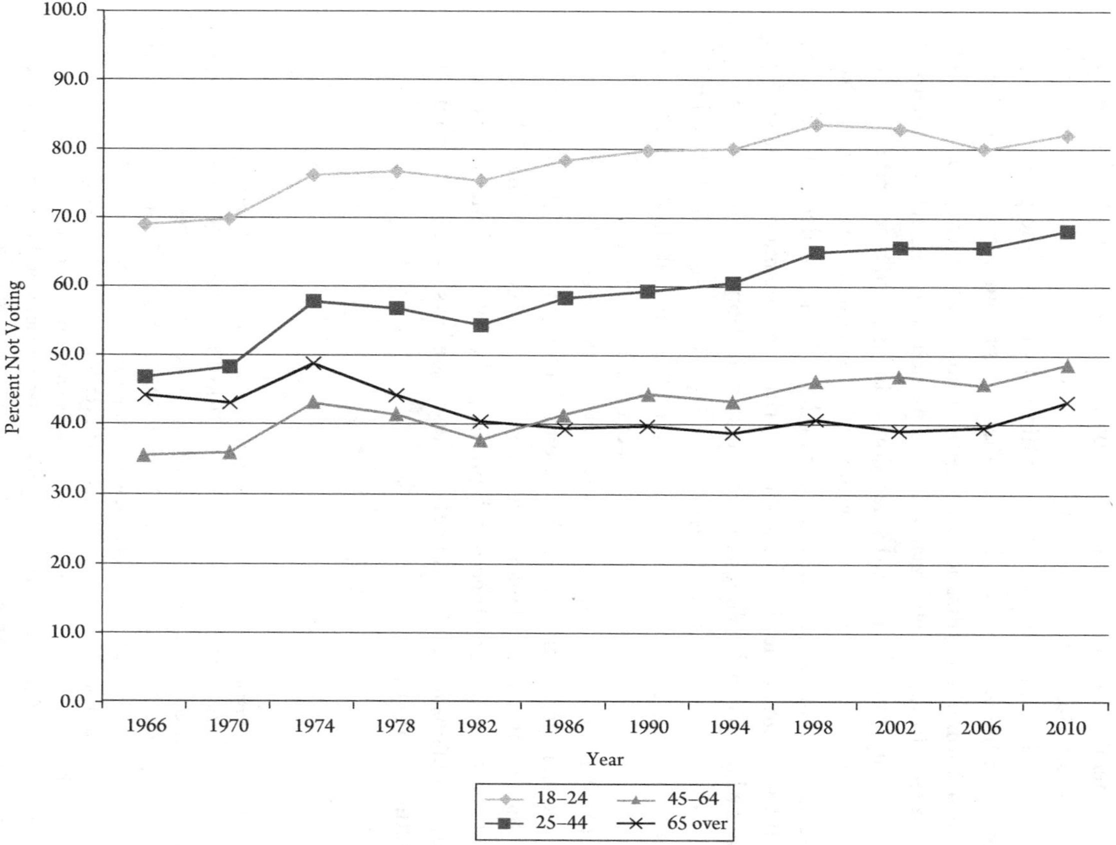

Figure 7.5 Nonvoting Among Age Groups in Midterm Elections, 1966–2010
Source: U.S. Census, "Voting and Registration in the Election of November 2012" found at http://www.census.gov/hhes/www/socdemo/voting/publications/p20/2012/tables.html

major new push for voter registration may come in the Hispanic-American community in which nonvoting rates are currently quite high.[36]

At the state level, there has been a recent movement to increase the stringency of state laws on participation. These include registration restrictions, proof of citizenship requirements, absentee ballot restrictions, early voting reductions, and voter identification requirements. The voter identification requirements have become the most commonplace. In 2012, 21 states had adopted some form of photo identification law, and three others have adopted strict identification requirements that did not mandate the presentation of photo ID at the polling place. Eleven other states required the presentation of a general form of identification (utility bill or bank statement).[37] It is unclear what effect these laws will have on voter participation, especially in tandem with the Supreme Court's 2013 decision striking down a central part of the Voting Rights Act of 1965 which required states, mostly in the South, to seek pre-clearance for changes in their voting laws. In a 5–4 decision in *Shelby County v. Holder*, Chief Justice Roberts, writing for the majority, stated "Our country has changed. While any racial discrimination in voting is too much, Congress must ensure that the legislation it passes to remedy that condition speaks to current conditions."[38] However, in 2016 several US Appeals Courts struck down key elements of voter identification laws in North Carolina, North Dakota, Texas, and Wisconsin as being inherently discriminatory against minority voters. Researchers Keith Bentele and Erin O'Brien showed that the recent passage of many voter access laws between 2006 and 2011 were highly partisan and designed to inhibit the participation of minority voters.[39] Thus, it remains to be seen what effect these state laws will have on nonvoting in future elections.

Michael Hanmer, *Discount Voting Voter Registration Reforms and Their Effects* (Cambridge: Cambridge University Press, 2009; Melanie Springer, *How the States Shaped the Nation: American Electoral Institutions and Voter Turnout, 1920–2000* (Chicago: University of Chicago Press, 2014).

[36] During presidential elections from 1980 through 2012, 52 percent of Hispanic Americans did not vote, compared with 41 percent of African Americans and 35 percent of non-Hispanic whites. The corresponding nonvoting numbers for midterm elections from 1982 through 2010 are 66 percent Hispanic Americans, 58 percent African Americans, and 50 percent non-Hispanic whites.

[37] National Conference of State Legislatures, "Voter Identification Requirements," found at http://www.ncsl.org/research/elections-and-campaigns/voter-id.aspx#State_Reqs.

[38] Adam Liptak, "Supreme Court Invalidates Key Part of the Voting Rights Act," *New York Times*, June 25, 2013, found at http://www.nytimes.com/2013/06/26/us/supreme-court-ruling.html?pagewanted=all&_r=0.

[39] Keith Bentele and Erin O'Brien, "Jim Crow 2.0? Why States Consider and Adopt Restrictive Voter Access Policies," *Perspectives on Politics* 11 (December 2013): 1088–1116.

International Affairs and Nonvoting

On April 23, 1975, Gerald Ford, speaking at Tulane University's convocation, stated, "Today, America can regain the sense of pride that existed before Vietnam. But it cannot be achieved by refighting a war that is finished as far as America is concerned . . . We, of course, are saddened indeed by the events in Indochina. But these events, tragic as they are, portend neither the end of the world nor of America's leadership in the world . . . We can and we should help others to help themselves. But the fate of responsible men and women everywhere, in the final decision, rests in their own hands, not in ours."[40] Just six days later, a frantic helicopter evacuation of remaining American personnel and South Vietnamese refugees began from Saigon. As Ford's remarks attest, US international efforts were more subdued in the aftermath of the Vietnam War than they had been in the previous two periods. Even with large increases in the defense budget begun under Carter and trademarked under Reagan, caution defined US international efforts. Nevertheless, the theory of uncertainty in the national campaign context suggests that war, no matter its size or intended duration, is still inherently uncertain. We hypothesize that war will decrease nonvoting, as people are unclear about future outcomes.

We consider the effects of the Persian Gulf War during the George H. W. Bush administration as an indicator of uncertainty in the national campaign context.[41] As seen in Table 7.2, the early stages of the Persian Gulf War had a substantial impact on nonvoting in the 1990 midterm elections. In August 1990, stating "a line has been drawn in the sand," President Bush sent US forces to Saudi Arabia in response to Iraq's invasion of its neighbor Kuwait.[42] Public opinion was generally favorable to Bush's decision, with 61 percent

[40] *Public Papers of the Presidents, Gerald Ford,* "Address at a Tulane University Convocation," April 23, 1975, found at the American Presidency Project: http://www.presidency.ucsb.edu/.

[41] Since there are no state-level aggregate data for this event, we turn to attitudinal data drawn from the 1990 American National Election studies. The question asked about the Persian Gulf was, "How strongly do you approve or disapprove of Bush's handling of the Persian Gulf crisis?" The variable is coded on a 7-point scale from +3 (strongly approve) through 0 (neutral) to -3 (strongly disapprove). States are assigned the mean value for respondents from the state. In those states in which no respondents were interviewed, we substitute the regional mean. Although the ANES samples are not state-representative, we conducted a comparison of state demographics found in the U.S. Census and state demographics as identified in the ANES data set. There are clear similarities in the backgrounds of the eligible electorate in a state relative to the backgrounds of ANES respondents in a state on age, sex, education, and mobility dimensions. Thus the measure, while less than ideal, does have merit.

[42] *Public Papers of the Presidents, George H.W. Bush,* "The President's News Conference," August 8, 1990, found at The American Presidency Project http://www.presidency.ucsb.edu/.

of Americans in agreement and 29 percent opposed. The Impact column in Table 7.2 shows that the mean approval of Bush's decision prompted nonvoting to decrease by 11 percentage points. Thus nonvoting, high in 1990 at 61 percent, would have been even higher had the international response not been made.

The Puzzle of Education and Participation

Throughout the 1970s and 1980s, education levels improved, although at a pace slower than during the 1950s and 1960s which, as noted in the previous chapter, saw the most dramatic improvement in education of any time in American history. From 1974 to 1990, high school graduates increased by 29 percent nationally, with 76 percent of Americans holding high school degrees by 1990.[43] The largest increase took place in the South, where there was a 40 percent increase in high school graduates across the period as compared with a 26 percent increase in the non-South. By 1990, 70 percent of southerners had graduated from high school. Thus the regional gap between the South and the rest of the country continued to shrink.

Still, the greater advances in education during the period occurred in the number of college graduates—a 55 percent increase in college graduates for the country as a whole (see Table 5.8). As another indicator, 20 percent of Americans held college degrees in 1990, as compared to 13 percent in 1974. Figure 7.6 shows that the increases in college graduation rates occurred in all regions and at very similar rates—with states in the East and the West doing slightly better than those in the South and Midwest, but not markedly so.

As seen in Table 7.1 and 7.2, throughout the third period the increase in education significantly decreases nonvoting in all years except 1984 and 1986. The "Impact" column shows that education has a sizable effect, but generally the effect is not substantial enough to offset the increases in nonvoting triggered by cable television in the 1980s. The relative effects of education and technology help resolve an empirical question researchers raised in the 1970s regarding increases in nonvoting at a time when education, especially college education, was expanding. Political scientist Richard Brody posed a simple puzzle: why did nonvoting increase when education was also increasing?[44] The results in Tables 7.1 and 7.2 indicate that at the aggregate

[43] Refer to Table 5.8.

[44] Richard Brody, "The Puzzle of Political Participation in America," in Anthony King, ed., *The New American Political System* (Washington, D.C.: American Enterprise Institute, 1978), 287–324. See also Brad Gomez, "Revisiting the 'Puzzle of Participation': A Dynamic Model of Education and

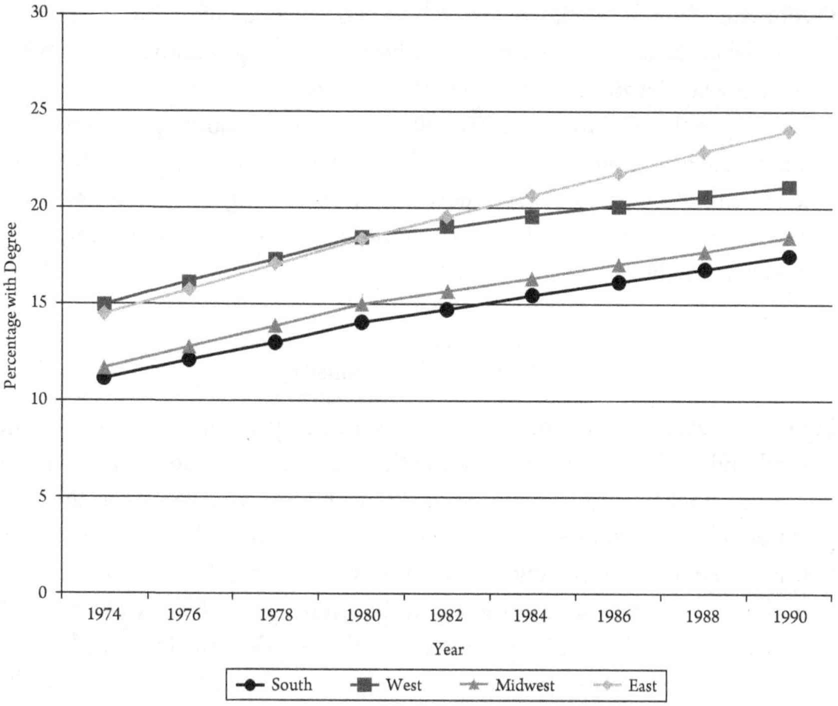

Figure 7.6 College Graduates by Region, 1974–1990

level, the link between education and turnout was never broken. Instead, during the 1970s and 1980s, communication technology was a countervailing element of the campaign context. Education did increase participation, but the expansion of cable television decreased participation at a stronger pace.

Party Competition and Regionalism Redefined

The post-Watergate period saw significant restructuring of party competition. The South continued to become more competitive as the Republicans' southern strategy entrenched the party in the region, especially at the presidential level. What were once inroads by the Eisenhower, Nixon, and Goldwater campaigns became permanent and broad-based support during the Reagan and George H. W. Bush elections of the 1980s. Post-Watergate meant something specific and welcome to the Republican Party in moving past both Nixon and Ford, whose credibility suffered after the Nixon pardon. Reagan became the anti-Nixon—another

Turnout Growth," unpublished manuscript, 2008. See http://myweb.fsu.edu/bgomez/Gomez_EducationTurnout_2008.pdf for another assessment of whether there ever was a puzzle.

Californian who was ebullient when Nixon was sullen, comfortable in front of a camera when Nixon sweated, passionately opposed to government even while running it when Nixon saw the benefit of government or at least did not challenge it. This began the growth of the Republican Party as a majority party resting on strong ideological tenets. It had been attempted with Goldwater, but Reagan succeeded in creating an electoral majority while advancing strident conservative views on abortion, labor, civil rights, education, AIDS, the environment, taxes, and military might.

Reagan's Regionalism

Figure 7.7 examines regional differences in party competition across the second and third periods. Bars below the zero point denote that there was greater competition in the non-South than the South. Bars above the zero point denote that there was greater competition in the South than the non-South. What is clear is how competitive races in the South became. The regional difference in competition is all but nonexistent from 1976 onward, except for 1980 when competitiveness in the South actually exceeds competitiveness in the non-South. In 1980, Reagan captured 51 percent of the vote in the South, the first time a Republican had received a majority in the South since 1872 (excluding Nixon's landslide reelection in 1972). Political scientists Earl Black and Merle Black clarified that Reagan's southern strength involved gaining a majority of white southerners and offering a "respectable version of the newest white people's party for many conservatives and some moderate whites."[45] Referring back to Table 5.6 presenting mean competition indicators by time period, the table shows the erosion of the Democratic share of the southern presidential vote. Democrats had already fallen below 50 percent support in presidential races in the post-war period. But they fell even further in the government reassessment period, receiving only 46 percent of the two-party vote across the period as a whole, even with southern Democrat Jimmy Carter's victory in 1976. Consistently after 1980, the Republican share of the southern presidential vote was never less than 49 percent. As Democratic control of the South faded, the competition index in presidential elections increased from 79 percent in the post-war period to 86 percent in the government reassessment period. (Recall that the higher the competition index, the greater is the level of competition between the parties in a state.) Referencing Table 5.7, the competition index in southern midterm

[45] Earl Black and Merle Black, *The Rise of Southern Republicans* (Cambridge: Harvard University Press, 2002), 217.

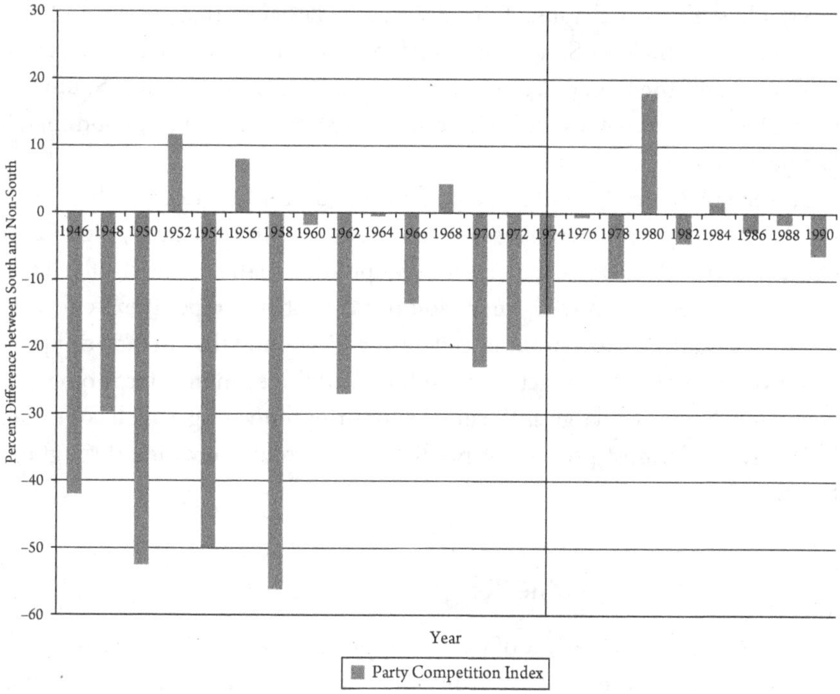

Figure 7.7 Regional Differences in Party Competition, 1946–1990

House elections also increased, although at a slower pace from 53 percent in the post-war period to 76 percent in the government reassessment period. Republicans began to pick up House seats held by long-time Democratic members who either retired or lost, and the Democratic share of the two-party vote dropped from 73 percent in the post-war period to 61 percent in the post-Watergate period.

In contrast to these developments in the South, the overall competition index for presidential elections in the non-South stayed flat at 83 percent, with little change in competitiveness in either the Midwest or the East compared to the post-war period (see Table 5.6). But hidden behind this constancy was a decrease in competition in the West. Republicans solidified gains in the West in presidential years, with the competition index declining from 85 percent to 79 percent. In midterm elections, competition declined in both the West and the East, with Republicans increasing their strength in the West and Democrats making headway in the East. From the second to the third period, the competition index dropped from 87 percent to 83 percent in midterm House elections in the West (see Table 5.7). The House midterm competition index in the East dropped even more sharply, by 9 percentage points from the post-war period (87 percent) to the government reassessment period (78 percent). To foreshadow the next chapter, Table 5.7 also makes clear that House midterm competition in the non-South continued to fall in the most recent time period across not only the West and the East but also the Midwest. The non-South was becoming a somewhat less cohesive political region in the third period than it had been during the second period.

As seen in Tables 7.1 and 7.2, competitiveness has little to do with nonvoting during the government reassessment period, with statistically significant effects only in 1980. Despite increased competition in the South, the flat levels of competitiveness across the non-South meant that competition's effect on nonvoting was much less pronounced during this period than in the prior periods. Even in 1980, its impact is much less than the economy, technology, or education. Nor is it as large as the impact for prior nonvoting, which continues to be the single most prominent predictor of current nonvoting throughout the period.

The "Reagan Revolution"

This relatively limited effect of party competition on nonvoting is an ironic feature of the third period, an irony that especially suffused Reagan's victory in 1980. Reagan offered what many touted as a "revolution," attacking not only the success of the New Deal and the Great Society but the very legitimacy of the national government and its ability to deliver on its mission. One can hardly imagine the term *revolution* tied to any of Reagan's immediate predecessors—Nixon, Ford, or Carter—who largely agreed on the role of the national government in domestic policy and advocated incremental advances in the national agenda. But Reagan's appeal was distinctly ideological and, combined with a mastery of image and mass communication, the name "Reagan" and the word "revolution" did fit together. Yet such fervor, radical thinking, and promised change typically bring people to the polls, both for and against the ideological driver. And competition is often fierce. But in 1980 this did not happen. To achieve Ronald Reagan's victory in 1980, Republican strategists worked to add just enough new people to the party base to win a majority in key states.[46] Unlike the Eisenhower effort in 1952, they did not seek to enlarge the base by adding new people to the voting public. Reagan Democrats became temporary Republicans, but nonvoting remained high, as it had in 1972 and 1976. Nonvoting continued to be elevated in 1984 and 1988 as Reagan and his successor, George H. W. Bush, won handily against luckless Democratic opponents. In none of the

[46] Gerald Pomper, "The Presidential Election," in G. Pomper, ed., *The Election of 1980* (Chatham, NJ: Chatham House, 1981), 65–96.

presidential elections of the period, not even 1980, was competition pushing people to vote.

Individual Nonvoting amidst the "Reagan Revolution"

The fact that the Reagan revolution did not bring increasing numbers of people to the polls is also important to individual nonvoting. Reagan made his political career on the notion that government was too large and intrusive. Carter had begun this reassessment of government by unsuccessfully trying to convince people that they relied too much on government. Rather than blaming the people for wanting too much, Reagan blamed government for doing too much. He summed this up in his first inaugural address: "Government is not the solution to our problem, government *is* the problem." In both Carter's and Reagan's outlook, government action was the central issue of the day. Even when George H. W. Bush offered a "kinder, gentler nation," it was with this reassessment of government in mind. To capture this reassessment, we introduce two variables for this historical period—individuals' views of government size and government spending.[47] We also add a government ethics variable in 1976 to understand whether the aftermath of Watergate and Ford's pardon of Nixon may have contributed to individuals' nonvoting. Did the public discourse about government reassessment influence individuals' nonvoting decisions?

Presidential Elections

Table 7.3 presents the results for individual nonvoting for presidential elections from 1976 to 1988. The government size, spending, and ethics variables have no effect on nonvoting. So while there was considerable discussion of the role of the national government during this period, it did not have a systematic effect on bringing people to the polls or keeping them away. This may help account for the high, stable nonvoting at the aggregate level. Politicians' very messages did not translate into encouraging participation. In general, it appears that while people do pay attention to aspects of the government in the national campaign context in making their participation decisions, the level of specificity mostly focuses

[47] The government size indicator is based on the question, "Is the government in Washington too strong?" The government spending indicator is based on a 7-point scale ranging from "government should provide many fewer services, reduce spending a lot" to "government should provide many more services, increase spending a lot."

on economic and international affairs, not on governmental ethics, policy, or size. The degree of uncertainty needs to be fairly high and broad before people take these matters into account in their uncertainty calculations. Campaigns may spend considerable time developing these issues as themes, but it does not mean that people see them as sufficiently novel or risky that they pay special attention to them.

Table 7.3 shows that unlike the government reassessment measures, the economic, media, and international indicators of the national campaign context influence individual nonvoting in each presidential election (except international involvement in 1988).[48] People who believe the economy is stable are less likely to vote than those who see economic change (whether strongly positive or strongly negative). As seen in the "change in likelihood" columns in Table 7.3, these effects range from a 22 percentage point difference in 1980 to a 76 percentage point difference in 1988. The impact of stagflation and subsequent economic instability, seen at the aggregate level, also plays out at the individual level. People who see uncertainty in the economy are more likely to vote. People who pay little attention to the media are much less likely to vote than those who pay considerable attention to the media. The effect is smaller than that found for economic conditions but still robust: the differences range from a 31 percentage points in 1984 to 47 percentage points in 1980. This is in contrast to the more specific effect of cable television in the aggregate results in Tables 7.1 and 7.2, which is the stronger determinant of nonvoting relative to economic conditions. Finally, the uncertainty within the international dimension strongly influences individual nonvoting. People who feel that US involvement should remain as it is are more likely to be nonvoters than those who feel that the US international posture should be more aggressive. The differences range from 20 percentage points in 1984 to 53 percentage points in 1980. Thus, not only do specific US foreign policy decisions affect aggregate nonvoting, but individuals' concerns about the world influence their participation decisions.

Continued examination of Table 7.3 shows that people's internal uncertainty about the candidates and who should win also affect individual nonvoting. Candidate comparisons influence individual nonvoting in 1980 and 1984, and ideological comparisons do so in 1980 and 1988. The 1980 result offers some

[48] The international involvement measure used in 1976, 1980, and 1988 is based on a question which asks respondents whether they agree with the statement, "The country is better off if we just stayed home and did not concern ourselves with problems in other parts of the world." Because of missing data issues, the international involvement variable used in 1984 is a 7-point scale measure based on a question about US cooperation with the Soviet Union: "Some people feel we should try to cooperate with the Soviet Union while others feel we should get much tougher in our dealings with them."

evidence of the ideological nature of Reagan's election. People who do not see the candidates ideologically are 32 percentage points more likely to be nonvoters than those who see strong ideological differences between Reagan and Carter. In 1988, perhaps Bush attacking Democratic opponent Michael Dukakis as a "Massachusetts liberal" paid off in bringing people to the polls. People who do not care who wins the election are also less likely to vote than those who do in each of the elections, except 1984. In general, people who do not resolve their internal uncertainty about the candidates are more likely not to vote than those who do.

The effects of the national campaign context and candidate awareness on individual nonvoting occur relative to the influence of personal resources, psychological involvement, campaign contact, and social connections. The patterns observed in Table 7.3 are quite similar to those found in Chapter 6. Age and education have very strong effects on individuals' participation decisions. People who are younger are much less likely to vote than those who are older; the difference ranges from 28 percentage points less likely in 1976 to 65 percentage points in 1988. Those who are less educated are consistently less likely to vote than those with high levels of education. In addition, people's psychological involvement in politics has a good deal to say about their nonvoting. People who are not interested in the campaign are from 34 percentage points (1976) to 72 percentage points (1988) less likely to vote than those who are very interested. Also, the efforts of campaigns to directly contact individuals have a strong effect on individual nonvoting. People who have not been contacted by one or both of the presidential campaigns are much less likely to vote than those who have received some sort of direct communication from a campaign.

During this period, social connections are somewhat better determinants of nonvoting than they were in the elections of 1968 and 1972. As shown in Table 7.3, people who are not married are less likely to vote in 1976 and 1980 but not thereafter. People who have lived in a community for a relatively short time are less likely to vote in 1980, 1984, and 1988. Consistent with results in Chapter 4, those who are unemployed are less likely to participate than those who have a job in 1976 and 1980.

Midterm Elections

Table 7.4 presents the results for midterm elections from 1978 through 1990. One of the most significant results at the midterm is a non-result. In preliminary estimates of the model, neither the government size nor the government spending variable had any impact on individual nonvoting in any

Table 7.3 **Effects of the National Campaign Context on Individual Nonvoting in Presidential Elections, 1976–1988 (Probit Maximum Likelihood Coefficients)**

Predictor	*1976*					*1980*			
	Maximum Likelihood Estimate	*MLE/ SE*		*Range of Value in the Variable*	*Change in Likelihood of the Variable*	*Maximum Likelihood Estimate*	*MLE/ SE*		*Range of Value in the Variable*
National Campaign Context									
Economic conditions	−0.111	−2.981	***	−2, 2	0.603	−0.090	−1.929	*	−2, 2
Media attention	−0.149	−4.274	***	0,4	0.357	−0.162	−3.496	***	0,4
Government ethics	0.012	0.172		0,1	0.012				
Government size	−0.057	−1.266		0,1	0.049	0.032	0.504		0,1
Government economic policy	−0.075	−1.283		1,3	0.157	n/a	n/a		
International involvement [a]	0.093	2.398	**	0,1	0.396	0.177	3.099	***	0,1
Candidate Awareness									
Candidate comparison	0.001	0.045		0,100	0.061	−0.004	−1.974	**	0,100
Ideological comparison	−0.036	−1.463		1,7	0.187	−0.067	−2.119	**	1,7
Care who wins	−0.122	−3.239	***	−1,1	0.244	−0.080	−1.675	*	−1,1
Personal Characteristics									
Youth	0.010	4.715	***	17,99	0.276	0.016	5.886	***	17,99
Education	−0.184	−3.725	***	0,3	0.215	−0.282	−4.386	***	0,3
Social Connections									
Marriage	−0.170	−2.240	**	0,1	0.138	−0.244	−2.455	***	0,1
Residential stability	−0.002	−1.393		0,99	0.273	−0.006	−4.179	***	0,99
Unemployment	0.128	1.724	*	0,1	0.046	0.215	2.057	**	0,1
Psychological Involvement									
Campaign interest	−0.169	−3.142	***	1,3	0.336	−0.441	−6.269	***	1,3
Party Mobilization and Competition									
Campaign contact	−0.331	−3.934	***	0,1	0.331	−0.381	−3.190	***	0,1
Closeness of race	−0.075	−1.003		0,1	0.076	0.070	0.690		0,1
Intercept	1.346	6.111	***			2.593	10.377	***	
Number of Cases	1658					1190			

	1984					1988				
Change in Likelihood of the Variable	*Maximum Likelihood Estimate*	*MLE/ SE*		*Range of Value in the Variable*	*Change in Likelihood of the Variable*	*Maximum Likelihood Estimate*	*MLE/ SE*		*Range of Value in the Variable*	*Change in Likelihood of the Variable*
0.224	−0.146	−3.036	***	−2, 2	0.721	−0.225	−5.194	***	−2, 2	0.761
0.472	−0.120	−2.477	**	0,4	0.311	−0.128	−2.805	***	0,4	0.365
0.032	0.074	1.069		0,1	0.094	−0.089	−1.571		0,1	0.100
	−0.046	−1.352		1,7	0.083	0.015	0.533		1,7	0.046
0.526	−0.049	−1.852	*	1,7	0.198	0.008	0.180		0,1	0.063
0.257	−0.003	−1.735	*	0,100	0.197	0.001	0.010		0,100	0.057
0.318	0.019	0.613		1,7	0.067	−0.086	−3.368	***	1,7	0.206
0.160	−0.074	−1.437		−1,1	0.181	−0.206	−4.774	***	−1,1	0.286
0.415	0.012	4.236	***	17,99	0.514	0.017	6.917	***	17,99	0.650
0.558	−0.261	−3.851	***	0,3	0.481	−0.348	−6.382	***	0,3	0.638
0.244	−0.038	−0.381		0,1	0.094	−0.062	−0.710		0,1	0.008
0.452	−0.003	−1.857	*	0,99	0.177	−0.003	−1.905	*	0,99	0.207
0.214	−0.033	−0.307		0,1	0.008	−0.054	−0.539		0,1	0.160
0.378	−0.219	−2.931	***	1,3	0.419	−0.442	−6.921	***	1,3	0.718
0.381	−0.464	−3.543	***	0,1	0.451	−0.510	−4.747	***	0,1	0.452
0.070	0.074	0.803		0,1	0.074	−0.167	−1.974	**	0,1	0.089
	0.823	2.576	***			2.896	10.780	***		
	731					1588				

Note: SE=standard error. Significance levels of the maximum likelihood estimates: * .10 level, critical value Z=1.65; **.05, critical value Z =1.96; *** 01, critical value Z=2.57.

[a]In 1976, 1980, and 1988 the international measure is based on the question, "Should the U.S. be involved in world affairs?" In 1984, the measure is based on the question, "How tough should the U.S. be toward the Soviet Union?"

midterm election year. We therefore deleted these variables from the models presented. Thus, the rhetoric associated with the reassessment of government had even less effect on nonvoting in congressional elections than in presidential contests.

The effects of the economy, media, and international affairs are more sporadic at the midterm than those observed in presidential elections.[49] Among these factors, economic conditions influence individual nonvoting in 1982 and 1990. The economic effect is largest in the 1982 election which, as discussed above, took place amidst a recession with high unemployment and resulted in Republicans losing 26 House seats. Individuals who see the economy as stable are 34 percentage points less likely to vote than those who feel the economy is sharply changing. This parallels the strong income effects at the aggregate level in 1982 shown in Table 7.2. It is also present in 1990 when the Iraqi invasion of Kuwait caused an oil price shock.[50] In addition to the economic effects, media attention affects individual nonvoting in the 1978 and 1982 elections. Unlike the strong influence of international affairs in presidential nonvoting, there is no effect of international involvement on individual nonvoting at the midterm.[51] The absence of this effect may result from the distinct difference between presidential campaigns, which are often waged on questions of America's role in the world, and congressional campaigns more typically focused on local issues.

In contrast, candidate comparisons have strong effects in each election. People who make only limited comparisons between the candidates are much less likely to vote than those who can make distinct comparisons between the congressional candidates; the differences range from 19 percentage points less likely in 1978 to 42 percentage points less likely in 1982. Consistent with the presidential elections, the likelihood of nonvoting increases if people do not care which candidate wins.[52] Thus, internal uncertainty about the candidates again drives nonvoting.

These campaign context and candidate factors play out relative to other influences. Psychological interest in politics has the single largest effects across the midterm elections. People who are not interested in the campaign are much less likely to vote than those who are interested—ranging from 67 percentage points less likely in 1978 to 80 percentage points less likely in 1982. This effect is

[49] Although the Iran-Contra scandal was revealed shortly before the 1986 election, no government ethics question was asked in the American National Election study of that year.

[50] *Congressional Quarterly Almanac* for 1978, 1986, and 1990 found at *Congressional Quarterly Almanac* online edition https://library.cqpress.com/cqalmanac/.

[51] Because of data availability, in the midterm models the international involvement measure is based on a 7-point scale question which asks whether the United States should greatly increase or decrease defense spending. The midpoint is "defense spending should remain the same."

[52] In other tests of the model, an indicator which measures people's views of the candidates' overall ideological positions was included but had no influence on individual nonvoting.

roughly double that found in presidential elections. Presumably, the much lower visibility of midterm congressional elections makes campaign interest critical to individual participation.

During this period, personal resources are also more important in midterm races than presidential ones. Being young increases the likelihood of not voting. As seen in Table 7.4, this effect ranges from a 38 percentage point difference in 1990 to a 68 percentage point difference in 1986. Being less educated also increases the likelihood of not voting, with the effect ranging from 49 percentage points in 1978 to 60 percentage points in 1982. Social connections have less influence than personal resources. Unemployment is the most important factor, with the unemployed being less likely to vote in each election than those who are employed, except 1982. Unlike in presidential races, campaign contact does not influence individual nonvoting, except for Democratic candidates in 1982 and Republican candidates in 1990. The difficulties congressional candidates face with making those kinds of direct connections, with less money and staff matched with a less interested eligible electorate, clarify why such an effect would be less likely in congressional midterm races.

Overall, these results provide a better understanding of the differences between individual nonvoting in presidential and midterm elections. Research has long noted that congressional elections are more local elections focused on narrower issues that hit closer to home.[53] Furthermore, they often occur with an inherent imbalance between venerable incumbent members of Congress and their invisible challengers. These obvious structural differences between the two offices, and the timing of the two races, permit congressional candidates to redirect attention from the national campaign context to the local campaign context. In some years when less is happening in the national sphere, they can accomplish this handily. In those years, resolving internal uncertainty about the candidates is the necessary condition for individual participation. If people cannot resolve this because they do not know the candidates or do not care who wins, then they are not likely to vote. In other midterm years, when national issues loom larger, people use their awareness of both the campaign context and the candidates in their participation decisions.

Personal Certainty amidst National Uncertainty

Many people look back longingly at the Reagan years as a unique period in American history characterized by prosperity and international dominance,

[53] Gary Jacobson, *The Politics of Congressional Elections* (New York: Pearson, 2012).

Table 7.4 **Effects of the National Campaign Context on Individual Nonvoting in Midterm Elections, 1978–1990 (Probit Maximum Likelihood Coefficients)**

Predictor	*1978*				*1982*		
	Maximum Likelihood Estimate	*MLE/SE*	*Range of Value in the Variable*	*Change in Likelihood of the Variable*	*Maximum Likelihood Estimate*	*MLE/SE*	*Range of Value in the Variable*
National Campaign Context							
Economic conditions	−0.041	−1.399	−2, 2	0.153	−0.085	−1.663 *	−2, 2
Media attention	−0.057	−1.951 **	0,4	0.276	−0.131	−2.641 ***	0,4
International involvement[1]	n/a	n/a			0.032	0.902	1,7
Candidate Awareness							
Candidate comparison	−0.007	−3.732 ***	0,100	0.185	−0.016	−5.300 ***	0,100
Democratic candidate recognition	−0.268	−1.144	0,1	0.268	0.382	0.651	0,1
Republican candidate recognition	0.183	0.492	0,1	0.183	−0.159	−0.286	0,1
Care who wins	−0.107	−3.236 ***	−1,1	0.215	−0.221	−4.323 ***	−1,1
Personal Characteristics							
Youth	0.012	6.556 ***	17,99	0.434	0.016	5.294 ***	17,99
Education	−0.161	−4.012 ***	0,3	0.488	−0.215	−3.233 ***	0,3
Social Connections							
Marriage	0.057	0.841	0,1	0.067	−0.190	−1.689 *	0,1
Residential stability	−0.001	−0.939	0,99	0.176	−0.007	−4.224 ***	0,99
Unemployment	0.148	2.310 **	0,1	0.144	0.109	0.952	0,1
Psychological Involvement							
Campaign interest	−0.318	−6.379 ***	1,3	0.666	−0.503	−6.289 ***	1,3
Democratic candidate contact	−0.020	−0.314	0,1	0.065	−0.249	−2.347 **	0,1
Republican candidate contact	−0.094	−1.575	0,1	0.117	−0.163	−1.592	0,1
Intercept	1.219	2.627 ***			1.076	1.626 ***	
Number of Cases	1548				993		

	1986					*1990*				
Change in Likelihood of the Variable	*Maximum Likelihood Estimate*	*MLE/ SE*		*Range of Value in the Variable*	*Change in Likelihood of the Variable*	*Maximum Likelihood Estimate*	*MLE/ SE*		*Range of Value in the Variable*	*Change in Likelihood of the Variable*
0.344	−0.051	−1.499		−2, 2	0.123	−0.061	−1.922	*	−2, 2	0.266
0.145	−0.060	−1.013		0,4	0.114	0.014	0.203		0,4	0.014
0.155	0.021	1.002		1,7	0.174	0.023	1.019		1,7	0.211
0.424	−0.006	−3.152	***	0,100	0.316	−0.007	−3.444	***	0,100	0.305
0.162	−0.225	−0.951		0,1	0.235	0.016	0.058		0,1	0.181
0.032	−0.044	−0.187		0,1	0.056	−0.231	−0.728		0,1	0.042
0.403	−0.161	−4.932	***	−1,1	0.329	−0.108	−3.079	***	−1,1	0.245
0.442	0.015	7.522	***	17,99	0.675	0.013	7.053	***	17,99	0.379
0.599	−0.169	−4.008	***	0,3	0.601	−0.138	−3.306	***	0,3	0.582
0.024	−0.064	−0.920		0,1	0.059	−0.001	−0.020		0,1	0.002
0.384	−0.003	−2.583	***	0,99	0.294	−0.002	−2.099	**	0,99	0.278
0.122	0.174	2.361	**	0,1	0.171	0.127	1.666	*	0,1	0.114
0.798	−0.367	−7.601	***	1,3	0.784	−0.350	−6.610	***	1,3	0.710
0.150	−0.101	−1.594		0,1	0.147	−0.074	−1.068		0,1	0.059
0.174	−0.029	−0.466		0,1	0.049	−0.162	−2.444	**	0,1	0.164
	1.76	4.5	***			1.62	3.817	***		
	1438					1269				

Note: SE=standard error. Significance levels of the maximum likelihood estimates: * .10 level, critical value Z=1.65; **.05, critical value Z =1.96; *** 01, critical value Z=2.57.

[1] The international measure is based on a 7-point question on whether to cut or increase defense spending.

featured between the bookends of two substandard administrations. Yet the Reagan years were actually quite consistent with the Carter and Bush years on the central dimensions of the national campaign context and their impact on nonvoting. Most fundamentally, the third period was an era of high and stable nonvoting. Back-to-back midterm and presidential elections in 1974, 1976, 1978, and 1980 set a floor under nonvoting. The 1974 House midterm elections established a high point for nonvoting, which had last been seen in 1946 and was quickly broken with still higher nonvoting in 1978. The 1976 and 1980 presidential elections returned to elevated nonvoting levels matching 1948, despite the fact that both were hard-fought contests. This floor was not lowered until the 1992 and 1994 elections.

This period of uniquely high nonvoting reflected that the overall national campaign context had a positive rather than a negative effect on nonvoting. Some of this was undoubtedly due to the lessening of uncertainty and novelty in the crisis-ridden 1960s and early 1970s. But, cable television was also a critical element of the national campaign context in increasing nonvoting. Moreover, its effect exceeded that of all other factors in the national campaign context. Unlike radio or television, which depressed nonvoting in the earlier periods, the expansion of cable television in the third period fueled nonvoting. While nearly every American household owned a television set, the purchase of cable television subscriptions and remote controls made the sets into different sources of political information. It allowed people to minimize uncertainty by ignoring it, turning to channels without political content and creating their own personal certainty that politics did not really matter.

Throughout the third period, economic conditions lessened nonvoting at both the aggregate and individual levels. But at the aggregate level, their impact did not offset the positive effect of cable television, except in 1978. Why is technology more important than economics? The relative influence of technology and economics on nonvoting is consistent across the three time periods: in each period, technology change has a greater impact on nonvoting than does economic change. This may reflect a distinction between immediate and proximate conditions for nonvoting within the national campaign context. Political information or its absence is an immediate condition. Some people gather political information through convenient forms of media in an effort to alleviate uncertainty surrounding politics. However, others may consciously seek to avoid political information, effectively living in a political news vacuum. Inside this vacuum, there is no compelling reason to vote. The economy is a more proximate condition, as people inferentially assess politics by judging the economy or their pocketbook. Thus the convenience and immediacy of communication technology makes it a more powerful predictor of nonvoting.

A fourth period began to emerge in the early 1990s. Within the national campaign context, the economy, which had been sluggish throughout the third period, became more robust. Globalization and advances in high-performance and personal computers sped up economic changes around the world. By the mid-1990s, the Internet became a new technological innovation that was arguably the most transformative source of political media, besting radio in the 1920s and television in the 1950s. Within the international dimension, the collapse of the Soviet Union in 1991 and the end of communism throughout Eastern Europe created a "new world order" that left the United States the single dominant world player.[54] Partisan politics became intensely polarized as parties developed regional superiority which aggregated to national parity. People responded to the resulting uncertainty with higher levels of electoral participation.

[54] George H. W. Bush, "Address Before a Joint Session of Congress on the Persian Gulf War and the Federal Budget Deficit," September 11, 1990, *Public Papers of the Presidents, George Bush,* found at American Presidency Project http://www.presidency.ucsb.edu/ws/index.php?pid=18820&st=new+world+order&st1=.

8

Information Technology Years: 1992–2012

The phrase "turn of the century" describes an unspecified set of years before and after a new century's beginning. There is no intrinsic importance to the actual turning of the calendar page from one century to the next, any more than there is from one year to the next. Nevertheless, the turn of a century creates a frame of reference for people's thinking about progress, modernity, and change. And as the twentieth century closed and the twenty-first opened, novelty punctuated the years surrounding both sides of the century mark. While there was no single date or event, over a set of years beginning in the early 1990s a fourth period emerged through a confluence of economic, technological, and international changes that were not seen during the third period. It was not simply that one of these dimensions changed, but that all of them changed in tandem. And the changes that occurred were truly novel, with events and inventions unfolding that few if any had imagined were possible. This was not the novelty of the 1960s when American politics seemed to come unhinged, amplifying people's interest in politics and voting. Instead, the novelty centered on highly improbable events that actually occurred and new technologies that combined to change American lives in unanticipated and ubiquitous ways. These created a highly uncertain national campaign context within which people decided whether to vote.

Beginning in the early 1990s, what many dubbed the "new economy" emerged in which information technology, enlarged service industries, and globalization intertwined. This supplanted the old industrial economy in which manufacturing dominated economic growth. By the middle 1990s, innovations in high-speed personal computers and the advent of the Internet combined with growth in other service industries, including financial, health, travel, and retail. Globalization accelerated the expansion of the new economy, and technology sped up globalization as capital and labor shifted around the world. Foreign direct investment was five times greater in the 10 years between 1993 and 2002 than it was between 1983 and 1992—on average $629 billion in the latter period compared to $121 billion in the earlier one.[1] It was nearly three times greater still in the next 10 years from 2003–2012—on average $1.5 trillion, even amidst a world-wide recession after 2008. Much of this was fed by the opening of the Chinese economy to private capital. In 1994, China's GDP stood at $500 billion; four years later it doubled to $1.1 trillion, and in 2004 doubled again to $2 trillion. During the period, China moved to become the second largest economy behind the United States, with real GDP growth over 10 percent annually.[2] By every measure, connections across the world were stronger and bigger from the mid-1990s onward than they had been before. Swings in one part of the world created reactions in all other parts of the world.

The technological advances were not simply drivers of a new global economy, but the personal computer–Internet nexus radically changed everyday life, and with it, political communication. While only 8 percent of American homes had computers in 1984, nearly 25 percent did a decade later and by 2000, half did—with most of these households also having Internet access. By 2012, nearly one-half of American adults owned smartphones.[3] People could access the Internet from anywhere at any time. This was perhaps the single largest technological advance of the twentieth century, more groundbreaking than even radio. While radio had permitted people throughout the country to listen to a program, the people themselves did not share with each other in the communication. The Internet connected people to one another in small and large numbers without concern for geographic distance or time. The advent of "social media" captured the difference between the Internet and older forms of communication.

Dramatic changes in international affairs also helped signal the beginning of a new period. The historic collapse of the Soviet Union in December 1991 ended the Cold War and redefined geopolitics, which had been divided by two superpowers since the 1950s. In one of the many telephone conversations between George H. W. Bush and Mikhail Gorbachev, Gorbachev spoke on December 13, 1991, calling to wish Bush a Merry Christmas: "The situation has become more difficult and complicated. This was unexpected for me. Perhaps it was not unexpected for others, but it was for me."[4] Gorbachev

[1] "Foreign Direct Investment, Net In-flows in current U.S. dollars," World Bank Data found at http://data.worldbank.org/indicator/BX.KLT.DINV.CD.WD/countries?page=3.

[2] International Monetary Fund data found at http://www.imf.org/external/index.htm.

[3] Aaron Smith, "Smartphone Ownership—2013 Update," Pew Research Center, June 5, 2013, 2, found at http://www.pewinternet.org/~/media/Files/Reports/2013/PIP_Smartphone_adoption_2013.pdf.

[4] "Memorandum of Telephone Conversation with President Mikhail Gorbachev of the former Soviet Union," December 13, 1991, 3:37–4:11pm, The Oval Office, http://bushlibrary.tamu.edu/research/pdfs/memcons_telcons/1991-12-13--Gorbachev.pdf.

resigned on Christmas Day, and the Soviet Union was formally dissolved two days later. With that, the us-against-them international politics that the United States had helped define now yielded to the United States being the sole military superpower.

Uncertainty matched this novelty. The personal computer–Internet nexus initially created uncertainty about whether the Internet would affect politics, but this quickly shifted to uncertainty over *how* the Internet would affect politics, and then to uncertainty about whether there were any ways the Internet would *not* affect politics. While the bipolar world of the Cold War era had been complex, it was also simple, as it defined most major and minor international conflicts as the good guys versus the bad guys. But with the end of the Cold War, there was considerable uncertainty about what role the United States would play in the world as the lone remaining military superpower, and who were its enemies. The arrival of China as an economic powerhouse defined a superpower of a different kind. Global terrorism directly challenged America's singular status, with the first World Trade Center bombing in 1993, US embassy bombings in Kenya and Tanzania in 1998, strikes on the USS Cole in 2000, and most frontally in the attacks on the World Trade Center and the Pentagon on September 11, 2001. These terrorist acts and nations actively developing nuclear war capabilities created as many unknowns in the absence of the Cold War as there had been at its height.

The emergence of the fourth period, then, which we call the information technology period, is in one sense the most difficult to discern and in other ways the easiest to interpret. It is difficult because there is no single event that delineates the end of the third period and the beginning of the fourth. There is no Roosevelt death or Nixon resignation. So, the days in the early 1990s do not appear distinctly different from one another—there is no natural before and after. Instead, over several years economic, technological, and international elements of uncertainty in the national campaign context that had not existed before—indeed had not been thought of before—were now commonplace. The uncertainty in the national campaign context thus shifted in ways that were not found in the third period and created a different basis from which people chose to participate in politics.[5]

[5] Unlike in the earlier periods, there was no sweeping legal change that expanded the eligible voting population. This may well happen if significant immigration reform is completed that provides citizenship for a portion of the Hispanic-American population. In addition, such reform might also have the impetus of increasing voting rates among Hispanic Americans in general, which have typically been quite low.

The National Campaign Context at the Turn of the Twenty-First Century

The novelty and uncertainty that characterized the information technology period emerged in the impact on nonvoting of the national campaign context. Referencing Table 5.1, it shows that the effect of the national campaign context is reversed from the government reassessment period. While the campaign context increased nonvoting in the government reassessment period, it generally diminishes it in the Internet period for presidential and midterm races both nationally and regionally. Referring back to Table 5.2, on average, nonvoting is 4 percentage points lower in presidential elections and 2 percentage points lower in midterm House elections than during the government reassessment period. As seen in Table 5.1, the national campaign context significantly diminishes nonvoting in the 1992, 2004, and 2008 presidential elections. From 1988 to 1992 there is a sizable drop in nonvoting of 6 percentage points for the nation as a whole, in the South, and in the non-South (see Table 2.1). This decline in nonvoting continues during the Internet period, with nonvoting falling another 3 percentage points for the nation as a whole, 6 percentage points in the South, and 1 percentage point in the non-South from 1992 to 2008. It ticks up only slightly in 2012 (see Table 2.1).

Table 5.1 also shows that during the Internet period, the national campaign context has greater influence on midterm House elections than presidential elections, posting strong and statistically significant effects on nonvoting across the country and regionally in all midterm elections except 2006. These midterm national effects are larger than those observed in the earlier periods and are associated with highly visible national campaigns or events that defied the more typically local nature of many House election cycles. In 1994, Newt Gingrich (R-Ga), then House Republican whip, led a well-orchestrated effort to offer the ideologically oriented "Contract with America," which resulted in Republican control of the House for the first time since 1954. In 1998, House Republicans clashed with Bill Clinton as they pushed his impeachment in votes just one month after the elections. The 2002 contests were caught up in the war on terror after the September 11, 2001 attacks. In 2006, Republicans' attempts to deflect attention from the Iraq war and focus on local concerns proved difficult as Democrats took back the majority in the House they had lost during Gingrich's triumph in 1994. The Great Recession and high unemployment rates across the country dominated the 2010 elections.

The strong national campaign effects during the fourth period are associated with what are among the most volatile midterms in American history. The president's party lost massive numbers of seats in three elections—1994, with 54 seats

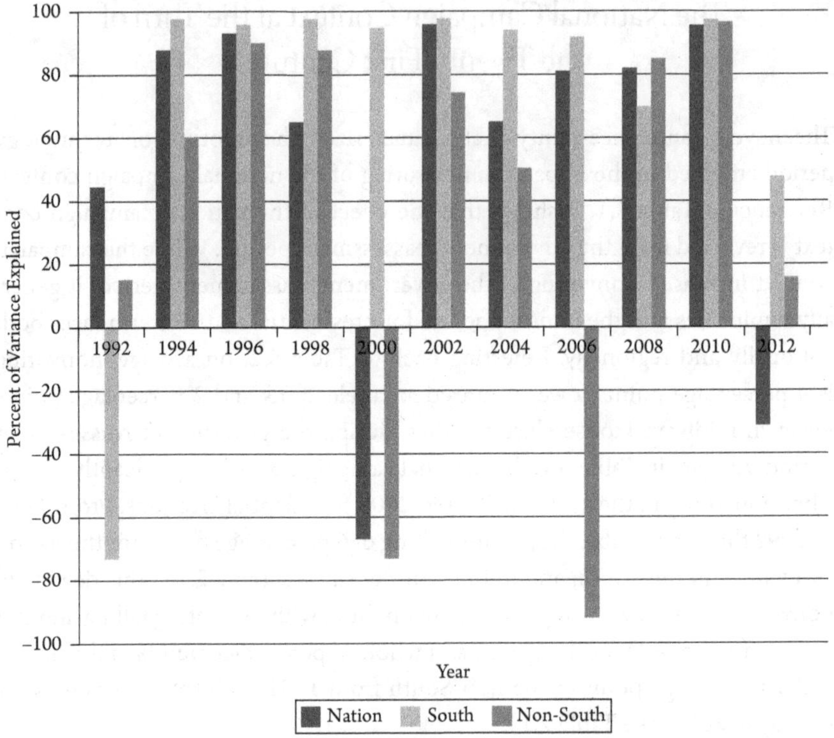

Figure 8.1 Net National and State Effects on Nonvoting, 1992–2012

changing from Democrats to Republicans; 2006, with 30 seats changing from Republicans to Democrats; and 2010, with 63 seats changing from Democratic to Republican hands. Indeed, the 2010 result was a historic swing exceeded only by the 1938 election when Republicans gained 72 seats. The volatility was also in evidence in 1998 and 2002, as the party of the president retained seats—only the second and third times this has occurred since 1934.[6]

In the Internet period, regional differences are also apparent. The nationalization of the South continues. Results in Table 5.1 indicate that national effects are substantially larger in the South than they are in the non-South. This is also seen in Figure 8.1, which shows that net national effects are greater in the South than in the non-South in all election years except 1992 and 2008. National effects in the South also are larger in midterm elections than presidential elections. In both elections, historic lows in nonvoting accompanied the national effects in the South. Returning to Table 2.1, in presidential elections, southern nonvoting drops 5 percentage points from 51 percent in 1988 to 46 percent in 1992 and

[6] Democrats gained 9 seats in 1934.

continues to fall, reaching historic lows in 2004 and 2008 (40 percent). As shown in Table 2.2, in midterm elections, nonvoting in the South falls 5 percentage points from 70 percent in 1990 to 65 percent in 1994, and it continues to decline to a historic low of 62 percent in 2010.

How do factors in the national campaign context influence nonvoting in ways distinct from the government reassessment period? We examine the influence on aggregate nonvoting of economic change, technological shock, and international conflict relative to youth, education, and party competition in elections from 1992 through 2012. To foretell the discussion below, economic conditions decrease nonvoting in especially dramatic ways after the 2008 Great Recession. Internet technology has a consistently strong influence in diminishing nonvoting in contrast to the positive effect of cable television in the government reassessment period. Disapproval of the Iraq War also decreases nonvoting.

Economic Bubbles and Crashes

Throughout the period, the "internationalization of financial markets and their greater speed and interconnectedness" created economic novelty and risk.[7] Businesses invested heavily in computer, telecommunication, and other information technology. As one example, in the span of five years between 1988 and 1993, business expenditures in communication increased nearly 25 percent.[8] This was more broadly reflected in equipment investment. From 1992 to 1998, real equipment investment averaged 11 percent per year, a rate greater than at any time since World War II. Economists Stacey Tevlin and Karl Whelan maintained that "declining computer prices, in conjunction with the increasing rates of replacement investment associated with the shift toward high-tech capital, were the crucial factors behind the investment boom of the 1990s." [9] This resulted from the confluence of rapid declines in computer prices and quicker depreciation of the hardware as it became obsolete more quickly than conventional equipment. Both low prices and fast depreciation made it attractive for companies to invest heavily. The prevailing viewpoint was that the diffusion of

7 Roger Congleton, "On the Political Economy of the Financial Crisis and Bailout of 2008–2009," *Public Choice* 140 (2009): 314.

8 U.S. Department of Commerce, "Business Expenditures for New Plant and Equipment: 1980 to 1994," *Statistical Abstract of the United States, 1995*, 559; found at http://www.census.gov/prod/1/gen/95statab/business.pdf.

9 Stacey Tevlin and Karl Whelan, "Explaining the Investment Boom of the 1990s," *Journal of Money, Credit, and Banking* 35 (February 2003): 18.

"the new technologies would accelerate productivity improvements, favoring a lasting era of sustained growth without inflation."[10]

The "investment boom" created a wave of optimism among consumers. Over 46 consecutive months from April 1997 through January 2001, the University of Michigan Index of Consumer Sentiment rose well above levels last seen in the 1960s. Real per capita income growth returned to levels above 2 percent per year. Unemployment, which peaked at 7.5 percent in 1992, declined throughout the remainder of the decade and was at a low 4 percent in the late 1990s, levels last seen in the 1960s and 1970s. Many tagged the economic growth as the "go-go '90s" and even the "Roaring Nineties."[11]

Yet, as economist Robert Shiller observed, since the 1890s each new major technological innovation has been accompanied by a run-up of stock prices followed by a crash. Shiller asserted that investors believe that stock prices will continue to rise as they underestimate the riskiness of the investment, and a bubble emerges. Thus, people minimize uncertainty by ignoring it. The new industry overshoots its market size and excess capacity builds, leading to a bust. [12] Alan Greenspan, then chairman of the Federal Reserve, identified this as a cycle of "irrational exuberance": "But how do we know when irrational exuberance has unduly escalated asset values, which then become subject to unexpected and prolonged contractions . . ."[13] Many people invested in technology companies with the idea that these stock prices could only go up. And indeed, as displayed in Figure 8.2, real growth in Internet-related stock prices increased 39 percent between 1995 and 1999. But, by the end of 2000, these stock prices had fallen by over 50 percent.[14] In 2001, real per capita growth slowed for the first time since 1994, exacerbated by the terrorist attacks of September 11, 2001. The slowdown continued with small upticks in unemployment through 2003. Thus the "Roaring 90s" roared only slightly longer than the "Roaring 20s"—seven years of economic growth that took off in earnest in 1993 and ended as the new century began.

[10] Eric Dor and Alain Durré, "Monetary Policy and the New Economy: Between Supply Shock and Financial Bubble," *Louvain Economic Review* 68 (2002): 221.

[11] Barbara Nagy, "The Go-go '90s: Part Savvy, Part Luck," *Hartford Courant* January 14, 2001. http://articles.courant.com/2001-01-14/news/0101102877_1_president-clinton-economists-overseas-rivals; Joseph Stiglitz, "The Roaring Nineties," *The Atlantic Monthly*, October 2002, found at http://www.theatlantic.com/past/docs/issues/2002/10/stiglizt.htm.

[12] Robert Shiller, *Irrational Exuberance*, 2nd ed. (Princeton: Princeton University Press, 2005).

[13] Alan Greenspan, "The Challenge of Central Banking in a Democratic Society," Boyer lecture, American Enterprise Institute, December 5, 1996, found at http://www.federalreserve.gov/boarddocs/speeches/1996/19961205.htm.

[14] Dor and Durré, 2002, 223.

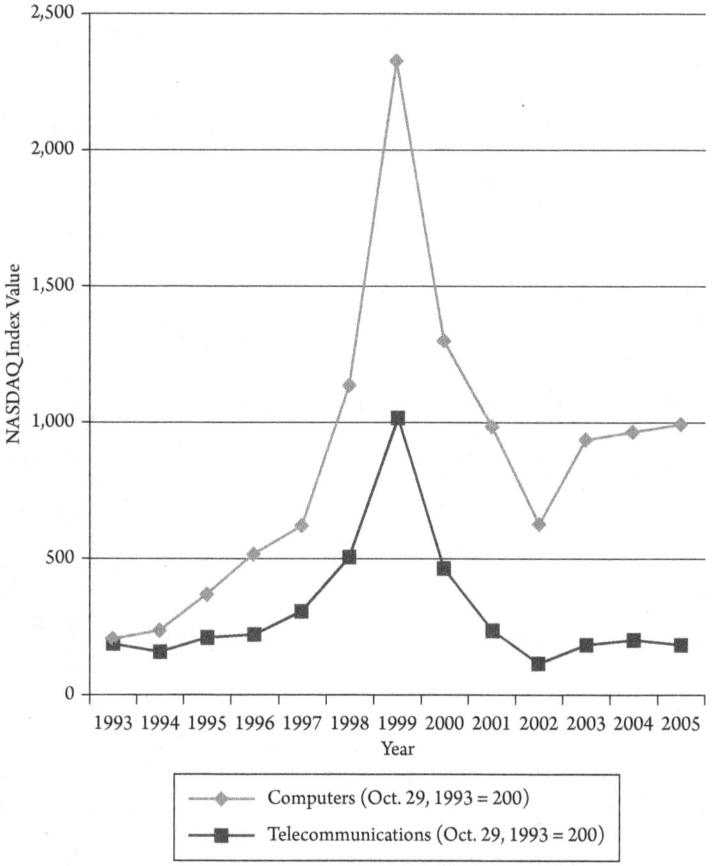

Figure 8.2 "Dot.com" Stock Prices, 1993–2005 Source: Telecommunication and Computer Indexes of the NASDAQ

Housing Crisis and Global Uncertainty

In the information technology period, the housing market also produced a bubble followed by a burst of historic proportions, suggesting that it is not simply new technologies but also new financial innovations combined with irrational exuberance that can produce economic extremes. As seen in Figure 8.3, from 1993 to 2007 home prices across the country increased 96 percent. In mid-2005, Greenspan observed that "at a minimum, there's a little 'froth' in this market. [While] we don't perceive that there is a national bubble, it's hard not to see that there are a lot of local bubbles."[15] In a special report, *The Economist*

[15] "Greenspan: Home-price Speculation Can't Last." *Boston Globe*, May 21, 2005, found at http://www.boston.com/business/globe/articles/2005/05/21/greenspan_home_price_speculation_cant_last/.

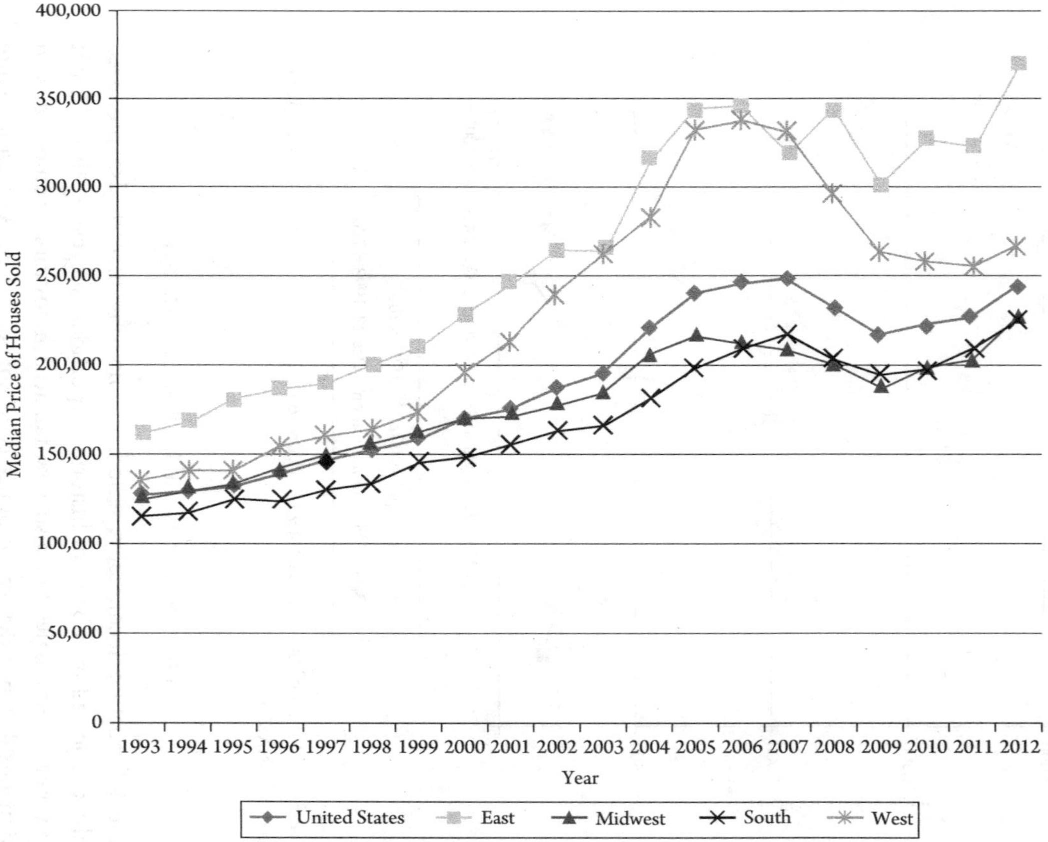

Figure 8.3 Housing Prices by Region, 1993–2012

Source: U.S. Census at http://www.census.gov/construction/nrs/historical_data/

magazine observed not just a sharp rise in housing prices in the United States from 1997 to 2005, but over 150 percent increases in Australia, Great Britain, Ireland, South Africa, and Spain. It concluded "the worldwide rise in house prices is the biggest bubble in history."[16] Like stockholders in "dot.com" companies, homeowners believed that the value of what was typically their single largest asset could not go down. Evidence from a 2003 survey of homeowners in four cities (Los Angeles, San Francisco, Boston, and Milwaukee) indicated that 90 percent believed that housing prices would increase over the next several years and by large amounts—10 percent in the next year and 14 percent over the next decade.[17]

As prices increased, lenders enlarged mortgage products designed to permit people who otherwise lacked sufficient capital to buy homes. With little or no down payment and adjustable-rate mortgages with low initial interest rates, more people bought houses. Sub-prime mortgages, which were 8 percent of originations in 2003, rose to more than 20 percent in 2005 and 2006.[18] As more people invested in housing, a larger market for mortgage-backed securities emerged. What had been government-secured mortgages since the 1930s expanded to private-label products. To reduce risk, lenders bundled these securities, insured them through third parties, and sold them to other financial institutions. Yet, assigning value and risk to them was inherently difficult, and this was compounded by the fact that lending institutions kept low reserves. In many cases the securities were given high bond ratings based on models that assumed the products' risk was less than in fact it was. But as long as foreclosures stayed low and home values rose, the twin questions of value and risk were not raised. By mid-2006, overheated housing prices began to fall as the inventory of both new and existing homes continued to grow. At the same time, many homeowners saw their adjustable-rate mortgages reset at higher rates, which in turn prompted higher monthly payments, delinquencies, and ultimately foreclosures. Foreclosures nearly doubled to almost 1 million between 2006 and 2007, mostly from sub-prime loans.[19]

What is most important about this increase in foreclosures, which totaled $250 billion by the end of 2007, is not actually the initial losses and slowdown in the housing market. By historic standards, if the problem had stopped there

[16] "In Come the Waves," *The Economist*, June 16, 2005, found at http://www.economist.com/node/4079027.

[17] Karl Case and Robert Shiller, "Is There a Bubble in the Housing Market?," *Brookings Papers on Economic Activity* 2003, No. 2, 323.

[18] "The State of the Nation's Housing 2008," Joint Center for Housing Studies, Harvard University, 2.

[19] "The State of the Nation's Housing 2008," 3, 20.

Table 8.1 **Effects of the National Campaign Context on Nonvoting, 1992–2006**

	1992				*1994*				*1996*				*1998*			
Predictor	***Coefficient***	***t-value***	***Mean***	***Impact***	***Coefficient***	***t-value***	***Mean***	***Impact***	***Coefficient***	***t-value***	***Mean***	***Impact***	***Coefficient***	***t-value***	***Mean***	***Impact***
Income Change	-0.002	–2.632	3620.882	–7.242	–0.003	–1.868	2830.875	–8.493	0.001	0.353	3289.804	3.290	–0.001	–1.277	4401.511	-4.402
Unemployment Change	–0.141	–0.577	1.611	–0.227	–1.294	–1.540	0.114	–0.148	–0.538	–1.333	1.713	–0.922	–1.375	–1.353	1.250	–1.719
Communication Technology	–0.083	–1.105	55.399	–4.598	–0.187	–1.977	60.124	–11.243	–0.041	–0.520	16.118	–0.661	–0.284	–2.156	26.436	–7.508
Competition	–0.112	–2.741	88.000	–9.856	–0.022	–0.625	82.629	–1.818	0.011	0.308	85.286	0.938	–0.066	–1.997	78.188	–5.160
Youth	–0.641	–1.617	13.883	–8.899	0.520	0.975	13.560	7.051	0.618	2.098	12.924	7.987	0.583	1.243	13.213	7.703
Education	–0.278	–2.699	57.332	–15.938	–0.255	–1.427	57.958	–14.779	–0.166	–1.523	59.593	–9.892	–0.053	–0.316	60.232	–3.192
Prior Nonvoting	0.803	12.727	45.825	36.797	0.688	8.476	59.948	41.244	0.800	10.777	39.774	31.819	0.700	7.892	57.466	40.226
Intercept	0.879	0.065			27.884	1.542			9.489	1.014			19.059	1.185		
N	51				50				51				50			
R^2	0.878				0.807				0.816				0.762			
Adjusted R^2	0.858				0.774				0.786				0.719			
Durbin h-statistic	0.501				0.507				0.303				0.997			

	2000				2002				2004				2006[a]			
Predictor	***Coefficient***	***t-value***	***Mean***	***Impact***	***Coefficient***	***t-value***	***Mean***	***Impact***	***Coefficient***	***t-value***	***Mean***	***Impact***	***Coefficient***	***t-value***	***Mean***	***Impact***
Income Change	−0.002	−1.002	5180.765	−10.362	−0.002	−1.967	4051.784	−8.104	−0.001	−2.571	3767.706	−2.729	−0.001	−1.528	5715.660	−5.716
Unemployment Change	−0.678	−0.895	1.251	−0.848	−0.341	−0.494	1.000	−0.341	−1.980	−4.133	1.322	−2.618	−2.403	−2.129	0.926	−2.225
Communication Technology	−0.194	−2.274	41.296	−8.011	−0.074	−0.569	49.835	−3.688	−0.233	−2.840	54.545	−12.709	−0.369	−2.154	58.101	−21.439
International Involvement									−0.087	−2.463	58.231	−5.066	−0.090	−1.091	60.774	−5.470
Competition	−0.047	−1.697	83.984	−3.947	−0.026	−0.849	76.694	−1.994	−0.130	−2.993	83.726	−10.884	−0.151	−2.476	83.377	−12.590
Youth	0.016	0.351	14.488	0.232	0.054	0.141	13.720	0.741	0.057	0.144	14.060	0.801	0.001	0.569	587700	470.160
Education	0.094	0.655	57.799	5.433	−0.282	−1.934	59.159	−16.683	−0.155	−1.356	58.578	−9.080	−0.107	−0.561	58.536	−6.263
Prior Nonvoting	0.849	10.179	46.273	39.286	0.572	6.712	59.210	33.868	0.665	7.649	44.234	29.416	0.543	3.258	58.251	31.630
Intercept	12.847	1.124			53.067	3.262			48.953	3.375			37.072	1.804		
N	51				50				51				50			
R^2	0.851				0.707				0.843				0.644			
Adjusted R^2	0.827				0.658				0.813				0.575			
Durbin h-statistic	0.681				1.105				1.296				0.366			

Note: Critical t-values are 1.679 at .10 probability; 2.009 at .05; 2.700 at .01. Critical value for Durbin h-statistic at .05 probability = 1.695.

[a] Total youth in the state population, rather than percent youth in the state population, used to estimate the model. See note 32.

Table 8.2 **Effects of the National Campaign Context on Nonvoting, 2008–2012**

Predictor	*2008*				*2010*				*2012*			
	Coefficient	*t-value*	*Mean*	*Impact*	*Coefficient*	*t-value*	*Mean*	*Impact*	*Coefficient*	*t-value*	*Mean*	*Impact*
Income Change	−0.001	−2.010	5301.412	−5.301	−0.002	−2.417	4167.320	−8.335	−0.001	−2.011	4613.469	−4.613
Unemployment Change	−1.294	−3.145	0.934	−1.209	−0.299	−0.930	4.537	−1.357	−0.422	−0.620	2.086	−0.880
Communication Technology	−0.092	−2.344	61.577	−5.665	−0.222	−2.181	73.756	−16.374	−0.189	−1.860	70.989	−13.417
International Involvement	−0.077	−1.651	77.780	−5.989								
Competition	−0.063	−1.827	82.062	−5.170	−0.161	−3.234	81.546	−13.129	−0.013	−0.220	81.054	−1.054
Youth	−0.083	−2.261	12.628	−1.048	0.182	0.358	13.327	2.426	−0.210	−0.386	13.050	−2.741
Education	−0.073	−1.139	59.145	−4.318	−0.250	−1.734	59.702	−14.926	−0.290	−2.678	57.910	−16.794
Prior Nonvoting	0.900	12.509	36.034	32.431	0.403	5.266	57.044	22.989	0.801	9.000	38.311	30.687
Intercept	11.187	1.053			75.473	4.212			24.723	1.86		
N	51				50				51			
R^2	0.866				0.664				0.828			
Adjusted R^2	0.840				0.609				0.8			
Durbin h-statistic	0.682				0.139				0.871			

Note: Critical t-values are 1.679 at .10 probability; 2.009 at .05; 2.700 at .01. Critical value for Durbin h-statistic at .05 probability = 1.695.

it would have resembled previous housing declines in the late 1970s and early 1980s.[20] By comparison, the collapse of the savings and loan industry in the 1990s, discussed in the previous chapter, produced then-record losses of $519 billion. Instead, as economist Olivier Blanchard observed, magnified by globalization, what occurred were "very large effects of a small trigger on world economic activity."[21] Blanchard estimated that the cumulative loss in world GDP was $4.7 trillion, and the loss to world stock markets exceeded $26 trillion by November 2008.[22] According to Blanchard, the amplification of the initial conditions into a full-blown crisis occurred for four reasons: "the underestimation of risk contained in newly issued assets; the opacity of the derived securities on the balance sheets of financial institutions; the connectedness between financial institutions, both within and across countries; and finally, the high leverage of the financial system as a whole."[23] Large financial institutions, heavily indebted with mortgage-backed securities, collapsed (Lehman Brothers), were sold to other companies (Merrill Lynch), received government support as "too big to fail" (e.g., AIG, Citigroup, Goldman Sachs, Morgan Stanley), or were placed in conservatorship (Fannie Mae and Freddie Mac).[24]

Bubbles, Crashes, and Nonvoting

Thus, during the Internet technology period there was evidence of both upside and downside economic uncertainty as people wondered how and when the economic expansion of the 1990s and the economic calamity of 2007–2008 would end. From the theory of uncertainty in the national campaign context, we hypothesize that these forms of uncertainty decrease nonvoting as people go to the polls in an attempt to grapple with the ambiguity of future economic outcomes. Table 8.1 displays the effects of economic uncertainty and other aspects of the national campaign context on nonvoting for elections from 1992 through 2006. Table 8.2 considers the elections after the worldwide crash, from 2008 through 2012. The results indicate that economic change decreases nonvoting in all but three of the 11 elections analyzed—1996, 1998, and 2000—in which there are no economic effects. Income change has consistent effects

[20] "The State of the Nation's Housing 2008," 10.

[21] Olivier Blanchard, "The Crisis: Basic Mechanisms and Appropriate Policies," IMF Working Paper, International Monetary Fund, April 2009, 4.

[22] Blanchard, 2009, 3–4.

[23] Blanchard, 2009, 4; 8.

[24] Dawn Kopecki, "U.S. Considers Bringing Fannie and Freddie onto Budget," Bloomberg News, September 11, 2008, found at http://www.bloomberg.com/apps/news?pid=newsarchive&sid=adr.czwVm3ws&refer=home.

on nonvoting throughout the period, while unemployment has the most pronounced effects beginning in 2004.

An examination of the "Impact" columns in the tables offers a comparison among several elections dominated by both bad and good economic news. During the 1992 election, mean change in income reduced nonvoting by 7 percentage points. During the 1994 election when the economy had significantly improved, mean income change decreased nonvoting by 8 percentage points. The tables also provide evidence of the bubbles. The 2004 and 2006 elections conducted as the housing bubble grew also saw significant negative effects of income and unemployment change on nonvoting. Mean income change and mean unemployment change reduce nonvoting by 3 percentage points in 2004, and unemployment reduces nonvoting by 2 percentage points in 2006. In 2008, 2010, and 2012, the impact of the Great Recession is in evidence as income change decreases nonvoting in each election with a 5 percentage point effect in 2008, an 8 percentage point effect in 2010, and a 5 percentage point effect in 2012. Unemployment change also reduces nonvoting by one percentage point in 2008. Thus, as in the earlier periods, sizable positive and negative changes in economic conditions decrease nonvoting.

The Internet, Cost-Free Information, and Nonvoting

During these years, uncertainty also surrounded the technological advances of the Internet. In 1962, J. C. R. Licklider, computer science pioneer noted in Chapter 7 for his predictions about cable television, wrote equally prescient memos discussing a "Galactic Network"—a globally connected set of computers that would allow people quick access to data and programs from any site in the world. What may have seemed like a work of science fiction began in earnest a few years later. In 1969, the Advance Research Projects Agency of the Defense Department supported the creation of a computer network for all researchers it funded at various sites so the scientists could share results. This network, called ARPANET, initially linked computers at four research sites but soon expanded across the globe over the next two decades. By 1982, the National Science Foundation funded the development of a standardized Internet protocol suite which permitted a world-wide network to be created. Commercial providers then began to emerge in the late 1980s and early 1990s as ARPANET itself was decommissioned in 1990. The High Performance Computing Act of 1991 provided incentives to accelerate the growth of high-speed computers, the infrastructure for a national network, and the first browser. What had connected four computer scientists in 1969 connected millions of people just 30 years later. And what was revolutionary in the 1990s was slow, dial-up connections to the network—the equivalent of grainy black-and-white television.

The Internet became an important new access point for information of all kinds, including political information. Some researchers have argued that the Internet has key similarities to cable television because people can seek information but they can also seek to avoid it.[25] According to this view, both offer a "high-choice environment." Yet, the Internet differs from cable television in two fundamental ways. First, the Internet provides both broadcasting and narrowcasting opportunities. People can seek out information that once only television news and newspapers provided. Stories can influence a much wider array of the population, notably when coverage of an event "goes viral." But the Internet also provides the ability for individuals, groups, and organizations to provide highly stylized and tailored information and opinion. Groups and organizations interested in specific candidates or policy agendas can offer websites that filter information and opinion in ways that are not available on cable television. While Fox News and MSNBC may stand broadly for voices on the right and left of American politics, they cannot provide this level of specificity.

Second, the Internet offers an immense volume of political information that is virtually cost-free. From mainstream sites, targeted sites, and social media links through Facebook and Twitter, political information is easy to obtain and often equally hard to ignore. Thus, the high-choice environment of the Internet is also a high-information and free-information environment. The sheer volume and diversity of information and opinion offered via the Internet makes it difficult to avoid political content. But, it also creates considerable uncertainty in the national campaign context. It upends previous models of how candidates communicate with the electorate and makes it more difficult for them to know what works. Its novelty also engages citizens as they navigate the unlimited supply of facts and viewpoints. From the theory of uncertainty in the national campaign context, we hypothesize that this technological shock increases public information about and interest in the election and thereby decreases nonvoting. This is consistent with research conducted by Caroline Tolbert and Ramona McNeal, who found that the Internet and, in particular, obtaining political news from the Internet, increases participation in US elections.[26] Other researchers

[25] Markus Prior, "News vs. Entertainment: How Increasing Media Choice Widens Gaps in Political Knowledge and Turnout," *American Journal of Political Science* 49 (July 2005): 577–592.

[26] Caroline Tolbert and Ramona McNeal, "Unraveling the Effects of the Internet on Political Participation." *Political Research Quarterly* 56 (June 2003): 175–185. See also, M. Kent Jennings and Vicki Zeitner, "Internet Use and Civic Engagement: A Longitudinal Analysis," *Public Opinion Quarterly* 67 (Autumn 2003): 311–334.

observed that social network communication, particularly among close friends on Facebook, along with emails from public officials urging people to vote also have small but positive influences on mobilizing people to vote.[27]

Tables 8.1 and 8.2 show that, unlike cable television, access to the Internet consistently decreases nonvoting. We begin to track the Internet's effect for the first time in 1996, when 16 percent of Americans had it in their homes. Not surprisingly, there is no effect of the Internet on nonvoting in the 1996 election when overall access was at this relatively low level. However, in each election thereafter except 2002, the Internet decreases nonvoting. For presidential elections, its impact is at its greatest in 2004 and 2012 when mean Internet access across the states prompts a 13 percentage point drop in nonvoting. For midterm elections, the impact of the Internet is much larger, including a 16 percentage point drop in nonvoting in 2010 and a 21 percentage point drop in 2006. One interesting side note is that cable television negatively influences nonvoting in 1994. With the ideologically focused Republican efforts to take the majority in the House, cable television actually boosted participation. This is the only time this occurs. Thus, the novelty of the Internet is an important feature of midterm elections in the fourth period. The Internet mitigates the low-information quality of these elections, as people are broadly exposed to political content in ways that are both accidental, as one of their friends posts something political on Facebook, and intentional, as people check a particular website.

After the Cold War

During the Internet technology period, three critical unknowns arose regarding the role of the United States in the world. First, the end of the Cold War removed communism as the chief enemy that the United States had fought since the late 1940s. Presidents could no longer define American national security with the Truman Doctrine. Second, the international sphere was radically altered after the September 11, 2001 terrorist attacks. As George W. Bush told a joint session of Congress on September 20, 2001, "Our war on terror begins with al-Qaeda, but it does not end there. It will not end until every terrorist group of global reach

[27] Robert Bond, Christopher Fariss, Jason Jones, Adam Kramer, Cameron Marlow, Jaime Settle, and James Fowler, "A 61-million-person Experiment in Social Influence and Political Mobilization," *Nature* 489 (13 September 2012): 295–298; Neil Malhorta, Melissa Michelson, and Ali Valenzuela, "Emails from Official Sources Can Increase Turnout," *Quarterly Journal of Political Science* 7 (2012): 321–332; although see David Nickerson, "Does Email Boost Turnout?" *Quarterly Journal of Political Science* 2 (2007): 369–379.

has been found, stopped, and defeated."[28] The war on terror replaced the war on communism, built on an omnipresent desire to protect Americans on American soil. Third, this perceived danger created the rationale for a broad new class of military and covert efforts. As Vice President Dick Cheney remarked, "the danger is that we'll get hit again—that we'll be hit in a way that will be devastating from the standpoint of the United States."[29] Almost any action could be justified as preventing the United States from being "hit again."

These three unknowns enveloped the Iraq War. Using the expansive nature of the war on terror as justification, the George W. Bush administration pursued an offensive war against Iraq as American troops invaded in March 2003. During the Cold War, the rationale for American military interventions had been defensive in nature and based on some provocation that threatened US national security. Now the intervention was preemptive, justified to prevent Saddam Hussein's use of "weapons of mass destruction" and end his alleged ties to al-Qaeda, even as United Nations weapons inspectors found no evidence of chemical or nuclear weapons and US intelligence agencies found no credible link between Hussein and al-Qaeda. Documented by British intelligence, the so-called Downing Street memo stated that "Bush wanted to remove Saddam, through military action, justified by the conjunction of terrorism and WMD. But the intelligence and facts were being fixed around the policy."[30] What at first seemed like a quick, bold victory turned into an indeterminate after-war against Iraqi insurgents. The days of Vietnam and the inability of the United States to extricate itself from an unpopular war returned. Figure 8.4 shows public attitudes toward the Iraq War from 2003 through 2012 as the war became increasingly unpopular.

The theory of uncertainty in the national campaign context hypothesizes that war is an important indicator of uncertainty, and as such it will decrease nonvoting as people are unsure of the war's outcomes. As Tables 8.1 and 8.2 reveal, high levels of uncertainty associated with the Iraq War do decrease nonvoting in 2004 and 2008, although not in 2006. The war effects are not as large as the economic or technology effects, but they are nevertheless significant. This is consistent with research that shows that the war depressed Bush's electoral margin

[28] *Public Papers of the Presidents, George W. Bush 2001*, "Address before a Joint Session of the Congress of the United States Response to the Terrorist Attacks of September 11," September 20, 2011, found at http://www.presidency.ucsb.edu/ws/index.php?pid=64731&st=&st1=#ixzz2iq06MSA9.

[29] "Cheney: Kerry Win Risks Terror Attack," CNN, September 7, 2004, found at http://www.cnn.com/2004/ALLPOLITICS/09/07/cheney.terror/.

[30] Matthew Rycroft, "The Secret Downing Street Memo," *The Times of London*, May, 1, 2005 found at http://downingstreetmemo.com/docs/memotext.pdf See also, *The Report of the Iraq Inquiry*, Committee of Privy Counsellors, House of Commons, United Kingdom, July 6, 2016 found at www.iraqinquiry.org.uk.

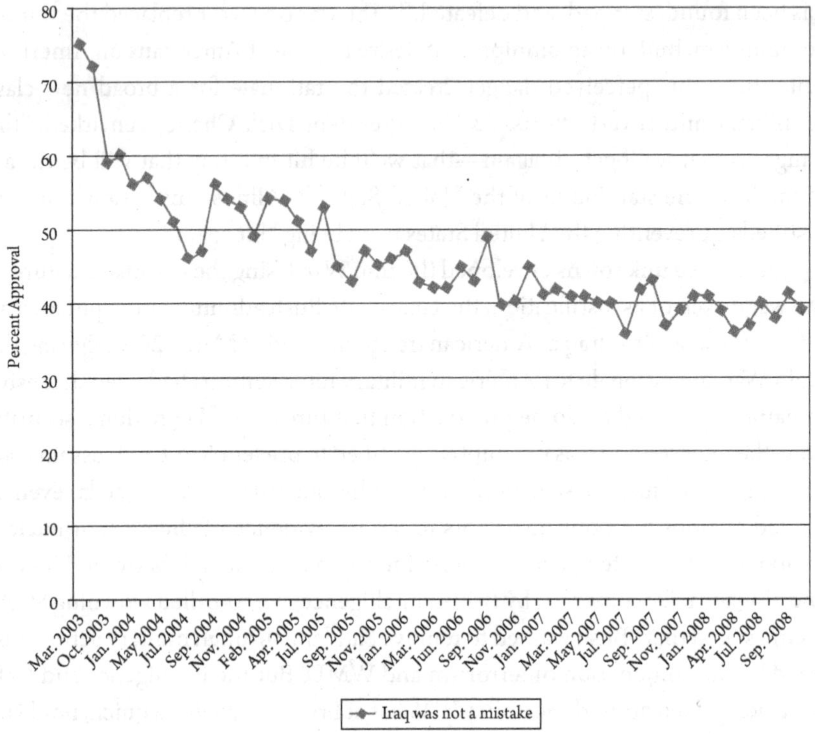

Figure 8.4 Public Approval of Iraq War, 2003–2008

in 2004 and Republican vote totals overall.[31] The international arena helps define uncertainty in the national campaign context that people assess in deciding whether to vote.

Youth, Education, and Low-Information Environments

In the information technology period, youth plays a slightly more active role in nonvoting than in the earlier period. The percentage of young people in a state's population increases nonvoting in 1996, but actually reduces it in 2008. This is

[31] David Karol and Edward Miguel, "The Electoral Cost of War: Iraq Casualties and the 2004 U.S. Presidential Election," *Journal of Politics* 69 (August 2007): 633–648; Herbert Weisberg and Dino Christenson, "Changing Horses in Wartime? The 2004 Presidential Election," *Political Behavior* 29 (2007): 279–304; Christian Grose and Bruce Oppenheimer, "The Iraq War, Partisanship, and Candidate Attributes: Variation in Partisan Swing in the 2006 U.S. House Elections," *Legislative Studies Quarterly* 32 (November 2007): 531–557.

the first time such a statistically significant negative effect exists since 1974.[32] This may reflect the appeal and the outreach to young people of the Obama campaign.

Relative to features of the campaign context, education as a personal resource of eligible voters has a more sporadic influence on nonvoting. Tables 8.1 and 8.2 show that education reduces nonvoting in four elections—1992, 2002, 2010, and 2012. The "Impact" column for these elections indicates that at the mean rate of higher education for the states, nonvoting drops by at least 15 percentage points. The inconsistent presence of an education effect may result in part from the leveling off of high school graduation rates. As those rates become high and flat, there is less inter-state variation. Referring back to Table 5.8, during the period, education rates reached historic levels: by 2012, 89 percent of Americans had graduated from high school and 31 percent had graduated from college. The regional education gap between the South and the rest of the country also reached an all-time low. High school graduation rates were on average 6 percentage points lower in the South than in the non-South, when they had been 11 percentage points lower in the prior period. College graduation rates were 3 percentage points lower in the South than in the non-South, a gap similar to that found in the prior period. Still, the variable we employ measures the difference between high school graduation rates and college graduation rates. These college graduation rates do fluctuate considerably across states and over time, so variation does remain in the education variable.

Party Polarization and the National Campaign Context

Changes in party competition combined with the economic, technological, and international aspects of the national campaign context draw a further distinction between the government reassessment period and the information technology period. Party competition shifted in two highly interrelated ways. First, regionalism in party politics, which had long been defined by a North–South divide, became increasingly multifaceted within the non-South. As discussed in the previous chapter, elements of this began during the government reassessment period but accelerated during the Internet period. There was an amalgam of gains and losses for the parties in each of the main regions of the country, confounded

[32] See Table 7.1. In 2006, we estimated the model with a variable measuring youth in the population rather than percent youth in the population. This provided for more robust estimates and the absence of autocorrelation among the error terms.

by differences in party success between presidential and midterm years. During the earlier period, Republicans had made inroads into the South at the presidential level, but Democrats still maintained an edge in southern midterms. During the Internet period, as a result of the 1994 House elections Democrats lost the advantage they had held in every election since 1930.[33] Democrats' mean support in midterm House elections in the South from 1994 to 2010 was 46 percent of the two-party vote compared with 61 percent in the government reassessment period. Republicans who had done extremely well in the West at the presidential level during the government reassessment period continued to be strong in the region but actually lost some ground. Meanwhile, Democrats who had done well in the West in midterm congressional elections in the government reassessment period did less well in the Internet period. Competition increased in the Midwest at the presidential level between the third and the fourth periods, but Republican strength in midterm races grew.

But the starkest transformation occurred in the East. The East, which was a competitive region during the government reassessment period, became the least competitive region during the Internet period, especially at the presidential level. Republicans lost considerable ground in these states, with mean two-party support of 38 percent in presidential races and 48 percent in House midterm contests. Even with former Governor of Massachusetts Mitt Romney running in 2012, Republicans won only 38 percent of the two-party vote in the East. The best Republicans did in the region during the period was George H. W. Bush who won 40 percent of the two-party vote in 1992 and George W. Bush who gained a similar tally in 2000. As a comparison, Democrats received 47 percent of the two-party vote in presidential elections in the South from 1992 to 2012. This provided little solace for either party. While Democrats were a true minority party in the South, Republicans were equally a minority party in the East. In both presidential and midterm races, the "Solid East" replaced the once "Solid South" for the Democratic Party.

Table 8.3 depicts these divisions in the non-South. The table presents inter-regional variation in party competition in presidential and midterm House elections measured by the standard deviation in the competition index across the regions. Among the regions outside the South, there is inter-regional variation in the Internet period that was last seen in the first period, but absent from the 2nd and 3rd periods. For presidential elections, there is a standard deviation of 4.9 in the latest period as compared with the standard deviation of 5.1 in the first period (from 1920–1944). The same comparison for midterm elections is a 5.5 standard deviation for the latest period and a 5.8 standard deviation for the first period.

[33] See Tables 5.6 and 5.7.

Table 8.3 **Regional Differences in Party Competition, 1920–2012 (Standard Deviations of Competition Index across Regions)**

Presidential Elections	*All Regions*	*Three Regions of Non-South*	*Midterm Elections*	*All Regions*	*Three Regions of Non-South*
1920	6.50	6.64			
1924	6.24	5.71	1922	14.33	8.01
1928	2.23	2.45	1926	10.67	5.35
1932	17.47	7.23	1930	12.97	6.15
1936	15.33	9.04	1934	21.86	7.21
1940	16.52	3.83	1938	20.74	3.44
1944	13.37	1.27	1942	20.16	5.04
Mean	**11.09**	**5.17**	**Mean**	**16.79**	**5.87**
1948	12.05	1.28	1946	15.30	6.94
1952	5.11	3.76	1950	19.92	2.31
1956	4.19	3.99	1954	19.51	1.59
1960	2.24	2.49	1958	22.49	4.97
1964	3.03	0.60	1962	10.54	1.41
1968	2.10	1.59	1966	5.17	0.37
1972	7.06	2.47	1970	9.10	4.05
Mean	**5.11**	**2.31**	**Mean**	**14.58**	**3.09**
1976	2.42	2.79	1974	6.74	4.90
1980	7.66	5.60	1978	4.39	3.14
1984	3.17	3.63	1982	2.47	2.15
1988	1.94	2.12	1986	6.01	6.82
Mean	**3.80**	**3.54**	1990	3.98	3.80
1992	4.25	4.00	**Mean**	**4.72**	**4.16**
1996	8.00	7.63	1994	4.43	4.30
2000	4.17	3.56	1998	5.41	5.35
2004	1.86	2.10	2002	8.72	9.03
2008	6.40	6.56	2006	6.41	6.69
2012	4.85	5.22	2010	3.92	3.91
Mean	**4.92**	**4.85**	**Mean**	**5.49**	**5.46**

As Tables 5.6 and 5.7 show, much of the increase in inter-regional difference is a result of the eastern states. As one example, the mean Democratic vote margin in presidential races from 1992 to 2012 was 62 percent when it had been at 50 percent in the government reassessment period. Paradoxically, the tally of these regional differences produced national party competition at all-time highs. The regional dominance of one party met the regional dominance of the other. During the Internet technology period, the mean Democratic share of the two-party vote in presidential elections is 50.7 percent in presidential elections and 47.2 percent in midterm elections. These are the closest average vote margins of any of the historic periods.

Second, party polarization, defined by "permanently competitive and ideologically charged politics," fueled but also was fueled by the combination of regional dominance and national competitiveness.[34] The historical reorientation of regional party competition and party polarization were inextricably intertwined. Political scientist Gary Jacobson noted that this growing divide resulted from a combination of candidate strategies, institutional behavior, activist interests, ideological fragmentation of the news media, and citizen preferences. The 1994 election set in motion a series of elections in which ideology was a litmus test for candidates and voters alike, as Republicans entered, in Jacobson's words, an era of "intentional polarization."[35] There was also a growing convergence between partisan and ideological preferences among ordinary citizens that did not exist in the 1970s and 1980s. People who identified as Democrats were consistently liberal on an array of issues while people who identified as Republicans were consistently conservative on these issues. In addition, within Congress, Republicans and Democrats took the opposite sides on issues more frequently than in any other time period.[36] Polarization in Congress produced high-wire attempts to refuse to increase the debt ceiling in 2011 and a government shutdown in 2013 as a maneuver against the Affordable Care Act. Mitch McConnell, Republican leader in the Senate summarized the approach, stating in October 2010 that "The single most important thing we want to achieve is for President Obama to be a one-term president."[37] At the same time, cable television and the Internet combined to provide politicians the opportunity to narrowcast. In addition, some networks and Internet sites slanted the factual accounts of events to

[34] Earl Black and Merle Black, *Divided America: The Ferocious Power Struggle in American Politics* (New York: Simon and Schuster, 2007).

[35] Gary Jacobson, *A Divider not a Uniter: George W. Bush and the American People* (New York: Pearson 2008), 291.

[36] Jacobson, 2008, 22–25.

[37] Major Garrett, "After the Wave," *The National Journal*, October 23, 2010, found at http://www.nationaljournal.com/magazine/after-the-wave-20101023.

reinforce their editorial bents, targeted audiences that fit a specific demographic and opinion profile, and created significant misperceptions among viewers in the process.[38] Thus, "changes in the preferences, behavior, and distribution of congressional voters gave the congressional parties more internally homogenous, divergent, and polarized electoral bases."[39] Although citizens objected to the resulting gridlock in government, they nevertheless contributed to it.

As seen in Tables 8.1 and 8.2, party competition has an effect on nonvoting in all presidential and midterm elections except 1994, 1996, 2002, and 2012. In examining the "Impact" columns, the effects of competition are uniform and robust in both presidential and midterm elections, ranging from 4 percentage points in 2000 to 13 percentage points in 2006 and 2010. This is in contrast with the minimal effects of competition on nonvoting in the government reassessment period and also provides further evidence of the new regionalism discussed above. It creates a type of uncertainty related to party competition that did not exist in earlier periods. Parties have a high degree of certainty that they will win key states in a particular region and lose other key states in a different region. But, they have a high degree of uncertainty about how they will fare nationally as these imbalances aggregate across the country. The influence of party competition is present even with the strong and consistent effect of prior nonvoting on current nonvoting in all elections during the Internet technology period. In examining the "Impact" columns in Tables 8.1 and 8.2, prior nonvoting has the single greatest impact on nonvoting of any factor in all elections.[40]

It is important to recognize that if past electoral history is any guide, this "new regionalism" in party competition is likely to be transitory. As one example in looking across the entire time frame of the book, the West, which was heavily Republican through 1930, became more Democratic during the New Deal only to return to its Republican roots by the 1950s. Yet, the West has become somewhat more competitive in presidential elections in the Internet period but less competitive as a region in the midterm House elections. The East, a competitive

[38] Steven Kull, Clay Ramsay, and Evan Lewis, "Misperceptions, the Media, and the Iraq War," *Political Research Quarterly* 118 (Winter 2003–2004): 569–598.

[39] Jacobson, 2008, 26.

[40] In earlier tests of the model, we also incorporated a dummy variable measure for states' early voting laws, which began in Texas in 1988 and grew to 37 states by 2012. As we did with state registration laws in Chapters 5 and 6, this was designed to determine the effect of state actions relative to the uncertainty of the national campaign context. In these tests, we observed no effect of early voting laws on nonvoting rates across the states. The variable was therefore not included in the final analysis in order to maximize the parsimony of the model. The results are consistent with the findings in Springer, who also observes no effect of early voting laws in elections from 1920 to 2000 (Melanie Springer, *How the States Shaped the Nation: American Electoral Institutions and Voter Turnout, 1920–2000* [Chicago: University of Chicago Press, 2014], 97–100).

region during the post-war and government reassessment periods, has seen a larger percentage of Democratic victories in the Internet period. As one comparison, modest Republican advantages in the presidential elections of 1980, 1984, and 1988 became strong Democratic advantages in presidential elections from 1992 through 2012.

Individual Nonvoters in Polarized Politics

We now turn to the impact on individual nonvoting in the Internet period of the uncertainty in the national campaign context and the climate of polarization. We would expect that with the high level of external uncertainty during this period—economic collapse, a technological revolution, and an interminable war—the campaign context and candidate comparisons would have strong effects on individual nonvoting. As seen in Tables 8.4 and 8.5, the economy influences individual nonvoting in all presidential elections in the period except 2000 and 2004. The economic effect is greatest in 2008 and 2012 amidst the Great Recession. In 2008, individuals who saw the economy as stable were 39 percentage points less likely to vote than those who saw economic change. In 2012, the difference is 49 percentage points. As shown in Table 8.6, the economy also influences individual nonvoting in the 1994 and 1998 midterm elections.[41] Of equal importance, the economy does not influence individual nonvoting in 2000, 2002, or 2004, when the economy was relatively stable with little change in personal income or unemployment from the year prior to the election.

Individuals' media attention strongly affects nonvoting in presidential elections. Following the aggregate analysis, we introduce Internet access as the media variable at the individual level beginning in the 1996 elections. Broad media attention influences individual nonvoting in 1992, but the effect is generally smaller than the effect of the Internet in the later elections. People who use only one form of media are 19 percentage points less likely to vote in 1992 than those who use multiple media sources. Beginning with 1996, Internet access significantly decreases individual nonvoting except in 2012. Those who do not use the Internet for political information are less likely to vote than those who do use the Internet, ranging from 29 percentage points less likely in 2008 to 35 percentage points less likely in 2000. This underscores similar results found at the aggregate level. Media also influences the 1994 midterm elections but has no effect in 1998 or 2002. The Internet variable is unavailable in the midterm studies, so we rely on the media exposure index. In 1994, those who rely on only one media source are 32 percentage points more likely to be nonvoters than those who rely on multiple media sources.

[41] There were no American National Election Studies in 2006 or 2010.

Table 8.4 **Effects of the National Campaign Context on Individual Nonvoting in Presidential Elections, 1992–1996 (Probit Maximum Likelihood Coefficients)**

Predictor	*1992*					*1996*				
	Maximum Likelihood Estimate	*MLE/SE*		*Range of Value in the Variable*	*Change in Likelihood of the Variable*	*Maximum Likelihood Estimate*	*MLE/SE*		*Range of Value in the Variable*	*Change in Likelihood of the Variable*
National Campaign Context										
Economic conditions	–0.172	–3.920	***	–2, 2	0.281	–0.099	–2.349	**	–2, 2	0.284
Media attention [a]	–0.138	–3.042	***	0,4	0.186	–0.177	–1.732	*	0,1	0.176
International involvement [b]	–0.066	–2.105	**	0,1	0.155	0.014	0.476		0,1	0.041
Candidate Awareness										
Candidate comparison	–0.006	–3.211	***	0,100	0.240	–0.003	–2.037	**	0,100	0.021
Ideological comparison	–0.061	–2.142	**	1,7	0.346	–0.019	–0.747		1,7	0.151
Care who wins	–0.192	–3.918	***	–1,1	0.334	–0.153	–3.485	***	–1,1	0.424
Ross Perot candidacy	0.001	0.923		0,100	0.067					
Personal Characteristics										
Youth	0.014	5.421	***	17,99	0.324	0.015	6.410	***	17,99	0.556
Education	–0.335	–5.716	***	0,3	0.575	–0.274	–5.048	***	0,3	0.558
Social Connections										
Marriage	–0.089	–0.981		0,1	0.102	–0.234	–2.777	***	0,1	0.170
Residential stability	–0.003	–2.572	***	0,99	0.241	0.001	0.080		0,99	0.193
Unemployment	0.115	1.125		0,1	0.168	0.012	0.120		0,1	0.198

(*continued*)

Table 8.4 **(Continued)**

Predictor	*1992*					*1996*				
	Maximum Likelihood Estimate	***MLE/SE***		***Range of Value in the Variable***	***Change in Likelihood of the Variable***	***Maximum Likelihood Estimate***	***MLE/SE***		***Range of Value in the Variable***	***Change in Likelihood of the Variable***
Psychological Involvement										
Campaign interest	–0.314	–4.660	***	1,3	0.660	–0.412	–6.924	***	1,3	0.801
Party Mobilization and Competition										
Campaign contact	–0.681	–4.831	***	0,1	0.686	–0.335	–3.374	***	0,1	0.318
Closeness of race	–0.150	–1.479		0,1	0.233	–0.089	–1.208		0,1	0.046
Intercept	1.985	7.269	***			1.581	6.733	***		
Number of Cases	1746					1388				

Note: SE=standard error. Significance levels of the maximum likelihood estimates: * .10 level, critical value Z=1.65; **.05, critical value Z =1.96; *** 01, critical value Z=2.57.

[a] In 1996, media attention is measured by internet access. The standard media exposure index is used in 1992.

[b] In 1992 and 1996, the international measure is based on a 7-point question on whether to cut or increase defense spending.

Table 8.5 **Effects of the National Campaign Context on Individual Nonvoting in Presidential Elections, 2000–2012 (Probit Maximum Likelihood Coefficients)**

	2000					2004					2008					2012				
Predictor	*Maximum Likelihood Estimate*	*MLE/ SE*		*Range of Value in the Variable*	*Change in Likelihood of the Variable*	*Maximum Likelihood Estimate*	*MLE/ SE*		*Range of Value in the Variable*	*Change in Likelihood of the Variable*	*Maximum Likelihood Estimate*	*MLE/ SE*		*Range of Value in the Variable*	*Change in Likelihood of the Variable*	*Maximum Likelihood Estimate*	*MLE/ SE*		*Range of Value in the Variable*	*Change in Likelihood of the Variable*
National Campaign Context																				
Economic Conditions	−0.044	−0.802		−2, 2	0.202	−0.040	−0.792		−2, 2	0.174	−0.020	−2.394	**	−2, 2	0.393	−0.181	−3.849	***	−2, 2	0.487
Media Attention	−0.342	−2.815	***	0,1	0.345	−0.259	−2.246	**	0,1	0.304	−0.285	−2.433	**	0,1	0.286	−0.077	−0.661		0,1	0.023
International involvement[a]	0.032	0.887		0,1	0.085	−0.070	−2.248	**	0,1	0.305	−0.092	−1.959	*	0,1	0.030	−0.051	−1.432		0,1	0.126
Candidate Awareness																				
Candidate comparison	−0.002	−0.996		0,100	0.106	−0.004	−2.164	**	0,100	0.302	−0.002	−1.672	*	0,100	0.167	−0.004	−1.938	*	0,100	0.234
Ideological comparison	−0.058	−1.661	*	1,7	0.500	−0.019	−0.628		1,7	0.013	−0.022	−1.789	*	1,7	0.419	−0.031	−1.035		1,7	0.166
Care who wins	−0.262	−4.516	***	−1,1	0.523	−0.279	−4.351	***	−1,1	0.540	−0.218	−3.776	***	−1,1	0.436	−0.200	−3.181	***	−1,1	0.381
Personal Characteristics																				
Youth	0.009	3.031	***	17,99	0.382	0.007	2.007	**	17,99	0.329	0.012	4.107	***	17,99	0.201	0.005	1.647	*	17,99	0.160
Education	−0.219	−3.143	***	0,3	0.428	−0.214	−3.202	***	0,3	0.402	−0.241	−3.781	***	0,3	0.573	−0.110	−1.751	*	0,3	0.290

(continued)

Table 8.5 **(Continued)**

Predictor	2000 Maximum Likelihood Estimate	MLE/SE	Range of Value in the Variable	Change in Likelihood of the Variable	2004 Maximum Likelihood Estimate	MLE/SE	Range of Value in the Variable	Change in Likelihood of the Variable	2008 Maximum Likelihood Estimate	MLE/SE	Range of Value in the Variable	Change in Likelihood of the Variable	2012 Maximum Likelihood Estimate	MLE/SE	Range of Value in the Variable	Change in Likelihood of the Variable
Social Connections																
Marriage	–0.093	–0.855	0,1	0.094	0.090	0.850	0,1	0.107	0.082	0.836	0,1	0.081	0.023	0.224	0,1	0.009
Residential stability	–0.001	–0.582	0,99	0.062	–0.002	–0.715	0,99	0.077	–0.003	–1.572	0,99	0.137	–0.005	–1.023	0,99	0.068
Unemployment	–0.012	–0.096	0,1	0.013	0.032	0.256	0,1	0.072	0.045	0.424	0,1	0.046	0.147	1.297	0,1	0.080
Psychological Involvement																
Campaign interest	–0.192	–2.333 **	1,3	0.331	–0.259	–2.246 **	1,3	0.572	–0.148	–2.100 **	1,3	0.319	–0.318	–4.342 ***	1,3	0.319
Party Mobilization and Competition																
Campaign contact	–0.493	–3.895 ***	0,1	0.506	–0.491	–4.603 ***	0,1	0.491	–0.435	–4.100 ***	0,1	0.436	–0.273	–2.444 **	0,1	0.222
Closeness of race	–0.251	–2.024 **	0,1	0.251	–0.078	–0.695	0,1	0.066	–0.164	–1.699 *	0,1	0.164	0.107	0.867	0,1	0.019
Intercept	0.997	3.521 ***			0.760	2.831 *			0.935	3.876 ***			–0.608	–1.589		
Number of Cases	733				937				940				1441			

Note: SE=standard error. Significance levels of the maximum likelihood estimates: * .10 level, critical value Z=1.65; **.05, critical value Z =1.96; *** 01, critical value Z=2.57.

[a] In 2000, 2004, and 2012, the international measure is based on a 7-point question on whether to cut or increase defense spending.

In 2008, the international measure is based on the question, "How involved should the U.S. be in world affairs?"

Table 8.6 **Effects of the National Campaign Context on Individual Nonvoting in Midterm Elections, 1994–2002 (Probit Maximum Likelihood Coefficients)**

Predictor	*1994*				*1998*				*2002*			
	Maximum Likelihood Estimate	*MLE/SE*	*Range of Value in the Variable*	*Change in Likelihood of the Variable*	*Maximum Likelihood Estimate*	*MLE/SE*	*Range of Value in the Variable*	*Change in Likelihood of the Variable*	*Maximum Likelihood Estimate*	*MLE/ SE*	*Range of Value in the Variable*	*Change in Likelihood of the Variable*
National Campaign Context												
Economic conditions	−0.082	−2.313 **	−2, 2	0.447	−0.077	−1.848 *	−2, 2	0.294	−0.013	−0.266	−2, 2	0.006
Media attention	−0.107	−1.679 *	0,4	0.317	−0.017	−0.255	0,4	0.154	−0.009	−0.133	0,4	0.051
Government ethics					0.092	1.096.	0,1	0.209				
International involvement [a]	−0.001	−0.061	1,7	0.122	−0.024	−0.443	1,7	0.016	0.053	1.109	1,7	0.095
Candidate Awareness												
Candidate comparison	−0.005	−2.435 **	0,100	0.614	−0.010	−3.886 ***	0,100	0.574	−0.013	−4.784 ***	0,100	0.475
Ideological comparison	−0.092	−3.031 ***	1.7	0.179	−0.086	−2.192 **	1.7	0.127	n/a	n/a		
Democratic candidate recognition	0.031	0.132	0,1	0.019	0.038	0.090	0,1	0.082	−0.441	−0.933	0,1	0.017
Republican candidate recognition	0.100	0.299	0,1	0.113	−0.479	−1.689 *	0,1	0.291	−0.432	−0.775	0,1	0.026
Care who wins	−0.146	−4.111 ***	−1,1	0.302	−0.155	−3.435 ***	−1,1	0.287	−0.117	−2.502 ***	−1,1	0.240

(continued)

Table 8.6 **(Continued)**

Predictor	1994					1998					2002				
	Maximum Likelihood Estimate	*MLE/SE*		*Range of Value in the Variable*	*Change in Likelihood of the Variable*	*Maximum Likelihood Estimate*	*MLE/SE*		*Range of Value in the Variable*	*Change in Likelihood of the Variable*	*Maximum Likelihood Estimate*	*MLE/ SE*		*Range of Value in the Variable*	*Change in Likelihood of the Variable*
Personal Characteristics															
Youth	0.015	7.476	***	17,99	0.704	0.018	7.158	***	17,99	0.534	0.012	4.370	***	17,99	0.496
Education	–0.217	–5.001	***	0,3	0.456	–0.149	–2.818	***	0,3	0.454	–0.265	–5.268	***	0,3	0.549
Social Connections															
Marriage	–0.002	–0.029		0,1	0.007	–0.229	–2.570	***	0,1	0.246	–0.267	–3.303	***	0,1	0.273
Residential stability	–0.001	–1.292		0,99	0.098	–0.003	–1.890	*	0,99	0.203	–0.001	–0.738		0,99	0.070
Unemployment	–0.150	–1.791	*	0,1	0.139	–0.180	–1.705	*	0,1	0.192	0.003	0.021		0,1	0.011
Psychological Involvement															
Campaign interest	–0.278	–5.451	***	1,3	0.574	–0.249	–3.660	***	1,3	0.644	–0.220	–3.137	***	1,3	0.580
Democratic candidate contact	–0.177	–2.552	***	0,1	0.176	n/a	n/a				n/a	n/a			
Republican candidate contact	–0.107	–1.679	***	0,1	0.180	n/a	n/a				n/a	n/a			
Intercept	1.677	3.867	***			2.046	3.829	***			1.956	2.445	**		
Number of Cases	1368					993					1008				

Note: SE=standard error. Significance levels of the maximum likelihood estimates: * .10 level, critical value Z=1.65; **.05, critical value Z =1.96; *** 01, critical value Z=2.57.

[a] In 1994, the international measure is based on a 7-point scale question on whether to cut or increase defense spending.

In 1998 and 2002, the international measure is based on the question, "How involved should the U.S. be in world affairs?" There are no American National Election Studies in 2006 and 2010.

International involvement plays a role in the 1992, 2004, and 2008 elections.[42] The largest effect is in 2004 when those who feel defense spending should remain stable are 31 percentage points less likely to vote than those who think defense spending should dramatically increase (decrease). This is likely an effect of the Iraq War and parallels the results found in aggregate nonvoting.[43] Unlike the strong effect in presidential elections of international involvement, international involvement has no effect on individual nonvoting at the midterms. This is consistent with the findings from the government reassessment period, when international affairs also affected presidential but not midterm elections (compare Table 7.3 with 7.4). The absence of an international-affairs effect reinforces the oft-quoted comment that "all politics is local" in congressional elections. Government ethics also has no effect in 1998 at the height of the Clinton impeachment imbroglio.[44]

During the Internet period, social connections have little impact on individual nonvoting, but people's personal backgrounds are influential. Young people are much less likely to vote than older people in all presidential and midterm House elections. However, in 2008 and 2012, the effect of the Obama candidacy is in evidence when the difference between young and old drops substantially. This parallels the aggregate results. The Obama campaign made a concerted and successful effort to bring more young people to the polls in both elections.[45] People who are less educated are also less likely to vote than those who are more educated across all presidential and midterm races.

Polarized Politics and Nonvoting

In addition to the effects of the campaign context, the individual-level results provide an opportunity to explore the impact of party polarization during the

[42] Because of data availability, international involvement is measured using a defense spending indicator in 1992, 1994, 1996, 2000, 2004, 2012. This measure is based on a 7-point scale question which asks respondents whether they fall on the scale from dramatic cuts to defense spending to dramatic increases. In 1998, 2002, and 2008, the indicator is based on the question, "How involved should the U.S. be in world affairs?"

[43] We do not include the government size and government spending variables used in Chapter 7 in the models here. Tests of the model including these variables from 1992 through 2012 revealed that they did not have a statistically significant effect on nonvoting in any election year. They were therefore removed from the model.

[44] This is the same government ethics measure used in the 1976 election after Watergate. It is based on a question which asks respondents whether politicians in Washington are mostly honest or mostly crooks.

[45] Tyler Kingkade, "Young Vote 2012 Turnout: Exit Polls Show Greater Share of the Electorate Than In 2008," *Huffington Post*, November 7, 2012, found at http://www.huffingtonpost.com/2012/11/07/youth-vote-2012-turnout-exit-polls_n_2086092.html.

Internet period. Across four key indicators—ideological comparisons between the candidates, caring which candidate wins, overall campaign interest, and candidate contact—voters and nonvoters are more politically connected in the Internet period than in the earlier periods. First, people draw more ideological comparisons during this period than in the earlier periods. In the Internet period, 18 percent of voters and 10 percent of nonvoters feel there are large ideological differences between the candidates. In contrast, during the post-war period, only 8 percent of voters and 5 percent of nonvoters see large ideological differences. Similarly, in the government reassessment period 7 percent of voters and 4 percent of nonvoters feel there are large ideological differences.[46] As seen in Tables 8.4 and 8.5, people's general ideological comparisons between the candidates affect nonvoting in 1992, 1994, 1998, 2000, and 2008.[47] These relative effects of ideology are larger in the Internet period than those found in the earlier periods. They range from a 13 percentage point difference in 1998 to a 50 percentage point difference in 2000. The effect in the earlier two periods was no greater than 32 percentage points in 1980.[48] As shown in Table 8.6, individuals who do not make ideological comparisons between the congressional candidates are significantly less likely to vote than those who do, in 1994 and 1998. The variable is not available in 2002. While the ideological effect is less than that found for the more general candidate comparison variable that is significant in all three midterm elections, it is nevertheless notable because ideology was not relevant at all to the midterms of the previous period.[49] Thus, people rely on ideological comparisons to alleviate their internal uncertainty about which candidate is best equipped to handle the external uncertainty in the national campaign context. In a polarized political environment, those comparisons are all the more crucial.

Second, more people care who wins in this period than in the earlier periods. During the Internet period, 88 percent of voters and 61 percent of nonvoters care a great deal about who will win; the corresponding numbers are 70 percent

[46] These entries and the other descriptive statistics to follow are mean results taken from American National Election Studies for individual election years. Far more people also saw moderate ideological differences (as compared to small or none) in the Internet period than in the two earlier periods: in the Internet period, 43 percent of voters and 28 percent of nonvoters saw moderate ideological differences between the candidates. In the post-war period, 35 percent of voters and 21 percent of nonvoters saw moderate ideological differences. And in the government reassessment period, 34 percent of voters and 18 percent of nonvoters saw these differences.

[47] General comparisons between the candidates also influence nonvoting in 1992, 1996, 2004, 2008, and 2012.

[48] See Table 7.3.

[49] In preliminary tests, an ideological comparison variable was included in estimates of individual nonvoting for election years from 1978 to 1990. It had no effect in any election year and was therefore deleted from the analyses of those years (see fn. 50 in Chapter 7).

of voters and 48 percent of nonvoters in the 1968 and 1972 elections in the post-war period, and 67 percent voters and 48 percent nonvoters in the government reassessment period. As presented in Tables 8.4 and 8.5, caring who wins the election negatively influences presidential nonvoting in each election of the period. These effects range from 33 percentage points in 1992 to 54 percentage points in 2004 and are greater than those found in the earlier two periods, when the largest effect of the care variable is 29 percentage points in the 1988 election (see Table 7.3). As shown in Table 8.6, caring who wins the election also strongly reduces nonvoting in the midterm elections of the period. The effect is somewhat smaller than that found in presidential years, ranging from 24 percentage points in 2002 to 30 percentage points in 1994. If people feel that the other party's candidate is unacceptable on personal or ideological grounds, then who wins is very important. In polarized politics, the stakes grow about who should win. People do not wish to risk the wrong candidate winning the election and being unable to meet the challenges of the external uncertainty in the national campaign context.

Third, during the Internet period more people are interested in election campaigns than in the earlier periods. Forty-six percent of voters and 19 percent of nonvoters report that they are very interested in the election. The corresponding numbers in the earlier periods are 41 percent of voters and 18 percent of nonvoters in the 1968 and 1972 elections, and 39 percent of voters and 17 percent of nonvoters in the government reassessment period. As shown in Tables 8.4 and 8.5, campaign interest reduces presidential nonvoting in each election year. And the relative influence of campaign interest during the Internet period is quite high, ranging from 32 percentage points in 2008 and 2012, to 80 percentage points in 1996. The largest relative effect of campaign interest in the other historical periods is 66 percentage points in 1968 (see Table 6.4). As seen in Table 8.6, campaign interest also reduces nonvoting in the three midterm election years. This works in tandem with the high degree of external uncertainty in the national campaign context during the period.

Finally, during the Internet period, campaign contact is at its highest level. Forty-three percent of voters and 16 percent of nonvoters reported contact by a candidate's campaign. This compares with 31 percent of voters and 14 percent of nonvoters in the 1968 and 1972 elections of the post-war period, and 33 percent of voters and 15 percent of nonvoters in the government reassessment period. The multivariate analysis shows that candidate contact significantly lowers nonvoting in each presidential election of the Internet period and in the 1994 midterm elections.[50] The relative effects of candidate contact ranges from 22 percentage points in 2012 to 69 percentage points in 1992. The largest

[50] Contact questions were not asked in 1998 or 2002.

relative effect in the other two periods is 45 percentage points in 1984 and 1988. In a polarized environment, it becomes important for the parties to directly contact their supporters because the central strategy for victory relies heavily on the party faithful.

The polarization sharpened political uncertainty because it was not just a matter of what would happen next, but what *should* happen next and, of equal importance, what should not happen next. Attached to the political unknowns was a heightened sense of political right and wrong. In a highly uncertain environment, politicians paradoxically claimed that there were a series of non-negotiable items about taxes, budgets, and health care that were off limits to compromise. The intensity of regional party dominance in the East, West, and South created few incentives for partisan compromise. Overall, the individual-level results point to the recasting of American politics in more ideological terms. It is not simply that partisan polarization affects the choices voters make between candidates. It also influences the choices people make about whether to vote at all.

The Speed of Uncertainty

Speed is the hallmark of the Internet technology period. High-speed computers permit analysts and investors to respond to minute-by-minute changes in economic outlooks. When the collapse occurred in 2008, it did so at a pace much faster than the unraveling of the economy in 1929. News that once took at least several hours, if not a day, to disseminate, now takes only minutes for people to be alerted to a shocking event as notifications ping people's smartphones. Global terrorism, as a central feature of the international sphere, turns lives and governments upside down in the second it takes to detonate a bomb.

Party polarization heightens people's awareness of both the speed and the uncertainty as one party loudly professes that it is the only group who can handle this hyper-uncertainty and stokes fear in people that the other party will preside over catastrophe. At the same time, the speed also heightens party polarization as the parties' leaders and elected officials are forced to respond in real time with limited reflection on how best to cope with sudden shifts and rattling news. This pushes politicians to retreat to easy, previously well-developed ideological takes on the rapidly changing circumstances. As one example, in June 2016 after an American citizen, pledging allegiance to the terrorist group ISIS, killed 49 people and wounded 53 others in an Orlando, Florida nightclub, 85 percent of Americans agreed that people who are on the US government's Terrorist Watchlist or no-fly list should be prevented from buying guns.[51] Yet,

[51] CNN-ORC Poll, June 20, 2016, found at http://i2.cdn.turner.com/cnn/2016/images/06/20/cnn_orc_poll_june_20.pdf.

Republican members of Congress overwhelmingly held to their prior orthodoxy of no restrictions of any kind on gun purchases.

The speed of uncertainty and party polarization help explain five central findings about nonvoting during the Internet technology period. First, there is an overall negative effect of the national campaign context on aggregate nonvoting (see Table 5.1). This is a shift from the positive effect found during the government reassessment period. The speed of uncertainty across economic, technological, and international dimensions made it difficult for people to ignore the national campaign context. Too, polarization sharpened political uncertainty, demanding people take sides on critical elements in the national campaign context.

Second, economic conditions influence nonvoting at both the aggregate and individual levels. At the aggregate level the effect of economic conditions across the period are similar to those found in the first and third periods, but they are not as great as those seen in the post-war period. It is perhaps surprising that the economic boom of the 1950s and 1960s produced greater negative effects on nonvoting than did the Depression, stagflation, and the Great Recession. It underscores how unique the post-war period was. It also suggests that protecting the good times may be somewhat more pivotal to participation than ending the bad times. At the same time, throughout the timespan of this study, it is obvious that economic bad times also significantly decrease nonvoting. At the individual level, economic conditions are weaker predictors in this period than they were in the government reassessment period. This may reflect that the stagflation was a singular focus of the elections in the 1970s and 1980s, while during the Internet period the economy moved in various directions—strongly positive in the early period, stable in the early 2000s, and sharply negative with the Great Recession.

Third, the results also show the influence of the Internet as a novel form of communication technology on nonvoting throughout the period. The instantaneous nature of communication via the Internet made this technological shock as fundamental as the first-time national coverage offered by radio and the introduction of visual images with television. At the aggregate level, the impact of the Internet on nonvoting in the early 2000s is generally equivalent to the corresponding introduction of radio in the 1920s and television in the 1950s. In each period, even though the effect in presidential elections is sizable, the effect is greater during the low-information midterm elections. At the aggregate level, as is true for the earlier three periods, the effect of media is greater than the effect of economic conditions. At the individual level, media attention is critical to nonvoting in each of the periods since the post-war era.

Fourth, the uncertainty associated with international involvements influences nonvoting in this period at the aggregate and individual levels. At the aggregate level, there is a negative effect of the Iraq War on nonvoting, as there had been in World War II. This is in contrast to the absence of an effect during the Korean War and a positive effect during the Vietnam War. At the individual level, consistent with the findings of the government reassessment period, international affairs affects nonvoting in presidential elections but not in midterm races. Individuals pay attention to the fast-paced events in the international arena when they are part of the campaign focus typical of presidential contests; they do not pay attention to foreign affairs when the focus is more local, typical of congressional races especially at the midterm. Thus, while war affects nonvoting, the specifics of the war, the uncertainty it creates, and its importance in the campaign are crucial to the kind of effect that is present.

Finally, the prominence of candidate comparisons, especially ideological comparisons, is apparent at the individual level in presidential and midterm elections. People see the candidates in sharper focus during this period than before. This too may be an indication of the polarization of the period, as picking the right candidate is key. It also underscores that people assess whether the candidates can handle the underlying uncertainty of the national campaign context as they decide whether to vote.

In the 2014 midterm elections nonvoting rose to 62.5 percent, a level last seen in 1930. Nonvoting was roughly as high at 61 percent in 1978 and 1990; nevertheless the nonvoting rate in 2014 was a dramatic increase relative to the declines that had occurred in 2002, 2006, and 2010. Given the nature of the national campaign context at the time, this increase, while unsettling, was not surprising. The economy was stable with moderate growth and low unemployment, and was not subject to the large swings that characterized the 2010 midterms. The Internet was close to a saturation point—present in most people's homes or through their cell phones. Although considerable concern prevailed in the international arena about terrorist groups and Russia, the United States was not at war after the last troops left Afghanistan and Iraq. So, the uncertainty within the national campaign context was lower than it had been in the earlier elections.

It is ultimately unclear what circumstances will occur in the next set of elections and when a new electoral period might emerge as the uncertainty in the national campaign context changes. The shift may occur with a significant mobilization of the Hispanic population, whether because of a very appealing or unappealing candidate, immigration reform, or both. It may also result from the growing income inequality in America as segments of the population worry about being permanently left behind in the economic system. There may be a revamping of election laws to provide people with Internet voting and thereby dramatically reduce nonvoting rates. Whatever the set of circumstances, a new period is certainly likely to emerge as the degree of external uncertainty shifts. What is not likely to change in such a new period are the fundamental effects of the economy, media, and international affairs on nonvoting. The uncertainty in the national campaign context will play an important role in how many people do not vote.

9

The National Campaign Context in Retrospect

In an October radio address prior to the 1944 presidential elections, Franklin Roosevelt told a nationwide audience, "Nobody will ever deprive the American people of the right to vote except the American people themselves, and the only way they could do this is by not voting . . . Candidates in every part of the United States are now engaged in running for office. All of us who are doing it are actuated by a normal desire to win. But, speaking personally, I should be very sorry to be elected President of the United States on a small turnout of voters. And by the same token, if I were to be defeated, I should be much happier to be defeated in a large outpouring of voters. Then there could not be any question of doubt in anybody's mind as to which way the masses of the American people wanted this election to go."[1]

The central conclusion of this book is that the "large outpouring of voters" occurs when there are high levels of uncertainty in the national campaign context. Neither politicians nor citizens control this uncertainty, but the election punctuates it. The hour the polls close on Election Day is fixed and irreversible. The election gives politicians and citizens the one chance to directly address, although not control, the external uncertainty. Politicians make multiple promises about how they are the best candidates to reduce the uncertainty—make the economy grow, win the war, calm the fears of the populace. Citizens evaluate these promises and the politicians who make them by assessing who would best handle the uncertainty. These evaluations only matter when citizens decide to participate in the election. This is their elemental uncertainty calculation. Although they will not know when they vote who will win, they have their greatest chance to address the uncertainty by deciding whom among the candidates best speaks to it. Those who vote may well be wrong—they bet on the wrong

[1] Franklin Roosevelt, "Radio Address from the White House," October 5, 1944, found at the American Presidency Project, www.presidency.ucsb.edu.

candidate, and even more uncertainty ensues. But remaining on the sidelines, the nonvoters leave the external uncertainty unchecked and the internal uncertainty about the candidates unresolved.

The uncertainty is not simply associated with a specific election year. It exists across American electoral history and defines political periods. While analysts frequently bracket political periods by changes in presidential administrations, this misses the broader economic, technological, international and legal shifts occurring in the national campaign context. To be sure, across 47 elections over 92 years there is variability and exceptions to general rules when the results for a specific election are inconsistent with adjacent elections. There are also differences across regions as patterns in the South often diverge from those in the rest of the country. But, this variability should not be surprising. Indeed, these temporal and regional nuances are at the very heart of the historical contribution of this study.

Even with anomalies found in individual elections, the analysis reveals three key generalizations regarding the uncertainty of the national campaign context that hold across the four time periods. Table 9.1 clarifies this with a summary of the aggregate impact results for the economy, technology, suffrage laws, international involvement, competition, and education. As we note below, youth performs poorly at the aggregate level and so is not included in the table. First, dramatic changes in economic conditions lower nonvoting rates. Economic volatility, regardless of whether the economy is spiking up or spiraling down, produces decreases in nonvoting. The uncertainty in the economy—about how to keep a strong economy growing or to bring a weak economy back—creates incentives for people to participate in the electoral process. However, economic swings are not always apparent during every election cycle. When the economy is flat or growing at a very slow pace, nonvoting is unaffected. Economic change has the greatest influence when uncertainty about the economy's direction is arguably at its highest—the depths of the Depression in 1934 and the recessions in 1958, 1962, 1982, 1990, and 2008; the inexplicable stagflation in 1978 and 1980; and the booms in 1942, 1952, 1964, and 1988.

These economic conditions also influence individual nonvoting. When people see economic conditions as stable, they are less likely to vote; when people see the economy as in flux, they are more likely to vote. Their perceptions tend to match the direction of the economy itself. The largest effects of the economy on individual nonvoting occur in 1982, 1984, 1988, 1994, 2008, and 2012, when economic conditions were unstable.

Second, technology shocks prompted by innovations in communication among radio, network television, and the Internet decrease nonvoting. Citizens reduce their internal uncertainty about the election by gathering information through these technological advances that provide free and ubiquitous

Table 9.1 **Summary of Impact of Selected Predictors on Nonvoting, 1920–2012**

Year	*Income Change*	*Unemployment Change*	*Communication Technology* [a]	*Enfranchisement Laws* [b]	*International Involvement* [c]	*Competition*	*Education*
1920	–0.316	0.844		24.242 *		–6.530 **	–3.801
1922	–1.427	–1.782		58.104 ***		–13.532 ***	–7.729 **
1924	–4.262	–0.671		–4.854		–4.862 *	–6.872 **
1926	–4.220 **	–2.653	–5.990	18.107		–4.567 **	–2.681
1928	–3.397 *	–1.527	–13.300 ***	21.573		1.316	–4.446
1930	–1.909	–4.323 **	–3.027			–4.269 *	–0.591
1932	–3.688	–4.025 *	–10.670 ***			3.082	–8.110 ***
1934	–3.127 **	–35.439 ***	–16.800 ***			–7.950 **	–0.133
1936	–3.998	–0.626	–10.657 **			–5.646 *	1.927
1938	–1.201	–3.819 *	–15.095 *			–7.562 *	–9.492 *
1940	–3.348 **	–3.843 ***	–14.385 ***			–0.624	–1.681
1942	–24.971 **	10.873	–8.828		–1.547 *	–4.090	1.257
1944	–6.549 *	1.286	–23.866 **		–10.017 *	–1.628	–2.574
1946	–3.497	–5.310	–13.375	–33.578		–8.932 ***	3.775
1948	–4.896	–3.571	5.222	17.316 ***		–0.084	0.053
1950	–0.251	–0.034	–7.666	17.842 *	–0.445	0.359	–4.242

(*continued*)

Table 9.1 **(Continued)**

Year	*Income Change*	*Unemployment Change*	*Communication Technology* [a]	*Enfranchisement Laws* [b]	*International Involvement* [c]	*Competition*	*Education*
1952	−19.987 *	−0.607	−3.668 *	110.209	1.071	−10.797 **	−5.482
1954	−6.558	−2.078	−7.429	18.895 **		−3.303	0.763
1956	−5.402 **	−0.746	−15.561 ***	97.104 **		−4.293	−1.332
1958	−24.883 **	−0.345	−27.211 **	59.839		−8.263 **	−10.097 *
1960	−6.434 *	−0.026	−23.742 ***	−39.341 ***		−4.381 **	−11.527 ***
1962	−24.162 ***	−0.006	−17.200	148.867 **		−9.717 ***	−7.499 *
1964	−18.282 **	−0.002	5.051	147.691 **		−0.747	−11.338 **
1966	−7.195	−0.151	−9.987	−175.106 *	9.224 *	−3.487	−12.533 *
1968	−11.100 **	−1.795 *	−17.899	−45.054 **	0.343	−11.878 *	−4.743
1970	−11.103 *	−0.065	−57.673 *	−22.745 *	2.839 *	−6.052 *	−21.548 ***
1972	−7.084	−0.871 *	88.579	49.210	−0.025	−7.446 **	−7.224 *
1974	6.542	0.274	−17.437	−10.927 *		−3.416	−15.945 *
1976	−2.138	−1.346 *	−1.960	−1.308		0.090	−13.347 **
1978	−17.749 *	−0.203 **	−73.079	5.282		0.321	−16.074 *
1980	−21.808 **	−0.099	27.929 **			−0.924 *	−13.974 **
1982	−13.762 **	0.326	23.587 **			−0.160	−15.133 **
1984	−4.379	−0.377 ***	7.798 **			1.379	5.317

1986	3.197		−1.548		9.341	*			4.451		−16.376	
1988	−5.560	***	−1.225	***	7.248	***			1.633		−10.210	***
1990	−18.998	*	−3.333	***	10.092		−10.708	**	4.093		−48.051	***
1992	−7.242	**	−0.227		−4.598				−9.856	***	−15.938	***
1994	−8.493	*	−0.148		−11.243	*			−1.818		−14.779	
1996	3.290		−0.922		−0.661				0.938		−9.892	
1998	−4.402		−1.719		−7.508	**			−5.160	*	−3.192	
2000	−10.362		0.848		−8.011	**			−3.947	*	5.433	
2002	−8.104	*	−0.341		−3.688				−1.994		−16.683	*
2004	−2.729	**	−2.618	***	−12.709	***	−5.066	**	−10.884	***	−9.080	
2006	−5.716		−2.225	**	−21.439	**	−5.470		−12.590	**	−6.263	
2008	−5.301	**	−1.209	***	−5.665	**	−5.989	*	−5.170	*	−4.318	
2010	−8.335	**	−1.357		−16.374	**			−13.129	***	−14.926	*
2012	−4.613	**	−0.880		−13.417	*			−1.054		−16.794	**

Note: Entries and significance levels are taken from Tables 5.3, 5.4, 6.1, 6.2, 7.1, 7.2, 8.1 and 8.2. Critical t-values are 1.679 at .10 probability; 2.009 at .05; 2.700 at .01.

[a]Communication technology is measured by radio in households from 1926–1950; television 1952–1978; cable television, 1980–1994; the Internet, 1996–2012.

[b]Enfranchisement laws involve women's suffrage from 1920–1928, voting rights for African Americans 1946–1972, 18-year right to vote 1974–1978. Youth is not included as an entry because it had a statistically significant effect on nonvoting in just 8 of 47 elections. See the text for more explanation.

[c]International involvement is measured by casualties in World War II (1942–1944), the Korean War (1950–1952), and the Vietnam War (1966–1972). It is measured by public opinion for the Persian Gulf War (1990), and the Iraq War (2004–2008).

information. In contrast, cable television increases nonvoting. People do not as readily reduce internal uncertainty through cable television as they enjoy the ability to pick and choose channels which may not have political content. Technology has its greatest effects as radio becomes a tool of political communication with fireside chats in 1934, as a device to communicate about the war in 1944, as television arrives in more and more living rooms with the 1958 midterms and in the first televised debates in 1960, and as the Internet becomes a viable political tool in 2004 and 2006. Cable television increases nonvoting most dramatically in 1980 and 1982 as cable enters more and more homes.

While we cannot analyze the effects of specific forms of mass communication at the individual level in the same way that we can at the aggregate level, we do know that the more individuals pay attention to multiple forms of media, the more likely they will vote. In addition, in the later years beginning in 1998, the Internet has a strong effect on decreasing individual nonvoting.

Third, in general, the increasing costs of war lower nonvoting. The uncertainty citizens face regarding the course of the war increases their participation in elections. This is true during World War II, the Persian Gulf War, and the Iraq War. No effect is found during the Korean War, and war deaths during the Vietnam War increased nonvoting as public support of the war dissipated. In addition, one of the central findings at the individual level is that the nature of US involvement in the international arena is quite important to people in their decisions about whether or not to vote in presidential elections but less in midterm congressional elections. People who see stability in US international affairs are generally less likely to vote than those who urge change. Taken together, the aggregate and individual-level findings amplify a growing body of political science research that demonstrates that the public pays far more attention to foreign policy matters in making electoral calculations than was originally assumed.[2]

Beyond these three generalizations, the uncertainty prompted by major changes in federal legal requirements have less consistent effects on nonvoting than the theory would suggest. The passage of the Voting Rights Act of 1965 had strong effects on decreasing nonvoting rates among African Americans beginning in 1966. Indeed in 2008 and 2012, with the Obama candidacy, white southerners had higher nonvoting rates than African-American southerners. But women's suffrage initially prompts a sharp spike in nonvoting as millions of eligible women did not vote. By the late 1920s, however, women were more integrated into the electorate. In contrast, the introduction of 18–20-year-olds initially prompted a drop in nonvoting in the 1974 midterm elections for their first midterm contests but

[2] For a discussion of this research, see Herbert Weisberg and Dino Christenson, "Changing Horses in Wartime? The 2004 Presidential Election," *Political Behavior* 29 (June 2007): 284.

a rise in nonvoting afterwards. The youngest eligible voters continue to have the highest nonvoting rates of any age group. Thus, legal changes as a disruption to the political status quo are less suitable indicators of uncertainty because they become entangled with the demographics and social profiles associated with the groups of citizens who become new members of the electorate.

Across the entire time period since the 1920s, demographic characteristics in the population do not automatically or consistently affect aggregate nonvoting. While youth is a strong determinant of individual nonvoting, the effect of young people in a state's population has more limited influence on aggregate nonvoting rates. It posts a statistically significant effect in just 8 of 47 elections from 1920 through 2012: 1922, 1924, 1938, 1956, 1964, 1974, 1996, and 2008. Indeed, in several years in the 1920s and 1930s and again during the Obama campaigns, young people in state electorates actually diminish nonvoting rates. Education has some of its largest effects as the ranks of the college-educated begin to expand in the late 1980s and early 1990s and continue into the twenty-first century. At the individual level, the effect of education is present in every election year.

Party competition does not always have an independent effect on nonvoting. In part this is true because there is any number of election years in which there is little competition. As one metric of this is the number of elections in which an incumbent president won reelection handily (1924, 1936, 1940, 1944, 1956, 1964, 1972, 1984, 1996) during the period. Competition has its largest effects in the 1950s through 1960 as Republican candidates began to vie in the South, and again as polarization heats up from 2004 onward. But it does not have strong effects in the 1940s nor in the 1970s and 1980s.

Thus, across an extended time period, uncertainty in the national campaign context helps explain how many people do not vote in the American states. The results indicate that dramatic shifts in that context push state nonvoting rates down, as presumably people see important reasons to go to the polls. Stable conditions in the campaign context push state nonvoting rates up or keep them steady, as presumably people are less convinced that voting is crucial. A thorough explanation for nonvoting rates across individual elections, then, must begin with an understanding of the changing circumstances within the national campaign context. In addition, key elements of the national campaign context also help explain the individuals who do not vote in American elections and reveal four different types of nonvoters. With the unavoidability of politics, many nonvoters are aware of sharply changing economic conditions, national events, and circumstances unfolding in the world. Even the politically ignorant nonvoters who do not pay much attention to politics or the candidates are nevertheless aware of key aspects of the national campaign context. Other nonvoters—the indifferent, the dissatisfied, and those with personal hardships—are not only aware of the national campaign context, but they also make comparisons between the candidates. Many of these nonvoters find the candidates wanting, whether because they do not see any difference between the candidates or because they see the candidates negatively. Thus, while these latter three groups of nonvoters, which comprise a majority of the nonvoting public, are aware of the external uncertainty in the campaign context, they do not resolve their internal uncertainty about a preferred candidate and so do not vote. This individual-level model suggests a correction to the personal resources model that indicates that people with limited personal resources are less likely to be aware of politics than others and therefore are more likely to be nonvoters. The uncertainty of the national campaign context pushes people across the personal resources spectrum to know more about the campaign context than would be presumed from the personal resources model alone. While it is true that people with certain resources such as age and education are more likely to vote than others, others do still vote.

The American Nonvoter

Uncertainty in the national campaign context, then, is as pivotal to understanding the American nonvoter as the psychological involvement, demographic characteristics, and social connections of individual citizens and the campaign mobilization of candidates and parties. One of the keys to understanding nonvoting goes beyond citizens and campaigners to the ever-changing economic, political, and technological environment within which they act. Novel events and conditions create high levels of external uncertainty in the national campaign context that catch citizens and candidates off guard. The higher the level of uncertainty, the more likely eligible voters go to the polls, regardless of their personal backgrounds or the skills and money available to campaigners. This is not to suggest that the other four explanations of nonvoting are unimportant, but rather that they must be viewed within this broader political context. What is actually happening in the national scene is as important to understanding American nonvoters as the individual qualities of the nonvoters themselves or the strategies of campaigners. Indeed, the individual qualities of voters vary in their importance as the national campaign context shifts. In addition, candidate strategies are directly tied to the vagaries of the campaign context and often fail when they do not take the often fast-changing environment into account.

American elections are often seen as low-turnout elections, but this view fails to consider the long sweep of electoral history in which nonvoting rates have moved up and down as the uncertainty of the national campaign context shifts. Over the nearly 100 years since women first gained the right to vote, Americans have, if nothing else, been quite consistent in their commitments to electoral politics—through the advent of radio, television, and the Internet, through one-party landslides and two-party duels. Sometimes that commitment reflects high levels of uncertainty and novelty in the national campaign context, and sometimes it does not. Of course there have been some very-low-turnout elections throughout this electoral history. The findings in this book may well help campaigners approach, particularly, groups of nonvoters who could well be prompted to vote. While we would not see the politically ignorant nonvoters discussed in Chapter 4 as especially good bets, the other types of nonvoters—indifferent, dissatisfied, and those with personal hardships—could well be attracted to the electoral process since they are paying attention to the national context and the candidates as the campaign proceeds.

American nonvoters are not neutral bystanders to the elections in which they do not participate. Many of them are interested in politics and know the candidates. When nonvoting declines in a given election, the drop is about something—the new voters have particular concerns about the uncertainty of the national campaign context, and preferences about which candidate will best handle it. These concerns may not be identical to those of people who vote election after election. Similarly, when nonvoting increases in a given election, this is also about something substantive—the spectators see little to worry about or may not be convinced that one candidate is that much better than the other in addressing the issues of the day. This too creates a bias when viewpoints and groups of people that are present in the body politic but silent at the polls are not directly accounted for in the policy directions that emerge from the final election results. It is difficult to assert how many people must vote in order for democratic government to survive. It is clear that everyone—nonvoters and voters alike—has a stake in the outcome when electoral decisions are made.

BIBLIOGRAPHY

Abramson, Paul and William Claggett. 1986. "Race-Related Differences in Self-Reported and Validated Turnout in 1984." *Journal of Politics* 48 (May): 412–422.

Achen, Christopher. 1982. *Interpreting and Using Regression*. Beverly Hills: Sage.

Achen, Christopher. 2000. "Why Lagged Dependent Variables Can Suppress the Explanatory Power of Other Independent Variables." Presented at the Annual Meeting of the Political Methodology Section of the American Political Science Association, Los Angeles, July.

Aldrich, John. 2011. *Why Parties?* Chicago: University of Chicago Press.

Aldrich, John, John Sullivan, and Eugene Borgida. 1989. "Foreign Affairs and Issue Voting: Do Presidential Candidates 'Waltz before a Blind Audience?'" *American Political Science Review* 83 (March): 123–131.

Alexopoulos, Michelle and Jon Cohen. 2009. "The Media is the Measure: Technical Change and Employment, 1909–1949." Working Paper 351, University of Toronto, Department of Economics, February 23, 1–48.

Alexopoulos, Michelle and Jon Cohen. 2009. "Uncertain Times, Uncertain Measures." Working Paper 352, University of Toronto, Department of Economics, February 11, 1–56.

Alexopoulos, Michelle and Jon Cohen. 2011. "Volumes of Evidence: Examining Technical Change in the Last Century through a New Lens." *The Canadian Journal of Economics* 44 (May): 413–450.

Alvarez, R. Michael and Charles Franklin. 1994. "Uncertainty and Political Perceptions." *Journal of Politics* 56 (August): 671–688.

Ansolabehere, Stephen and Eitan Hersh. 2012. "Validation: What Big Data Reveal About Survey Misreporting and the Real Electorate." *Political Analysis* 20 (Autumn): 437–459.

Avey, Michael. 1989. *The Demobilization of American Voters*. New York: Greenwood Press.

Bachmann, Rudiger and Christian Bayer. 2013. "Wait and See Business Cycles." *Journal of Monetary Economics* 60 (September): 704–719.

Baek, Mijeong. 2009. "A Comparative Analysis of Political Communication Systems and Voter Turnout." *American Journal of Political Science* 53 (April): 376–393.

Baker, Scott, Nicholas Bloom, and Steven Davis. 2015. "Measuring Economic Policy Uncertainty." Working Paper 21633, National Bureau of Economic Research, October 2015.

Barsky, Robert and Lutz Kilian. 2001. "Do We Really Know that Oil Caused the Great Stagflation? A Monetary Alternative." *NBER Macroeconomics Annual* 16: 137–183.

Barsky, Robert and Lutz Kilian. 2004. "Oil and the Macroeconomy since the 1970s." *The Journal of Economic Perspectives* 18 (Autumn): 115–134.

Bartels, Larry. 1986. "Issue Voting Under Uncertainty: An Empirical Test." *American Journal of Political Science* 30 (November): 709–728.

Bartels, Larry. 1998. "Electoral Continuity and Change, 1868–1996." *Electoral Studies* 17: 301–326.

Bekaert, Geert, Marie Hoerova, and Marco Lo Duca. 2013. "Risk, Uncertainty, and Monetary Policy." *Journal of Monetary Economics* 60 (October): 771–788.

Bendor, Jonathan, Daniel Biermeier, and Michael Ting. 2003. "A Behavioral Model of Turnout." *American Political Science Review* 97 (May): 261–280.

Berinsky, Adam. 2009. *In Time of War: Understanding Public Opinion from World War II to Iraq*. Chicago: University of Chicago Press.

Bernanke, Ben. 1983. "Irreversibility, Uncertainty, and Cyclical Investment." *The Quarterly Journal of Economics* 98 (February): 85–106.

Bernanke, Ben, Mark Gertler, and Mark Watson. 1997. "Systematic Monetary Policy and the Effects of Oil Price Shocks." *Brookings Papers on Economic Activity* 1997: 91–157.

Bernstein, Barton. 1971. "Election of 1952." In A. Schlesinger, ed. *History of American Presidential Elections, 1789–1968*, vol. IV. New York: Chelsea House, 3215–3266.

Bimber, Bruce. 2003. *Information and American Democracy Technology in the Evolution of Political Power*. Cambridge: Cambridge University Press.

Black, Earl and Merle Black. 2002. *The Rise of Southern Republicans*. Cambridge: Harvard University Press.

Black, Earl and Merle Black. 2007. *Divided America: The Ferocious Power Struggle in American Politics*. New York: Simon and Schuster.

Blanchard, Olivier. 1993. "Consumption and the Recession of 1990–1991." *American Economics Review* 83 (May): 270–275.

Blanchard, Olivier. 2009. "The Crisis: Basic Mechanisms and Appropriate Policies." IMF Working Paper, International Monetary Fund, April 2009, 1–22.

Blanchard, Olivier. 2009. "(Nearly) nothing to fear but fear itself." Economist, January 29, 2009, found at http://www.economist.com/node/13021961/print.

Bloom, Nicholas. 2009. "The Impact of Uncertainty Shocks." *Econometrica* 77 (May): 623–685.

Bloom, Nicholas. 2014. "Fluctuations in Uncertainty." *Journal of Economic Perspectives* 28 (Spring): 153–176.

Bloom, Nick, Stephen Bond, and John van Reenen. 2007. "Uncertainty and Investment Dynamics." *The Review of Economic Studies* 74 (April): 391–415.

Bobic, Igor. 2014. "Scott Brown wants to secure the border from Ebola." *Huffington Post*, October 9, found at http://www.huffingtonpost.com/2014/10/09/scott-brown-ebola_n_5959200.html.

Bond, Robert, Christopher Fariss, Jason Jones, Adam Kramer, Cameron Marlow, Jaime Settle, and James Fowler. 2012. "A 61-million-person Experiment in Social Influence and Political Mobilization." *Nature* 489 (13 September): 295–298.

Boyne, Roy. 2003. *Risk*. Buckingham, UK: Open University Press.

Brody, Richard. 1978. "The Puzzle of Political Participation in America." In A. King, ed. *The New American Political System*. Washington, D.C.: American Enterprise Institute, 287–324.

Bruno, Michael. 1980. "Import Prices and Stagflation in the Industrial Countries: A Cross-Section Analysis." *The Economic Journal* 90 (September): 479–492.

Bruno, Michael. 1984. "Raw Materials, Profits, and the Productivity Slowdown." *Quarterly Journal of Economics* 99 (February): 1–30.

Burden, Barry, ed. 2003. *Uncertainty in American Politics*. Cambridge: Cambridge University Press.

Burden, Barry and Jacob Neiheisel. 2013. "Election Administration and the Pure Effect of Voter Registration on Turnout." *Political Research Quarterly* 66 (March): 77–90.

Burden, Barry and Amber Wichowsky. 2014. "Economic Discontent as a Mobilizer: Unemployment and Turnout." *Journal of Politics* 76 (October 2014): 887–898.

Burnham, Walter Dean. 1970. *Critical Elections and the Mainsprings of American Politics*. New York: W.W. Norton.

Burns, Arthur. 1978. *Reflections of an Economic Policy Maker: Speeches and Congressional Statements: 1969–1978*. Washington, D.C.: American Enterprise Institute.

Case, Karl and Robert Shiller. 2003. "Is There a Bubble in the Housing Market?" *Brookings Papers on Economic Activity* No. 2, 299–342.

Claggett, William, William Flanigan, and Nancy Zingale. 1984. "Nationalization of the American Electorate." *American Political Science Review* 78 (March): 77–91.

Cioffi-Revilla, Claudio. 1998. *Uncertainty and Politics*. Cambridge: Cambridge University Press.

Condon, Stephanie. 2012. "Noonan: Romney Campaign is a 'rolling calamity.'" CBS News, September 25, found at http://www.cbsnews.com/news/noonan-romney-campaign-is-a-rolling-calamity/.

Confessore, Nicholas. 2014. "A National Strategy Funds State Political Monopolies." *New York Times*, January 12. A-1, A-20–21.

Congleton, Roger. 2009. "On the Political Economy of the Financial Crisis and Bailout of 2008–2009." *Public Choice* 140: 287–317.

Converse, Philip, Warren Miller, Jerrold Rusk, and Arthur Wolfe. 1969. "Continuity and Change in American Politics." *American Political Science Review* 63 (December): 1083–1105.

Converse, Philip and Richard Niemi. 1971. "Non-voting Among Young Adults in the United States." In William Crotty, ed. *Political Parties and Political Behavior*, 2nd ed. Boston: Allyn and Bacon, 443–466.

Coolidge, Calvin. 1929. *The Autobiography of Calvin Coolidge*. New York: Cosmopolitan Book Corporation.

Craig, Douglas. 2000. *Fireside Politics: Radio and Political Culture in the United States, 1920–1940*. Baltimore: Johns Hopkins University Press.

Cunningham, Sean. 2014. *American Politics in the Postwar Sunbelt: Conservative Growth in a Battleground Region*. Cambridge: Cambridge University Press.

Curry, Timothy and Lynn Shibut. 2000. "The Cost of the Savings and Loan Crisis: Truth and Consequences." *FDIC Banking Review* 13 (December), found at http://www.fdic.gov/bank/analytical/banking/2000dec/brv13n2_2.pdf.

Davis, Otto, Melvin Hinich, and Peter Ordeshook. 1970. "An Expository Development of a Mathematical Model of the Electoral Process." *American Political Science Review* 64 (June): 426–448.

De Haven-Smith, Lance. 2005. *The Battle for Florida*. Gainesville: University Press of Florida.

Dor, Eric and Alain Durré. 2002. "Monetary Policy and the New Economy: Between Supply Shock and Financial Bubble." *Louvain Economic Review* 68: 221–237.

Downs, Anthony. 1957. *An Economic Theory of Democracy*. New Haven: Yale University Press.

Edelman, Murray. 1964. *The Symbolic Uses of Politics*. Urbana: University of Illinois Press.

Engstrom, Erik and Samuel Kernell. 2014. *Party Ballots, Reform, and the Transformation of America's Electoral System*. New York: Cambridge University Press.

Ferejohn, John and Morris Fiorina. 1974. "The Paradox of Not Voting: A Decision Theoretic Analysis." *American Political Science Review* 68 (June): 525–536.

Fiorina, Morris. 1981. *Retrospective Voting in American National Elections*. New Haven: Yale University Press.

Fowler, James. 2006. "Habitual and Behavioral Turnout." *Journal of Politics* 68 (May): 335–344.

Francis, Wayne, Lawrence Kenny, Rebecca Morton, and Amy Schmidt. 1994. "Retrospective Voting and Political Mobility." *American Journal of Political Science* 38 (November): 999–1024.

Frankel, Max. 1971. "'Japan Inc.' and 'Nixon Shocks,'" *New York Times*, November 25, 2.

Franklin, Mark. 2004. *Voter Turnout and the Dynamics of Electoral Competition in Established Democracies Since 1945*. Cambridge: Cambridge University Press.

Friedman, Emily. 2012. "Romney says he was completely wrong about the 47 percent remark." ABC News. October 5, found at http://abcnews.go.com/blogs/politics/2012/10/romney-says-he-was-completely-wrong-about-47-percent-comments/.

Gardner, Jennifer. 1994. "The 1990–91 Recession: How Bad was the Labor Market?" *Monthly Labor Review* 117 (June): 3–11.

Gerber, Alan and Donald Green. 2000. "The Effect of a Nonpartisan Get-Out-the-Vote Drive: An Experimental Study of Leafletting." *Journal of Politics* 62 (August): 846–857.

Gerber, Alan, Donald Green and Christopher Latimer. 2008. "Social Pressure and Voter Turnout: Evidence from a Large-Scale Field Experiment." *American Political Science Review* 102 (February): 33–48.

Gimpel, James. 1996. *National Elections and the Autonomy of American State Party Systems.* Pittsburgh: University of Pittsburgh Press.

Gimpel, James and Jason Schuknecht. 2003. *Patchwork Nation: Sectionalism and Political Change in American Politics.* Ann Arbor, MI: University of Michigan Press.

Glasgow, Garrett and R. Michael Alvarez. 2000. "Uncertainty in Candidate Personality Traits." *American Politics Research* 28 (January): 26–49.

Godbout, Jean-Francois and Eric Belanger. 2007. "Economic Voting and Political Sophistication in the United States: A Reassessment." *Political Research Quarterly* 60 (September): 541–554.

Goldstein, Kenneth and Travis Ridout. 2002. "The Politics of Participation: Mobilization and Turnout over Time." *Political Behavior* 24 (March): 3–29.

Gomez, Brad. 2008. "Revisiting the 'Puzzle of Participation': A Dynamic Model of Education and Turnout Growth." Unpublished manuscript.

Gomez, Brad and Matthew Wilson. 2001. "Political Sophistication and Economic Voting in the American Electorate." *American Journal of Political Science* 45 (October): 899–914.

Graber, Doris. 2001. *Processing Politics: Learning from Television in the Internet Age.* Chicago: University of Chicago Press.

Gray, Jack. 2000. "Meta-Risk." *Journal of Portfolio Management* 26 (Spring): 18–25.

Green, Donald and Alan Gerber. 2010. "Introduction to Social Pressure and Voting: New Experimental Evidence." *Political Behavior* 32 (September): 331–336.

Green, Donald and Alan Gerber. 2015. *Get Out the Vote: How to Increase Voter Turnout.* 3rd ed. Washington, D.C.: Brookings Institution.

Green, Donald and Ron Shachar. 2000. "Habit Formation and Political Behaviour: Evidence of Consuetude in Voter Turnout." *British Journal of Political Science* 30 (October): 561–573.

Greenspan, Alan. 1996. "The Challenge of Central Banking in a Democratic Society." Boyer lecture, American Enterprise Institute, found at http://www.federalreserve.gov/boarddocs/speeches/1996/19961205.htm.

"Greenspan: Home-price Speculation Can't Last." *Boston* Globe, May 21, 2005, found at http://www.boston.com/business/globe/articles/2005/05/21/greenspan_home_price_speculation_cant_last/.

Gronke, Paul, Eva Galanes-Rosenbaum, and Peter Miller. 2008. "Early Voting and Voter Turnout." In Bruce Cain, Todd Donovan, and Caroline Tolbert, eds., *Democracy in the States: Experiments in Election Reform.* Washington, D.C.: Brookings Institution Press, 68–82.

Grose, Christian and Bruce Oppenheimer. 2007. "The Iraq War, Partisanship, and Candidate Attributes: Variation in Partisan Swing in the 2006 U.S. House Elections." *Legislative Studies Quarterly* 32 (November): 531–557.

Grubb, D., R. Jackman, R, and R. Layard. 1982. "Causes of the Current Stagflation." *Review of Economic Studies* 49: 707–730.

Hanmer, Michael. 2009. *Discount Voting: Voter Registration Reforms and Their Effects.* Cambridge: Cambridge University Press.

Havier, Ernest. 1920. "Tammany Puzzled by Women Voters." *New York Times.* October 17, E7.

Highton, Benjamin. 1997. "Easy Registration and Voter Turnout." *Journal of Politics* 59 (May): 565–575.

Highton, Benjamin and Raymond Wolfinger. 1998. "Estimating the Effects of the National Voter Registration Act of 1993." *Political Behavior* 20 (June): 79–104.

Hogan, Michael. 1987. *The Marshall Plan: America, Britain, and the Reconstruction of Western Europe, 1947–1952.* Cambridge: Cambridge University Press.

Holbrook, Thomas and Scott McClurg. 2005. "The Mobilization of Core Supporters: Campaigns, Turnout, and Electoral Composition in United States Presidential Elections." *American Journal of Political Science* 49 (October): 689–703.

Hout, Michael and David Knoke. 1975. "Change in Voting Turnout, 1952–1971." *Public Opinion Quarterly* 39 (Spring): 52–68.

Jacobson, Gary. 2008. *A Divider, not a Uniter: George W. Bush and the American People.* New York: Pearson.

Jacobson, Gary. 2012. *The Politics of Congressional Elections,* 8th ed. New York: Pearson.

Jedrzejczak, Antonina. 2010. "Here are the Greatest Moments in CNN History." *Business Insider,* found at http://www.businessinsider.com/here-are-some-of-the-greatest-moments-in-cnn-history-2010-6?op=1.

Jennings, M. Kent and Vicki Zeitner. 2003. "Internet Use and Civic Engagement: A Longitudinal Analysis." *Public Opinion Quarterly* 67 (Autumn): 311–334.

Johnston, John. 1972. *Econometrics Methods.* New York: McGraw-Hill.

Kahn, Herman. 1971. "Thinking More Unthinkable Thoughts" *New York Times,* September 13, 37.

Karol, David and Edward Miguel. 2007. "The Electoral Cost of War: Iraq Casualties and the 2004 U.S. Presidential Election." *Journal of Politics* 69 (August): 633–648.

Katz, Jonathan and Gabriel Katz. 2010. "Correcting for Survey Misreports Using Auxiliary Information with an Application to Estimating Turnout." *American Journal of Political Science* 54 (July): 815–835.

Keele, Luke and Nathan Kelly. 2006. "Dynamic Models for Dynamic Theories: The Ins and Outs of Lagged Dependent Variables." *Political Analysis* 14 (Spring): 186–205.

Key, V. O. 1955. "A Theory of Critical Elections." *Journal of Politics* 17 (February): 3–18.

Key, V. O. 1956. *American State Politics: An Introduction.* New York: Alfred A. Knopf.

King, Gary. 1997. *A Solution to the Ecological Inference Problem.* Princeton: Princeton University Press.

King, Gary and Lyn Ragsdale. 1988. *The Elusive Executive.* Washington, D.C.: CQ Press.

Kirkendall, Richard. 1971. "Election of 1948." In A. Schlesinger, ed. *History of American Presidential Elections, 1789–1968,* vol. IV. New York: Chelsea House, 099–3145.

Knack, Stephen. 1995. "Does 'Motor Voter' Work? Evidence from State-Level Data." *Journal of Politics* 57 (August): 795–811.

Knight, Frank. 1921. *Risk, Uncertainty, and Profit.* Boston: Houghton Mifflin.

Kouser, J. Morgan. 1974. *The Shaping of Southern Politics.* New Haven: Yale University Press.

Kull, Steven, Clay Ramsay, and Evan Lewis. 2003–2004. "Misperceptions, the Media, and the Iraq War." *Political Research Quarterly* 118 (Winter): 569–598.

Lanoue, David. 1994. "Retrospective and Prospective Voting in Presidential-Year Elections." *Political Research Quarterly,* 47 (March): 193–205.

Lazarsfeld, Paul, Bernard Berelson, and Helen Gaudet. 1948. *The People's Choice.* New York: Columbia University Press.

Lindley, Dennis. 2007. *Understanding Uncertainty.* Hoboken, NJ: Wiley-Interscience.

Ledbetter, James. 2011. *Unwarranted Influence: Dwight Eisenhower and the Military- Industrial Complex.* New Haven: Yale University Press.

Leighley, Jan and Jonathan Nagler. 2014. *Who Votes Now? Demographics, Issues, Inequality, and Turnout in the United States.* Princeton: Princeton University Press.

Ljung, G. M. and George Box. 1978. "On a Measure of a Lack of Fit in Time Series Models." *Biometrika* 65 (2): 297–303.

Litan, Robert and Alice Rivlan. 2001. "Projecting the Economic Impact of the Internet." *American Economic Review* 91 (May): 313–317.

Lyons, William and Robert Alexander. 2000. "The Tale of Two Electorates: Generational Replacement and the Decline of Voting in Presidential Elections." *Journal of Politics* 62 (November): 1014–1034.

Machina, Mark and Viscusi, W. Kip. 2014. *Handbook of the Economics of Risk and Uncertainty.* Amsterdam: Elsevier.

Maddala, G. S. 2001. *Introduction to Econometrics.* 3rd ed. New York: Wiley.

Malhorta, Neil, Melissa Michelson, and Ali Valenzuela. 2012. "Emails from Official Sources Can Increase Turnout." *Quarterly Journal of Political Science* 7: 321–332.

Mann, Thomas and Norman Ornstein. 2013. *It's Even Worse than it Looks*. New York: Basic Books.

March, James and Zur Shapira. 1988. "Managerial Perspectives on Risk and Risk- Taking." In J. March ed., *Decisions and Organizations*. Oxford: Basil Blackwell, 76–97.

Mark, David. 2006. *Going Dirty: The Art of Negative Campaigning*. New York: Rowman and Littlefield.

Matland, Richard and Gregg Murray. 2012. "An Experimental Test of Mobilization Effects in a Latino Community." *Political Research Quarterly* 65 (March): 192–205.

Mayer, William. 2010. "Retrospective Voting in Presidential Primaries." *Presidential Studies Quarterly* 40 (December): 660–685.

Mayhew, David. 1974. *Congress: The Electoral Connection*. New Haven: Yale University Press.

Mayhew, David. 2002. *Electoral Realignments: A Critique of an American Genre*. New Haven: Yale University Press.

Mayhew, David. 2013. *Partisan Balance: Why American Parties Don't Kill the U.S. Constitutional System*. Princeton: Princeton University Press.

McCracken, Paul. 1978. "Towards Full Employment and Price Stability." *Nebraska Journal of Economics and Business* 17 (Autumn): 5–19.

McCullough, David. 1992. *Truman*. New York: Simon and Schuster.

McDonald, Michael. 2002. "The Turnout Rate Among Eligible Voters in the States, 1980–2000." *State Politics and Policy Quarterly* 2 (Summer): 199–212.

McDonald, Michael and Samuel Popkin. 2001. "The Myth of the Vanishing Voter." *American Political Science Review* 95 (December): 963–974.

McGinnis, Joe. 1969. *The Selling of the President* New York: Penguin Books.

McGraw, Kathleen, Edward Hasecke, and Kimberly Conger. 2003. "Ambivalence, Uncertainty, and Processes of Candidate Evaluation." *Political Psychology* 24 (September): 421–448.

Merriam, Charles and Harold Gosnell. 1924. *Non-voting: Causes and Methods of Control*. Chicago: University of Chicago Press.

Miller, Warren and J. Merrill Shanks. 1996. *The New American Voter*. Cambridge: Harvard University Press.

Moore, Don. 1992. "The 1924 Radio Election." *Monitoring Times*, July 1992, found at http://www.pateplumaradio.com/genbroad/elec1924.html.

Mueller, John. 1973. *War, Presidents and Public Opinion*. New York: John Wiley.

Mycoff, Jason, Michael Wagner, and David Wilson. 2009. "The Empirical Effects of Voter-ID Laws: Present or Absent?" *PS: Political Science and Politics* 42 (January): 121–126.

Nardulli, Peter, Jon Dalager, and Donald Greco. 1996. "Voter Turnout in U.S. Presidential Elections: A Historical View and Some Speculation." *PS: Political Science and Politics* 29 (September): 480–490.

Nickerson, David. 2007. "Does Email Boost Turnout?" *Quarterly Journal of Political Science* 2: 369–379.

Noonan, Peggy. 2012. "Time for an Intervention." *Wall Street Journal*, September 18, , found at http://blogs.wsj.com/peggynoonan/2012/09/18/time-for-an-intervention.

Oberholzer-Gee, Felix and Joel Waldfogel. 2009. "Media Markets and Localism: Does Local News in Espanol Boost Hispanic Voter Turnout?" *The American Economics Review* 99 (December): 2120–2128.

Parsons, Patrick. 2003. "The Evolution of the Cable-Satellite Distribution System." *Journal of Broadcasting and Electronic Media* 47 (1): 1–17.

Patterson, Thomas. 2002. *The Vanishing Voter*. New York: Vintage Books.

Peterson, Wallace. 1980. "Stagflation and the Crisis of Capitalism." *Review of Social Economy* 38 (December): 277–287.

Pietrusza, David. 2008. *1920: The Year of the Six Presidents*. New York: Basic Books.

Piven, Frances Fox and Richard Cloward. 1988. *Why Americans Don't Vote*. New York: Pantheon Books.

Piven, Frances Fox and Richard Cloward. 2000. *Why Americans Still Don't Vote*. Boston: Beacon Press.

Pomper, Gerald. 2001. "The Presidential Election." In G. Pomper, ed. *The Election of 1980*. Chatham, NJ: Chatham House, 65–96.

Powell, Colin. "Oral History of the Gulf War." Frontline, found at http://www.pbs.org/wgbh/pages/frontline/gulf/oral/powell/1.html.

Plutzer, Eric. 2002. "Becoming a Habitual Voter: Inertia, Resources, and Growth in Young Adulthood." *American Political Science Review* 96 (March): 41–56.

Prior, Markus. 2005. "News vs. Entertainment: How Increasing Media Choice Widens Gaps in Political Knowledge and Turnout." *American Journal of Political Science* 49 (July): 577–592.

Prior, Markus. 2007. *Post-Broadcast Democracy*. Cambridge: Cambridge University Press.

Public Papers of the Presidents, Dwight Eisenhower, 1954. Washington, D.C.: U.S. Government Printing Office, 1955.

Ragsdale, Lyn. 1998. *Vital Statistics on the American Presidency*, rev. ed. Washington, D.C.: CQ Press.

Ragsdale, Lyn. 2009. *Vital Statistics on the American Presidency*, 3rd ed. Washington, D.C.: CQ Press.

Ragsdale, Lyn and Jerrold Rusk. 1993. "Who are Nonvoters? Profiles from the 1990 Senate Elections." *American Journal of Political Science* 37 (August): 721–746.

Ragsdale, Lyn and Jerrold Rusk. 1995. "Candidates, Issues, and Participation in Senate Elections." *Legislative Studies Quarterly* 20 (August): 305–327.

Raskin, A. H. 1971. "Dr. Nixon Prescribes Shock Therapy: The Freeze." *New York Times*, August 22, E1.

Renner, Tari. 1999. "Electoral Congruence and the Autonomy of American State Party Systems." *American Politics Research* 27 (January): 122–132.

Report of the Iraq Inquiry. 2016. Committee of the Privy Counsellors, House of Commons, United Kingdom, July 6, found at www.iraqinquiry.org.uk.

Riker, William and Peter Ordeshook. 1968. "A Theory of the Calculus of Voting." *American Political Science Review* 62 (March): 25–42.

Rosenstone, Steven and John Mark Hansen. 2003. *Mobilization, Participation and Democracy in America*. New York: Longman.

Rolfe, D. Meredith. 2013. *Voter Turnout: A Social Theory of Political Participation*. New York: Cambridge University Press.

Romer, Christina. 1990. "The Great Crash and the Onset of the Great Depression." *The Quarterly Journal of Economics* 3 (August): 597–624.

Rucker, Philip. 2012. "Mitt Romney Thought He Could Win." *Washington Post*, November 7, found at http://www.washingtonpost.com/blogs/post-politics/wp/2012/11/07/mitt-romney-thought-he-would-win/.

Rudel, Anthony. 2008. *Hello Everybody: The Dawn of American Radio*. New York: Houghton Mifflin Harcourt.

Rusk, Jerrold. 1970. "The Effect of the Australian Ballot on Split-Ticket Voting." *American Political Science Review* 64 (December): 1220–1238.

Rusk, Jerrold. 1974. "Comment: The American Electoral Universe: Speculation and Evidence." *American Political Science Review* 68 (September): 1028–1049.

Rusk, Jerrold. 2001. *A Statistical History of the American Electorate*. Washington, D.C.: CQ Press.

Rusk, Jerrold and John Stucker. 1978. "The Effect of the Southern System of Election Laws on Voting Participation." In Joel Silbey, Allan Bogue, and William Flanigan, eds., *The History of American Voting Behavior*. Princeton: Princeton University Press, 198–250.

Rusk, Jerrold and John Stucker. 1991. "Legal-Institutional Factors and Voting Participation: The Impact of Women's Suffrage on Voter Turnout." In William Crotty, ed. *Political Participation and American Democracy*. New York: Greenwood Press, 113–138.

Sanders, Mitchell. 2001. "Uncertainty and Turnout." *Political Analysis* 9 (Winter): 45–57.

Schlesinger, Arthur, Jr. 1957. *The Crisis of the Old Order*. Boston: Houghton Mifflin.

Schlesinger, Arthur, Jr., ed. 1971. *The History of American Presidential Elections*, 5 vols. New York: Chelsea House

Shafer, Byron and Richard Spady. 2014. *The American Political Landscape*. Cambridge: Harvard University Press.

Shaffer, Stephen. 1981. "A Multivariate Explanation of Decreasing Turnout in Presidential Elections, 1960–1976." *American Journal of Political Science* 25 (February): 68–95.

Shiller, Robert. 2005. *Irrational Exuberance*, 2nd ed. Princeton: Princeton University Press.

Sigelman, Lee, Philip Roeder, Malcolm Jewell, and Michael Baer. 1985. "Voting and Non-Voting: A Multi-Election Perspective." *American Journal of Political Science* 29 (November): 749–765.

Silver, Brian, Barbara Anderson, and Paul Abramson. 1986. "Who Overreports Voting? *American Political Science Review* 80 (June): 613–624.

Smith, Aaron and Maeve Duggan. 2012. "The State of the 2012 Election—Mobile Politics." PEW Internet and American Life Project, October 9, found at http://pewinternet.org/Reports/2012/Election-2012-Mobile.aspx.

Springer, Melanie. 2014. *How the States Shaped the Nation: American Electoral Institutions and Voter Turnout, 1920–2000*. Chicago: University of Chicago Press.

"The State of the Nation's Housing 2008." Joint Center for Housing Studies, Harvard University, 1–40.

Stokes, Donald. 1969. "A Variance Components Model of Political Effects." In J. M. Claunch, ed. *Mathematical Applications in Political Science*. Dallas: Southern Methodist University Press, 61–85.

Stokes, Donald. 1975. "Parties and the Nationalization of Electoral Forces." In W. N. Chambers and W. D. Burnham, eds. *The American Party Systems*. New York: Oxford University Press, 182–202.

Sundquist, James. 1983. *Dynamics of the Party System: Alignment and Realignment of Political Parties in the United States*, 2nd ed. Washington, D.C.: Brookings Institution.

Teixeira, Ruy. 1987. *Why Americans Don't Vote: Turnout Decline in the United States 1960–1984*. Westport, CT: Greenwood Press

Teixeira, Ruy. 1992. *The Disappearing American Voter*. Washington, D.C.: Brookings Institution.

Teixeira, Ruy, ed. 2012. *America's New Swing Region: Changing Politics and Demographics in the Mountain West*. Washington, D.C.: Brookings Institution Press.

Tevlin, Stacey and Karl Whelan, "Explaining the Investment Boom of the 1990s." *Journal of Money, Credit, and Banking* 35 (February 2003): 1–22.

Tolbert, Caroline and Ramona McNeal. 2003. "Unnraveling the Effects of the Internet on Political Participation." *Political Research Quarterly* 56: 175–185.

Truman, Harry. 1955. *Memoirs*. 2 vols. New York: Doubleday.

U.S. Census Bureau. *Current Population Reports*, P20-542, "Voting and Registration in the Election of November 2000," issued February 2002.

U.S. Census Bureau. http://www.census.gov/population/www/socdemo/voting.html, Voting and Registration, Historical Time Series Tables, Table A-1; A-9.

U.S. Census Bureau. Statistical Abstract of the United States. Various years.

U.S. Department of Defense, Federal Voting Assistance Program, "Voting Residency Guidelines under the Uniformed and Overseas Citizens Absentee Voting Act of 2004." found at http://www.fvap.gov/laws/legal.html#1.

U.S. Department of Labor, Bureau of Labor Statistics, Report HS-29, "Employment Status of the Civilian Population: 1929–2002." Found at http://stats.bls.gov.

U.S. House of Representatives, Clerk of the House, "Election Statistics (1920–2004)," found at http://clerk.house.gov/members/electionInfo/index.html.

Verba, Sidney and Norman Nie. 1972. *Participation in America*. New York: Harper and Row.

Verba, Sidney, Kay Schlozman and Henry Brady. 1995. *Voice and Equality*. Cambridge: Harvard University Press.

Whaley, Robert. 2000. "The Investor Fear Gauge." *Journal of Portfolio Management* 21 (Spring): 12–17.

Wattenberg, Martin. 2002. *Where Have All the Voters Gone?* Cambridge: Harvard University Press.

Wattenberg, Martin. 2005. "Elections: Turnout in the 2004 Presidential Elections." *Presidential Studies Quarterly* 35 (March 2005): 136–146.

Weisberg, Herbert. 2007. "Electoral Democracy during Wartime: The 2004 U.S. Election." *Political Behavior* 29 (June 2007): 143–149.

Weisberg, Herbert and Dino Christenson. 2007. "Changing Horses in Wartime? The 2004 Presidential Election." *Political Behavior* 29 (June 2007): 279–304.

White, Theodore H. 1961. *The Making of the President 1960*. New York: Atheneum Publishers

Wolfinger, Ray and Steven Rosenstone. 1980. *Who Votes*? New Haven: Yale University Press.

INDEX

Numbers in *italics* indicate figures and tables.